A RENAISSANCE
TREASURY

A Collection of Representative Writings
of the Renaissance
on the Continent of Europe

A RENAISSANCE
TREASURY

Edited by HIRAM HAYDN
and JOHN CHARLES NELSON

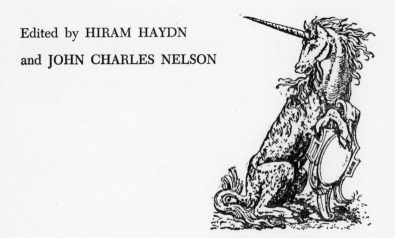

Doubleday & Company, Inc., Garden City, New York, 1953

Acknowledgments

Thanks are due the following authors and publishers for permission to reprint the selections indicated:

Columbia University Press, for selections from *Three Copernican Treatises,* translated by Edward Rosen.

The Johns Hopkins Press, for selections from *Four Treatises of Theophrastus Von Hohenheim Called Paracelsus,* translated by C. Lilian Temkin, George Rosen, Gregory Zilboorg, and Henry E. Sigerist.

Isaac Don Levine, as editor of the Macaulay Drama Library, for the translation by Stark Young of Machiavelli's *Mandragola,* published by Macaulay, 1927.

The Macmillan Company, New York, and Eyre & Spottiswoode (Publishers) Limited, London, for seven sonnets from *Sonnets pour Hélène,* by Pierre de Ronsard, translated by Humbert Wolfe. The Macmillan Company, for selections from *The Epitome of Andreas Vasalius,* translated by L. R. Lind.

Estate of Curtis Hidden Page, for seven poems from *Songs and Sonnets of Pierre de Ronsard,* by Curtis Hidden Page.

Philosophical Library, Inc., for selections from *Johannes Kepler: Life and Letters,* by Carola Baumgardt.

The University of Chicago Press, for selections from *The Renaissance Philosophy of Man,* edited by Ernst Cassirer, Paul Oskar Kristeller, and John Herman Randall, Jr.

The University of Wisconsin Press, for four poems by Joachim Du Bellay, from *French Lyrics in English Verse,* translated by William Frederic Giese.

Library of Congress Catalog Card Number 53–9988

Design: Diana Klemin

Introduction

This book is especially intended for that real person who, though neither a scholar nor a specialist, still entertains a curiosity about and an interest in the Renaissance. This book is intended for the browser, the dipper, and the lazy evening reader. It has been put together, in other words, with the conviction that, of all the periods in the history of Western man that still haunt the imaginations of many people, the Renaissance is the most compelling. It has also been put together with the conviction that there are not a few but many Americans who, despite all the pressures and distractions of our time, still like to sit down beside a good lamp and invite their minds to that extra act of stretching that involves entering a recognizable but not wholly familiar world—entering it at a leisurely pace and sojourning in it for a while, exploring it, so to speak, on their own.

These are the reasons that there are in this book so few annotations and explanations of references that may be unfamiliar to the casual reader. Yet at the same time we believe that quite possibly college instructors in the period of the Renaissance may find this book most satisfactory for their students, too, since it is a part of their own work to supply the interpretive and documentary elements. At any rate, we have kept to a minimum those selections in which local or "timely" references are needed to make the meaning of the text clear. Quite possibly some of the specific objects of satiric treatment in, say, the fables by Bruno and Despériers will be missed by the non-specialist reader; but surely the general intent will come through, and there will be other sorts of incidental enjoyment. In most of our selections, to be sure, we do not believe that this problem exists to any appreciable degree.

The Renaissance, however defined and differently limited in length by various historians, is a vast period, even when its development in England is not under consideration. There are no English selections in this book. The Renaissance in England was the period from the reign of Henry VIII through that of Elizabeth, and its literature is readily and widely available, but there have been only a few books containing comprehensive selections from the literature of the Continental Renaissance.

In selecting from that literature, then, we have included writings ranging from the mid-fourteenth century all the way to the mid-seventeenth century. We have found a certain appropriateness in beginning the book with Petrarch looking back toward the last great artist of the Middle Ages (who, in a sense, might also be called the first great artist of the Renaissance), Dante—and in ending the book

vii

with Galileo and Kepler looking forward to worlds firmly established in their minds but for various reasons quite inacceptable to many of their contemporaries.

We are fully aware that some of the notable figures of the Continental Renaissance are not represented in this volume—for example, from the Italian Renaissance there is nothing of Marsilio Ficino and nothing of Pietro Aretino. And although there are plenty of great names in the Table of Contents (perhaps more than there could be in a comparable volume covering any other single period)—even with these, the selections are frequently not the most famous ones.

An explanation is therefore in order—an explanation of our bases for selection. These bases are readability and representativeness. It is our conviction that literary works that still have life after four, five, or six hundred years possess that life to the degree that they are readable. (We believe that the so-called "unread classics" are not alive but rather in a state of preservation resembling that to be found in an Egyptian sarcophagus.) Within our frame of reference, then, the reader may quarrel with our judgment and with our taste, but let him not object to the absence of weighty but largely unreadable "masterpieces." Incidentally, prose heavily outweighs the poetry in the volume—indeed overwhelmingly, except in Italy. The most important reason for this is the difficulty of securing first-rate translations of poems, but this very problem is, of course, really a part of the larger problem of readability. As a rule, we have found it advisable to retain for subtle reasons of rhyme, meter, etc., the original spelling of the poetic translations, but have modernized old spelling in prose translations.

The matter of representativeness is not quite so easy to state clearly and simply. The Renaissance was a great eclectic period. Diversity in temperament and outlook is matched by variety in form and expression. The literature of the Renaissance really comprises a world in miniature. It is, in its striking diversity, that microcosm that Renaissance writers were so fond of referring to. Conflicts and even polar opposites of theme and treatment and attitude are everywhere apparent. The literature of these centuries is full of theses and antitheses: beauty and ugliness, refinement and coarseness, authoritarianism and libertarianism. The fifteenth-century glorification of man found, for example, in Pico, and the sixteenth-century reaction apparent equally in the early Protestant doctrine of man's total depravity and in Machiavelli's low estimate of human nature are antithetical; and yet even the middle ground is not empty, for there stands Montaigne, quite content to know that man is neither a god nor a beast.

Perhaps it is high time to state what we, the editors of this book, mean when we speak of the Renaissance on the continent of Europe. We have not, in our selections, been concerned with any particular one of the prevalent theories as to what the Renaissance really was. Learned opinion on this matter stretches all the way from the conviction that the Renaissance was a fairly short historical phenomenon, during which there was a rebirth of creative activity in the arts and a fresh interest in the life and learning of classical antiquity, to the opinion that the Renaissance was the greatest single turning point in the history of Western man and indeed the period in which "modern man" was born. Various scholars believe, on the one hand, that the concept of the Renaissance is really an illusion, a convenient designation of an historical period marked by little important change in attitudes and ways of life from those of the Middle Ages, and, on the other hand, that it was a conscious and extensive revolt from everything characteristic of the Middle Ages.

Whatever the right of this matter—if there can be said to be a right—this has not been our concern in editing this book. What has had our earnest and exclusive attention is, to repeat, the literature of these three hundred years (which provide at least as good a beginning and terminus to what is called the Renaissance as any other dates) that seems to us for whatever reasons to be representative of some important aspect of the period—and good and lively to read today.

The order of our selections is not strictly chronological. We have divided the book into four parts: Italy, Spain, France, and, fourth, Middle and Eastern Europe. This is roughly the order of progression in the flowering of the arts, including literature, in the countries of the European continent during the Renaissance. But within each of these four parts we decided not to follow precise chronology. There have been several reasons for this decision. In the section called "Italy," which contains more poetry than do the other sections, we have attempted to provide a pleasant balance between prose and poetry, and between various kinds of prose in the order as well as in the number of selections. For example, if one moves (as many orderly readers may, not skipping here and there) from the inspired flights of Michelangelo's poetic imagination to the forthright and highly colored story of Cellini's life, and in turn to the religious fervor of Savonarola, one is immediately aware of that complexity and diversity to which we have already referred. On the other hand, in the last section we have followed a particular order because in this section so arranging the selections provides an opportunity for the reader, if he will, to move in a kind of logical progression from the stern new doctrine of Calvin and Luther to the half-mocking, half-traditional mind of Erasmus, and from his brand of skepticism and independence to that of Cornelius Agrippa, who is also interested in the occult; he, in turn, appropriately introduces this side of that strange vagabond, half charlatan and half scientist, Paracelsus—and Paracelsus, with his interest in medicine, makes it appropriate to move on to Vesalius, the founder of the science of anatomy and a true scientist in the modern sense, thence to the new voices of Galileo and Kepler.

Whether or not the Renaissance was indeed the period in which "modern man" was born, it is perhaps worth mentioning that, for all the opposite tendencies, there runs from the very first selection to the very last a constantly re-emergent current that carries the ideal of human freedom. On the first page of the book, so to speak, we see Dante in revolt against one kind of authoritarianism, and the book concludes with Kepler exhorting the booksellers to keep an open mind to the free traffic of ideas and not to act as censors or the allies of censors. The great modern heritage of individual freedom—of thought, of expression, of religion, and of political conviction—saturates the book and finds articulate spokesmen in figures as diverse as Luther and Montaigne, Agrippa and Kepler, Cellini and Erasmus.

Finally, it is perhaps not out of place to describe one of the particular sources of pleasure that has come to the editors in compiling this book, and that they believe may come to many readers. We have pointed out that it is a book to browse in and that those who do not like poetry may still find rewarding the basic scientific texts they read here; that those who are bored with essays may still be enchanted by the tales of Boccaccio, Rabelais, and Margaret of Navarre; that those who, for instance, find little satisfaction in the harsh injunctions of a Calvin or the mysticism of a Loyola may take great pleasure in the bland and casual, yet incisive, ruminations of Montaigne or the dry cynicism and political earnestness of Machiavelli. We have also demonstrated that we have been at some pains to arrange the book carefully in terms of the logical reader who likes to go through from beginning to end. But I think that the deepest satisfaction of all lies in the opportunity to have a sense of consorting with great minds. This sense is inherent in a great deal of the literature selected for inclusion. It is, however, perhaps peculiarly evident in the few collections of letters that have found their way into the book. The active imagination cannot fail to be excited at the invitation to read a letter written by Petrarch to Boccaccio about Dante. Again, to read Erasmus advising Agrippa how to behave is to have a deeper and also more amusing insight into the mind of a man whose very name has come to be synonymous with

x   tolerance, balance, and flexibility—for in these letters one finds these qualities, to be sure, but one also has a wonderfully vivid sense of the fears and the timidities that lead to the homilies he delivers to Agrippa. Finally, through all the formalities of the exchange between Galileo and Kepler, one has a most lively impression of the differences in character and yet the commonness of purpose to be found in these two men facing a hostile world—hostile, because it found them radical and dangerous.

So much for what we have tried to do. We would only say in conclusion that we hope we are right about that reader we described at the beginning of this introductory piece: that this book will discover him, reproduced in good number, and that he will find it as satisfying to read as we have found it to put together.

Hiram Haydn and John Charles Nelson

Contents

INTRODUCTION   vii

ITALY

FRANCESCO PETRARCA
Petrarch's Attitude toward Dante—A Letter to Giovanni Boccaccio   3
Eleven sonnets and two odes   4

GIOVANNI BOCCACCIO
The Decameron: *The Confession of Master Ciappelletto*   12
Andreuccio of Perugia   22
Alibech   32

LORENZO DE' MEDICI
Triumph of Bacchus and Ariadne   36
Sonnet   37

POLIZIANO
A Ballata   39

GIORGIO VASARI
Life of Leonardo da Vinci   41

MICHELANGELO BUONARROTTI
Three Sonnets   45

BENVENUTO CELLINI
From Autobiography   47

GIROLAMO SAVONAROLA
The Triumph of the Cross   62

LUDOVICO ARIOSTO
From Orlando Furioso   67

GIOVANNI PICO DELLA MIRANDOLA
From Oration on the Dignity of Man   91

NICCOLÒ MACHIAVELLI
Mandragola   99
From The Prince   134
From Discourses on the First Decade of Titus Livius   142

xiii

PIETRO POMPONAZZI
From On the Immortality of the Soul   149

FRANCESCO GUICCIARDINI
From Counsels and Reflections   157

TORQUATO TASSO
Aminta   164

BALDASSARE CASTIGLIONE
From The Book of the Courtier   193

GIORDANO BRUNO
The Mercurial Ass   208

SPAIN

ANONYMOUS
Lazarillo de Tormes   217

JUAN LUIS VIVES
A Fable about Man   224

ST. IGNATIUS LOYOLA
From Spiritual Exercises   230

MIGUEL DE CERVANTES SAAVEDRA
Don Quixote de la Mancha: *Of the good success which the valorous Don Quixote had in the most terrifying and never-to-be-imagined adventure of the wind-mills. How Don Quixote set free many miserable creatures, who were carrying, much against their wills, to a place they did not like* . . .   234

LOPE DE VEGA
The History of Mireno   245

FRANCE

PIERRE DE RONSARD
Fourteen poems   255

FRANÇOIS RABELAIS
Gargantua and Pantagruel: *How a Monk of Sevillé Saved the Close of the*

Abbey from Being Ravaged by the Enemy. How Gargantua Did Eat up Six Pilgrims in a Sallad. How Gargantua Caused to Be Built for the Monk the Abbey of Theleme. The Inscription Set upon the Great Gate of Theleme. How the Thelemites Were Governed, and of Their Manner of Living. Of the Nativity of the Most Dread and Redoubted Pantagruel. Of the Infancy of Pantagruel. Of the Acts of the Noble Pantagruel in His Youthful Age. How Panurge Related the Manner How He Escaped out of the Hands of the Turks. How Pantagruel with His Tongue Covered a Whole Army, and What the Author Saw in His Mouth 262

JOACHIM DU BELLAY
Four poems 288

MARGARET QUEEN OF NAVARRE
The Heptameron: *Novel LXX* 291

MICHEL DE MONTAIGNE
Essays: *Of three commerces or societies. Of experience* 306

JEAN BODIN
On the Idea of a Golden Age 331

BONAVENTURE DES PÉRIERS
Cymbalum Mundi, the Third Dialogue 337

PIERRE CHARRON
From A Treatise on Wisdom 342

MIDDLE AND EASTERN EUROPE

JUSTUS LIPSIUS
From Two Books of Constancy 349

MARTIN LUTHER
Concerning Christian Liberty 356

JOHN CALVIN
From Instruction and Confession of Faith 369

DESIDERIUS ERASMUS
From The Praise of Folly 377

xv

CORNELIUS AGRIPPA
Selected Letters and Other Writings 389

PARACELSUS
The Sixth Defence 398
On the Miners' Sickness and Other Miners' Diseases 401
The Diseases That Deprive Man of His Reason 403
A Book on Nymphs, Sylphs, Pygmies, and Salamanders, and on Other
Spirits 407

ANDREAS VESALIUS
The Epitome of His Books on the Fabric of the Human Body 412

NIKOLAUS COPERNICUS
From The Commentariolus 417
The Narratio Prima of Rheticus: The Arrangement of the Universe 419

JOHANNES KEPLER AND GALILEO GALILEI
Letters 423

BIOGRAPHICAL SKETCHES 429

ITALY

FRANCESCO PETRARCA

GIOVANNI BOCCACCIO

LORENZO DE' MEDICI

POLIZIANO

GIORGIO VASARI

MICHELANGELO BUONARROTTI

BENVENUTO CELLINI

GIROLAMO SAVONAROLA

LUDOVICO ARIOSTO

GIOVANNI PICO DELLA MIRANDOLA

NICCOLÒ MACHIAVELLI

PIETRO POMPONAZZI

FRANCESCO GUICCIARDINI

TORQUATO TASSO

BALDASSARE CASTIGLIONE

GIORDANO BRUNO

FRANCESCO PETRARCA

Petrarch's Attitude toward Dante—
A Letter to Giovanni Boccaccio
Translated by John Charles Nelson

. . . Those who hate me say that I hate and despise him [Dante], expressly to bring upon me the hate of the common people, by whom he is very well liked—a new kind of iniquity and remarkable art of injury! Let truth itself reply to them on my behalf.

In the first place there is no cause whatever for me to hate a man who was pointed out to me only once, in my early childhood. He lived with my father and my grandfather, younger than the latter, but older than the former, and was expelled from the country's borders with them on the same day and by the same civil commotion. Often in such circumstances great friendships are contracted among companions in hardship; and that happened particularly to them, who were joined not only by a similar fortune, but by great affinity of interests and disposition. However, he [Dante] resisted the exile to which my father, devoted to other cares and anxious about his family, had to submit; and then applied himself more passionately to his purpose, disregarding everything and desirous only of fame. In that act I can scarcely admire and praise him enough: neither the injustice of his fellow-citizens, nor exile, nor poverty, nor the stings of enmity, nor love for his wife, nor compassion toward his children could dissuade him from that path once taken. . . .

The second part of the calumny by which I am reproached is that which bases its argument upon the fact that from childhood, when one is usually most eager for such things, I who took delight in collecting books by every means never possessed his book; and that although I was always most ardent in searching for other books, even when there was scarcely any hope of finding them, with new

3

and strange conduct I was lukewarm only with regard to this one, easily obtainable. I confess the fact, but deny that I did it with the intent which they attribute to me. Being given at that time to the same style, I too exercised my talent in the common tongue; I thought nothing more elegant nor had I yet learned to seek a higher goal. But I feared that if I were steeped in his writings or another's I should against my will and unawares become an imitator, as that age is responsive and inclined to admire everything. That I disdained with the audacity of youth, and assumed such confidence and exaltation as to think that my own talent would suffice without the aid of any mortal to realize a certain style of my own in that genre. Others must judge whether I believed correctly. . . .

Now that I am far from those concerns, which I have left completely, and the fear which I had is removed, I accept all others with all my heart—him above the rest. As before I submitted myself to the judgment of others, I now judge the others in silence, and though I judge the rest variously, I do not hesitate to give him the prize of vernacular eloquence. Therefore those who say that I slander his fame are liars. . . .

For my part, I admire and esteem him; I do not despise him. And I think I can say with every right that had he lived till this time, he would have been friendlier to few than to me—this I say, if I should have liked his habits as much as I like his genius. . . .

Others accuse me of envy: those, to wit, who envy me and my name. . . . And whom at length would he envy who does not envy Virgil? When it happens that I do not envy the applause and hullabaloo of dyers and inn-keepers and other such admirers, whose praise is vituperation, and I am happy to be without it in the company of Virgil himself and of Homer. For I know how the praise of the ignorant is valued by learned people. . . .

Sonnets and Odes during the Life of Laura

Translated by John Nott

Each creature, on whose wakeful eyes
   The bright sun pours his golden fire,
     By day a destin'd toil pursues;
And, when heav'n's lamps illume the skies,
   All to some haunt for rest retire,
4   Till a fresh dawn that toil renews.

But I, when a new morn doth rise,
   Chasing from earth its murky shades,
     While ring the forests with delight,
Find no remission of my sighs;
   And, soon as night her mantle spreads,
     I weep, and wish returning light.

Again when eve bids day retreat,
   O'er other climes to dart its rays;
     Pensive those cruel stars I view,
Which influence thus my am'rous fate;
   And imprecate that beauty's blaze,
     Which o'er my form such wildness threw.

No forest surely in its glooms
   Nurtures a savage so unkind
     As she, who bids these sorrows flow:
Me, nor the dawn, nor sleep o'ercomes;
   For, though of mortal mould, my mind
     Feels more than passion's mortal glow.

Ere up to you, bright orbs, I fly,
   Or to Love's bow'r speed down my way,
     While here my mould'ring limbs remain;
Let me her pity once espy:
   Thus, rich in bliss, one little day
     Shall recompense whole years of pain.

Be Laura mine at set of sun;
   Let heav'n's fires only mark our loves,
     And the day ne'er its light renew;
My fond embrace may she not shun;
   Nor, Phœbus-like, through laurel groves
     May I a nymph transform'd pursue!

But I shall cast this mortal veil on earth,
And stars shall gild the noon, ere such bright scenes have birth.

Anonymous translation

Alone, and lost in thought, the desert glade
   Measuring I roam with ling'ring steps and slow,
   And still a watchful glance around me throw,
5   Anxious to shun the print of human tread:

No other means I find, no surer aid
   From the world's prying eye to hide my woe:
   So well my wild disorder'd gestures show,
   And love-lorn looks, the fire within me bred,
That well I deem each mountain, wood and plain,
   And river knows, what I from men conceal,
   What dreary hues my life's sad prospects dim.
Yet whate'er wild or savage paths I've ta'en,
   Where'er I wander, love attends me still,
   Soft whisp'ring to my soul, and I to him.

Anonymous translation

Loose to the breeze her golden tresses flow'd
   Wildly in thousand mazy ringlets blown,
   And from her eyes unconquer'd glances shone,
   Those glances now so sparingly bestow'd.
And true or false, meseem'd some signs she show'd
   As o'er her cheek soft pity's hue was thrown:
   I, whose whole breast with love's soft food was sown,
   What wonder if at once my bosom glow'd?
Graceful she mov'd, with more than mortal mien,
   In form an angel: and her accents won
   Upon the ear with more than human sound.
A spirit heav'nly pure, a living sun,
   Was what I saw; and if no more 'twere seen,
   T'unbend the bow will never heal the wound.

Translated by Penn

That window where my Sun is often seen
   Refulgent, and the world's at morning's hours;
   And that, where Boreas blows, when Winter lowers,
And the short days reveal a clouded scene;
That bench of stone where, with a pensive mien,
   My Laura sits, forgetting beauty's powers;
   Haunts where her shadow strikes the walls or flowers,
And her feet press the paths or herbage green:
   The place where Love assail'd me with success;
And Spring, the fatal time that, first observed,
   Revives the keen remembrance every year;
6 With looks and words, that o'er me have preserved

A power, no length of time can render less,
Call to my eyes the sadly-soothing tear.

Translated by C. B. Cayley

Sweet, cool and limpid wave,
  Where she her beauties brought,
    Who to me seems all womankind alone—
And you, fair boughs, that gave,
  As by these sighs I'm taught,
    The prop, she leaned her lovely flank upon—
    Ye flowers and sods whereon
Her graceful garb was laid—
  That heavenly bosom's screen—
  Thou sacred air serene,
Whence Love my heart pierced from fair eyes conveyed—
    O grant you audience all,
    To this my last and lamentable call.

Yet, if it be my fate,
  And this be heaven's endeavour,
    That Love upon my tears should seal my eyes,
'Midst you let this poor weight
  Find hiding-place by favour,
    When tow'rd its goal my soul nakedly flies.
    Less threat'ning Death will rise,
If this hope fall not short
  Before yon pass of dread;
  For no way can be sped
My weary spirit tow'rd a softer pit,
    From bones and aching members, can it flit.

A time may come, perchance,
  When tow'rd the wonted bower
    Returneth meek that creature wild and bright;
Then may she bend her glance,
  Where in that blessed hour
    She saw me, and again require that sight
    In blitheness; but, oh spite,
She'll 'mid those rocks discern
  That I am clay; and Love
  Will then her bosom move
To sigh so gently that my peace she'll earn.
    For heav'n will violence bear,
    When tow'rd her eyes she draws her veil thrice fair.

7

From those fine boughs (how sweet
    To memory is the story!)
        There fell about her lap a rain of flowers;
And there she kept her seat,
    Meek in exceeding glory,
        Covered already by those amorous showers;
        Her skirt this blossom dowers,
This her pale tresses crave,
    Which now like burnished gold
    And pearl are to behold;
One settles in the ground, one on the wave,
    One, fondly wandering,
    Circleth and saith, methinks, "Love here is king."

How often then said I,
    All overwhelmed with fear,
        "No doubt, but she was born in Paradise."
My brain had so thrown-by
    All but her heavenly cheer,
        Aspect, and words, and sweetly-smiling eyes!
        And these in such a guise
Had the true scene effaced,
    That I said sighing then,
    "Whence came I here, and when?"
Thinking it heaven, not earth, where I was placed.
        Henceforth that verdure so
        Delights me, that no peace I elsewhere know.

If thou'dst apparel as thou hast good-will,
        Thou could'st have boldly broke
        Out from the woods, and gone amidst the folk.

Translated by John Nott

Warfare I cannot wage, yet know not peace;
    I fear, I hope, I burn, I freeze again;
    Mount to the skies, then bow to earth my face;
    Grasp the whole world, yet nothing I obtain.
His pris'ner Love nor frees, nor will detain;
    In toils he holds me not, nor will release;
    He slays me not, nor yet will he unchain;
    Nor joy allows, nor lets my sorrow cease.
Sightless I see my fair; though mute, I mourn;
    I scorn existence, and yet court its stay;
    Detest myself, and for another burn;

By grief I'm nurtur'd; and, though tearful, gay;
  Death I despise, and life alike I hate:
  Such, lady, dost thou make my wayward state!

Anonymous translation

Glad flow'rs and herbs, that on your favour'd bed,
  Where pensive oft she sits, my lady bear;
  Plains, that of her sweet voice the accents hear,
  And of her lovely foot preserve the tread;
Shrubs timely shap'd, leaves green and crude that spread,
  Ye violets, pale and love-lorn that appear:
  And ye, thick woods, that high and proudly rear,
  Cheer'd by the sun's enlivening beams, your head;
O thou sweet country; and thou limpid stream,
  That, as she bathes, o'er all her charms canst rove,
  And borrowest of that living light a gleam;
How does each chaste dear act my envy move!
  No rock have you, but by long use shall seem
  To share my flames, and burn with my hot love.

Sonnets and Odes after the Death of Laura

Translated by Langhorne

Fall'n the fair column, blasted is the bay,
  That shaded once my solitary shore!
  I've lost what hope can never give me more,
Though sought from Indus to the closing day.
My twofold treasure death has snatch'd away,
  My pride, my pleasure, left me to deplore:
What fields far-cultur'd, nor imperial sway,
  Nor orient gold, nor jewels can restore.
O destiny severe of human kind!
  What portion have we unbedew'd with tears?
The downcast visage and the pensive mind
  Through the thin veil of smiling life appears;
And in one moment vanish into wind
9   The hard-earn'd fruits of long laborious years.

Translated by Barbarina Lady Dacre

The eyes, the face, the limbs of heavenly mould,
 So long the theme of my impassioned lay,
 Charms which so stole me from myself away,
 That strange to other men the course I hold:
The crisped locks of pure and lucid gold,
 The lightning of the angelic smile, whose ray
 To earth could all of Paradise convey,
 A little dust are now, to feeling cold.
And yet I live—but that I live bewail,
 Sunk the loved light that through the tempest led
 My shattered bark, bereft of mast and sail.
Hushed be the song that breathed love's purest fire:
 Lost is the theme on which my fancy fed,
 And turned to mourning my once tuneful lyre.

Translated by John Nott

My fancy bore me to that region, where
 Dwells her I seek, on earth yet cannot find;
 Again I saw her amid those, consign'd
 To the third heav'n, less haughty, and more fair.
She took my hand, and thus did she declare:
 "Still shalt thou dwell with me, if hope prove kind;
 " 'Twas I, who in such warfare held thy mind,
 "Whose day was clos'd ere evening could appear:
"No human thought may scan the bliss I prove;
 "I only wait for thee, and to resume
 "My fair veil cast on earth thou so didst love."
How could she quit my hand, why mute become?
 For words thus chastely, piteously exprest,
 Had nearly render'd me heav'n's lasting guest.

Anonymous translation

Nor stars through heav'n's grey vault that twinkle clear,
 Nor barks swift gliding through the level main,
 Nor armed knights that prick along the plain,
 Nor through thick woods the gay and bounding deer;
Nor tidings glad when first they strike the ear,
10 Nor loftier notes to pour of love's soft reign,

Nor beauteous dames that tune their happier strain
  In verdant fields, or some pure fountain near;
Nor these or aught besides can touch my heart,
  So deep she buried it and with her bore;
  Who light and mirror of my eyes had been.
Nor ever do I wish from life to part;
  Life so long loath'd by me; who pant once more
  To see her, whom 'twere best I ne'er had seen.

Translated by John Nott

My verdurous, and bloomy prime was past;
  More faintly glow'd my bosom's scorching flame;
  And to that portion of my days I came,
  When life declining to its end doth haste:
My hostile fair suspicion had nigh ceas'd,
  Of insecurity did little dream;
  Ofttimes my tender sorrows were her theme,
  On which some courteous merriment she cast:
Now time at length that sober period brought,
  When chastity might fondness safely greet,
  And social lovers speak each inmost thought:
Then death, invidious of a joy so sweet
  E'en in expectance, cross'd me on my road,
  And, like an armed foe, despoil'd me of my good.

Translated by John Nott

Still do I weep the days that are gone by,
  When sublunary things my fondness sway'd,
  And no bold flight, though having wings, I made,
  Haply to give of me examples high.
Thou, who my impious, foul misdeeds dost spy,
  Dread Lord of heaven immortal, viewless! aid
  The soul that's frail, that has from duty stray'd;
  And its defect O let thy grace supply!
Thus if life's warfare, and its storm I prov'd,
  Peace, and a harbour may in death be mine:
  Though vain my stay, I'll worthily depart.
For that short period ere I'm hence remov'd,
  And at the last, extend thy hand divine:
11   Thou know'st, that thou alone giv'st hope unto my heart.

GIOVANNI BOCCACCIO

The Decameron
Translated by John Payne

THE CONFESSION OF MASTER CIAPPELLETTO

"It is a seemly thing, dearest ladies, that whatsoever a man doth, he give it beginning from the holy and admirable name of Him who is the maker of all things. Wherefore, it behoving me, as the first, to give commencement to our storytelling, I purpose to begin with one of His marvels, to the end that, this being heard, our hope in Him, as in a thing immutable, may be confirmed and His name be ever praised of us. It is manifest that, like as things temporal are all transitory and mortal, even so both within and without are they full of annoy and anguish and travail and subject to infinite perils, against which it is indubitable that we, who live enmingled therein and who are indeed part and parcel thereof, might avail neither to endure nor to defend ourselves, except God's especial grace lent us strength and foresight; which latter, it is not to be believed, descendeth unto us and upon us by any merit of our own, but of the proper motion of His own benignity and the efficacy of the prayers of those who were mortals even as we are and having diligently ensued His commandments, what while they were on life, are now with Him become eternal and blessed and unto whom we—belike not daring to address ourselves unto the proper presence of so august a judge—proffer our petitions of the things which we deem needful unto ourselves, as unto advocates informed by experience of our frailty. And this more we discern in Him, full as He is of compassionate liberality towards us, that, whereas it chanceth whiles (the keenness of mortal eyes availing not in any wise to penetrate the secrets of the Divine intent), that we peradventure, beguiled by report, make such an one our advocate unto His majesty, who is outcast from His presence with an eternal banishment—nevertheless He, from whom nothing is hidden, having regard rather to the purity of the suppliant's intent than to his ignorance or to the reprobate estate of him whose intercession he invoketh, giveth ear unto those who pray unto the latter, as if he were in very deed blessed in His aspect. The which will manifestly appear from the story which I purpose to relate; I say manifestly, ensuing, not the judgment of God, but that of men.

It is told, then, that Musciatto Franzesi, being from a very rich and considerable merchant in France become a knight and it behoving him thereupon go into Tuscany with Messire Charles Sansterre, brother to the king of France, who had been required and bidden thither by Pope Boniface, found his affairs in one part and another sore embroiled (as those of merchants most times are), and was unable lightly or promptly to disentangle them; wherefore he bethought himself to commit them unto divers persons and made shift for all, save only he abode in doubt whom he might leave sufficient to the recovery of the credits he had given to certain Burgundians. The cause of his doubt was that he knew the Burgundians to be litigious, quarrelsome fellows, ill-conditioned and disloyal, and could not call one to mind, in whom he might put any trust, curst enough to cope with their perversity. After long consideration of the matter, there came to his memory a certain Master Ciapperello da Prato, who came often to his house in Paris and whom, for that he was little of person and mighty nice in his dress, the French, knowing not what Cepparello meant and thinking it be the same with Cappello, to wit, in their vernacular, Chaplet, called him, not Cappello, but Ciapelletto, and accordingly as Ciappelletto he was known everywhere, whilst few knew him for Master Ciapperello.

Now this said Ciappelletto was of this manner life, that, being a scrivener, he thought very great shame whenas any of his instruments was found (and indeed he drew few such) other than false; whilst of the latter he would have drawn as many as might be required of him and these with a better will by way of gift than any other for a great wage. False witness he bore with especial delight, required or not required, and the greatest regard being in those times paid to oaths in France, as he recked nothing of forswearing himself, he knavishly gained all the suits concerning which he was called upon to tell the truth upon his faith. He took inordinate pleasure and was mighty diligent in stirring up troubles and enmities and scandals between friends and kinsfolk and whomsoever else, and the greater the mischiefs he saw ensue thereof, the more he rejoiced. If bidden to manslaughter or whatsoever other
13 naughty deed, he went about it with a will, without ever saying nay

thereto; and many a time of his proper choice he had been known to wound men and do them to death with his own hand. He was a terrible blasphemer of God and the saints, and that for every trifle, being the most choleric man alive. To church he went never and all the sacraments thereof he flouted in abominable terms, as things of no account; whilst, on the other hand, he was still fain to haunt and use taverns and other lewd places. Of women he was as fond as dogs of the stick; but in the contrary he delighted more than any filthy fellow alive. He robbed and pillaged with as much conscience as a godly man would make oblation to God; he was a very glutton and a great wine bibber, insomuch that bytimes it wrought him shameful mischief, and to boot, he was a notorious gamester and a caster of cogged dice. But why should I enlarge in so many words? He was belike the worst man that ever was born. His wickedness had long been upheld by the power and interest of Messer Musciatto, who had many a time safeguarded him as well from private persons, to whom he often did a mischief, as from the law, against which he was a perpetual offender.

This Master Ciappelletto, then, coming to Musciatto's mind, the latter, who was very well acquainted with his way of life, bethought himself that he should be such an one as the perversity of the Burgundians required and accordingly, sending for him, he bespoke him thus: 'Master Ciappelletto, I am, as thou knowest, about altogether to withdraw hence, and having to do, amongst others, with certain Burgundians, men full of guile, I know none whom I may leave to recover my due from them more fitting than thyself, more by token that thou dost nothing at this present; wherefore, an thou wilt undertake this, I will e'en procure thee the favour of the Court and give thee such part as shall be meet of that which thou shalt recover.'

Don Ciappelletto, who was then out of employ and ill provided with the goods of the world, seeing him who had long been his stay and his refuge about to depart thence, lost no time in deliberation, but, as of necessity constrained, replied that he would well. They being come to an accord, Musciatto departed and Ciappelletto, having gotten his patron's procuration and letters commendatory from the king, betook himself into Burgundy, where well nigh none knew him, and there, contrary to his nature, began courteously and blandly to seek to get in his payments and do that wherefor he was come thither, as if reserving choler and violence for a last resort. Dealing thus and lodging in the house of two Florentines, brothers, who there lent at usance and who entertained him with great honour for the love of Messer Musciatto, it chanced that he fell 14 sick, whereupon the two brothers promptly fetched physicians and servants to tend him and furnished him with all that behoved unto the recovery of his health.

But every succour was in vain, for that, by the physicians' report, the good man, who was now old and had lived disorderly, grew daily worse, as one who had a mortal sickness; wherefore the two brothers were sore concerned and one day, being pretty near the chamber where he lay sick, they began to take counsel together, saying one to the other, 'How shall we do with yonder fellow? We have a sorry bargain on our hands of his affair, for that to send him forth of our house, thus sick, were a sore reproach to us and a manifest sign of little wit on our part, if the folk, who have seen us first receive him and after let tend and medicine him with such solicitude, should now see him suddenly put out of our house, sick unto death as he is, without it being possible for him to have done aught that should displease us. On the other hand, he hath been so wicked a man that he will never consent to confess or take any sacrament of the church; and he dying without confession, no church will receive his body; nay, he will be cast into a ditch, like a dog. Again, even if he do confess, his sins are so many and so horrible that the like will come of it, for that there is nor priest nor friar who can or will absolve him thereof; wherefore, being unshriven, he will still be cast into the ditches. Should it happen thus, the people of the city, as well on account of our trade, which appeareth to them most iniquitous and of which they missay all day, as of their itch to plunder us, seeing this, will rise up in riot and cry out, "These Lombard dogs, whom the church refuseth to receive, are to be suffered here no longer";—and they will run to our houses and despoil us not only of our good, but may be of our lives, to boot; wherefore in any case it will go ill with us, if yonder fellow die.'

Master Ciappelletto, who, as we have said, lay near the place where the two brothers were in discourse, being quick of hearing, as is most times the case with the sick, heard what they said of him and calling them to him, bespoke them thus: 'I will not have you anywise misdoubt of me nor fear to take any hurt by me. I have heard what you say of me and am well assured that it would happen even as you say, should matters pass as you expect; but it shall go otherwise. I have in my lifetime done God the Lord so many an affront that it will make neither more nor less, an I do Him yet another at the point of death; wherefore do you make shift to bring me the holiest and worthiest friar you may avail to have, if any such there be, and leave the rest to me, for that I will assuredly order your affairs and mine own on such wise that all shall go well and
15 you shall have good cause to be satisfied.'

The two brothers, albeit they conceived no great hope of this, nevertheless betook themselves to a brotherhood of monks and demanded some holy and learned man to hear the confession of a Lombard who lay sick in their house. There was given them a venerable brother of holy and good life and a past master in Holy Writ, a very reverend man, for whom all the townsfolk had a very great and special regard, and they carried him to their house; where, coming to the chamber where Master Ciappelletto lay and seating himself by his side, he began first tenderly to comfort him and after asked him how long it was since he had confessed last; whereto Master Ciappelletto, who had never confessed in his life, answered, 'Father, it hath been my usance to confess every week once at the least and often more; it is true that, since I fell sick, to wit, these eight days past, I have not confessed, such is the annoy that my sickness hath given me.' Quoth the friar, 'My son, thou hast done well and so must thou do henceforward. I see, since thou confessest so often, that I shall be at little pains either of hearing or questioning.' 'Sir,' answered Master Ciappelletto, 'say not so; I have never confessed so much nor so often but I would still fain make a general confession of all my sins that I could call to mind from the day of my birth to that of my confession; wherefore I pray you, good my father, question me as punctually of everything, nay, everything, as if I had never confessed; and consider me not because I am sick, for that I had far liefer displease this my flesh than, in consulting its ease, do aught that might be the perdition of my soul, which my Saviour redeemed with His precious blood.'

These words much pleased the holy man and seemed to him to argue a well-disposed mind; wherefore, after he had much commended Master Ciappelletto for that his usance, he asked him if he had ever sinned by way of lust with any woman. 'Father,' replied Master Ciappelletto, sighing, 'on this point I am ashamed to tell you the truth, fearing to sin by way of vainglory.' Quoth the friar, 'Speak in all security, for never did one sin by telling the truth, whether in confession or otherwise.' 'Then,' said Master Ciappelletto, 'since you certify me of this, I will tell you; I am yet a virgin, even as I came forth of my mother's body.' 'O blessed be thou of God!' cried the monk. 'How well hast thou done! And doing thus, thou hast the more deserved, inasmuch as, an thou wouldst, thou hadst more leisure to do the contrary than we and whatsoever others are limited by any rule.'

After this he asked him if he had ever offended against God in the sin of gluttony; whereto Master Ciappelletto answered, sighing, Ay had he, and that many a time; for that, albeit, over and above the Lenten fasts that are yearly observed of the devout, he had been wont to fast on bread and water three days at the least in every week—he had oftentimes (and especially whenas he had endured any fatigue, either praying or going a-pilgrimage) drunken the water with as much appetite and as keen a relish as great drinkers do wine. And many a time he had longed to have such homely salads of potherbs as women make when they go into the country; and whiles eating had given him more pleasure than himseemed it should do to one who fasteth for devotion, as did he. 'My son,' said the friar, 'these sins are natural and very slight and I would not therefore have thee burden thy conscience withal more than behoveth. It happeneth to every man, how devout soever he be, that, after long fasting, meat seemeth good to him. and after travail, drink.'

'Alack, father mine,' rejoined Ciappelletto, 'tell me not this to comfort me; you must know I know that things done for the service of God should be done sincerely and with an ungrudging mind; and whoso doth otherwise sinneth.' Quoth the friar, exceeding well pleased, 'I am content that thou shouldst thus apprehend it and thy pure and good conscience therein pleaseth me exceedingly. But, tell me, hast thou sinned by way of avarice, desiring more than befitted or withholding that which it behoved thee not to withhold?' 'Father mine,' replied Ciappelletto, 'I would not have you look to my being in the house of these usurers; I have nought to do here; nay, I came hither to admonish and chasten them and turn them from this their abominable way of gain; and methinketh I should have made shift to do so, had not God thus visited me. But you must know that I was left a rich man by my father, of whose good, when he was dead, I bestowed the most part in alms, and after, to sustain my life and that I might be able to succour Christ's poor, I have done my little traffickings, and in these I have desired to gain; but still with God's poor have I shared that which I gained, converting my own half to my occasion and giving them the other, and in this so well hath my Creator prospered me that my affairs have still gone from good to better.'

'Well hast thou done,' said the friar; 'but hast thou often been angered?' 'Oh,' cried Master Ciappelletto, 'that I must tell you I have very often been! And who could keep himself therefrom, seeing men do unseemly things all day long, keeping not the commandments of God neither fearing His judgments? Many times a day I had liefer been dead than alive, seeing young men follow after vanities and hearing them curse and forswear themselves, haunting the taverns, visiting not the churches and ensuing rather the ways of the world than that of God.' 'My son,' said the friar, 'this is a righteous anger, nor for my part might I enjoin thee any penance therefor. But

17

hath anger at any time availed to move thee to do any manslaughter or to bespeak any one unseemly or do any other unright?' 'Alack, sir,' answered the sick man, 'you, who seem to me a man of God, how can you say such words? Had I ever had the least thought of doing any one of the things whereof you speak, think you I believe that God would so long have forborne me? These be the doings of outlaws and men of nought, whereof I never saw any but I said still, "Go, may God amend thee!"'

Then said the friar, 'Now tell me, my son (blessed be thou of God), hast thou never borne false witness against any or missaid of another, or taken others' good, without leave of him to whom it pertained?' 'Ay, indeed, sir,' replied Master Ciappelletto; 'I have missaid of others; for that I had a neighbour aforetime, who, with the greatest unright in the world, did nought but beat his wife, insomuch that I once spoke ill of him to her kinsfolk, so great was the compassion that overcame me for the poor woman, whom he used as God alone can tell, whenassoever he had drunken overmuch.' Quoth the friar, 'Thou tellest me thou hast been a merchant. Hast thou never cheated any one, as merchants do whiles?' 'I' faith, yes, sir,' answered Master Ciappelletto; 'but I know not whom, except it were a certain man, who once brought me monies which he owed me for cloth I had sold him and which I threw into a chest, without counting. A good month after, I found that they were four farthings more than they should have been; wherefore, not seeing him again and having kept them by me a full year, that I might restore them to him, I gave them away in alms.' Quoth the friar, 'This was a small matter, and thou didst well to deal with it as thou didst.'

Then he questioned him of many other things, of all which he answered after the same fashion, and the holy father offering to proceed to absolution, Master Ciappelletto said, 'Sir, I have yet sundry sins that I have not told you.' The friar asked him what they were, and he answered, 'I mind me that one Saturday, after none, I caused my servant sweep out the house and had not that reverence for the Lord's holy day which it behoved me have.' 'Oh,' said the friar, 'that is a light matter, my son.' 'Nay,' rejoined Master Ciappelletto, 'call it not a light matter, for that the Lord's Day is greatly to be honoured, seeing that on such a day our Lord rose from the dead.' Then said the friar, 'Well, hast thou done aught else?' 'Ay, sir,' answered Master Ciappelletto; 'once, unthinking what I did, I spat in the church of God.' Thereupon the friar fell a-smiling and said, 'My son, that is no thing to be recked of; we who are of the clergy, we spit there all day long.' 'And you do very ill,' rejoined Master Ciappelletto; 'for that there is nought which it so straitly behoveth to keep clean as the holy temple wherein is rendered sacrifice to God.'

Brief, he told him great plenty of such like things and presently fell a-sighing and after weeping sore, as he knew full well to do, whenas he would. Quoth the holy friar, 'What aileth thee, my son?' 'Alas, sir,' replied Master Ciappelletto, 'I have one sin left, whereof I never yet confessed me, such shame have I to tell it; and every time I call it to mind, I weep, even as you see, and meseemeth very certain that God will never pardon it me.' 'Go to, son,' rejoined the friar; 'what is this thou sayest? If all the sins that were ever wrought or are yet to be wrought of all mankind, what while the world endureth, were all in one man and he repented him thereof and were contrite therefor, as I see thee, such is the mercy and loving-kindness of God that, upon confession, He would freely pardon them to him. Wherefore do thou tell it in all assurance.' Quoth Master Ciappelletto, still weeping sore, 'Alack, father mine, mine is too great a sin, and I can scarce believe that it will ever be forgiven me of God, except your prayers strive for me.' Then said the friar, 'Tell it me in all assurance, for I promise thee to pray God for thee.'

Master Ciappelletto, however, still wept and said nought; but, after he had thus held the friar a great while in suspense, he heaved a deep sigh and said, 'Father mine, since you promise me to pray God for me, I will e'en tell it you. Know, then, that when I was little, I once cursed my mother.' So saying, he fell again to weeping sore. 'O my son,' quoth the friar, 'seemeth this to thee so heinous a sin? Why, men blaspheme God all day long and He freely pardon-eth whoso repenteth him of having blasphemed Him; and deemest thou not He will pardon thee this? Weep not, but comfort thyself; for, certes, wert thou one of those who set Him on the cross, He would pardon thee, in favour of such contrition as I see in thee.' 'Alack, father mine, what say you?' replied Ciappelletto. 'My kind mother, who bore me nine months in her body, day and night, and carried me on her neck an hundred times and more, I did passing ill to curse her and it was an exceeding great sin; and except you pray God for me, it will not be forgiven me.'

The friar, then, seeing that Master Ciappelletto had no more to say, gave him absolution and bestowed on him his benison, holding him a very holy man and devoutly believing all that he had told him to be true. And who would not have believed it, hearing a man at the point of death speak thus? Then, after all this, he said to him, 'Master Ciappelletto, with God's help you will speedily be whole; but, should it come to pass that God call your blessed and well-disposed soul to Himself, would it please you that your body be

19 buried in our convent?' 'Ay, would it, sir,' replied Master Ciappel-

letto. 'Nay, I would fain not be buried otherwhere, since you have promised to pray God for me; more by token that I have ever had a special regard for your order. Wherefore I pray you that whenas you return to your lodging, you must cause bring me that most veritable body of Christ, which you consecrate a-mornings upon the altar, for that, with your leave, I purpose (all unworthy as I am) to take it and after, holy and extreme unction, to the intent that, if I have lived as a sinner, I may at the least die like a Christian.' The good friar replied that it pleased him much and that he said well and promised to see it presently brought him; and so was it done.

Meanwhile, the two brothers, misdoubting them sore lest Master Ciappelletto should play them false, had posted themselves behind a wainscot, that divided the chamber where he lay from another, and listening, easily heard and apprehended that which he said to the friar and had whiles so great a mind to laugh, hearing the things which he confessed to having done, that they were like to burst and said, one to other, 'What manner of man is this, whom neither old age nor sickness nor fear of death, whereunto he seeth himself near, nor yet of God, before whose judgment-seat he looketh to be ere long, have availed to turn from his wickedness nor hinder him from choosing to die as he hath lived?' However, seeing that he had so spoken that he should be admitted to burial in a church, they recked nought of the rest.

Master Ciappelletto presently took the sacrament and, growing rapidly worse, received extreme unction, and a little after evensong of the day he had made his fine confession, he died; whereupon the two brothers, having, of his proper monies, taken order for his honourable burial, sent to the convent to acquaint the friars therewith, bidding them come thither that night to hold vigil, according to usance, and fetch away the body in the morning, and meanwhile made ready all that was needful thereunto.

The holy friar, who had shriven him, hearing that he had departed this life, betook himself to the prior of the convent and, letting ring to chapter, gave out to the brethren therein assembled that Master Ciappelletto had been a holy man, according to that which he had gathered from his confession, and persuaded them to receive his body with the utmost reverence and devotion, in the hope that God should show forth many miracles through him. To this the prior and brethren credulously consented and that same evening, coming all whereas Master Ciappelletto lay dead, they held high and solemn vigil over him and on the morrow, clad all in albs and copes, book in hand and crosses before them, they went, chanting the while, for

20 his body and brought it with the utmost pomp and solemnity to

their church, followed by well nigh all the people of the city, men and women.

As soon as they had set the body down in the church, the holy friar, who had confessed him, mounted the pulpit and fell a-preaching marvellous things of the dead man and of his life, his fasts, his virginity, his simplicity and innocence and sanctity, recounting, amongst other things, that which he had confessed to him as his greatest sin and how he had hardly availed to persuade him that God would forgive it him; thence passing on to reprove the folk who hearkened, 'And you, accursed that you are,' quoth he, 'for every waif of straw that stirreth between your feet, you blaspheme God and the Virgin and all the host of heaven.' Moreover, he told them many other things of his loyalty and purity of heart; brief, with his speech, whereto entire faith was yielded of the people of the city, he so established the dead man in the reverent consideration of all who were present that, no sooner was the service at an end, than they all with the utmost eagerness flocked to kiss his hands and feet and the clothes were torn off his back, he holding himself blessed who might avail to have never so little thereof; and needs must they leave him thus all that day, so he might be seen and visited of all.

The following night he was honourably buried in a marble tomb in one of the chapels of the church and on the morrow the folk began incontinent to come and burn candles and offer up prayers and make vows to him and hang images of wax at his shrine, according to the promise made. Nay, on such wise waxed the fame of his sanctity and men's devotion to him that there was scarce any who, being in adversity, would vow himself to another saint than him; and they styled and yet style him Saint Ciappelletto and avouch that God through him hath wrought many miracles and yet worketh them every day for whoso devoutly commendeth himself unto him.

Thus, then, lived and died Master Cepperello da Prato and became a saint, as you have heard; nor would I deny it to be possible that he is beatified in God's presence, for that, albeit his life was wicked and perverse, he may at his last extremity have shown such contrition that peradventure God had mercy on him and received him into His kingdom; but, for that this is hidden from us, I reason according to that which is apparent and say that he should rather be in the hands of the devil in perdition than in Paradise. And if so it be, we may know from this how great is God's lovingkindness towards us, which, having regard not to our error, but to the purity of our faith, whenas we thus make an enemy (deeming him a friend) of His our intermediary, giveth ear unto us, even as if we had recourse unto one truly holy, as intercessor for His favour. Wherefore, to the end that by His grace we may be preserved safe and sound in this present adversity and in this so joyous company, let us, magnifying His name, in which we have begun our diversion, and holding Him in reverence, commend ourselves to Him in our necessities, well assured of being heard." And with this he was silent.

ANDREUCCIO OF PERUGIA

"The stones found by Landolfo," began Fiammetta, to whose turn it came to tell, "have brought to my mind a story scarce less full of perilous scapes than that related by Lauretta, but differing therefrom inasmuch as the adventures comprised in the latter befell in the course of belike several years and these of which I have to tell in the space of a single night, as you shall hear.

There was once in Perugia, as I have heard tell aforetime, a young man, a horse-courser, by name Andreuccio di Pietro, who, hearing that horses were going cheap at Naples, put five hundred gold florins in his purse and betook himself thither with other merchants, having never before been away from home. He arrived there one Sunday evening, towards vespers, and having taken counsel with his host, sallied forth next morning to the market, where he saw great plenty of horses. Many of them pleased him and he cheapened one and another, but could not come to an accord concerning any. Meanwhile, to show that he was for buying, he now and again, like a raw unwary clown as he was, pulled out the purse of florins he had with him, in the presence of those who came and went. As he was thus engaged, with his purse displayed, it chanced that a Sicilian damsel, who was very handsome, but disposed for a small matter to do any man's pleasure, passed near him, without his seeing her, and catching sight of the purse, said straightway in herself, 'Who would fare better than I, if yonder money were mine!' And passed on.

Now there was with her an old woman, likewise a Sicilian, who, seeing Andreuccio, let her companion pass on and running to him, embraced him affectionately, which when the damsel saw, she stepped aside to wait for her, without saying aught. Andreuccio, turning to the old woman and recognizing her, gave her a hearty greeting and she, having promised to visit him at his inn, took leave, without holding over-long parley there, whilst he fell again to chaffering, but bought nothing that morning. The damsel, who had noted first Andreuccio's purse and after her old woman's acquaint-

22

ance with him, began cautiously to enquire of the latter, by way of casting about for a means of coming at the whole or part of the money, who and whence he was and what he did there and how she came to know him. The old woman told her every particular of Andreuccio's affairs well nigh as fully as he himself could have done, having long abidden with his father, first in Sicily and after at Perugia, and acquainted her, to boot, where he lodged and wherefore he was come thither.

The damsel, being thus fully informed both of his name and parentage, thereby with subtle craft laid her plans for giving effect to her desire and returning home, set the old woman awork for the rest of the day, so she might not avail to return to Andreuccio. Then, calling a maid of hers, whom she had right well lessoned unto such offices, she despatched her, towards evensong, to the inn where Andreuccio lodged. As chance would have it, she found him alone at the door and enquired at him of himself. He answered that he was the man she sought, whereupon she drew him aside and said to him, 'Sir, an it please you, a gentlewoman of this city would fain speak with you.' Andreuccio, hearing this, considered himself from head to foot and himseeming he was a handsome varlet of his person, he concluded (as if there were no other well-looking young fellow to be found in Naples) that the lady in question must have fallen in love with him. Accordingly, he answered without further deliberation that he was ready and asked the girl when and where the lady would speak with him; whereto she answered, 'Sir, whenas it pleaseth you to come, she awaiteth you in her house'; and Andreuccio forthwith rejoined, without saying aught to the people of the inn, 'Go thou on before; I will come after thee.'

Thereupon the girl carried him to the house of her mistress, who dwelt in a street called Malpertugio, the very name whereof denoteth how reputable a quarter it is. But he, unknowing neither suspecting aught thereof and thinking to go to a most honourable place and to a lady of quality, entered the house without hesitation—preceded by the serving-maid, who called her mistress and said, 'Here is Andreuccio'—and mounting the stair, saw the damsel come to the stairhead to receive him. Now she was yet in the prime of youth, tall of person, with a very fair face and very handsomely dressed and adorned. As he drew near her, she came down three steps to meet him with open arms and clasping him round the neck, abode awhile without speaking, as if hindered by excess of tenderness; then kissed him on the forehead, weeping, and said, in a somewhat broken voice, 'O my Andreuccio, thou art indeed welcome.'

He was amazed at such tender caresses and answered, all confounded, 'Madam, you are well met.' Thereupon, taking him by the

23

hand, she carried him up into her saloon and thence, without saying another word to him, she brought him into her chamber, which was all redolent of roses and orange flowers and other perfumes. Here he saw a very fine bed, hung round with curtains, and store of dresses upon the pegs and other very goodly and rich gear, after the usance of those parts; by reason whereof, like a freshman as he was, he firmly believed her to be no less than a great lady. She made him sit with her on a chest that stood at the foot of the bed and bespoke him thus, 'Andreuccio, I am very certain thou marvellest at these caresses that I bestow on thee and at my tears, as he may well do who knoweth me not and hath maybe never heard speak of me; but I have that to tell thee which is like to amaze thee yet more, namely, that I am thy sister; and I tell thee that, since God had vouchsafed me to look upon one of my brothers (though fain would I see you all) before my death, henceforth I shall not die disconsolate; and as perchance thou hast never heard of this, I will tell it thee.

Pietro, my father and thine, as I doubt not thou knowest, abode long in Palermo and there for his good humour and pleasant composition was and yet is greatly beloved of those who knew him; but, among all his lovers, my mother, who was a lady of gentle birth and then a widow, was she who most affected him, insomuch that, laying aside the fear of her father and brethren, as well as the care of her own honour, she became so private with him that I was born thereof and grew up as thou seest me. Presently, having occasion to depart Palermo and return to Perugia, he left me a little maid with my mother nor ever after, for all that I could hear, remembered him of me or her; whereof, were he not my father, I should blame him sore, having regard to the ingratitude shown by him to my mother (to say nothing of the love it behoved him bear me, as his daughter, born of no serving-wench nor woman of mean extraction) who had, moved by very faithful love, without anywise knowing who he might be, committed into his hands her possessions and herself no less. But what [skilleth it]? Things ill done and long time passed are easier blamed than mended; algates, so it was.

He left me a little child in Palermo, where being grown well nigh as I am now, my mother, who was a rich lady, gave me to wife to a worthy gentleman of Girgenti, who, for her love and mine, came to abide at Palermo and there, being a great Guelph, he entered into treaty with our King Charles, which, being discovered by King Frederick, ere effect could be given to it, was the occasion of our being enforced to flee from Sicily, whenas I looked to be the greatest lady was ever in the island; wherefore, taking such few things as we might (I say few, in respect of the many we had) and leaving our lands and palaces, we took refuge in this city, where we found

King Charles so mindful of our services that he hath in part made good to us the losses we had sustained for him, bestowing on us both lands and houses, and still maketh my husband, thy kinsman that is, a goodly provision, as thou shalt hereafter see. On this wise come I in this city, where, Godamercy and no thanks to thee, sweet my brother, I now behold thee.' So saying, she embraced him over again and kissed him on the forehead, still weeping for tenderness.

Andreuccio, hearing this fable so orderly, so artfully delivered by the damsel, without ever stammering or faltering for a word, and remembering it to be true that his father had been in Palermo, knowing, moreover, by himself the fashions of young men and how lightly they fall in love in their youth and seeing the affectionate tears and embraces and the chaste kisses that she lavished on him, held all she told him for more than true; wherefore, as soon as she was silent, he answered her, saying, 'Madam, it should seem to you no very great matter if I marvel, for that in truth, whether it be that my father, for whatsoever reason, never spoke of your mother nor of yourself, or that if he did, it came not to my notice, I had no more knowledge of you than if you had never been, and so much the dearer is it to me to find you my sister here, as I am alone in this city and the less expected this. Indeed, I know no man of so high a condition that you should not be dear to him, to say nothing of myself, who am but a petty trader. But I pray you make me clear of one thing; how knew you that I was here?' Whereto she made answer, 'A poor woman, who much frequenteth me, gave me this morning to know of thy coming, for that, as she telleth me, she abode long with our father both at Palermo and at Perugia; and but that meseemed it was a more reputable thing that thou shouldst visit me in my own house than I thee in that of another, I had come to thee this great while agone.' After this, she proceeded to enquire more particularly of all his kinsfolk by name, and he answered her of all, giving the more credence, by reason of this, to that which it the less behoved him to believe.

The talk being long and the heat great, she called for Greek wine and confections and let give Andreuccio to drink, after which he would have taken leave, for that it was supper-time; but she would on no wise suffer it and making a show of being sore vexed, embraced him and said, 'Ah, woe is me! I see but too clearly how little dear I am to thee! Who would believe that thou couldst be with a sister of thine, whom thou hast never yet seen and in whose house thou shouldst have lighted down, whenas thou camest hither, and offer to leave her, to go sup at the inn? Indeed, thou shalt sup with me, and albeit my husband is abroad, which grieveth me mightily, 25 I shall know well how to do thee some little honour, such as a woman may.' To which Andreuccio, unknowing what else he should say, answered, 'I hold you as dear as a sister should be held; but, an I go not, I shall be expected to supper all the evening and shall do an unmannerliness.' 'Praised be God!' cried she. 'One would think I had no one in the house to send to tell them not to expect thee; albeit thou wouldst do much greater courtesy and indeed but thy duty an thou sentest to bid thy companions come hither to supper; and after, an thou must e'en begone, you might all go away together.'

Andreuccio replied that he had no desire for his companions that evening; but that, since it was agreeable to her, she might do her pleasure of him. Accordingly, she made a show of sending to the inn to say that he was not to be expected to supper, and after much other discourse, they sat down to supper and were sumptuously served with various meats, whilst she adroitly contrived to prolong the repast till it was dark night. Then, when they rose from table and Andreuccio would have taken his leave, she declared that she would on no wise suffer this, for that Naples was no place to go about in by night, especially for a stranger, and that, whenas she sent to the inn to say that he was not to be expected to supper, she had at the same time given notice that he would lie abroad. Andreuccio, believing this and taking pleasure in being with her, beguiled as he was by false credence, abode where he was, and after supper they held much and long discourse, not without reason, till a part of the night was past, when she withdrew with her women into another room, leaving Andreuccio in her own chamber, with a little lad to wait upon him, if he should lack aught.

The heat being great, Andreuccio, as soon as he found himself alone, stripped to his doublet and putting off his hosen, laid them at the bedhead; after which, natural use soliciting him to rid himself of the overmuch burden of his stomach, he asked the boy where this might be done, who showed him a door in one corner of the room and said, 'Go in there.' Accordingly he opened the door and passing through in all assurance, chanced to set foot on a plank, which, being broken loose from the joist at the opposite end, [flew up] and down they went, plank and man together. God so favoured him that he did himself no hurt in the fall, albeit he fell from some height; but he was all bemired with the ordure whereof the place was full; and in order that you may the better apprehend both that which hath been said and that which ensueth, I will show you how the place lay. There were in a narrow alley, such as we often see between two houses, a pair of rafters laid from one house to another, and thereon sundry boards nailed and the place of session set up; 26 of which boards that which gave way with Andreuccio was one.

Finding himself, then, at the bottom of the alley and sore chagrined at the mishap, he fell a-bawling for the boy; but the latter, as soon as he heard him fall, had run to tell his mistress, who hastened to his chamber and searching hurriedly if his clothes were there, found them and with them the money, which, in his mistrust, he still foolishly carried about him. Having now gotten that for which, feigning herself of Palermo and sister to a Perugian, she had set her snare, she took no more reck of him, but hastened to shut the door whereby he had gone out when he fell.

Andreuccio, getting no answer from the boy, proceeded to call loudlier, but to no purpose; whereupon, his suspicions being now aroused, he began too late to smoke the cheat. Accordingly, he scrambled over a low wall that shut off the alley from the street, and letting himself down into the road, went up to the door of the house, which he knew very well, and there called long and loud and shook and beat upon it amain, but all in vain. Wherefore, bewailing himself, as one who was now fully aware of his mischance, 'Ah, woe is me!' cried he. 'In how little time have I lost five hundred florins and a sister!' Then, after many other words, he fell again to battering the door and crying out and this he did so long and so lustily that many of the neighbours, being awakened and unable to brook the annoy, arose and one of the courtezan's waiting-women, coming to the window, apparently all sleepy-eyed, said peevishly, 'Who knocketh below there?'

'What?' cried Andreuccio. 'Dost thou not know me? I am Andreuccio, brother to Madam Fiordaliso.' Whereto quoth she, 'Good man, an thou have drunken overmuch, go sleep and come back to-morrow morning. I know no Andreuccio nor what be these idle tales thou tellest. Begone in peace and let us sleep, so it please thee.' 'How?' replied Andreuccio. 'Thou knowest not what I mean? Certes, thou knowest; but, if Sicilian kinships be of such a fashion that they are forgotten in so short a time, at least give me back my clothes and I will begone with all my heart.' 'Good man,' rejoined she, as if laughing, 'methinketh thou dreamest'; and to say this and to draw in her head and shut the window were one and the same thing. Whereat Andreuccio, now fully certified of his loss, was like for chagrin to turn his exceeding anger into madness and bethought himself to seek to recover by violence that which he might not have again with words; wherefore, taking up a great stone, he began anew to batter the door more furiously than ever.

At this many of the neighbours, who had already been awakened and had arisen, deeming him some pestilent fellow who had trumped up this story to spite the woman of the house and provoked at the
27 knocking he kept up, came to the windows and began to say, no

otherwise than as all the dogs of a quarter bark after a strange dog, ''Tis a villainous shame to come at this hour to decent women's houses and tell these cock-and-bull stories. For God's sake, good man, please you begone in peace and let us sleep. An thou have aught to mell with her, come back to-morrow and spare us this annoy to-night.' Taking assurance, perchance, by these words, there came to the window one who was within the house, a bully of the gentlewoman's, whom Andreuccio had as yet neither heard nor seen, and said, in a terrible big rough voice, 'Who is below there?'

Andreuccio, hearing this, raised his eyes and saw at the window one who, by what little he could make out, himseemed should be a very masterful fellow, with a bushy black beard on his face, and who yawned and rubbed his eyes, as he had arisen from bed or deep sleep; whereupon, not without fear, he answered, 'I am a brother of the lady of the house.' The other waited not for him to make an end of his reply, but said, more fiercely than before, 'I know not what hindereth me from coming down and cudgelling thee what while I see thee stir, for a pestilent drunken ass as thou must be, who will not let us sleep this night.' Then, drawing back into the house, he shut the window; whereupon certain of the neighbours, who were better acquainted with the fellow's quality, said softly to Andreuccio, 'For God's sake, good man, begone in peace and abide not there to-night to be slain; get thee gone for thine own good.'

Andreuccio, terrified at the fellow's voice and aspect and moved by the exhortations of the neighbours, who seemed to him to speak out of charity, set out to return to his inn, in the direction of the quarter whence he had followed the maid, without knowing whither to go, despairing of his money and woebegone as ever man was. Being loathsome to himself, for the stench that came from him, and thinking to repair to the sea to wash himself, he turned to the left and followed a street called Ruga Catalana, that led towards the upper part of the city. Presently, he espied two men coming towards him with a lantern and fearing they might be officers of the watch or other ill-disposed folk, he stealthily took refuge, to avoid them, in a hovel, that he saw hard by. But they, as of malice aforethought, made straight for the same place and entering in, began to examine certain irons which one of them laid from off his shoulder, discoursing various things thereof the while.

Presently, 'What meaneth this?' quoth one. 'I smell the worst stench meseemeth I ever smelt.' So saying, he raised the lantern and seeing the wretched Andreuccio, enquired, in amazement, 'Who is there?' Andreuccio made no answer, but they came up to him with the light and asked him what he did there in such a pickle; whereupon he related to them all that had befallen him, and they, conceiving where this might have happened, said, one to the other, 'Verily, this must have been in the house of Scarabone Buttafuoco.' Then, turning to him, 'Good man,' quoth one, 'albeit thou hast lost thy money, thou hast much reason to praise God that this mischance betided thee, so that thou fellest nor couldst after avail to enter the house again; for, hadst thou not fallen, thou mayst be assured that, when once thou wast fallen asleep, thou hadst been knocked on the head and hadst lost thy life as well as thy money. But what booteth it now to repine? Thou mayst as well look to have the stars out of the sky as to recover a farthing of thy money; nay, thou art like to be murdered, should yonder fellow hear that thou makest any words thereof.' Then they consulted together awhile and presently said to him, 'Look you, we are moved to pity for thee; wherefore, an thou wilt join with us in somewhat we go about to do, it seemeth to us certain that there will fall to thee for thy share much more than the value of that which thou hast lost.' Whereupon Andreuccio, in his desperation, answered that he was ready.

Now there had been that day buried an archbishop of Naples, by name Messer Filippo Minutolo, and he had been interred in his richest ornaments and with a ruby on his finger worth more than five hundred florins of gold. Him they were minded to despoil and this their intent they discovered to Andreuccio, who, more covetous than well-advised, set out with them for the cathedral. As they went, Andreuccio still stinking amain, one of the thieves said, 'Can we not find means for this fellow to wash himself a little, be it where it may, so he may not stink so terribly?' 'Ay can we,' answered the other. 'We are here near a well, where there useth to be a rope and pulley and a great bucket; let us go thither and we will wash him in a trice.' Accordingly they made for the well in question and found the rope there, but the bucket had been taken away; wherefore they took counsel together to tie him to the rope and let him down into the well, so he might wash himself there, charging him shake the rope as soon as he was clean, and they would pull him up.

Hardly had they let him down when, as chance would have it, certain of the watch, being athirst for the heat and with running after some rogue or another, came to the well to drink, and the two rogues, setting eyes on them, made off incontinent, before the officers saw them. Presently, Andreuccio, having washed himself at the bottom of the well, shook the rope, and the thirsty officers, laying by their targets and arms and surcoats, began to haul upon the rope, thinking the bucket full of water at the other end. As soon as Andreuccio found himself near the top, he let go the rope and laid hold of the marge with both hands; which when the officers saw, overcome with sudden affright, they dropped the rope, without saying a word, and took to their heels as quickliest they might. At this Andreuccio marvelled sore, and but that he had fast hold of the marge, would have fallen to the bottom, to his no little hurt or maybe death. However, he made his way out and finding the arms, which he knew were none of his companions' bringing, he was yet more amazed; but, knowing not what to make of it and misdoubting [some snare], he determined to begone without touching aught and accordingly made off he knew not whither, bewailing his ill-luck.

As he went, he met his two comrades, who came to draw him forth of the well; and when they saw him, they marvelled exceedingly and asked him who had drawn him up. Andreuccio replied that he knew not and told them orderly how it had happened and what he had found by the wellside, whereupon the others, perceiving how the case stood, told him, laughing, why they had fled and who these were that had pulled him up. Then, without farther parley, it being now middle night, they repaired to the cathedral and making their way thereinto lightly enough, went straight to the archbishop's tomb, which was of marble and very large. With their irons they raised the lid, which was very heavy, and propped it up so as a man might enter; which being done, quoth one, 'Who shall go in?' 'Not I,' answered the other. 'Nor I,' rejoined his fellow; 'let Andreuccio enter.' 'That will I not,' said the latter; whereupon the two rogues turned upon him and said, 'How! Thou wilt not? Cock's faith, an thou enter not, we will clout thee over the costard with one of these iron bars till thou fall dead.'

Andreuccio, affrighted, crept into the tomb, saying in himself the while, 'These fellows will have me go in here so they may cheat me, for that, when I shall have given them everything, they will begone about their business, whilst I am labouring to win out of the tomb, and I shall abide empty-handed.' Accordingly, he determined to make sure of his share beforehand; wherefore, as soon as he came to the bottom, calling to mind the precious ring whereof he had heard them speak, he drew it from the archbishop's finger and set it on his own. Then he passed them the crozier and mitre and gloves and stripping the dead man to his shirt, gave them everything, saying that there was nothing more. The others declared that the ring must be there and bade him seek everywhere; but he replied that he found it not and making a show of seeking it, kept them in play awhile. At last, the two rogues, who were no less wily than himself, bidding him seek well the while, took occasion to pull away the prop that held up the lid and made off, leaving him shut in the tomb.

30   What became of Andreuccio, when he found himself in this

plight, you may all imagine for yourselves. He strove again and again to heave up the lid with his head and shoulders, but only wearied himself in vain; wherefore, overcome with chagrin and despair, he fell down in a swoon upon the archbishop's dead body; and whoso saw him there had hardly known which was the deader, the prelate or he. Presently, coming to himself, he fell into a passion of weeping, seeing he must there without fail come to one of two ends, to wit, either he must, if none came thither to open the tomb again, die of hunger and stench, among the worms of the dead body, or, if any came and found him there, he would certainly be hanged for a thief.

As he abode in this mind, exceeding woebegone, he heard folk stirring in the church and many persons speaking and presently perceived that they came to do that which he and his comrades had already done; whereat fear redoubled upon him. But, after the new-comers had forced open the tomb and propped up the lid, they fell into dispute of who should go in, and none was willing to do it. However, after long parley, a priest said, 'What fear ye? Think you he will eat you? The dead eat not men. I will go in myself.' So saying, he set his breast to the marge of the tomb and turning his head outward, put in his legs, thinking to let himself drop. Andreuccio, seeing this, started up and catching the priest by one of his legs, made a show of offering to pull him down into the tomb. The other, feeling this, gave a terrible screech and flung precipitately out of the tomb; whereupon all the others fled in terror, as they were pursued by an hundred thousand devils, leaving the tomb open.

Andreuccio, seeing this, scrambled hastily out of the tomb, rejoiced beyond all hope, and made off out of the church by the way he had entered in. The day now drawing near, he fared on at a venture, with the ring on his finger, till he came to the sea-shore and thence made his way back to his inn, where he found his comrades and the host, who had been in concern for him all that night. He told them what had betided him and themseemed, by the host's counsel, that he were best depart Naples incontinent. Accordingly, he set out forthright and returned to Perugia, having invested his money in a ring, whereas he came to buy horses."

ALIBECH

John Payne's translation supplemented by other hands

Dioneo, who had diligently hearkened to the queen's story, seeing
that it was ended and that it rested with him alone to tell, without
awaiting commandment, smilingly began to speak as follows:
"Charming ladies, maybe you have never heard tell how one putteth
the devil in hell; wherefore, without much departing from the tenor
of that whereof you have discoursed all this day, I will e'en tell it
you. Belike, having learned it, you may catch the spirit thereof and
come to know that, albeit Love sojourneth liefer in jocund palaces
and luxurious chambers than in the hovels of the poor, yet none the
less doth he whiles make his power felt midmost thick forests and
rugged mountains and in desert caverns; whereby it may be understood that all things are subject to his puissance.

To come, then, to the fact, I say that in the city of Capsa in
Barbary there was aforetime a very rich man, who, among his other
children, had a fair and winsome young daughter, by name Alibech.
She, not being a Christian and hearing many Christians who abode
in the town mightily extol the Christian faith and the service of God,
one day questioned one of them in what manner one might avail to
serve God with the least hindrance. The other answered that they
best served God who most strictly eschewed the things of the world,
as those did who had betaken them into the solitudes of the deserts
of Thebaïs. The girl, who was maybe fourteen years old and very
simple, moved by no ordered desire, but by some childish fancy, set
off next morning by stealth and all alone, to go to the desert of
Thebaïs, without letting any know her intent. After some days, her
desire persisting, she won, with no little toil, to the deserts in question and seeing a hut afar off, went thither and found at the door
a holy man, who marvelled to see her there and asked her what
she sought. She replied that, being inspired of God, she went seeking to enter into His service and was now in quest of one who
should teach her how it behoved to serve Him.

The worthy man, seeing her young and very fair and fearing
lest, an he entertained her, the devil should beguile him, commended her pious intent and giving her somewhat to eat of roots
of herbs and wild apples and dates and to drink of water, said to
her, 'Daughter mine, not far hence is a holy man, who is much better
master than I of that which thou goest seeking; do thou betake
thyself to him'; and put her in the way. However, when she reached

the man in question, she had of him the same answer and faring farther, came to the cell of a young hermit, a very devout and good man, whose name was Rustico and to whom she made the same request as she had done to the others. He, having a mind to make a trial of his own constancy, sent her not away, as the others had done, but received her into his cell, and the night being come, he made her a little bed of palm-fronds and bade her lie down to rest thereon. This done, temptations tarried not to give battle to his powers of resistance and he, finding himself grossly deceived by these latter, turned tail, without awaiting many assaults, and confessed himself beaten; then, laying aside devout thoughts and orisons and mortifications, he fell to revolving in his memory the youth and beauty of the damsel and bethinking himself what course he should take with her, so as to win to that which he desired of her, without her taking him for a debauched fellow.

Accordingly, having sounded her with sundry questions, he found that she had never known man and was in truth as simple as she seemed; wherefore he bethought him how, under colour of the service of God, he might bring her to his pleasures. In the first place, he showeth her with many words how great an enemy the devil was of God the Lord and after gave her to understand that the most acceptable service that could be rendered to God was to put back the devil into hell, whereto he had condemned him. The girl asked him how this might be done; and he, 'Thou shalt soon know that; do thou but as thou shalt see me do.' So saying, he proceeded to put off the few garments he had and abode stark naked, as likewise did the girl, whereupon he fell on his knees, as he would pray, and caused her abide over against himself.

And thus kneeling, Rustico being kindled more than ever in his desire from seeing her so beautiful, there came the resurrection of the flesh, observing which, Alibech was astonished and said: 'Rustico, what is that there, which I see of thine, that thus sticketh out, and that I have not?' 'O my daughter,' said Rustico, 'this is the devil, of which I spoke to thee, and which thou now seest: he giveth me great annoyance, so much that I scarce can suffer it.' Then said the maiden, 'O praised be God, for I see that I am better off than thee, as I have not that devil.' Said Rustico, 'Thou speakest true; but thou hast another thing which I have not, and hast it instead of this.' Said Alibech: 'How now?' To whom Rustico replied: 'Thou hast hell; and I tell thee, that I believe God hath sent thee here for the welfare of my soul; since, should this devil yet worry me, if thou wishest to take pity upon me and suffer me to put him in hell, thou shalt give me the greatest consolation, and shalt do God great pleasure and service; if thou art come to these parts to do what thou sayest.' The maiden in good faith replied, 'O my father, since I have hell, let the devil be put there when it shall please thee.' Then Rustico said: 'Blessed be thou, my daughter: let us then go ahead and put him there, that he may then leave me alone.' And so saying, having lain the young girl over one of their little beds, he taught her how she should stay to imprison that thing accursed by God.

The girl, who had never before put any devil into hell, at first felt a little discomfort; for which she said to Rustico, 'Certainly, my father, this devil must be a bad thing, and truly the enemy of God, for hell itself, let alone all else, acheth when he is put inside there.' Said Rustico, 'Daughter, it will not always happen thus': and to do in such wise that this should not happen, before they got them up from the bed, they put him there six times; with the result that for a time they so drew out the pride from his head, that he willingly remained in peace. But pride returning thereafter over and again, and the obedient lass always disposing herself to remove it, it happened that the game began to please her; and she began to say to Rustico, 'Well I see that those good men in Capsa said the truth, that serving God was such a sweet thing, and for certain I remember not that ever I did aught else that were of such pleasure and delight, as putting the devil in hell; and therefore I judge every other person, who attendeth to aught but the service of God, to be a beast.' For this reason she oftentimes went to Rustico, and told him, 'My father, I am come here to serve God, and not to be idle; let us go and put the devil in hell.' Which doing, she sometimes said, 'Rustico, I know not why the devil should flee hell, for if he stayed there so willingly as hell receiveth him, he would never go out again.' So then Rustico inviting the young girl often, and she comforting him in the service of God, she so took the fluff from his doublet, that he felt cold when another would have sweat; and consequently he began to say to the maiden that the devil was not to be punished, nor put again into hell, save only when for pride he should raise his head; 'and we, by the grace of God, have so disillusioned him, that he prayeth God that he may bide in peace'; and thus he imposed silence for some time on the girl. Who, when she saw that Rustico required her not to put the devil in hell, said to him one day, 'Rustico, if thy devil is punished, and giveth thee no more worry, yet my hell leaveth me not be: therefore thou shalt do well if with thy devil thou helpest me to quiet the wrath of my hell, as I with my hell have helped to take the pride from thy devil.'

Rustico, who lived on roots and water, could ill avail to answer her calls and told her that it would need overmany devils to appease hell, but he would do what he might thereof. Accordingly he satisfied her bytimes, but so seldom it was but casting a bean into the

34

lion's mouth; whereas the girl, herseeming she served not God as diligently as she would fain have done, murmured somewhat. But, whilst this debate was toward between Rustico his devil and Alibech her hell, for overmuch desire on the one part and lack of power on the other, it befell that a fire broke out in Capsa and burnt Alibech's father in his own house, with as many children and other family as he had; by reason whereof she abode heir to all his good. Thereupon, a young man called Neerbale, who had spent all his substance in gallantry, hearing that she was alive, set out in search of her and finding her, before the court had laid hands upon her father's estate, as that of a man dying without heir, to Rustico's great satisfaction, but against her own will, brought her back to Capsa, where he took her to wife and succeeded, in her right, to the ample inheritance of her father.

There, being asked by the women at what she served God in the desert, she answered (Neerbale having not yet lain with her) that she served Him at putting the devil in hell and that Neerbale had done a grievous sin in that he had taken her from such service. The ladies asked, 'How putteth one the devil in hell?' And the girl, what with words and what with gestures, expounded it to them; whereat they set up so great a laughing that they laugh yet and said, 'Give yourself no concern, my child; nay, for that is done here also and Neerbale will serve our Lord full well with thee at this.' Thereafter, telling it from one to another throughout the city, they brought it to a common saying there that the most acceptable service one could render to God was to put the devil in hell, which byword, having passed the sea hither, is yet current here. Wherefore do all you young ladies, who have need of God's grace, learn to put the devil in hell, for that this is highly acceptable to Him and pleasing to both parties and much good may grow and ensue thereof."

LORENZO
DE' MEDICI

Triumph of Bacchus and Ariadne
Translated by John Addington Symonds

Fair is youth and void of sorrow;
  But it hourly flies away.—
  Youths and maids, enjoy to-day;
Nought ye know about to-morrow.

This is Bacchus and the bright
  Ariadne, lovers true!
They, in flying time's despite,
  Each with each find pleasure new;
These their Nymphs, and all their crew
  Keep perpetual holiday.—
  Youths and maids, enjoy to-day;
Nought ye know about to-morrow.

These blithe Satyrs, wanton-eyed,
  Of the Nymphs are paramours:
Through the caves and forests wide
  They have snared them mid the flowers.
Warmed with Bacchus, in his bowers,
  Now they dance and leap alway.—
  Youths and maids, enjoy to-day;
Nought ye know about to-morrow.

These fair Nymphs, they are not loth
  To entice their lovers' wiles.
None but thankless folk and rough
  Can resist when Love beguiles.
Now enlaced with wreathèd smiles,
  All together dance and play.—
  Youths and maids, enjoy to-day;
Nought ye know about to-morrow.

See this load behind them plodding
  On the ass, Silenus he,
Old and drunken, merry, nodding,
  Full of years and jollity;
Though he goes so swayingly,
  Yet he laughs and quaffs alway.—
  Youths and maids, enjoy to-day;
Nought ye know about to-morrow.

Midas treads a wearier measure:
  All he touches turns to gold:
If there be no taste of pleasure,
  What's the use of wealth untold?
What's the joy his fingers hold,
  When he's forced to thirst for aye?—
  Youths and maids, enjoy to-day;
Nought ye know about to-morrow.

Listen well to what we're saying;
  Of to-morrow have no care!
Young and old together playing,
  Boys and girls, be blithe as air!
Every sorry thought forswear!
  Keep perpetual holiday.—
  Youths and maids, enjoy to-day;
Nought ye know about to-morrow.

Ladies and gay lovers young!
  Long live Bacchus, live Desire!
Dance and play, let songs be sung;
  Let sweet Love your bosoms fire;
  In the future come what may!—
  Youths and maids, enjoy to-day;
Nought ye know about to-morrow.

Sonnet
Translated by William Roscoe

Seek he who will in grandeur to be blest,
  Place in proud halls, and splendid courts, his joy,
  For pleasure or for gold, his arts employ,
37   Whilst all his hours unnumbered cares molest.

—A little field in native flowerets drest,
   A rivulet in soft murmurs gliding by,
   A bird whose love-sick note salutes the sky,
   With sweeter magic lull my cares to rest.
And shadowy woods, and rocks, and towering hills,
   And caves obscure, and nature's free-born train,
   And some lone nymph that timorous speeds along,
Each in my mind some gentle thought instils
   Of those bright eyes that absence shrouds in vain;
   —Ah gentle thoughts! soon lost the city cares among.

POLIZIANO

A BALLATA

Translated by John Addington Symonds

I went a-roaming, maidens, one bright day,
In a green garden in mid month of May.

Violets and lilies grew on every side
  Mid the green grass, and young flowers wonderful,
Golden and white and red and azure-eyed;
  Toward which I stretched my hands, eager to pull
  Plenty to make my fair curls beautiful,
To crown my rippling curls with garlands gay.

I went a-roaming, maidens, one bright day,
In a green garden in mid month of May.

But when my lap was full of flowers I spied
  Roses at last, roses of every hue;
Therefore I ran to pluck their ruddy pride,
  Because their perfume was so sweet and true
  That all my soul went forth with pleasure new,
With yearning and desire too soft to say.

I went a-roaming, maidens, one bright day,
In a green garden in mid month of May.

I gazed and gazed. Hard task it were to tell
  How lovely were the roses in that hour:
One was but peeping from her verdant shell,
  And some were faded, some were scarce in flower.
  Then Love said: Go, pluck from the blooming bower
Those that thou seest ripe upon the spray.

I went a-roaming, maidens, one bright day,
In a green garden in mid month of May.

For when the full rose quits her tender sheath,
39   When she is sweetest and most fair to see,

Then is the time to place her in thy wreath,
  Before her beauty and her freshness flee.
  Gather ye therefore roses with great glee,
Sweet girls, or ere their perfume pass away.

I went a-roaming, maidens, one bright day,
In a green garden in mid month of May.

GIORGIO
VASARI

Lives of the Most Eminent Painters, Sculptors, and Architects
Translated by E. H. and E. W. Blashfield and A. A. Hopkins

LEONARDO DA VINCI

The richest gifts are occasionally seen to be showered, as by celestial influence, on certain human beings, nay, they sometimes supernaturally and marvellously congregate in one sole person; beauty, grace, and talent being united in such a manner, that to whatever the man thus favoured may turn himself, his every action is so divine as to leave all other men far behind him, and manifestly to prove that he has been specially endowed by the hand of God himself, and has not obtained his pre-eminence by human teaching, or the power of man. This was seen and acknowledged by all men in the case of Leonardo da Vinci, in whom, to say nothing of his beauty of person, which yet was such that it has never been sufficiently extolled, there was a grace beyond expression which was rendered manifest without thought or effort in every act and deed, and who had besides so rare a gift of talent and ability, that to whatever subject he turned his attention, however difficult, he presently made himself absolute master of it. Extraordinary power was in his case conjoined with remarkable facility, a mind of regal boldness and magnanimous daring; his gifts were such that the celebrity of his name extended most widely, and he was held in the highest estimation, not in his own time only, but also, and even to a greater extent, after his death, nay, this he has continued, and will continue to be by all succeeding ages. . . .

In conversation Leonardo was indeed so pleasing that he won the hearts of all hearers, and though possessing so small a patrimony only that it might almost be called nothing, while he yet worked very little, he still constantly kept many servants and horses, taking extraordinary delight in the latter: he was indeed fond of all animals, ever treating them with infinite kindness and consideration; as a proof of this it is related, that when he passed places where birds were sold, he would frequently take them from their cages, and having paid the price demanded for them by the sellers, would then let them fly into the air, thus restoring to them the liberty they had lost. Leonardo was in all things so highly favoured by nature, that to whatever he turned his thoughts, mind, and spirit, he gave proof in all of such admirable power and perfection, that whatever he did bore an impress of harmony, truthfulness, goodness, sweetness and grace, wherein no other man could even equal him.

Leonardo, with his profound intelligence of art, commenced various undertakings, many of which he never completed, because it appeared to him that the hand could never give its due perfection to the object or purpose which he had in his thoughts, or beheld in his imagination; seeing that in his mind he frequently formed the idea of some difficult enterprise, so subtle and so wonderful that, by means of hands, however excellent or able, the full reality could never be worthily executed and entirely realized. His conceptions were varied to infinity; philosophizing over natural objects; among others, he set himself to investigate the properties of plants, to make observations on the heavenly bodies, to follow the movements of the planets, the variations of the moon, and the course of the sun. . . .

For the Dominican monks of Santa Maria delle Grazie at Milan, he also painted a Last Supper, which is a most beautiful and admirable work; to the heads of the Apostles in this picture the master gave so much beauty and majesty that he was constrained to leave that of Christ unfinished, being convinced that he could not impart to it the divinity which should appertain to and distinguish an image of the Redeemer. But this work, remaining thus in its unfinished state, has been ever held in the highest estimation by the Milanese, and not by them only, but by foreigners also: Leonardo succeeded to perfection in expressing the doubts and anxiety experienced by the Apostles, and the desire felt by them to know by whom their Master is to be betrayed; in the faces of all appear love, terror, anger, or grief and bewilderment, unable as they are to fathom the meaning of their Lord. Nor is the spectator less struck with admiration by the force and truth with which, on the other hand, the master has exhibited the impious determination, hatred, and treachery of Judas. The whole work indeed is executed with inexpressible diligence even in its most minute part; among other things may be mentioned the table-cloth, the texture of which is copied with such exactitude, that the linen-cloth itself could scarcely look more real.

It is related that the Prior of the Monastery was excessively importunate in pressing Leonardo to complete the picture; he could in no way comprehend wherefore the artist should sometimes remain half a day together absorbed in thought before his work, without making any progress that he could see; this seemed to him a strange waste of time, and he would fain have had him work away as he could make the men do who were digging in his garden, never laying the pencil out of his hand. Not content with seeking to hasten Leonardo, the Prior even complained to the Duke, and tormented him to such a degree that the latter was at length compelled to send for Leonardo, whom he courteously entreated to let the work be finished, assuring him nevertheless that he did so because compelled by the importunities of the Prior. Leonardo, knowing the Prince to be intelligent and judicious, determined to explain himself fully on the subject with him, although he had never chosen to do so with the Prior. He therefore discoursed with him at some length respecting art, and made it perfectly manifest to his comprehension, that men of genius are sometimes producing most when they seem to be labouring least, their minds being occupied in the elucidation of their ideas, and in the completion of those conceptions to which they afterwards give form and expression with the hand. He further informed the Duke that there were still wanting to him two heads, one of which, that of the Saviour, he could not hope to find on earth, and had not yet attained the power of presenting it to himself in imagination, with all that perfection of beauty and celestial grace which appeared to him to be demanded for the due representation of the Divinity incarnate. The second head still wanting was that of Judas, which also caused him some anxiety, since he did not think it possible to imagine a form of feature that should properly render the countenance of a man who, after so many benefits received from his master, had possessed a heart so depraved as to be capable of betraying his Lord and the Creator of the world; with regard to that second, however, he would make search, and, after all—if he could find no better, he need never be at any great loss, for there would always be the head of that troublesome and impertinent Prior. This made the Duke laugh with all his heart, he declared Leonardo to be completely in the right, and the poor Prior, utterly confounded, went away to drive on the digging in his garden, and left Leonardo in peace: the head of Judas was then finished so successfully, that it is indeed the true image of treachery and wickedness; but that of the Redeemer remained, as we have said, incomplete. The admirable excellence of this picture, the beauty of its composition, and the care with which it was executed, awakened in the King of France, a desire to have it removed into his own kingdom, insomuch that he made many attempts to discover architects, who might be able to secure it by defences of wood and iron, that it might be transported without injury. He was not to be deterred by any consideration of the cost that might be incurred, but the painting, being on the wall, his Majesty was compelled to forego his desire, and the Milanese retained their picture.

MICHELANGELO BUONARROTTI

Sonnets
Translated by John Addington Symonds

BEAUTY AND THE ARTIST

A heart of flaming sulphur, flesh of tow,
    Bones of dry wood, a soul without a guide
    To curb the fiery will, the ruffling pride
    Of fierce desires that from the passions flow;
A sightless mind that weak and lame doth go
    Mid snares and pitfalls scattered far and wide;—
    What wonder if the first chance brand applied
    To fuel massed like this should make it glow?
Add beauteous art, which, brought with us from heaven,
    Will conquer nature;—so divine a power
    Belongs to him who strives with every nerve.
If I was made for art, from childhood given
    A prey for burning beauty to devour,
    I blame the mistress I was born to serve.

CELESTIAL LOVE

I saw no mortal beauty with these eyes
    When perfect peace in thy fair eyes I found;
    But far within, where all is holy ground,
    My soul felt Love, her comrade of the skies:
For she was born with God in Paradise;
    Else should we still to transient loves be bound;
    But, finding these so false, we pass beyond
    Unto the Love of Loves that never dies.
45 Nay, things that die, cannot assuage the thirst

Of souls undying; nor Eternity
Serves Time, where all must fade that flourisheth.
Sense is not love, but lawlessness accurst:
This kills the soul; while our love lifts on high
Our friends on earth—higher in heaven through death.

LOVE IS A REFINER'S FIRE

It is with fire that blacksmiths iron subdue
Unto fair form, the image of their thought:
Nor without fire hath any artist wrought
Gold to its utmost purity of hue.
Nay, nor the unmatched phœnix lives anew,
Unless she burn: if then I am distraught
By fire, I may to better life be brought
Like those whom death restores nor years undo.
The fire whereof I speak, is my great cheer;
Such power it hath to renovate and raise
Me who was almost numbered with the dead;
And since by nature fire doth find its sphere
Soaring aloft, and I am all ablaze,
Heavenward with it my flight must needs be sped.

BENVENUTO CELLINI

Autobiography
Translated by John Addington Symonds

NECROMANCY

It happened through a variety of singular accidents that I became
intimate with a Sicilian priest, who was a man of very elevated
genius and well instructed in both Latin and Greek letters. In the
course of conversation one day we were led to talk about the art
of necromancy; apropos of which I said: "Throughout my whole life
I have had the most intense desire to see or learn something of this
art." Thereto the priest replied: "A stout soul and a steadfast must
the man have who sets himself to such an enterprise." I answered
that of strength and steadfastness of soul I should have enough and
to spare, provided I found the opportunity. Then the priest said:
"If you have the heart to dare it, I will amply satisfy your curiosity."
Accordingly we agreed upon attempting the adventure.

The priest one evening made his preparations, and bade me find
a comrade, or not more than two. I invited Vincenzio Romoli, a very
dear friend of mine, and the priest took with him a native of Pistoja,
who also cultivated the black art. We went together to the Coliseum;
and there the priest, having arrayed himself in necromancer's robes,
began to describe circles on the earth with the finest ceremonies
that can be imagined. I must say that he had made us bring precious
perfumes and fire, and also drugs of fetid odour. When the pre-
liminaries were completed, he made the entrance into the circle; and
taking us by the hand, introduced us one by one inside it. Then he
assigned our several functions; to the necromancer, his comrade, he
gave the pentacle to hold; the other two of us had to look after the
fire and the perfumes; and then he began his incantations. This
lasted more than an hour and a half; when several legions appeared,

and the Coliseum was all full of devils. I was occupied with the precious perfumes, and when the priest perceived in what numbers they were present, he turned to me and said: "Benvenuto, ask them something." I called on them to reunite me with my Sicilian Angelica. That night we obtained no answer; but I enjoyed the greatest satisfaction of my curiosity in such matters. The necromancer said that we should have to go a second time, and that I should obtain the full accomplishment of my request; but he wished me to bring with me a little boy of pure virginity.

I chose one of my shop-lads, who was about twelve years old, and invited Vincenzio Romoli again; and we also took a certain Agnolino Gaddi, who was a very intimate friend of both. When we came once more to the place appointed, the necromancer made just the same preparations, attended by the same and even more impressive details. Then he introduced us into the circle, which he had reconstructed with art more admirable and yet more wondrous ceremonies. Afterwards he appointed my friend Vincenzio to the ordering of the perfumes and the fire, and with him Agnolino Gaddi. He next placed in my hand the pentacle, which he bid me turn toward the points he indicated, and under the pentacle I held the little boy, my workman. Now the necromancer began to utter those awful invocations, calling by name on multitudes of demons who are captains of their legions, and these he summoned by the virtue and potency of God, the Uncreated, Living, and Eternal, in phrases of the Hebrew, and also of the Greek and Latin tongues; insomuch that in a short space of time the whole Coliseum was full of a hundredfold as many as had appeared upon the first occasion. Vincenzio Romoli, together with Agnolino, tended the fire and heaped on quantities of precious perfumes. At the advice of the necromancer, I again demanded to be reunited with Angelica. The sorcerer turned to me and said: "Here you what they have replied; that in the space of one month you will be where she is?" Then once more he prayed me to stand firm by him, because the legions were a thousandfold more than he had summoned, and were the most dangerous of all the denizens of hell; and now that they had settled what I asked, it behoved us to be civil to them and dismiss them gently. On the other side, the boy, who was beneath the pentacle, shrieked out in terror that a million of the fiercest men were swarming round and threatening us. He said, moreover, that four huge giants had appeared, who were striving to force their way inside the circle. Meanwhile the necromancer, trembling with fear, kept doing his best with mild and soft persuasions to dismiss them. Vincenzio Romoli, who quaked like an aspen leaf, looked after the perfumes. Though I was quite as frightened as the rest of them, I tried to show it less, and inspired them all with marvellous courage; but the truth is that I had given myself up for dead when I saw the terror of the necromancer. The boy had stuck his head between his knees, exclaiming: "This is how I will meet death, for we are certainly dead men." Again I said to him: "These creatures are all inferior to us, and what you see is only smoke and shadow; so then raise your eyes." When he had raised them he cried out: "The whole Coliseum is in flames, and the fire is advancing on us"; then covering his face with his hands, he groaned again that he was dead, and that he could not endure the sight longer. The necromancer appealed for my support, entreating me to stand firm by him, and to have assafetida flung upon the coals; so I turned to Vincenzio Romoli, and told him to make the fumigation at once. While uttering these words I looked at Agnolino Gaddi, whose eyes were starting from their sockets in his terror, and who was more than half dead, and said to him: "Agnolo, in time and place like this we must not yield to fright, but do the utmost to bestir ourselves; therefore, up at once, and fling a handful of that assafetida upon the fire." Agnolo, at the moment when he moved to do this, let fly such a volley from his breech, that it was far more effectual than the assafetida. The boy, roused by that great stench and noise, lifted his face a little, and hearing me laugh, he plucked up courage, and said the devils were taking to flight tempestuously. So we abode thus until the matin-bells began to sound. Then the boy told us again that but few remained, and those were at a distance. When the necromancer had concluded his ceremonies, he put off his wizard's robe, and packed up a great bundle of books which he had brought with him; then, all together, we issued with him from the circle, huddling as close as we could to one another, especially the boy, who had got into the middle, and taken the necromancer by his gown and me by the cloak. All the while that we were going toward our houses in the Banchi, he kept saying that two of the devils he had seen in the Coliseum were gambolling in front of us, skipping now along the roofs and now upon the ground. The necromancer assured me that, often as he had entered magic circles, he had never met with such a serious affair as this. He also tried to persuade me to assist him in consecrating a book, by means of which we should extract immeasurable wealth, since we could call up fiends to show us where treasures were, whereof the earth is full; and after this wise we should become the richest of mankind; love affairs like mine were nothing but vanities and follies without consequence. I replied that if I were a Latin scholar I should be very willing to do what he suggested. He continued to persuade me by arguing that Latin scholarship was of no importance, and that, if he wanted, he could

49

have found plenty of good Latinists; but that he had never met with a man of soul so firm as mine, and that I ought to follow his counsel. Engaged in this conversation, we reached our homes, and each one of us dreamed all that night of devils.

ESCAPE FROM CASTEL SANT' ANGELO

The castellan was subject to a certain sickness, which came upon him every year and deprived him of his wits. The sign of its approach was that he kept continually talking, or rather jabbering, to no purpose. These humours took a different shape each year; one time he thought he was an oil-jar; another time he thought he was a frog, and hopped about as frogs do; another time he thought he was dead, and then they had to bury him; not a year passed but he got some such hypochondriac notions into his head. At this season he imagined that he was a bat, and when he went abroad to take the air, he used to scream like bats in a high thin tone; and then he would flap his hands and body as though he were about to fly. The doctors, when they saw the fit was coming on him, and his old servants, gave him all the distractions they could think of; and since they had noticed that he derived much pleasure from my conversation, they were always fetching me to keep him company. At times the poor man detained me for four or five stricken hours without ever letting me cease talking. He used to keep me at his table, eating opposite to him, and never stopped chatting and making me chat; but during these discourses I contrived to make a good meal. He, poor man, could neither eat nor sleep; so that at last he wore me out. I was at the end of my strength; and sometimes when I looked at him, I noticed that his eyeballs were rolling in a frightful manner, one looking one way and the other in another.

He took it into his head to ask me whether I had ever had a fancy to fly. I answered that it had always been my ambition to do those things which offer the greatest difficulties to men, and that I had done them; as to flying, the God of Nature had gifted me with a body well suited for running and leaping far beyond the common average, and that with the talents I possessed for manual art I felt sure I had the courage to try flying. He then inquired what methods I should use; to which I answered that, taking into consideration all flying creatures, and wishing to imitate by art what they derived from nature, none was so apt a model as the bat. No sooner had the poor man heard the name bat, which recalled the humour he was suffering under, than he cried out at the top of his voice: "He says

50

true—he says true; the bat's the thing—the bat's the thing!" Then he turned to me and said: "Benvenuto, if one gave you the opportunity, should you have the heart to fly?" I said that if he would set me at liberty, I felt quite up to flying down to Prati, after making myself a pair of wings out of waxed linen. Thereupon he replied: "I too should be prepared to take flight; but since the Pope has bidden me guard you as though you were his own eyes, and I know you a clever devil who would certainly escape, I shall now have you locked up with a hundred keys in order to prevent you slipping through my fingers." I then began to implore him, and remind him that I might have fled, but that on account of the word which I had given him I would never have betrayed his trust: therefore I begged him for the love of God, and by the kindness he had always shown me, not to add greater evils to the misery of my present situation. While I was pouring out these entreaties, he gave strict orders to have me bound and taken and locked up in prison. On seeing that it could not be helped, I told him before all his servants: "Lock me well up, and keep good watch on me; for I shall certainly contrive to escape." So they took and confined me with the utmost care.

I then began to deliberate upon the best way of making my escape. No sooner had I been locked in, than I went about exploring my prison; and when I thought I had discovered how to get out of it, I pondered the means of descending from the lofty keep, for so the great round central tower is called. I took those new sheets of mine, which, as I have said already, I had cut in strips and sewn together; then I reckoned up the quantity which would be sufficient for my purpose. Having made this estimate and put all things in order, I looked out a pair of pincers which I had abstracted from a Savoyard belonging to the guard of the castle. This man superintended the casks and cisterns; he also amused himself with carpentering. Now he possessed several pairs of pincers, among which was one both big and heavy. I then, thinking it would suit my purpose, took it and hid it in my straw mattress. The time had now come for me to use it; so I began to try the nails which kept the hinges of my door in place. The door was double, and the clinching of the nails could not be seen; so that when I attempted to draw one out, I met with the greatest trouble; in the end, however, I succeeded. When I had drawn the first nail, I bethought me how to prevent its being noticed. For this purpose I mixed some rust, which I had scraped from old iron, with a little wax, obtaining exactly the same colour as the heads of the long nails which I had extracted. Then I set myself to counterfeit these heads and place them on the holdfasts; for each nail I extracted I made a counterfeit in wax. I left the hinges

51

attached to their door-posts at top and bottom by means of some of the same nails that I had drawn; but I took care to cut these and replace them lightly, so that they only just supported the irons of the hinges.

All this I performed with the greatest difficulty, because the castellan kept dreaming every night that I had escaped, which made him send from time to time to inspect my prison. The man who came had the title and behaviour of a catchpole. He was called Bozza, and used always to bring with him another of the same sort, named Giovanni and nicknamed Pedignone; the latter was a soldier, and Bozza a serving-man. Giovanni never entered my prison without saying something offensive to me. He came from the district of Prato, and had been an apothecary in the town there. Every evening he minutely examined the holdfasts of the hinges and the whole chamber, and I used to say: "Keep a good watch over me, for I am resolved by all means to escape." These words bred a great enmity between him and me, so that I was obliged to use precautions to conceal my tools, that is to say, my pincers and a great big poniard and other appurtenances. All these I put away together in my mattress, where I also kept the strips of linen I had made. When day broke, I used immediately to sweep my room out; and though I am by nature a lover of cleanliness, at that time I kept myself unusually spic and span. After sweeping up, I made my bed as daintily as I could, laying flowers upon it, which a Savoyard used to bring me nearly every morning. He had the care of the cistern and the casks, and also amused himself with carpentering; it was from him I stole the pincers which I used in order to draw out the nails from the holdfasts of the hinges.

Well, to return to the subject of my bed; when Bozza and Pedignone came, I always told them to give it a wide berth, so as not to dirty and spoil it for me. Now and then, just to irritate me, they would touch it lightly, upon which I cried: "Ah, dirty cowards! I'll lay my hand on one of your swords there, and will do you a mischief that will make you wonder. Do you think you are fit to touch the bed of a man like me? When I chastise you I shall not heed my own life, for I am certain to take yours. Let me alone then with my troubles and my tribulations, and don't give me more annoyance than I have already; if not, I shall make you see what a desperate man is able to do." These words they reported to the castellan, who gave them express orders never to go near my bed, and when they came to me, to come without swords, but for the rest to keep a watchful guard upon me.

52 Having thus secured my bed from meddlers, I felt as though the

main point was gained; for there lay all things needful to my venture. It happened on the evening of a certain feast-day that the castellan was seriously indisposed; his humours grew extravagant; he kept repeating that he was a bat, and if they heard that Benvenuto had flown away, they must let him go to catch me up, since he could fly by night most certainly as well or better than myself; for it was thus he argued: "Benvenuto is a counterfeit bat, but I am a real one; and since he is committed to my care, leave me to act; I shall be sure to catch him." He had passed several nights in this frenzy, and had worn out all his servants, whereof I received full information through divers channels, but specially from the Savoyard, who was my friend at heart.

On the evening of that feast-day, then, I made my mind up to escape, come what might; and first I prayed most devoutly to God, imploring His Divine Majesty to protect and succour me in that so perilous a venture. Afterwards I set to work at all the things I needed, and laboured the whole of the night. It was two hours before daybreak when at last I removed those hinges with the greatest toil; but the wooden panel itself and the bolt too offered such resistance that I could not open the door; so I had to cut into the wood; yet in the end I got it open, and shouldering the strips of linen which I had rolled up like bundles of flax upon two sticks, I went forth and directed my steps toward the latrines of the keep. Spying from within two tiles upon the roof, I was able at once to clamber up with ease. I wore a white doublet with a pair of white hose and a pair of half boots, into which I had stuck the poniard I have mentioned.

After scaling the roof, I took one end of my linen roll and attached it to a piece of antique tile which was built into the fortress wall; it happened to jut out scarcely four fingers. In order to fix the band, I gave it the form of a stirrup. When I had attached it to that piece of tile, I turned to God and said: "Lord God, give aid to my good cause; you know that it is good; you see that I am aiding myself." Then I let myself go gently by degrees, supporting myself with the sinews of my arms, until I touched the ground. There was no moonshine, but the light of a fair open heaven. When I stood upon my feet on solid earth, I looked up at the vast height which I had descended with such spirit, and went gladly away, thinking I was free. But this was not the case; for the castellan on that side of the fortress had built two lofty walls, the space between which he used for stable and henyard; the place was barred with thick iron bolts outside. I was terribly disgusted to find there was no exit from this trap; but while I paced up and down debating

53 what to do, I stumbled on a long pole which was covered up with

straw. Not without great trouble I succeeded in placing it against the wall, and then swarmed up it by the force of my arms until I reached the top. But since the wall ended in a sharp ridge, I had not strength enough to drag the pole up after me. Accordingly I made my mind up to use a portion of the second roll of linen which I had there; the other was left hanging from the keep of the castle. So I cut a piece off, tied it to the pole, and clambered down the wall, enduring the utmost toil and fatigue. I was quite exhausted, and had, moreover, flayed the inside of my hands, which bled freely. This compelled me to rest awhile, and I bathed my hands in my own urine. When I thought that my strength was recovered, I advanced quickly toward the last rampart, which faces toward Prati. There I put my bundle of linen lines down upon the ground, meaning to fasten them round a battlement, and descend the lesser as I had the greater height. But no sooner had I placed the linen, than I became aware behind me of the sentinel, who was going the rounds. Seeing my designs interrupted and my life in peril, I resolved to face the guard. This fellow, when he noticed my bold front, and that I was marching on him with a weapon in hand, quickened his pace and gave me a wide berth. I had left my lines some little way behind; so I turned with hasty steps to regain them; and though I came within sight of another sentinel, he seemed as though he did not choose to take notice of me. Having found my lines and attached them to the battlement, I let myself go. On the descent, whether it was that I thought I had really come to earth and relaxed my grasp to jump, or whether my hands were so tired that they could not keep their hold, at any rate I fell, struck my head in falling, and lay stunned for more than an hour and a half, so far as I could judge.

It was just upon daybreak, when the fresh breeze which blows an hour before the sun revived me; yet I did not immediately recover my senses, for I thought my head had been cut off and fancied that I was in purgatory. With time, little by little, my faculties returned, and I perceived that I was outside the castle, and in a flash remembered all my adventures. I was aware of the wound in my head before I knew my leg was broken; for I put my hands up, and withdrew them covered with blood. Then I searched the spot well, and judged and ascertained that I had sustained no injury of consequence there; but when I wanted to stand up, I discovered that my right leg was broken three inches above the heel. Not even this dismayed me: I drew forth my poniard with its scabbard; the latter had a metal point ending in a large ball, which had caused the fracture of my leg; for the bone, coming into violent contact with the ball, and not being able to bend, had snapped at that point. I threw the sheath away, and with the poniard cut a piece of the linen which I had left. Then I bound my leg up as well as I could, and crawled on all fours with the poniard in my hand toward the city gate. When I reached it, I found it shut; but I noticed a stone just beneath the door which did not appear to be very firmly fixed. This I attempted to dislodge; after setting my hands to it, and feeling it move, it easily gave way, and I drew it out. Through the gap thus made I crept into the town.

I had crawled more than five hundred paces from the place where I fell, to the gate by which I entered. No sooner had I got inside than some mastiff dogs set upon me and bit me badly. When they returned to the attack and worried me, I drew my poniard and wounded one of them so sharply that he howled aloud, and all the dogs, according to their nature, ran after him. I meanwhile made the best way I could on all fours toward the church of the Trespontina.

On arriving at the opening of the street which leads to Sant' Agnolo, I turned off in the direction of San Piero; and now the dawn had risen over me, and I felt myself in danger. When therefore I chanced to meet a water-carrier driving his donkey laden with full buckets, I called the fellow, and begged him to carry me upon his back to the terrace by the steps of San Piero, adding: "I am an unfortunate young man, who, while escaping from a window in a love-adventure, have fallen and broken my leg. The place from which I made my exit is one of great importance; and if I am discovered, I run risk of being cut to pieces; so for heaven's sake lift me quickly, and I will give you a crown of gold." Saying this, I clapped my hand to my purse, where I had a good quantity. He took me up at once, hitched me on his back, and carried me to the raised terrace by the steps to San Piero. There I bade him leave me, saying he must run back to his donkey.

I resumed my march, crawling always on all fours, and making for the palace of the Duchess, wife of Duke Ottavio and daughter of the Emperor. She was his natural child, and had been married to Duke Alessandro. I chose her house for refuge, because I was quite certain that many of my friends, who had come with that great princess from Florence, were tarrying there; also because she had taken me into favour through something which the castellan had said in my behalf. Wishing to be of service to me, he told the Pope that I had saved the city more than a thousand crowns of damage, caused by heavy rain on the occasion when the Duchess made her entrance into Rome. He related how he was in despair, and how I put heart into him, and went on to describe how I had pointed several large pieces of artillery in the direction where the

55

clouds were thickest, and whence a deluge of water was already pouring; then, when I began to fire, the rain stopped, and at the fourth discharge the sun shone out; and so I was the sole cause of the festival succeeding, to the joy of everybody. On hearing this narration the Duchess said: "That Benvenuto is one of the artists of merit, who enjoyed the good-will of my late husband, Duke Alessandro, and I shall always hold them in mind if an opportunity comes of doing such men service." She also talked of me to Duke Ottavio. For these reasons I meant to go straight to the house of her Excellency, which was a very fine palace situated in Borgio Vecchio.

I should have been quite safe from recapture by the Pope if I could have stayed there; but my exploits up to this point had been too marvellous for a human being, and God was unwilling to encourage my vainglory; accordingly, for my own good, He chastised me a second time worse even than the first. The cause of this was that while I was crawling on all fours up those steps, a servant of Cardinal Cornaro recognised me. His master was then lodging in the palace; so the servant ran up to his room and woke him, crying: "Most reverend Monsignor, your friend Benvenuto is down there; he has escaped from the castle, and is crawling on all fours, streaming with blood; to all appearances he has broken a leg, and we don't know whither he is going." The Cardinal exclaimed at once: "Run and carry him upon your back into my room here." When I arrived, he told me to be under no apprehension, and sent for the first physicians of Rome to take my case in hand. Among them was Maestro Jacomo of Perugia, a most excellent and able surgeon. He set the bone with dexterity, then bound the limb up, and bled me with his own hand. It happened that my veins were swollen far beyond their usual size, and he too wished to make a pretty wide incision; accordingly the blood sprang forth so copiously, and spurted with such force into his face, that he had to abandon the operation. He regarded this as a very bad omen, and could hardly be prevailed upon to undertake my cure. Indeed, he often expressed a wish to leave me, remembering that he ran no little risk of punishment for having treated my case, or rather for having proceeded to the end with it. The Cardinal had me placed in a secret chamber, and went off immediately to beg me from the Pope.

THE CASTING OF THE "PERSEUS"

Abandoned thus to my own resources, I took new courage, and
56 banished the sad thoughts which kept recurring to my mind, making

me often weep bitter tears of repentance for having left France; for though I did so only to revisit Florence, my sweet birthplace, in order that I might charitably succour my six nieces, this good action, as I well perceived, had been the beginning of my great misfortune. Nevertheless, I felt convinced that when my Perseus was accomplished, all these trials would be turned to high felicity and glorious well-being.

Accordingly I strengthened my heart, and with all the forces of my body and my purse, employing what little money still remained to me, I set to work. First I provided myself with several loads of pinewood from the forests of Serristori, in the neighbourhood of Montelupo. While these were on their way, I clothed my Perseus with the clay which I had prepared many months beforehand, in order that it might be duly seasoned. After making its clay tunic (for that is the term used in this art) and properly arming it and fencing it with iron girders, I began to draw the wax out by means of a slow fire. This melted and issued through numerous air-vents I had made; for the more there are of these, the better will the mould fill. When I had finished drawing off the wax, I constructed a funnel-shaped furnace all round the model of my Perseus. It was built of bricks, so interlaced, the one above the other, that numerous apertures were left for the fire to exhale at. Then I began to lay on wood by degrees, and kept it burning two whole days and nights. At length, when all the wax was gone, and the mould was well baked, I set to work at digging the pit in which to sink it. This I performed with scrupulous regard to all the rules of art. When I had finished that part of my work, I raised the mould by windlasses and stout ropes to a perpendicular position, and suspending it with the greatest care one cubit above the level of the furnace, so that it hung exactly above the middle of the pit, I next lowered it gently down into the very bottom of the furnace, and had it firmly placed with every possible precaution for its safety. When this delicate operation was accomplished, I began to bank it up with the earth I had excavated; and, ever as the earth grew higher, I introduced its proper air-vents, which were little tubes of earthenware, such as folk use for drains and such-like purposes. At length, I felt sure that it was admirably fixed, and that the filling-in of the pit and the placing of the air-vents had been properly performed. I also could see that my work-people understood my method, which differed very considerably from that of all the other masters in the trade. Feeling confident, then, that I could rely upon them, I next turned to my furnace, which I had filled with numerous pigs of copper and other bronze stuff. The pieces were piled according to the laws of art, that is to say, so resting one upon the other that the flames could play

57

freely through them, in order that the metal might heat and liquefy the sooner. At last I called out heartily to set the furnace going. The logs of pine were heaped in, and, what with the unctuous resin of the wood and the good draught I had given, my furnace worked so well that I was obliged to rush from side to side to keep it going. The labour was more than I could stand; yet I forced myself to strain every nerve and muscle. To increase my anxieties, the workshop took fire, and we were afraid lest the roof should fall upon our heads; while, from the garden, such a storm of wind and rain kept blowing in, that it perceptibly cooled the furnace.

Battling thus with all these untoward circumstances for several hours, and exerting myself beyond even the measure of my powerful constitution, I could at last bear up no longer, and a sudden fever, of the utmost possible intensity, attacked me. I felt absolutely obliged to go and fling myself upon my bed. Sorely against my will having to drag myself away from the spot, I turned to my assistants, about ten or more in all, what with master-founders, hand-workers, country-fellows, and my own special journeymen, among whom was Bernardino Mannellini of Mugello, my apprentice through several years. To him in particular I spoke: "Look, my dear Bernardino, that you observe the rules which I have taught you; do your best with all despatch, for the metal will soon be fused. You cannot go wrong; these honest men will get the channels ready; you will easily be able to drive back the two plugs with this pair of iron crooks; and I am sure that my mould will fill miraculously. I feel more ill than I ever did in all my life, and verily believe that it will kill me before a few hours are over." Thus, with despair at heart, I left them, and betook myself to bed.

No sooner had I got to bed, than I ordered my servingmaids to carry food and wine for all the men into the workshop; at the same time I cried: "I shall not be alive to-morrow." They tried to encourage me, arguing that my illness would pass over, since it came from excessive fatigue. In this way I spent two hours battling with the fever, which steadily increased, and calling out continually, "I feel that I am dying." My housekeeper, who was named Mona Fiore da Castel del Rio, a very notable manager and no less warm-hearted, kept chiding me for my discouragement; but, on the other hand, she paid me every kind attention which was possible. However, the sight of my physical pain and moral dejection so affected her, that, in spite of that brave heart of hers, she could not refrain from shedding tears; and yet, so far as she was able, she took good care

I should not see them. While I was thus terribly afflicted, I beheld the figure of a man enter my chamber, twisted in his body into the form of a capital S. He raised a lamentable, doleful voice, like one who announces their last hour to men condemned to die upon the scaffold, and spoke these words: "O Benvenuto! your statue is spoiled, and there is no hope whatever of saving it." No sooner had I heard the shriek of that wretch than I gave a howl which might have been heard from the sphere of flame. Jumping from my bed, I seized my clothes and began to dress. The maids, and my lad, and every one who came around to help me, got kicks or blows of the fist, while I kept crying out in lamentation "Ah! traitors! enviers! This is an act of treason, done by malice prepense! But I swear by God that I will sift it to the bottom, and before I die will leave such witness to the world of what I can do as shall make a score of mortals marvel."

When I had got my clothes on, I strode with soul bent on mischief toward the workshop; there I beheld the men, whom I had left erewhile in such high spirits, standing stupefied and downcast. I began at once and spoke: "Up with you! Attend to me! Since you have not been able or willing to obey the directions I gave you, obey me now that I am with you to conduct my work in person. Let no one contradict me, for in cases like this we need the aid of hand and hearing, not of advice." When I had uttered these words, a certain Maestro Alessandro Lastricati broke silence and said: "Look you, Benvenuto, you are going to attempt an enterprise which the laws of art do not sanction, and which cannot succeed." I turned upon him with such fury and so full of mischief, that he and all the rest of them exclaimed with one voice: "On then! Give orders! We will obey your least commands, so long as life is left in us." I believe they spoke thus feelingly because they thought I must fall shortly dead upon the ground. I went immediately to inspect the furnace, and found that the metal was all curdled; an accident which we express by "being caked." I told two of the hands to cross the road, and fetch from the house of the butcher Capretta, a load of young oak-wood, which had lain dry for above a year; this wood had been previously offered me by Madame Ginevra, wife of the said Capretta. So soon as the first armfuls arrived, I began to fill the grate beneath the furnace. Now oak-wood of that kind heats more powerfully than any other sort of tree; and for this reason, where a slow fire is wanted, as in the case of gun-foundry, alder or pine is preferred. Accordingly, when the logs took fire, oh! how the cake began to stir beneath that awful heat, to glow and sparkle in a blaze! At the same time I kept stirring up the channels, and sent men upon the roof to stop the conflagration, which had gathered force from the increased combustion in the furnace; also I caused

59

boards, carpets, and other hangings to be set up against the garden, in order to protect us from the violence of the rain.

When I had thus provided against these several disasters, I roared out first to one man and then to another: "Bring this thing here! Take that thing there!" At this crisis, when the whole gang saw the cake was on the point of melting, they did my bidding, each fellow working with the strength of three. I then ordered half a pig of pewter to be brought, which weighed about sixty pounds, and flung it into the middle of the cake inside the furnace. By this means, and by piling on wood and stirring now with pokers and now with iron rods, the curdled mass rapidly began to liquefy. Then, knowing I had brought the dead to life again, against the firm opinion of those ignoramuses, I felt such vigour fill my veins, that all those pains of fever, all those fears of death, were quite forgotten.

All of a sudden an explosion took place, attended by a tremendous flash of flame, as though a thunderbolt had formed and been discharged amongst us. Unwonted and appalling terror astonied every one, and me more even than the rest. When the din was over and the dazzling light extinguished, we began to look each other in the face. Then I discovered that the cap of the furnace had blown up, and the bronze was bubbling over from its source beneath. So I had the mouths of my mould immediately opened, and at the same time drove in the two plugs which kept back the molten metal. But I noticed that it did not flow as rapidly as usual, the reason being probably that the fierce heat of the fire we kindled had consumed its base alloy. Accordingly I sent for all my pewter platters, porringers, and dishes, to the number of some two hundred pieces, and had a portion of them cast, one by one, into the channels, the rest into the furnace. This expedient succeeded, and every one could now perceive that my bronze was in most perfect liquefaction, and my mould was filling; whereupon they all with heartiness and happy cheer assisted and obeyed my bidding, while I, now here, now there, gave orders, helped with my own hands, and cried aloud: "O God! Thou that by Thy immeasurable power didst rise from the dead, and in Thy glory didst ascend to heaven!" . . . even thus in a moment my mould was filled; and seeing my work finished, I fell upon my knees, and with all my heart gave thanks to God.

After all was over, I turned to a plate of salad on a bench there, and ate with hearty appetite, and drank together with the whole crew. Afterwards I retired to bed, healthy and happy, for it was now two hours before morning, and slept as sweetly as though I had never felt a touch of illness. My good housekeeper, without my giving any orders, had prepared a fat capon for my repast. So that, when I rose, about the hour for breaking fast, she presented herself with a smiling countenance, and said: "Oh! is that the man who felt that he was dying? Upon my word, I think the blows and kicks you dealt us last night, when you were so enraged, and had that demon in your body as it seemed, must have frightened away your mortal fever! The fever feared that it might catch it too, as we did!" All my poor household, relieved in like measure from anxiety and overwhelming labour, went at once to buy earthen vessels in order to replace the pewter I had cast away. Then we dined together joyfully; nay, I cannot remember a day in my whole life when I dined with greater gladness or a better appetite.

After our meal I received visits from the several men who had assisted me. They exchanged congratulations, and thanked God for our success, saying they had learned and seen things done which other masters judged impossible. I too grew somewhat glorious; and deeming I had shown myself a man of talent, indulged a boastful humour. So I thrust my hand into my purse, and paid them all to their full satisfaction.

GIROLAMO SAVONAROLA

The Triumph of the Cross
Translated by O'Dell Travers Hill

Book *Introduction.* I undertake to defend the glorious triumph of the
One Cross against the impious volubility of the sophists and wise men
of the world. The enterprise is bold and beyond my strength, but
I hope God will aid me in a work, in these days, so useful to His
glory; for although it may seem superfluous to reproduce the proofs
of the faith so happily founded and established by the innumerable
miracles of our Lord, by the literary monuments of the Fathers and
Doctors of the Church, yet many men are so deeply plunged in the
mire of vice that they do not see the light of truth, that they regard
heavenly things as ridiculous, and despise Divine marvels as absurd
dreams. We, inflamed by zeal for the house of God, will exert ourselves to rouse these souls slumbering in the shadow of death, and
recall to their memory the authentic deeds of the past.

Although it may not be possible to demonstrate the faith by the
causes and principles of nature, however, its manifested effects will
furnish us with proofs so solid that every sensible man will be compelled to admit them.

But the faith does not depend upon proofs; for, says the Apostle,
faith is a gift which God bestows on man through grace alone, lest
any one should boast. We will, therefore, only bring forward these
proofs to confirm those who hesitate, and to dispose them to receive
the supernatural gift of faith, and at the same time to arm the faithful against the assaults of impiety, and to prevent the impious from
undertaking anything against souls so simple whom it would be
wicked to deceive. And as to what is said that faith has no merit
when it is demonstrated by human reason, it does not follow that we
here derogate from the mystery of grace, for this adage only
refers to men who to believe will be vanquished by the arms of
reason alone; but those are to be praised who by virtue of the Divine

62

gift, having already embraced the faith of Jesus Christ, still seek for solid reasons to assure themselves in it, and to confirm their brethren.

The prince of apostles exhorts to do this when he says, "Sanctify the Lord God in your hearts, and be ready always to give an answer to every man that asketh you a reason of the hope which is in you."

Therefore, as we wish in this book to proceed only by reasonings, we shall invoke no authority, but act as if it were only necessary to believe our own reason and experience; for all men are compelled, under pain of folly, to consent to natural reason.

As we address ourselves to the learned of the times, who generally disdain familiar language destitute of ornament, we shall on their account abandon for a little our usual simplicity.

Chapter *On the mode of proceeding in this work.* It is necessary that we
One should attain to the knowledge of invisible things by means of visible, for all our knowledge commences with the senses, and the senses only apprehend external accidents; but the intellect by its subtlety penetrates to the very substance of things, whence it elevates itself to the knowledge of that which is immaterial and invisible: for while man seeks the substance and propriety, order, causes, and movement of visible things, he is led by induction to the knowledge of invisible things, and even raises himself to God; so that by the accidents, the movements, and the exterior operations of man we arrive at a knowledge of our own soul. This is the reason why the philosophers in contemplating the universe, that is the heavens, their ornaments and the influence of the stars, the properties, action, and mixture of elements, the varieties, the movements, and the passions of composite beings, and in fine, the admirable order, the grandeur, and the beauty of this visible world, elevated their regard still higher to seek invisible things; and, having found them, they endeavoured to penetrate into their nature and properties; and now as they have learnt that nature is the work of God, and that through the creation we may arrive at a knowledge of the power and glory of a Creator—so we wish to show that the works which the Church has done, and which are perceived by the senses and reason, are Divine works, and that by them we can learn the majesty and glory of the invisible Jesus Christ. Also as these philosophers have collected and put before our eyes all the things which God has created in the universe, we must present in a tableau all that Christ has done in the world; and as the philosophers
63 were constrained by the marvels of nature to recognise that God

is the first cause of all created beings, and that nature is the work of an infallible intelligence, that is a Divine—so do we find from the admirable works of the Church that the same Jesus Christ crucified is the first cause of these works, and that His operations are the operations of a God who cannot be deceived.

However, we do not say that our faith is born out of these reasons so proposed, and that the Christian soul is impelled towards belief by the virtue of argumentation, for then faith would be no more than human opinion; but we believe, thanks to the power of that light which God has supernaturally infused into us, and reason only serves to confirm that belief, that to preserve this Divine gift is not idleness, but gravity and wisdom.

In order to present to the eyes of men a grand synthesis of the works of the Church in the present and the past, we describe them under the figure of a triumphal chariot, having some kind of similitude with the universe.

Chapter Two *Concerning the triumph of the Cross—whence the proofs of the faith are drawn.* As the power, the wisdom, and the goodness of God are infinite, the contemplation of a single creature can only give us an imperfect idea of Him. So the philosophers arrived at a knowledge of God through contemplating the order of the universe; but this order results not from one thing, but from innumerable things, which they could easily embrace at one view, since all beings in creation are dependent upon one another, and are united together by a natural tie. In the same manner, an isolated view of one of the works of Jesus Christ cannot give us instantly the intelligence of His virtue and wisdom, but if we offer to view all His works at once, and the effects they have produced, to draw not one proof but many, every intellect will be compelled to recognise that the Christ crucified is the true God; for if a single proof will not suffice, all the proofs united will have the power to convince every man who is not foolishly obstinate.

But because the past and present works of Christ do not offer themselves easily to the view, like objects of nature, which are linked together in admirable order under the vault of heaven, it has seemed good to present them under the image of a triumphant chariot, in order to render them palpable to the most vulgar mind, and that we may contemplate them not only one after another, but in their harmonious whole.

Let us represent to ourselves, first, a chariot with four wheels, and
upon this chariot Christ borne in triumph, crowned with thorns, and

showing, after having conquered the pains of death, the sacred wounds of his pale and bleeding body: the arms, with which he has subdued the world and led captivity captive. Let there shine on his head a triple sun, representing the Holy Trinity: let that radiant globe shed an ineffable splendour over Christ and His Church: let Christ bear in His left hand His cross and all the instruments of His passion, and press with His right hand the books of the Old and New Testament. Let the apostles and preachers march immediately before the chariot, as if they were drawing it, preceded by patriarchs, prophets, and an innumerable crowd of Old Testament saints: let a crowd also of martyrs, of all conditions and of both sexes, surround that triumphal chariot, and around them all the holy doctors with their books open in their hands, followed by an immense number of every rank and nation—Jews, Greeks, Latins, barbarians, learned and ignorant, of every age, applauding the triumph of Christ. And outside this triumphal band let there be seen the enemies of Christ, who with all their strength persecute the Church: the emperors, kings, princes, and the mighty of this age: the sages, the philosophers, the heretics, and the wicked of all nations and tongues, slaves and free, men and women; and near this crowd let there be the relics and idols of the gods reversed and destroyed; the heretical books delivered up to the flames, their impious dogmas confounded, and their false worship reduced to nothing.

This chariot thus represented before us will be, so to speak, a universe whence we shall draw a new philosophy.

For the first cause, and for things invisible, to the knowledge of which the philosophers were compelled to attain by means of visible things, we place, in fact, upon the head of Christ the radiant globe which represents the Trinity, which we confess to be the sovereign God and the Christ (invisible to us) dominating over the whole, and surrounded by the homage of a chorus of angels and saints.

All these visible beings whom we have placed on the chariot and about the chariot, will conduct us to the knowledge and the science of these invisible beings.

And just as the philosophers establish, after God, the heavens as the principal generating cause of all, we will place, after God, the Cross and the suffering of Christ as principal cause of the grace bestowed on the Church and of our salvation. After the heavens come the elements (of nature), and that is why after the Cross and suffering come the sacraments of the Church. And in the same manner as the elements draw all their virtue from heaven, so the sacraments draw all their virtue from the suffering of Christ. After 65 the elementary principles in the constitution of the universe, come all the seeds, all the germs, and all the particular agents of propagation; and so, in the same manner, in our Triumph of the Cross, we place as seed the evangelical teaching and the example of the holy. As to particular agents, they are apostles, partriarchs, martyrs, and doctors, who during their lives have, in Christ, regenerated the whole universe, and by whose merits and example the Church becomes daily fecund in renowned and fruitful works. Then in this material world come the effects which in our work are represented by that immense multitude of men, of every condition, converted to Christ by the example and exhortation of holy men whose lives have been pious and pure.

Seeing that in Nature every movement passes from one contrary to another, so that the generation of one being is but the corruption of another, and that in every act of generation, opposing principles are necessary with the triumph of the stronger principle over the weaker, therefore we have placed around our chariot all the enemies of Christ and the Church, and we have represented the Christ as a valiant captain, triumphant over His enemies, and putting them and their errors to flight. Also, as the philosophers, having the universe before their eyes, and considering its phenomena, have been ravished with admiration, and seized with an ardour to know, and have arrived step by step from effects to the cause, from inferior things to superior, and, in fine, have attained to the notion even of invisible natures, and of the majesty of God—so also we arrive gradually to a knowledge of the Divinity of Christ, and of the invisible marvels which are in Him, by carefully studying His symbolical image, and the triumph of His past and present effects and all their causes.

LUDOVICO ARIOSTO

Orlando Furioso
Translated by Sir John Harington

Angelica

Canto Of Dames, of Knights, of armes, of loves delight,
One Of courtesies, of high attempts I speake,
Then when the Moores transported all their might
On Africke seas, the force of France to breake:
Incited by the youthfull heate and spight
Of Agramant their King, that vow'd to wreake
The death of King Trayano (lately slaine)
Upon the Romane Emperour Charlemaine.

I will no less Orlandos acts declare,
(A tale in prose ne verse yet sung or said)
Who fell bestraught with love, a hap most rare,
To one that erst was counted wise and stayd:
If my sweet Saint that causeth my like care,
My slender muse affoord some gracious ayd,
I make no doubt but I shall have the skill,
As much as I have promist to fulfill.

Orlando who long time had loved deare,
Angelica the faire: and for her sake,
About the world, in nations far and neare,
Did high attempts performe and undertake,
Return'd with her into the West that yeare,
That Charles his power against the Turks did make:
And with the force of Germanie and France,
Neare Pyren Alpes his standard did advance.

To make the Kings of Affrike and of Spaine,
67 Repent their rash attempts and foolish vaunts,

One having brought from Affrike in his traine,
All able men to carry sword or launce,
The other mov'd the Spaniards now againe
To overthrow the goodly Realme of Fraunce.
And hither (as I said) Orlando went,
But of his coming straight he did repent.

For here (behold how humane judgements are,
And how the wiser sort art oft mistaken)
His Ladie whom he guarded had so farre,
Nor had in fights nor dangers great forsaken,
Without the dint of sword or open warre,
Amid his friends away from him was taken.
For Charles the great, a valiant Prince and wise,
Did this to quench a broile that did arise.

Betweene Orlando and Renaldo late,
There fell about Angelica some brall,
And each of them began t'other hate,
This Ladies love had made them both so thrall.
But Charles who much mislikes that such debate
Betweene such friends should rise, on cause so small,
To Namus of Bavier in keeping gave her,
And suffred neither of them both to have her.

But promist he would presently bestow
The damsell faire, on him that in that fight,
The plainest proofe should of his prowesse show,
And danger most the Pagans with his might,
But (ay the while) the Christians take the blow,
Their souldiers slaine, their Captaines put to flight,
The Duke himself a prisner there was taken,
His tent was quite abandon'd and forsaken.

Where when the damsell faire a while had stayd,
That for the victor pointed was a pray,
She tooke her horse, ne farther time delayd,
But secretly convay'd herselfe away,
For she foresaw, and was full sore afrayd,
That this to Charles would prove a dismall day.
And riding through a wood, she hapt to meet
A Knight that came against her on his feet.

His curats on, his helmet not undone,
His sword and target ready to the same,
And through the wood so swiftly he did runne,
68 As they that go halfe naked for a game.

But never did a shepheards daughter shunne
More speedily a snake that on her came,
Then faire Angelica did take her flight,
When as she once had knowledge of the Knight.

This valiant Knight was Lord of Clarimount,
Duke Ammons sonne, as you shall understand,
Who having lost his horse of good account,
That by mishap was slipt out of his hand,
He follow'd him, in hope againe to mount,
Untill this Ladies sight did make him stand,
Whose face and shape proportion'd were so well,
They seem'd the house where love itselfe did dwell.

But she that shuns Renaldo all she may,
Upon her horses necke doth lay the raine,
Through thicke and thin she gallopeth away,
Ne makes the choise of beaten way or plaine,
But gives her palfrey leave to chuse the way,
And being mov'd with feare and with disdaine,
Now up, now downe, she never leaves to ride,
Till she arrived by a river side.

Fast by the streame Ferraw she sees an one,
(Who noyd, in part with dust, and part with sweat)
Out of the battell hither came alone,
With drinke his thirst, with aire to swage his heat;
And minding backe againe to have bene gone,
He was detain'd with an unlookt for lot,
Into the streame by hap his helmet fell,
And how to get it out he cannot tell.

And hearing now the noise and mournfull crie
Of one with piteous voice demaunding ayd,
Seeing the damsell eke approching nie,
That nought but helpe against Renaldo prayd,
What wight it was, he guessed by and by,
Though looking pale, like one that had bene frayd,
And though she had not late bene in his sight,
He thought it was Angelica the bright.

And being both a stout and courteous Knight,
And love a little kindling in his brest,
He promist straight to aide her all he might,
And to performe what ever she request.
And though he want an helmet, yet to fight
With bold Renaldo he will do his best.

69

And both the one, the other straight defied,
Oft having either others value tried.

Betweene them two a combat fierce began,
With strokes that might have pierst the hardest rocks:
While they thus fight on foote, and man to man,
And give and take so hard and heavy knocks,
Away the damsell posteth all she can,
Their paine and travell she requites with mocks.
So hard she rode while they were at their fight,
That she was cleane escaped out of sight.

When they long time contended had in vaine,
Who should remaine the master in the field,
And that with force, with cunning, nor with paine,
The one of them could make the other yeeld,
Renaldo first did move the Knight of Spaine
(Although he us'd such curtesie but seeld)
To make a truce; ne was he to be blamed,
For love his heart to other fight inflamed.

You thought (said he) to hinder me alone,
But you have hurt yourselfe as much or more,
You see the faire Angelica is gone,
So soone we leese that earst we sought so sore.
Had you me tane or slaine, your gaine were none,
Sith you were nere the nere your love therfore,
For while we two have made this little stay,
She lets us both alone and goes her way.

But if you love the Ladie, as you say,
Then let us both agree to find her out,
To have her first will be our wisest way,
And when of holding her there is no doubt,
Then by consent let her remaine his pray,
That with his sword can prove himselfe most stout,
I see not else after our long debate,
How either of us can amend his state.

Ferraw (that felt small pleasure in the fight)
Agreed a sound and friendly league to make:
They lay aside all wrath and malice quight,
And at the parting from the running lake,
The Pagan would not let the Christen Knight
To follow him on foote, for manners sake:
But prayes him mount behind his horses backe,
70 And so they seeke the damsell by the tracke.

O auncient Knights of true and noble hart,
They rivals were, one faith they liv'd not under,
Beside they felt their bodies shrewdly smart
Of blowes late given, and yet (behold a wonder)
Through thicke and thin, suspition set apart,
Like friends they ride, and parted not asunder,
Untill the horse with double spurring drived,
Unto a way, which parts in two, arrived.

And being neither able to descrie
Which way was gone Angelica the bright,
Because the tracke of horses feet, whereby
They seeke her out, appeare alike in sight:
They part, and either will his fortune try,
The left hand one, the other takes the right.
The Spaniard when he wandred had a while,
Came whence he went, the way did him beguile. . . .

But follow we Angelica that fled.

That fled through woods and deserts all obscure,
Through places uninhabited and wast,
Ne could she yet repute herselfe secure,
But farther still she gallopeth in hast.
Each leafe that stirres in her doth feare procure,
And maketh her affrighted and agast:
Each noise she heares, each shadow she doth see,
She doth mistrust it should Renaldo be.

Like to a fawne, or kid of bearded goate,
That in the wood a tyger fierce espide,
To kill her dam, and first to teare the throate,
And then to feed upon the hanch or side,
Both feare lest she might light on such a lot,
And seeke itself in thickest brackes to hide,
And thinkes each noise the wind or aire doth cause,
Itselfe in danger of the tygers clawes.

That day and night she wandred here and there,
And halfe the other day that did ensue,
Untill at last she was arrived where
A fine yong grove with pleasant shadow grew,
Neare to the which two little rivers were,
Whose moisture did the tender herbes renew,
And make a sweete and very pleasing sound,
71 By running on the sand and stonie ground.

Here she at last her selfe in safetie thought,
As being from Renaldo many a mile,
Tyr'd with annoy the heate and travell brought,
She thinkes it best with sleepe the time beguile,
And having first a place convenient sought,
She lets her horse refresh his limbes the while,
Who fed upon the bankes well cloth'd with grasse,
And dranke the river water clere as glasse.

Hard by the brooke an arbor she descride,
Wherein grew faire and very fragrant floures,
With roses sweet, and other trees beside,
Wherewith the place adornes the native boures,
So fenced in with shades on either side,
Safe from the heate of late or early houres,
The boughes and leaves so cunningly were mixt,
No sunne, no light, could enter them betwixt.

Within, the tender herbes a bed do make,
Inviting folke to take their rest and ease:
Here meanes this Ladie faire a nap to take,
And fals to sleepe, the place so well doth please.
Not long she lay, but her a noise did wake,
The trampling of a horse did her disease,
And looking out as secret as she might,
To come all arm'd she saw a comely Knight.

She knowes not yet if he be foe or friend,
Twixt hope and feare she doubtfully doth stand,
And what he meanes to do she doth attend,
And who it was she faine would understand.
The Knight did to the river side descend,
And resting downe his head upon his hand,
All in a muse he sitteth still alone,
Like one transform'd into a marble stone.

He tarri'd in this muse an houre and more,
With looke cast downe in sad and heavie guise,
At last he did lament his hap so sore,
Yet in so sweete and comely mournefull wise,
So hard a heart no tyger ever bore,
But would have heard such plaints with watrish eies.
His heart did seeme a mountaine full of flame,
His cheekes a streame of teares to quench the same.

Alas (said he) what meanes this divers passion?
I burne as fire, and yet as frost I freese,

I still lament, and yet I move compassion,
I come too late, and all my labour leese.
I had but words and lookes for shew and fashion,
But others get the game, and gainefull fees:
If neither fruite nor floure come to my part,
Why should her love consume my carefull hart?

Like to the rose I count the virgine pure,
That grow'th on native stem in garden faire,
Which wile it stand with wals environ'd sure,
Where heardmen with their heards cannot repaire
To favor it, seemeth to allure
The morning deaw, the heate, the earth, the aire.
Yong gallant men, and lovely dames delight
In their sweet sent, and in their pleasing sight.

But when at once tis gathered and gone,
From proper stalke, where late before it grew,
The love, the liking little is or none,
Both favour, grace and beautie all adew.
So when a virgin grants to one alone
The precious floure for which so many sew,
Well he that getteth it may love her best,
But she forgoes the love of all the rest.

She may deserve his love, but others hate,
To whom of love she shewd herselfe so scant,
(Oh then my cruell fortune or my fate)
Others have store, but I am starv'd with want:
Then leave to love this ladie so ungrate:
Nay live to love (behold I soone recant)
Yea first let life from these my limbs be rent,
Ere I to change my love shall give consent.

Orlando's dream

Canto   Now in this time to Paris siege was layd,
Eight   By famous Agramant Trajanos sonne,
      Of which as last they grew so sore afraid,
      The towne had almost of the Turks been wonne,
      Had not their vowes procur'd them heav'nly ayd,
      They had bin ruin'd all and quite undone,
      The force of France had welnigh then bin foyled,
73   The holy Empire had almost bin spoyled.

For when that now the City was on fire,
And when all hope of humane helpe was past,
Then might God forgetting wrath and ire,
Upon their teares, repentance true and fast,
At Charles his humble prayer and desire,
With helpe from heav'n releev'd them at the last,
And sent such raine to aide the noble Prince,
As seld was seene before, and never since.

Now lay Orlando on his restlesse bed,
And thinks with sleepe to rest his troubled sprite,
But still a thousand thoughts possest his head,
Troubling his mind, and sleepe expelling quite:
As circles in a water cleare are spread,
When sun doth shine by day, and moone by night
Succeeding one another in a ranke,
Till all by one and one do touch the banke.

So when his mistriss entred in his thought,
(As lightly she was never thence away)
The thought of her in him such circles wrought,
As kept him waking ever night and day,
To thinke how he from India had her brought,
And that she should thus on the sodaine stray,
Nor that he could of her true notice know,
Since Charles at Burdels had the overthrow.

The griefe hereof did him most neerely tuch,
And cause'd him often to himselfe to say,
What beast would have been overrul'd so much?
That when I might have made her with me stay,
(For why her love and zeale to me was such,
That in her life she never said me nay)
Yet I must suffer Namus for to guard her,
As though my selfe but little did reguard her.

I should to Charles myselfe have rather scused,
And as I did, have kept the damsell still,
Or if excuses all had bin refused,
I might instead of reason pleaded will:
And rather then have bin so much abused,
All those that should resist me slay and kill,
At least I might have got her safer keeping,
And not have let her thus be lost with sleeping.

Where bidest thou, where wanderst thou my deare?
So yong, so lovely, and so faire of hew?

Even a lambe when starres do first appeare,
(Her dame and shepheard being out of vew)
Bleateth aloud to make the shepheard heare,
And in her kind her evill hap doth rew,
Untill the wolfe doth find her to her paine,
The filly shepheard seeking her in vaine.

Where is my love, my joy, my lifes delight?
Wanderst thou still? do not the wolves offend thee?
Or need'st not thou the service of thy Knight?
And keepest thou the flowre did so commend thee?
That flowre that me may make a happy wight,
That flowre for which I ever did defend thee,
That I forbare, to please thy mind (too chast)
Is not that flowre (alas) now gone and past?

O most unfortunate and wretched I,
If they have tane that sweet and precious floure,
What can I do in such a case but dy?
Yea I would kill my selfe this present houre,
I would this world and that to come defy,
Earth first my coarse, and Hell my soule devoure,
And this unto himselfe Orlando said,
With care and sorrowes being overlaid.

Now was the time when man and bird and beast,
Gives to his travel'd body due repose,
When some on beds, and some on boords do rest,
Sleepe making them forget both friends and foes.
But cares do thee Orlando so molest,
That scarce thou canst thine eyes a little close,
And yet that fugitive and little slumber,
With dreams unpleasant thee doth vex and cumber.

He dreamt that standing by a pleasant greene,
Upon a bank with fragrant flowers all painted,
He saw the fairest sight that erst was seene,
I meane that face with which he was acquainted,
And those two stars that Cupid fits between
Whence came that shaft whose head his heart hath tainted,
The sight whereof did breed in him that pleasure,
That he prefer'd before all worldly treasure.

He thought himselfe the fortunatest wight
That ever was, and eke the blessedst lover:
But lo a storme destroy'd the flowers quite,
75 And all the pleasant banke with haile did cover:

Then suddenly departed his delight,
Which he remain'd all hopelesse to recover;
She being of this tempest so afraid,
That in the wood to save herselfe she straid.

And there (unhappy wretch) against his will,
He lost his Lady in unlucky howre:
But her to find againe he travel'd still,
Employing to her safety all his powre,
The woods and deserts he with plaints doth fill,
And cride, alas turn'd is my sweet to sowre:
And while these same and such like words he said,
He thought he heard her voice demaunding aid.

At this same voice (well knowne) a while he staid,
Then follow'd as the sound him guided most,
With this mischance his mind was much dismaid,
His body sore with toile and travell tost:
When straight he heard another voice, that said,
Now hope no more, for all thy hope is lost.
And of the sodaine waking with the sound,
His eies all full of watry teares he found.

The Palace of Atlanta

Canto Faire Ceres when she hastned backe againe,
Twelve From great Idea homeward to returne,
There where Enceladus with endles paine,
Doth beare mount Ætna that doth ever burne,
When she had sought her daughter long in vaine,
Whose losse so strange did make the mother mourne,
She spoiles for spite her brest, cheeks, eyes and heare,
At last two boughs from Pyne tree she doth teare.

In Vulcans forge she sets on fire the brands,
And gives them powre for ever to be light,
And taking one a peece in both her hands,
And drawne in coach by yoaked serpents might,
She searcheth woods and fields and seas and lands,
And brooks and streames and dens devoyd of light,
And hearing here on earth no news to like her,
At last she went to hell itselfe to seeke her.

Were good Orlandos powre to be compared,
As well with Ceres as his loving minde,
He would no paine, no place, nor time have spared,
76 His deare belov'd Angelyca to finde,

To go to rocks and caves he would have dared,
And place to saints, and place to fiends assign'd,
He onely wanted one of Ceres waggons,
In which she carried was with flying draggons.

How he did search all France before he told,
Now Italy to search in his intent,
And Germany and Castill new and old,
And then to Affrica to passe he ment,
And as he thus determined, behold
He heard a voice that seemed to lament,
And drawing nye, to understand what tyding,
On a great horse he saw a horseman ryding.

Perforce he bare upon his saddle bow,
A Lady sorrowfull and sore afrayd,
That cryde aloud still making open show,
Of inward griefe, and thus to him she said,
O worthy wight (Lord of Anglante) know
I dye, I dye without you bring me ayd,
And then he thought comming more nie to vew her,
It was Angelyca, and that he knew her.

I say not that it was, but that it seem'd,
To be Angelyca that thus was cary'd,
But he that justly great disgrace it deem'd,
Thus in his sight, to have his mistresse hary'd,
Whose love above all treasures he esteem'd,
To take revenge hereof he nothing tary'd,
But put his spurres to Brilliadores sides,
And in great hast to that same horseman rydes.

With many bloodie words and cruell threats,
He bids that horseman to come backe againe,
But he at naught his words and speeches sets,
Rejoycing in so rich a gotten gayne,
The vilen still ground of Orlando gets,
Untill they came into a faire large plaine,
Wherein a house of great estate was built,
The gate hereof in gorgeous sort was gilt.

The building all of marble faire was wrought,
Most costly carv'd and cunningly contrived,
To this faire house, his pray the foule thiefe brought,
Straight after him Orlando there arrived:
Then he alights and all about he sought,
77 For him that had him of his joy deprived,

He maketh search in chambers all about,
And galleries and halls to finde them out.

Each roome he finds set forth with rich aray,
With beds of silke, and gold of curious art,
But yet he finds not that desired pray,
The want whereof did sore torment his heart.
There might he finde with like affliction stray,
Gradasso, Sacrapant and Brandimart,
And feirce Ferraw possest with strange confusion,
Procured in that place by strong illusion.

They all complaine in anger and in rage,
How of this house the master them hath used,
One lost his horse, another lost his page,
Another doubts his mistresse is abused:
Thus are they kept like birds within a cage,
And stand with sense and wits and words confused
And manie with this strange deception carried,
Within this place both weeks & months had tarrid.

Orlando when he saw he could not learne,
Where this same theefe his mistress had convaid,
Thought she was carride out at some posterne;
Wherefore within no longer time he staid,
But walkes about the castle to discerne,
It that were true of which he was afraid:
But as he walked up and downe the plaine,
He thought he heard her call him backe againe.

And to a window casting up his eye,
He thought he saw her face full of divinity,
And that he heard her plainly thus to crie,
O noble wight of proved magnanimitie,
Helpe now, or never helpe, alas shall I
In mine Orlandos sight leese my virginitie?
Kill me, or let a thousand deaths befall me,
Rather then let a villaine so to thrall me.

These wofull speeches once or twise repeted,
Caus'd him returne into the house againe,
And searching once againe he chafte and freted,
(Hope still asswaging somewhat of his paine)
And oft he heard the voice that counterfeted
The speech of his Angelica most plaine,
From side to side he follow'd still the sound,
78 But of Angelica no signe he found.

Now while Orlando tarrid in this trance,
In hope for to avenge his mistresse harmes,
Rogero (who I told you had this chaunce)
To see his Bradamant in gyants armes,
(Drawne to this place with such another daunce)
Namely by force of some unusuall charmes,
Saw first the gyant in this castle enter,
And after him he boldly doth adventer.

But when he came within the castle walls,
And made much narrow search, as in such case,
In garrets, towrs, in parlers and in halls,
And under staires and many a homely place,
Oft casting doubts what hurt his love befalls,
Or lest the theefe were gone in this meane space,
Forthwith he walketh out into the plaine,
And heares a voice recall him backe againe.

That voice that lately did Orlando make
Returne in hope Angelica to finde,
Rogero now for Bradamant doth take,
Whose love no lesse possest his carefull minde:
And when the voice unto Gradasso spake,
Or Sacrapant, or Brandimart most kinde,
To every one of these it plainely seemed,
To be her voice whom each one best esteemed.

Atlanta had procur'd this strange invention,
Thereby to keepe Rogero from mischance,
Because he saw it was the heavens intention,
That he by treason should be kil'd in France,
Ferraw and those of whom I last made mention,
Whith all whom vallew highest did advance,
To keepe him companie he here detained,
With good provision while they here remained.

And while these knights with strange enchantments bound
Do here abide, behold the Indian queene
Angelica that late her ring had found,
(Whose vertue can her cause to go unseene,
And also frustrate magick still profound)
Now longing home, where long she had not been,
And being now of needful things provided,
Yet wants she one that her might home have guided.

Orlandos company she would have had,
79 Or Sacrapant, she car'd not which of twaine,

Not that of eithers love she would be glad,
For them and all the world she did disdaine,
But (for the way was dangerous and bad,
In time of warre to travell France and Spaine)
She wisht for her owne safetie and her case,
To have the company of one of these.

Wherefore a while she travels up and downe,
To seeke for them that long in vaine had sought her,
And passing many woods and many a towne,
Unto this place at last good fortune brought her,
Where when she saw these knights of great renowne,
Thus seek for her, she scant abstaines from laughter,
To see Atlantas cunning and dissembling,
Her person and her voice so right resembling.

Herselfe unseene sees them and all the rest,
Now meanes she sure to take one of them two,
But yet she knowes not which (her doubtfull brest
Did stay as unresolved what to do).
Orlandos valour could defend her best,
But then this doubt is added thereunto,
That when she once so highly had prefard him,
She shall not know againe how to discard him.

But Sacrapant although she should him lift
High up to heaven, yet maketh she no doubt,
But she will find some fleight and pretie shift,
With her accustom'd coyness him to lout:
To him she goes, resolved of this drift,
And straight the precious ring she taketh out
From of her mouth, which made her go concealed,
With mind to him alone to be revealed.

But straight came in Orlando and Ferraw,
That both desired, her to have enjoy'd,
Thus all of them at once their goddesse saw,
Not being now by magick art annoyd,
For when the ring on finger she did draw,
She made unwares all their enchantments voyd,
These three were all in complete armor, save
Ferraw no headpeece had, nor none would have.

The cause was this, he solemnely had sworne,
Upon his head no helmet should be set,
But that that was by stout Orlando worne,
Which he did erst from Trajans brother get,
Ferraw to weare a helmet had forborne,

Since with the ghost of Argall he had met:
Thus in this sort they came together armed,
By vertue of her ring now all uncharmed.

All three at once do now the damsell view,
All three at once on her would straight have seased,
All three her faithfull lovers were she knew,
Yet with all three at once she is displeased,
And from all three she straight herselfe withdrew,
Who (haply) one at once would her have pleased,
From henceforth none of them she thinks to need,
But that the ring shall serve in all their steed.

She hastens hence and will no longer stay,
Disdaine and feare together make her swift,
Into a wood she leades them all the way,
But when she saw there was none other shift,
Into her mouth the ring she doth convay,
That ever holpe her at the deadest lift,
And out of all their sights forthwith she vanish'd,
And leaves them all with wonder halfe astonish'd.

Orlando's madness

Canto Thus on went he, till him the way did bring
Twenty- Unto a shadie cave and pleasant spring.
three

This was a place, wherein above the rest,
This loving paire, leaving their homely host,
Spent time in sports that may not be exprest,
Here in the parching heate they tarrid most,
And here Medore (that thought himselfe most blest)
Wrote certaine verses as in way of bost:
Which in his language doubtlesse sounded prittie,
And thus I turne them to an English dittie.

Ye pleasant plants, greene herbs, and waters faire,
And cave with smell, and gratefull shadow mixt,
Where sweet Angelica, daughter and heire
Of Galafronne, on whom in vaine were fixt
Full many hearts, with me did oft repaire
Alone, and naked lay mine armes betwixt;
I poore Medore, can yeeld but praise and thanks,
For these great pleasures found amid your banks.

And pray each Lord whom Cupid holds in pay,
81 Each Knight, each dame, and ev'ry one beside,

Of gentle or meane sort that passe this way,
As fancie or his fortune shall him guide,
That to the plants, herbs, spring, and cave he say,
Long may the Sun and Moon maintaine your pride,
And the faire crew of Nymphs make such purveyance
As hither come no heards to your annoyance.

It written was there in th'Arabian tong,
Which tong Orlando perfect understood,
As having learnt it when he was but yong,
And oft the skill thereof had done him good,
But at this time it him so deeply stoong,
It had bin well that he it never coud,
And yet we see, to know men still are glad,
And yet we see much knowledge makes men mad.

Twise, thrise, yea five times he doth reade the rime,
And though he saw and knew the meaning plaine,
Yet, that his love was guilty of such crime,
He will not let it sinke into his braine,
Oft he perused it, and ev'ry time
It doth increase his sharpe tormenting paine,
And ay the more he on the matter mused,
The more his wits and senses were confused.

Ev'n then was he of wit welnigh bestraught,
So quite he was giv'n over unto griefe,
(And sure if we beleeve as proofe hath taught,
This torture is of all the rest the chiefe)
His sprite was dead, his courage quaild with thought,
He doth despaire and looke for no reliefe;
And sorrow did his senses so surprise,
That words his toong, and teares forsooke his eyes.

The raging pang remained still within,
That would have burst out all at once too fast:
Ev'n so we see the water tarry in
A bottle little mouth'd, and big in wast,
That though you topsie turvy turne the brim,
The liquor bides behind with too much hast,
And with the striving oft is in such taking,
As scant a man can get it out with shaking.

At last he comes unto himselfe anew,
And in his mind another way doth frame,
That that which there was written was not trew,
But writ of spite his Ladie to defame,

Or to that end, that he the same might vew,
And so his heart with jealousie inflame:
Well be't who list (quoth he) I see this clearly,
He hath her hand resembled passing nearly.

With this small hope, with this poore little sparke,
He doth some deale revive his troubled sprite,
And for it was now late, and waxed darke,
He seekes some place where he may lie that night,
At last he heares a noise of dogs that barke,
He smels some smoke, and sees some candle light,
He takes his Inne, with will to sleepe, not eate,
As fild with griefe, and with none other meate.

But lo his hap was at that house to host,
Where faire Angelica had layne before,
And where her name on ev'ry doore and post,
With true love knots was joyned to Medore,
That knot his name whom he detested most,
Was in his eye and thought still evermore:
He dares not aske, nor once the matter tuch,
For knowing more of that he knowes too much.

But vaine it was himselfe to so beguile,
For why his host unasked by and by,
That saw his guest sit there so sad the while,
And thinks to put him from his dumps thereby,
Beginneth plaine without all fraud or guile,
Without concealing truth or adding lie,
To tell that tale to him without regard,
Which divers had before with pleasure heard.

As thus, how at Angelicas request
He holpe unto his house to bring Medore,
Who then was sorely wounded in his brest,
And she with surgery did heale his sore:
But while with her owne hands the wound she drest,
Blind Cupid wounded her as much or more,
That when her skill and herbs had cur'd her patient,
Her curelesse wound in love made her unpatient.

So that, admit she were the greatest Queene
Of fame, and living in those Eastern parts,
Yet so with fancie she was overseene,
To marry with a page of meane desarts;
Thus love (quoth he) will have his godhead seene,
In famous Queens, and highest Princes harts:

83

This said (to end the tale) he shew'd the jewell
That she had giv'n him, which Orlando knew well.

This tale, and chiefly this same last conclusion,
Was ev'n a hatchet to cut off all hope,
When love had after many a vaine collusion,
Now for his farewell lent him such a rope
To hang himselfe, and drowne him in confusion,
Yet faine he would denie his sorrow scope,
And though a while to shew it he forbeares,
It breaketh out at last in sighs and teares.

And as it were inforst he gives the raine
To raging griefe, upon his bed alone,
His eyes do shed a very showre of raine,
With many a scalding sigh and bitter grone,
He slept as much as if he had then laine
Upon a bed of thornes, and stuft with stone.
And as he lay thereon and could not rest him,
The bed itselfe gave matter to molest him.

Ah wretch I am (thus to himselfe he sed)
Shall I once hope to take repose and rest me
In that same house? yea ev'n in that same bed
Where my ungrateful love so leudly drest me?
Nay, let me first an hundred times be ded,
First wolves devoure and vultures shall digest me.
Strait up he starts, and on he puts his clothes,
And leaves the house, so much the bed he lothes.

He leaves his host, nor once doth take his leave,
He far'd so ill, he bids them not farewell,
He leaves the towne, his servants he doth leave,
He rides, but where he rides he cannot tell.
And when alone himselfe he doth perceave
To weepe and waile, nay ev'n to houle and yell,
He doth not cease to give his griefe a vent,
That inwardly so sore did him torment.

The day the night to him were both aleeke,
Abroade upon the cold bare earth he lies,
No sleepe, no food he takes, nor none would seek,
All sustenance he to himselfe denies.
Thus he began, and ended halfe the weeke,
And he himselfe doth marvell, whence his eyes
Are fed so long with such a spring of water,
84 And to himselfe thus reasons on the matter.

No, no, these be no teares that now I shed,
These be no teares, nor can teares run so rife,
But fire of frenzie drawth up to my head,
My vitall humor that should keepe my life:
This streame will never cease till I be dead,
Then welcome death and end my fatall strife:
No comfort in this life my wo can minish,
But thou who canst both life and sorrow finish.

These are not sighs, for sighs some respite have,
My gripes, my pangs, no respite do permit,
The blindfold boy made me a seeing slave,
When from her eyes my heart he first did hit.
Now all inflam'd, I burne, I rage and rave,
And in the midst of flame consume no whit:
Love sitting in my heart a master crewell,
Blowes with his wings feeds with his will the fewell.

I am not I, the man that earst I was,
Orlando, he is buried and dead,
His most ungratefull love (ah foolish lasse)
Hath kild Orlando, and cut off his head:
I am his ghost, that up and downe must passe,
In this tormenting hell for ever led,
To be a fearfull sample and a just,
To all such fooles as put in love their trust.

Thus wandring still in wayes that have no way,
He hapt againe to light upon the cave,
Where (in remembrance of their pleasant play)
Medoro did that epigram ingrave.
To see the stones againe, his woes display,
And her ill name, and his ill hap deprave,
Did on the sudden all his sence inrage,
With hate, with fury, with revenge and rage.

Straightwayes he draweth forth his fatall blade,
And hewes the stones, to heav'n the shivers flee,
Accursed was that fountaine, cave and shade,
The arbor and the flowres and ev'ry tree:
Orlando of all places havocke made,
Where he those names together joyn'd may see,
Yea to the spring he did perpetuall hurt,
By filling it with leaves, boughs, stones, and durt.

And having done this foolish franticke feate,
85 He layes him downe all weary on the ground,

Distemper'd in his bodie with much heate,
In mind with paines that no tongue can expound,
Three dayes he doth not sleepe, nor drinke, nor eate,
But lay with open eyes as in a sound.
The fourth with rage, and not with reason waked,
He rents his clothes, and runs about starke naked.

His helmet here he flings, his poulderns there;
He casts away his curats and his shield:
His sword he throws away, he cares not where,
He scatters all his armor in the field:
No ragge about his bodie he doth beare,
As might from cold or might from shame him shield,
And save he left behind this fatall blade,
No doubt he had therewith great havocke made.

But his surpassing force did so exceed,
All common men, that neither sword nor bill,
Nor any other weapon he did need,
Meere strength suffic'd him to do what he will,
He rootes up trees as one would root a weed:
And ev'n as birders laying nets with skill,
Pare slender thornes away with easie strokes,
So he did play with ashes, elmes and okes.

The heardmen and the shepheards that did heare,
The hideous noise and unacquainted sound,
With feare and wonder great approched neare,
To see, and know, what was hereof the ground.
But now I must cut off this treatise heare,
Lest this my booke do grow beyond his bound;
And if you take some pleasure in this text,
I will go forward with it in the next.

Astolfo's journey to the moon in search of Orlando's wit

Canto Foure horses fierce, as red as flaming fire,
Thirty- Th'Apostle doth into the charet set,
four Which when he framed had to his desire,
Astolfo in the carre by him he set,
Then up they went, and still ascending higher,
Above the firie region they did get,
Whose nature so th' Apostle then did turn,
That though they went through fire, they did not burn.

I say although the fire were wondrous hot,
86 Yet in their passage they no heat did feel,

So that it burn'd them, nor offends them not;
Thence to the Moone he guides the running wheel,
The Moone was like a glasse all void of spot,
Or like a peece of purely burnisht steel,
And look'd, although to us it seem'd so small,
Welnigh as big as earth and sea and all.

Here had Astolfo cause of double wonder,
One, that that region seemeth there so wide,
That unto us that are so farre asunder,
Seems but a little circle, and beside,
That to behold the ground that him lay under,
A man had need to have been sharply ey'd,
And bend his browes, and mark ev'n all they might,
It seem'd so small, now chiefly wanting light.

'Twere infinite to tell what wondrous things
He saw, that passed ours not few degrees,
What towns, what hils, what rivers, and what springs,
What dales, what pallaces; what goodly trees,
But to be short, at last his guide him brings
Unto a goodly valley, where he sees
A might masse of things strangely confus'd,
Things that on earth were lost, or were abus'd.

A store-house strange, that what on earth is lost,
By fault, by time, by fortune, there is found,
And like a merchandize is there ingrost,
In stranger sort then I can well expound;
Nor speak I sole of wealth, or things of cost,
In which blind fortunes power doth most abound,
But ev'n of things quite out of fortunes power,
Which wilfully we wast each day and houre.

The precious time that fooles mis-spend in play,
The vaine attempts that never take effect,
The vowes that sinners make, and never pay,
The counsels wise that carelesse men neglect,
The fond desires that lead us oft astray,
The praises that with pride the heart infect,
And all we lose with folly and mis-spending,
May there be found unto this place ascending.

Now as Astolfo by those regions past,
He asked many questions of his guide,
And as he on one side his eye did cast,
A wondrous hill of bladders he espied;
87 And he was told they had been in time past,

The pompous crowns and scepters full of pride,
Of monarchs of Assyria and of Greece,
Of which now scantly there is left a peece.

He saw great store of baited hooks with gold,
And those were gifts that foolish men preferd
To give to Princes covetous and old,
With fondest hope of future vaine reward;
Then were there ropes all in sweet garlands rold,
And those were all false flatteries he hard,
Then heard he crickets songs, like to the verses
The servant in his masters praise reherses.

There did he see fond loves, that men pursue,
To look like golden gives with stones all set,
Then things like Eagles Talents he did view,
Those offices that favourites do get:
Then saw he bellowes large that much wind blew,
Large promises that Lords make, and forget,
Unto their Ganimeds in flowre of youth,
But after nought but beggery ensu'th.

He saw great Cities seated in faire places,
That overthrowne quite topsie turvie stood,
He ask'd and learn'd, the cause of their defaces
Was treason, that doth never turne to good:
He saw foule serpents with faire womens faces,
Of coyners and of theeves the cursed brood,
He saw fine glasses all in peeces broken,
Of service lost in Court, a wofull token.

Of mingled broth he saw a mighty masse
That to no use all spilt on ground did lie,
He ask'd his teacher, and he heard it was
The fruitless almes that men give when they die:
Then by a faire green mountaine he did passe,
That once smelt sweet, but now it stinks perdye,
This was that gift (be't said without offence)
That Constantine gave Silvester long since.

Of birdlime-rods he saw no little store,
And these (O Ladies faire) your beauties be,
I do omit ten thousand things and more
Like unto these, that there the Duke did see:
For all that here is lost, there evermore
Is kept, and thither in a trice doth flee,
Howbeit more nor lesse there was no folly,
88 For still that here with us remaineth wholly.

He saw some of his own lost time and deeds,
But yet he knew them not to be his own,
They seem'd to him disguis'd in so strange weeds,
Till his instructer made them better known:
But last, the thing which no man thinks he needs,
Yet each man needeth most, to him was shown,
By name mans wit, which here we leese so fast,
As that one substance all the other past.

It seem'd to be a body moist and soft,
And apt to mount by ev'ry exhalation,
And when it hither mounted was aloft,
It there was kept in pots of such a fashion,
As we call jarrs, where oyle is kept in oft:
The Duke beheld (with no small admiration)
The jarrs of wit, amongst which one had writ
Upon the side thereof Orlandos wit.

This vessell bigger was than all the rest,
And ev'ry vessell had ingrav'n with art
His name that erst the wit therein possest:
There of his own the Duke did find a part,
And much he mus'd, and much himselfe he blest,
To see some names of men of great desert,
That think they have great store of wit, and boast it,
When here it plaine appear'd they quite had lost it.

Some lose their wit with love, some with ambition,
Some running to the sea, great wealth to get,
Some following Lords, and men of high condition,
And some in faire jewels rich and costly set:
One hath desire to prove a rare Magician,
And some with Poetrie their wit forget,
Another thinks to be an Alcumist,
Till all be spent, and he his number mist.

Astolfo takes his own before he goes,
For so th' Evangelist doth him permit;
He set the vessels mouth but to his nose,
And to his place he snuft up all his wit:
Long after wise he liv'd, as Turpin showes,
Untill one fault he after did commit:
By name the love of one faire Northerne lasse,
Sent up his wit into the place it was.

The vessell where Orlandos wit was clos'd,
Astolfo took, and thence with him did beare:
89 It was far heavier then he had suppos'd,

So great a quantity of wit was there;
But yet ere back their journey they dispos'd,
The holy Prophet brought Astolfo, where
A pallace (seldome seen by mortall man)
Was plac'd, by which a thick dark river ran.

GIOVANNI PICO DELLA MIRANDOLA

Oration on the Dignity of Man
Translated by Elizabeth Livermore Forbes

I have read in the records of the Arabians, reverend Fathers, that Abdala the Saracen, when questioned as to what on this stage of the world, as it were, could be seen most worthy of wonder, replied: "There is nothing to be seen more wonderful than man." In agreement with this opinion is the saying of Hermes Trismegistus: "A great miracle, Asclepius, is man." But when I weighed the reason for these maxims, the many grounds for the excellence of human nature reported by many men failed to satisfy me—that man is the intermediary between creatures, the intimate of the gods, the king of the lower beings, by the acuteness of his senses, by the discernment of his reason, and by the light of his intelligence the interpreter of nature, the interval between fixed eternity and fleeting time, and (as the Persians say) the bond, nay, rather the marriage song of the world, on David's testimony but little lower than the angels. Admittedly great though these reasons be, they are not the principal grounds, that is, those which may rightfully claim for themselves the privilege of the highest admiration. For why should we not admire more the angels themselves and the blessed choirs of heaven? At last it seems to me I have come to understand why man is the most fortunate of creatures and consequently worthy of all admiration and what precisely is that rank which is his lot in the universal chain of Being—a rank to be envied not only by brutes but even by the stars and by minds beyond this world. It is a matter past faith and a wondrous one. Why should it not be? For it is on this very account that man is rightly called and judged a great miracle and a wonderful creature indeed.

But hear, Fathers, exactly what this rank is and, as friendly auditors, conformably to your kindness, do me this favor. God the
91 Father, the supreme Architect, had already built this cosmic home

we behold, the most sacred temple of His godhead, by the laws of His mysterious wisdom. The region above the heavens He had adorned with Intelligences, the heavenly spheres He had quickened with eternal souls, and the excrementary and filthy parts of the lower world He had filled with a multitude of animals of every kind. But, when the work was finished, the Craftsman kept wishing that there were someone to ponder the plan of so great a work, to love its beauty, and to wonder at its vastness. Therefore, when everything was done (as Moses and Timaeus bear witness), He finally took thought concerning the creation of man. But there was not among His archetypes that from which He could fashion a new offspring, nor was there in His treasurehouses anything which He might bestow on His new son as an inheritance, nor was there in the seats of all the world a place where the latter might sit to contemplate the universe. All was now complete; all things had been assigned to the highest, the middle, and the lowest orders. But in its final creation it was not the part of the Father's power to fail as though exhausted. It was not the part of His wisdom to waver in a needful matter through the poverty of counsel. It was not the part of His kindly love that he who was to praise God's divine generosity in regard to others should be compelled to condemn it in regard to himself.

At last the best of artisans ordained that that creature to whom He had been able to give nothing proper to himself should have joint possession of whatever had been peculiar to each of the different kinds of being. He therefore took man as a creature of indeterminate nature and, assigning him a place in the middle of the world, addressed him thus: "Neither a fixed abode nor a form that is thine alone nor any function peculiar to thyself have we given thee, Adam, to the end that according to thy longing and according to thy judgment thou mayest have and possess what abode, what form, and what functions thou thyself shalt desire. The nature of all other beings is limited and constrained within the bounds of laws prescribed by Us. Thou, constrained by no limits, in accordance with thine own free will, in whose hand We have placed thee, shalt ordain for thyself the limits of thy nature. We have set thee at the world's center that thou mayest from thence more easily observe whatever is in the world. We have made thee neither of heaven nor of earth, neither mortal nor immortal, so that with freedom of choice and with honor, as though the maker and molder of thyself, thou mayest fashion thyself in whatever shape thou shalt prefer. Thou shalt have the power to degenerate into the lower forms of life, which are brutish. Thou shalt have the power, out of thy soul's judgment, to be reborn into the higher forms, which are divine."

O supreme generosity of God the Father, O highest and most
marvelous felicity of man! To him it is granted to have whatever
he chooses, to be whatever he wills. Beasts as soon as they are
born (so says Lucilius) bring with them from their mother's womb
all they will ever possess. Spiritual beings, either from the beginning or soon thereafter, become what they are to be for ever and
ever. On man when he came into life the Father conferred the seeds
of all kinds and the germs of every way of life. Whatever seeds
each man cultivates will grow to maturity and bear in him their own
fruit. If they be vegetative, he will be like a plant. If sensitive, he
will become brutish. If rational, he will grow into a heavenly being.
If intellectual, he will be an angel and the son of God. And if,
happy in the lot of no created thing, he withdraws into the center of
his own unity, his spirit, made one with God, in the solitary darkness of God, who is set above all things, shall surpass them all. Who
would not admire this our chameleon? Or who could more greatly
admire aught else whatever? It is man who Asclepius of Athens,
arguing from his mutability of character and from his self-trans-
forming nature, on just grounds says was symbolized by Proteus in
the mysteries. Hence those metamorphoses renowned among the
Hebrews and the Pythagoreans.

For the occult theology of the Hebrews sometimes transforms
the holy Enoch into an angel of divinity whom they call "Mal'akh
Adonay Shebaoth," and sometimes transforms others into other
divinities. The Pythagoreans degrade impious men into brutes and,
if one is to believe Empedocles, even into plants. Mohammed, in
imitation, often had this saying on his tongue: "They who have
deviated from divine law become beasts," and surely he spoke
justly. For it is not the bark that makes the plant but its senseless
and insentient nature; neither is it the hide that makes the beast
of burden but its irrational, sensitive soul; neither is it the orbed
form that makes the heavens but their undeviating order; nor is it
the sundering from body but his spiritual intelligence that makes
the angel. For if you see one abandoned to his appetites crawling on
the ground, it is a plant and not a man you see; if you see one
blinded by the vain illusions of imagery, as it were of Calypso, and,
softened by their gnawing allurement, delivered over to his senses,
it is a beast and not a man you see. If you see a philosopher de-
termining all things by means of right reason, him you shall
reverence: he is a heavenly being and not of this earth. If you see
a pure contemplator, one unaware of the body and confined to the
inner reaches of the mind, he is neither an earthly nor a heavenly
being; he is a more reverend divinity vested with human flesh.

93   Are there any who would not admire man, who is, in the sacred

writings of Moses and the Christians, not without reason described sometimes by the name of "all flesh," sometimes by that of "every creature," inasmuch as he himself molds, fashions, and changes himself into the form of all flesh and into the character of every creature? For this reason the Persian Euanthes, in describing the Chaldaean theology, writes that man has no semblance that is inborn and his very own but many that are external and foreign to him; whence this saying of the Chaldaeans: "Hanorish tharah sharinas," that is, "Man is a being of varied, manifold, and inconstant nature." But why do we emphasize this? To the end that after we have been born to this condition—that we can become what we will—we should understand that we ought to have especial care to this, that it should never be said against us that, although born to a privileged position, we failed to recognize it and became like unto wild animals and senseless beasts of burden, but rather the saying of Asaph the prophet should apply: "Ye are all angels and sons of the Most High," and that we may not, by abusing the most indulgent generosity of the Father, make for ourselves that freedom of choice He has given into something harmful instead of salutary. Let a certain holy ambition invade our souls, so that, not content with the mediocre, we shall pant after the highest and (since we may if we wish) toil with all our strength to obtain it.

Let us disdain earthly things, despise heavenly things, and, finally, esteeming less whatever is of the world, hasten to that court which is beyond the world and nearest to the Godhead. There, as the sacred mysteries relate Seraphim, Cherubim, and Thrones hold the first places; let us, incapable of yielding to them, and intolerant of a lower place, emulate their dignity and their glory. If we have willed it, we shall be second to them in nothing.

But how shall we go about it, and what in the end shall we do? Let us consider what they do, what sort of life they lead. If we also come to lead that life (for we have the power), we shall then equal their good fortune. The Seraph burns with the fire of love. The Cherub glows with the splendor of intelligence. The Throne stands by the steadfastness of judgment. Therefore if, in giving ourselves over to the active life, we have after due consideration undertaken the care of the lower beings, we shall be strengthened with the firm stability of Thrones. If, unoccupied by deeds, we pass our time in the leisure of contemplation, considering the Creator in the creature and the creature in the Creator, we shall be all ablaze with Cherubic light. If we long with love for the Creator himself alone, we shall speedily flame up with His consuming fire into a Seraphic likeness. Above the Throne, that is, above the just judge, God sits as Judge of the ages. Above the Cherub, that is, above him

94

who contemplates, God flies, and cherishes him, as it were, in watching over him. For the spirit of the Lord moves upon the waters, the waters, I say, which are above the firmament and which in Job praise the Lord with hymns before dawn. Whoso is a Seraph, that is, a lover, is in God and God in him, nay, rather, God and himself are one. Great is the power of Thrones, which we attain in using judgment, and most high the exaltation of Seraphs, which we attain in loving.

But by what means is one able either to judge or to love things unknown? Moses loved a God whom he saw and, as judge, administered among the people what he had first beheld in contemplation upon the mountain. Therefore, the Cherub as intermediary by his own light makes us ready for the Seraphic fire and equally lights the way to the judgment of the Thrones. This is the bond of the first minds, the Palladian order, the chief of contemplative philosophy. This is the one for us first to emulate, to court, and to understand; the one from whence we may be rapt to the heights of love and descend, well taught and well prepared, to the functions of active life. But truly it is worth while, if our life is to be modeled on the example of the Cherubic life, to have before our eyes and clearly understood both its nature and its quality and those things which are the deeds and the labor of Cherubs. But since it is not permitted us to attain this through our own efforts, we who are but flesh and know of the things of earth, let us go to the ancient fathers who, inasmuch as they were familiar and conversant with these matters, can give sure and altogether trustworthy testimony. Let us consult the Apostle Paul, the chosen vessel, as to what he saw the hosts of Cherubim doing when he was himself exalted to the third heaven. He will answer, according to the interpretation of Dionysius, that he saw them being purified, then being illuminated, and at last being made perfect. Let us also, therefore, by emulating the Cherubic way of life on earth, by taming the impulses of our passions with moral science, by dispelling the darkness of reason with dialectic, and by, so to speak, washing away the filth of ignorance and vice, cleanse our soul, so that her passions may not rave at random nor her reason through heedlessness ever be deranged.

Then let us fill our well-prepared and purified soul with the light of natural philosophy, so that we may at last perfect her in the knowledge of things divine. And lest we be satisfied with those of our faith, let us consult the patriarch Jacob, whose form gleams carved on the throne of glory. Sleeping in the lower world but keeping watch in the upper, the wisest of fathers will advise us. But he will advise us through a figure (in this way everything was wont to come to those men) that there is a ladder extending from the lowest earth to the highest heaven, divided in a series of many steps, with the Lord seated at the top, and angels in contemplation ascending and descending over them alternately by turns.

If this is what we must practice in our aspiration to the angelic way of life, I ask: "Who will touch the ladder of the Lord either with fouled foot or with unclean hands?" As the sacred mysteries have it, it is impious for the impure to touch the pure. But what are these feet? What these hands? Surely the foot of the soul is that most contemptible part by which the soul rests on matter as on the soil of the earth, I mean the nourishing and feeding power, the tinder of lust, and the teacher of pleasurable weakness. Why should we not call the hands of the soul its irascible power, which struggles on its behalf as the champion of desire and as plunderer seizes in the dust and sun what desire will devour slumbering in the shade? These hands, these feet, that is, all the sentient part whereon resides the attraction of the body which, as they say, by wrenching the neck holds the soul in check, lest we be hurled down from the ladder as impious and unclean, let us bathe in moral philosophy as if in a living river. Yet this will not be enough if we wish to be companions of the angels going up and down on Jacob's ladder, unless we have first been well fitted and instructed to be promoted duly from step to step, to stray nowhere from the stairway, and to engage in the alternate comings and goings. Once we have achieved this by the art of discourse or reasoning, then, inspired by the Cherubic spirit, using philosophy through the steps of the ladder, that is, of nature, and penetrating all things from center to center, we shall sometimes descend, with titanic force rending the unity like Osiris into many parts, and we shall sometimes ascend, with the force of Phoebus collecting the parts like the limbs of Osiris into a unity, until, resting at last in the bosom of the Father who is above the ladder, we shall be made perfect with the felicity of theology. . . .

When we have been so soothingly called, so kindly urged, we shall fly up with winged feet, like earthly Mercuries, to the embraces of our blessed mother and enjoy that wished-for peace, most holy peace, indivisible bond, of one accord in the friendship through which all rational souls not only shall come into harmony in the one mind which is above all minds but shall in some ineffable way become altogether one. This is that friendship which the Pythagoreans say is the end of all philosophy. This is that peace which God creates in his heavens, which the angels descending to earth proclaimed to men of good will, that through it men might ascend to heaven and become angels. Let us wish it for every home into which we go; let us wish it for our own soul, that through it she shall herself be made the house of God, and to the end that as soon as she has cast out her uncleanness through moral philosophy and dialectic, adorned herself with manifold philosophy as with the splendor of a courtier, and crowned the pediments of her doors with the garlands of theology, the King of Glory may descend and, coming with his Father, make his stay with her. If she show herself worthy of so great a guest, she shall, by the boundless mercy which is his, in golden raiment like a wedding gown, and surrounded by a varied throng of sciences, receive her beautiful guest not merely as a guest but as a spouse from whom she will never be parted. She will desire rather to be parted from her own people and, forgetting her father's house and herself, will desire to die in herself in order to live in her spouse, in whose sight surely the death of his saints is precious—death, I say, if we must call death that fulness of life, the consideration of which wise men have asserted to be the aim of philosophy. . . .

But indeed not only the Mosaic and Christian mysteries but also the theology of the ancients show us the benefits and value of the liberal arts, the discussion of which I am about to undertake. For what else did the degrees of the initiates observed in the mysteries of the Greeks mean? For they arrived at a perception of the mysteries when they had first been purified through those expiatory sciences, as it were, moral philosophy and dialectic. What else can that perception possibly be than an interpretation of occult nature by means of philosophy? Then at length to those who were so disposed came that ΕΠΟΠΤΕΙΑ, that is to say, the observation of things divine by the light of theology. Who would not long to be initiated into such sacred rites? Who would not desire, by neglecting all human concerns, by despising the goods of fortune, and by disregarding those of the body, to become the guest of the gods while yet living on earth, and, made drunk by the nectar of eternity, to be endowed with the gifts of immortality though still a mortal being? Who would not wish to be so inflamed with those Socratic frenzies sung by Plato in the *Phaedrus*, that, by the oarage of feet and wings escaping speedily from hence, that is, from a world set on evil, he might be borne on the fastest of courses to the heavenly Jerusalem? Let us be driven, Fathers, let us be driven by the frenzies of Socrates, that they may so throw us into ecstasy as to put our mind and ourselves in God. Let us be driven by them, if we have first done what is in our power. For if through moral philosophy the forces of our passions have by a fitting agreement become so intent on harmony that they can sing together in undisturbed concord, and if through dialectic our reason has moved progressively in a rhythmical measure, then we shall be stirred by the frenzy of the Muses and drink the heavenly harmony with our inmost hearing. Thereupon Bacchus, the leader of the Muses, by showing in his mysteries, that is, in the visible signs of nature, the invisible things of God to us who study philosophy, will intoxicate us with the fulness of God's house, in which, if we prove faithful, like Moses, hallowed theology shall come and inspire us with a doubled frenzy. For, exalted to her lofty height, we shall measure therefrom all things that are and shall be and have been in indivisible eternity; and, admiring their original beauty, like the seers of Phoebus, we shall become her own winged lovers. And at last roused by ineffable love as by a sting, like burning Seraphim rapt from ourselves, full of divine power we shall no longer be ourselves but shall become He Himself Who made us. . . .

NICCOLÒ MACHIAVELLI

Mandragola
Translated by Stark Young

INTERLOCUTORS

Callimaco, Siro, Messer Nicia, Ligurio, Sostrata, Brother Timoteo,
A Lady, Lucrezia

SONG SUNG BY NYMPHS AND SHEPHERDS

Since life is short and the woes are many
That all who live and breathe must fear
We go passing the years, consuming them
Against our wills.
We know the deceit of the world, the ills
That mortals all must bear.

To flee this sorrow we have chosen
A solitary life; in joys
And festival always we are,
Happy nymphs and laughing boys.
We come here now
With this our harmony
Only to honor this bright day
And this sweet company.

Now once again hath brought us here
The name of him who governs you
In whom we see all good appear,
In whom the eternal virtues shine.
For such a grace divine,

For such a happy state,
Joy is your due!
Rejoice, thank him who them has given you.

God save you, worthy listeners. Since it is clear that your gracious-
ness depends on our pleasing you, we wish, if you will be so kind as
not to make a noise, that you may hear a new case born on this earth
of ours. You see this apparatus that is shown you here. This is your
Florence. Another time it will be Rome or Pisa, and that's enough
itself to make you split your jaws with laughter. The door that you
see here on the right is the house of the doctor, who is much studied
in the law: that street there crammed into the corner is the Street
of Love, where he who falls will never rise again. You will recognize
by his friar's habit the prior who belongs in the church there
opposite, if you do not go away too soon.

A young gentleman, Callimaco by name, new come from Paris,
lives at that door on the left. He among all the other worthy gentlemen, by his carriage and sweet ways, must take the prize for gentleness. A lady young and lovely was greatly loved by him and by him
deceived, as you shall hear; and I should like it well if you too were
deceived like her.

The tale is called Mandragola: the argument, I fancy, you will
see in the playing of it. The author is of little fame: but if you will
not laugh at him, he'll gladly stand for the wine. A lover with weak
hams, a doctor of little wit, an evil-living friar, a malicious parasite,
let them for this day be your entertainment.

And if this matter—wishing only to be light-hearted—be not
worthy of a man who wishes to seem wise and grave, make this
excuse for it, that it only tries with these vain thoughts to make his
sad days more sweet: else he shall have nowhere to turn his face;
for he has been prohibited from showing with other ventures other
virtue, as not being worthy of his labors.

The reward hoped for is that everyone stand aside and smirk,
speaking ill of what he sees and hears. This is the reason why,
without any doubt, the antique virtue deserts our present century:
for nobody, when he sees that everyone does nothing but find fault,
is going to groan and heave, making with infinite pains a work that
the wind wastes and the mists will hide.

If, however, anyone has in mind to speak ill, take him by the hair
and push him aside. I warn him, I say to such a one that somebody

else knows how to speak ill as well as he, that the very first art he learned in fact was this; and that in all the world wherever Italian is spoken, he esteems nobody; though he might pay reverence to the man who can wear a better mantle than he.

But let us leave saying ill to such as like it, and return to our case, and not lose too much time. We must not give too much weight to words, nor esteem that monster who haply knows not whether he may be alive or dead. Callimaco is coming out, and has Siro his servant with him, and will set forth everything in due course. Listen everyone and look for no more argument just now.

ACT ONE

SCENE I—Callimaco and Siro

Callimaco: Siro, don't go away; I want you a little.

Siro: Here I am.

Callimaco: I fancy you wondered at my leaving Paris so suddenly, and now you wonder at my being here a month without doing anything.

Siro: That's the truth.

Callimaco: If I've not told you before now what I'm going to tell you, it hasn't been because I didn't trust you, but because I think that when there's something we don't want known, it's better not to tell it, unless we're obliged to. But now I think I need your help and so I want to tell you everything.

Siro: I'm your servant; servants ought never to ask their masters questions or pry into any of their actions; but when of themselves the masters tell something, then the servants should serve them faithfully; so I have done and I will do.

Callimaco: I know that. I fancy you've heard me say a thousand times (but it's nothing to me that you've heard it a thousand times) how when I was ten years old, my father and mother being dead, I was sent by my guardians to Paris, where I have been for twenty years. And because at the end of ten years, there began through the death of King Charles the wars in Italy, which ruined this province, I decided to live in Paris and not come back to my own country, thinking I could live safer in that place than here.

Siro: That's right.

Callimaco: I ordered all my goods here to be sold, except the house, and arranged to live there, and there have been another ten years with the greatest happiness.

Siro: So I know.

Callimaco: I divided my time partly in studies, partly in pleasure and partly in affairs; and managed so that one never got in the way of another. And thus, as you know, I lived very quietly, pleasing everyone and contriving to offend none, so that I seemed to be liked by townsmen, by gentlemen, by the working people, by the rich and by the poor.

Siro: That's true.

Callimaco: But since it seemed to fortune that I was having much too fair sailing in this world, she caused me to meet in Paris a certain Camillo Calfucci.

Siro: I begin to guess your trouble.

Callimaco: He, like other Florentines, was often invited to my house; and in talking together one day it happened that we fell into a dispute as to where the more beautiful women were to be found, in Italy or in France; and since I couldn't talk on the subject of the Italians, because I had left there when I was so small, another Florentine who was present took the French side and Camillo the Italian; and after many arguments right and left, Camillo, in something of a temper, said that if all the women in Italy should prove to be monsters, this one kinswoman of his could redeem the honor of them all.

Siro: Now I know what you're coming to.

Callimaco: He named Donna Lucrezia, wife of Messer Nicia Calfucci, of whom he sang so many praises for both her beauty and her habits that he left us all gaping, and he gave me such a wish to see her that I dropped every other consideration; I thought of neither war nor peace in Italy, but got ready to come here. And when I arrived I found the fame of Donna Lucrezia a long way under the truth—something that happens all too rarely—and now I'm so bitten with desire for her that I can get no peace.

Siro: If you'd told me of this in Paris, I'd have known how to advise you; but now I don't know what to say.

Callimaco: I haven't told you this to get your advice. It's partly to let off steam myself, and partly because I want you to be ready to help me when I need you.

Siro: I'm the readiest man in the world. But what hope have you?

Callimaco: Alas, none or very little and I tell you this: first of all her very nature is against me; for 'tis most honest and every way strange to these love matters; she has a very rich husband, who lets himself be governed by her in everything; and if he's not young neither is he so very old as he seems; she has no kin or neighbors with whom she goes to parties and festivals and other pleasures that young women delight in; no workmen or mechanics are about her house, and she hasn't a servant or a maid who is not in awe of her; so that there is no opening anywhere for bribes or corruption.

Siro: Well, then, what do you think you're going to do?

Callimaco: There's nothing so desperate, and never was, that you couldn't find some way of hope, however weak and vain, and your great wish and great desire keep it from seeming so.

Siro: Just the same, what makes you hope?

Callimaco: Two things: one the simplicity of Messer Nicia, for though he's a doctor, he's the greatest simpleton and fool in Florence. The other is the wish both he and she have for children, for she's been married six years and has not had a child, and with all that wealth they are dying for one.

Siro: Have you tried anything yet?

Callimaco: Yes, I have, but it's only a little thing.

Siro: What?

Callimaco: You know Ligurio, how he comes constantly to dine with me. He was a marriage agent once; and so is given to begging suppers and dinners. Ligurio is a likable man, Messer Nicia is very friendly with him, and Ligurio gets round him most seasonably; and though Messer Nicia won't ask him to a meal, he lends him money. I have made me a friend of Ligurio and have told him about my love; he has promised heart and soul to help me.

Siro: Look out that he don't cheat you, you can't trust these gluttons.

Callimaco: That's right. Nevertheless when you confide in a man you've got to believe that he'll serve you in good faith. I've promised him, if it succeeds, that he'll get a good fat purse of money; if it doesn't succeed, he'll sponge a sup or a dinner, which I shouldn't eat alone anyhow.

Siro: What has he promised to do so far?

Callimaco: He has promised to persuade Messer Nicia to take his lady to the baths this May.

Siro: And what's that to you?

Callimaco: What is it? Perhaps in such a place I can make her change her state of mind. In these places you do nothing if not make a holiday; and I'll go there and I'll lead them into every pleasure I can think of, I'll spare no magnificence, believe me. And something may come of it, time will tell.

Siro: That suits me.

Callimaco: This morning when Ligurio left me he promised to see Messer Nicia about this and let me know.

Siro: Here they are together.

103 Callimaco: I'll draw aside and wait for Ligurio when the doctor

leaves him. You go on in the house about your business, and if
I want anything I'll say so.

Siro: I'm off.

SCENE II—Nicia and Ligurio

Nicia: I think your advice is good, and I spoke yesterday evening
with the lady. She said she'd give me an answer to-day, but to
tell you the truth I'm not going on very happy legs just now.

Ligurio: Because?

Nicia: Because I don't go about willingly picking bombs. And I
don't like having to hoodwink my wife, my servants and the
whole house. Besides I spoke last night to several doctors; one
said I should go to San Filipo, the other to Poretta, the other to
the Villa; and they all seemed to me a lot of old crows; to tell you
the truth these doctors of medicine don't know what they are
about.

Ligurio: What troubles you is what you said first, you're not used to
letting the cupola out of your sight, you won't leave Florence.

Nicia: You are wrong there. When I was younger I traveled a lot;
there was never a festival at Prato that I was not on hand; and not
a castle anywhere around where I had not been; and what's more
I've been to Pisa and Leghorn. Come off!

Ligurio: At Leghorn you saw the sea?

Nicia: You know well enough I saw it.

Ligurio: How much bigger is it than the Arno?

Nicia: Than the Arno? It's four times as big, six, seven times, I'd
say; you see nothing but water, water, water.

Ligurio: I'm surprised, then, when you've seen so much of the world,
you'd make such a fuss about going to the baths.

Nicia: Ah, your mouth's full of mother's milk: it seems to you nothing at all, does it, to turn a house upside down? But, alas, I've
such a wish to have children that I'll do anything. You talk about
it a little with your master; see where he advises me to go; and
I'll go speak with the lady and be with you anon.

Ligurio: That's good.

SCENE III—Ligurio and Callimaco

Ligurio: I don't believe there was ever such a stupid man in the
world as that one; and look how fortune has favored him! He's
rich, he has a beautiful wife, wise, well-behaved and fit to govern a kingdom. It seems to me you don't often see the proverb

about marriage come true that says: God made human beings, and they couple themselves. For often you see a most worthy man married to a beast, and on the contrary a sensible woman married to a madman. But there's one good thing about this particular madness: Callimaco can hope to get something out of it. Yonder he comes. What are you waiting for, Callimaco?

Callimaco: I saw you with the doctor and was waiting till you left him to hear what you did.

Ligurio: What quality of man he is you know: of little prudence and less wits, he leaves Florence most unwillingly. But I've got him heated up; and he's agreed at last to do anything. We'll pull our plot through, I think, but that's not saying whether or not we'll get what we want out of it.

Callimaco: Why?

Ligurio: How do I know! You know how every kind of people go to these baths; what if a man turned up who pleased Donna Lucrezia more than you do, who was richer in gold than you are and more rich in grace; so that perchance our labor is all vain; what if the crowd of rivals made her still more difficult; what if when you were fast friends at last she turned to another, not to you?

Callimaco: I know that's true. But what must I do? What line can I take? Where can I turn? I must do something, be it great or be it small, be it curst or infamous; better die than live thus. If I could sleep at night, if I could eat, if I could talk, if I could take pleasure in anything, I'd be more patient biding my time. But there's no remedy here; and if I cannot live in hope some way or other, I'll die anyhow; and seeing I have to die, I'm not for fearing anything but for clinching some scheme, bestial, raw or wicked.

Ligurio: Don't talk like that; curb this rash soul.

Callimaco: You see well how by curbing it I only feed myself on kindred thoughts; and so perforce must we go on with our sending those people to the baths, or launch some other plot, so that I can feed on a hope, if not true at least false, that will soften my pangs a little.

Ligurio: You are right, and I'm for doing it.

Callimaco: I believe it, for you and the likes of you live by cozening people. But I don't think I'll be one of such; for if you played me a trick and I found it out, I'd turn it to my own uses, be sure; and you'd lose the use of my house and the hope of ever having what I have promised you for the future.

Ligurio: Never doubt my faith; even it if were not so profitable as I wish and hope, your blood is mixed with mine, and I want you to have your desire almost as much as you do. But enough of this. The doctor has commissioned me to find a physician and learn

what baths would be good to go to. I would have you do my way,
and this is it: say that you have studied medicine and have had
some experience in Paris. He'll swallow it easily, because he's
stupid and because you have a polished wit and could say something in the learned style.

Callimaco: And how shall this serve us?

Ligurio: Serve to send him to those baths we want, and to clinch as
well another plan I've thought of, which will be shorter, more
certain and more successful than the baths.

Callimaco: What are you saying?

Ligurio: I'm saying that if you pluck up your spirits and trust in me
I'll have this thing done before this time to-morrow. Even if he
were the man, which he is not, to investigate whether you are a
doctor or not, the short time, the very thing itself, will keep him
from speaking of it, and our plot from being spoiled even if he
does speak of it.

Callimaco: You save my life; this promise is too great and feeds me
with too great a hope! What shall I do?

Ligurio: You'll know when the time comes: for the present it's
enough that I tell you; for we've time only to do, not to talk. Go
into the house and wait for me there; and I'll go find the doctor;
and if I bring him to you, you go on minding what I say, and
suit yourself to that.

Callimaco: I'll do it, though you are filling me with a hope that I
fear me will go up in smoke.

SONG

He who hath never felt thy power, O Love,
Hopes all in vain, in vain, to rise
On that true faith that is heaven's highest prize;
Nor knows not what it may be
To live and die together,
To follow loss, to flee prosperity;
Nor how the soul may love its own self less
Than the beloved's soul, nor that distress
When fear and hope steal our heart's fire and pith,
Nor knows how men and gods alike
Do fear the arms that thou are armored with.

ACT TWO

SCENE I—Ligurio, Nicia and Siro, who answers from the house

Ligurio: As I've told you I think God has sent that man to us so that
   your desire may be fulfilled. In Paris he has had the greatest
   experience; and you needn't wonder why he has never practiced
   his art in Florence, why should he? First because he's rich, and
   second, because he's on the point any minute of going back to
   Paris.
Nicia: Very well. I shouldn't want to be led into a tangle and left
   high and dry.
Ligurio: Don't doubt him; all you have to fear is that he won't take
   the case, but if he does take it, he won't leave you till he sees it
   through to the end.
Nicia: For that I trust you; but as for his science, I tell you straight,
   as I'll tell him indeed, though he be such a man of learning, that
   he won't sell me any bladder-rattles, I'm not so easy.
Ligurio: I'll take you to him so that you can talk with him yourself;
   and if when you've talked with him he does not seem to you for
   presence, learning and address a man to take off your hat to, say
   that I'm not I.
Nicia: So be it then, by all the holy angels; let's go. But where is he?
Ligurio: He lives in this square; that's his door you see opposite you.
Nicia: Right off, be quick.
Ligurio: Done.
Siro: What is it?
Ligurio: Is Callimaco here?
Siro: Yes, he is.
Nicia: Why don't you say Master Callimaco?
Ligurio: He cares nothing for such twaddle.
Nicia: That's not the way to talk; do your duty, and if he takes it ill,
   pay no attention.

SCENE II—Callimaco, Nicia and Ligurio

Callimaco: Who is it wants me?
Nicia: Bona dies, domine magister.
Callimaco: Et vobis, domine doctor.
Ligurio: How does it strike you?
107   Nicia: Good, by the apostles!

Ligurio: If you want me to stay by you, speak as I tell you, otherwise we are minding two fires.

Callimaco: What's your good business?

Nicia: How do I know? I'm looking for two things that another man, perchance, would flee; to make trouble for myself and for others. I have no children and I want some, and to possess that trouble I come to bother you.

Callimaco: May it never displease me to give pleasure to you and to all men so virtuous and good as you are; I have not labored so many years in Paris to learn my arts if not to serve such men as you.

Nicia: Gran mercé; and when you have need of my arts I will serve you freely. But let us go back to our matter. Have you thought what baths would be good to bring my wife with child? I know that Ligurio here has told you what he has to tell you.

Callimaco: That is true; but if I am to comply with your wishes, I must first know the cause of your wife's sterility; for it may proceed from many causes. Nam causae sterilitatis sunt, aut in semine, aut in matrice, aut in instrumentis seminariis, aut in virga, aut in causa extrinseca.

Nicia: This is the most learned man to be found anywhere.

Callimaco: This sterility might otherwise be caused by an impotence in you, and if this should be the case, there would not be any remedy.

Nicia: I impotent? Oh, you make me laugh! I don't believe there's a lustier and redder-blooded man in Florence than I am.

Callimaco: If that be true, be of good cheer, we'll find you some remedy.

Nicia: Would there be any other remedy beside the baths? For I've no mind for a bother like this myself and the lady would go most unwillingly from Florence.

Ligurio: Yes, there is. I'm going to answer you. Callimaco is so very considerate that he's too much so. Have you not told me you could prescribe a certain potion that without fail could make her conceive?

Callimaco: I have; but I am reserved with men that I know but little; I would not have them think me a charlatan.

Nicia: Don't doubt me; for you've already filled me with such admiration that there is nothing I would not believe or do at your hands.

Ligurio: I think you should see a specimen of her . . .

Callimaco: Undoubtedly; one may not do less.

Ligurio: Call Siro and let him go home with the doctor for it, and
come back here; we'll wait for you in the house.

Callimaco: Siro, go with him; and if it pleases you, Messer Nicia, come back at once, and we'll think of something fitting.

Nicia: How, if it pleases me! I'll be here again in an instant; for I have more faith in you than a Hun has in a sword.

SCENE III—Nicia and Siro

Nicia: This master of yours is a very worthy man.

Siro: More than you can say.

Nicia: The king of France sets great store by him?

Siro: Enough.

Nicia: And for that reason he ought gladly to be in France.

Siro: So he thinks.

Nicia: He does quite right. In this country there is nothing but scum; nobody prizes any virtue. If he were here there wouldn't be a man who would look him in the face. I don't know what to think of it, for I've burst a gut to learn the little I know, and if I had to live by it, I'd grow fat, I can tell you.

Siro: Don't you make a hundred ducats a year?

Nicia: Go on, not a hundred lire, not a hundred groats! It's this way: anybody in this country who hasn't got the estate of the likes of us, finds not a dog that would bark at him; and we are good for nothing but to go to burials, or to wedding parties or to stay all day on the bench of the Proconsolo and loll. But I don't care, you know where you can stick the whole business. I don't need anybody. If there's anybody worse off than I am let him be worse off. But still I wouldn't want what I say to be heard, or I'd be getting a dig behind that would make me sweat.

Siro: No doubt.

Nicia: We are at the house; wait for me here; I'll be back at once.

SCENE IV—Siro alone

Siro: If all the doctors were like this one we should work wonders. This wretched Ligurio and this madman my master are up to something, they're getting him where they can put some shame or other on him! And truly I'd like it too, if I could believe it wouldn't get out, for if it were heard of, I'd be in danger of my life, and my master of both his life and his property. He has already become a physician; I don't know what his game is or what the trick means. But here's the doctor with a vessel in his hand. Who wouldn't laugh at the old bird?

SCENE V—Nicia and Siro

Nicia: I've done everything your way, in this I want you to do
mine. If I had thought I wouldn't have children, I'd sooner have
taken a peasant to wife, for— Are you there, Siro? Then follow me.
What a bother I've undergone to make this woman of mine give
me this specimen! And it's not because she's not crazy to have
children, it's on her mind more than it is on mine; but if I ask her
to do the least little thing, oh, that's another story!
Siro: Have patience; women must be brought with soft words where
you want them.
Nicia: Soft words, after she's rasped me so. Hurry, tell your master
and Ligurio that I'm here.
Siro: Here they are coming out.

SCENE VI—Ligurio, Callimaco and Nicia

Ligurio: The doctor will be easy to persuade, the trouble will be
the lady, and for that we'll find ways.
Callimaco: Have you the specimen?
Nicia: Siro has it under—
Callimaco: Give it here. Oh, this specimen shows a weakness of the
kidneys.
Nicia: And seems to me muddy, and yet it's quite fresh.
Callimaco: Don't be surprised. Nam mulieris urinae sunt semper
majoris glossitici, et albedinis, et minoris pulchritudinis, quam
virorum. Hujus autem, inter caetera, causa est amplitudo ca-
nalium, mixtio eorum ex matrice quae exeunt cum urina.
Nicia: Oh, belly of St. Puccio, how I dote upon this man! Look how
bravely he carries off these things!
Callimaco: I'm afraid she's poorly covered at night; and for that
reason it is raw.
Nicia: She's got a good quilt for her back but she stays four hours
on her knees stringing pater nosters before she'll come to bed,
and she's a regular beast for standing the cold.
Callimaco: In sum, doctor, either you have faith in me or you have
not; I on my part will give you the remedy, you, if you have faith
in me, will take it; and if this day a year from now your lady has
not her little son in her arms, I'll give you two thousand ducats.
Nicia: Only say the word, for I honor you above all men and believe you more than I do my confessor.
Callimaco: You must hear that there's nothing more certain to bring
on conception than a potion made of mandragola. It's a thing

I've experimented with twice a couple of times and always found it true; if it were not so the queen of France would be sterile and countless other princesses of that realm.

Nicia: Is it possible?

Callimaco: It's just as I tell you; and fortune has wished you so well that I happened to have brought here with me all those things that are put into that potion, and you can have it at your will.

Nicia: When might I take it?

Callimaco: This evening after dinner; because the moon is propitious, and the time could never be more fit.

Nicia: Don't bother about that. You prescribe it by all means, I'll make her take it.

Callimaco: Now you must think of this point; the man that first lies with her after she has taken this potion, dies in eight days; nothing in the world could save him.

Nicia: O pox, I don't want such a torment as that on my hands: you won't stick that on me! You've given me loads enough to carry.

Callimaco: Be easy, there's a remedy.

Nicia: What?

Callimaco: Make another sleep with her right off, so that he will draw to himself by passing the night with her all the infection of the mandragola; after that you can lie with her without danger.

Nicia: I don't want to do this.

Callimaco: Why?

Nicia: Because I don't want to make my wife a whore and me a cuckold.

Callimaco: What are you saying, doctor? You are not the wise man I took you for; do you hesitate to do what the king of France has done and do many noble gentlemen of his?

Nicia: Do you want me to do such a crazy thing? If I tell her about it she won't want to do it; if I don't tell her I'll be betraying her. It's a case for the magistrate; I don't want to put my head in that noose.

Callimaco: If that's all that worries you leave the affair to me.

Nicia: What will you do?

Callimaco: I'll tell you. I'll give you the potion this evening after dinner; you give it to her to drink, and put her at once to bed. Later we'll disguise ourselves, Ligurio, Siro and I, and go hunting in the New Market and the Old Market and the first fine lad we find idle, we'll kidnap him, and with a few cracks on the head will take him into the house, and into your room in the dark; there we'll put him in bed, telling him what he has to do: there won't be any trouble about that. Then in the morning you send him off before daybreak; make your wife go bathe; lie with her at your pleasure and with naught of danger.

Nicia: I'm agreed, since you say that the king and the leading nobles have tried this way; but for the love of God keep it secret.

Callimaco: Who would ever tell it?

Nicia: One trouble remains and a grave one.

Callimaco: What?

Nicia: To make my wife agree to it; for I don't think she'll ever come around to such a thing.

Callimaco: True, but I shouldn't want a wife that I couldn't persuade to do my way.

Ligurio: I've thought of a remedy for that.

Nicia: What?

Ligurio: Work through the confessor.

Callimaco: Who would persuade the confessor?

Ligurio: You, I, money, our wickedness, yours.

Nicia: I wager, if for no other reason than just because I say so, she will not want to go to the confessor.

Ligurio: And there's a remedy for that too.

Callimaco: Tell me?

Ligurio: Take her to her mother.

Nicia: She has faith in her.

Ligurio: And I know that her mother is of our opinion. Let's get on, for it will soon be evening. You go, Callimaco, and we will join you at home two hours from now, see that you have the potion ready. We'll go to the mother's house, the doctor and I, and explain to her; then we will go to the friar, and tell him all of what we have done.

Callimaco: Hey, don't leave me alone!

Ligurio: You seem to me all ready and set.

Callimaco: Where do you want me to go now?

Ligurio: Here, there, this way, that way, Florence is a big place.

Callimaco: I'm dead.

SONG

How happy is that's born a fool
And swallows all that he doth hear,
Ambition doth not rule,
His days, he feels not fear,
Which are the seeds of woe;
112 This doctor of ours so

Bursting is he for sons,
He would believe an ass could fly;
And all else is oblivion's,
And for this he would live or die.

ACT THREE

SCENE I—Sostrata, Nicia and Ligurio

Sostrata: I've always heard it said that the part of a wise man is to make the best of his ills. If you have no other remedy to bring you children and you want to take this one, it need not weigh on your conscience.

Nicia: So be it.

Ligurio: You go find your daughter, and Messer Nicia and I will find Brother Timoteo her confessor, and tell him our case, so that you'll not have to tell him. You'll see what he will say to you.

Sostrata: So be it. Your way is there, I'm going to find Lucrezia, and take her at all costs to speak with the friar.

SCENE II—Nicia and Ligurio

Nicia: Perhaps you are surprised, Ligurio, that you have to spin so many lies to persuade my wife, but if you knew all you wouldn't be surprised at it.

Ligurio: I fancy it may be because all women are suspicious.

Nicia: It's not that. She used to be the sweetest person in the world and the easiest to get on with; but hearing a neighbor of hers say that if she vowed to hear forty mornings the first mass of the Servi, she would find herself with child, she made the vow and went perhaps twenty mornings. Then one of those beastly friars began to hang around her and she ended by not going back again. It's a bad thing when those who ought to set a good example act like that. How say you?

Ligurio: It's the devil to pay if that be true.

Nicia: Since then she has her ears up like a rabbit, and anything you tell her to do, she puts a thousand difficulties in the way.

Ligurio: I'm not surprised. But that vow, how is it to be fulfilled?

Nicia: It's dispensed with.

Ligurio: Good. But give me, if you have it, twenty-five ducats; for we must spend something in these matters and make a friend of the friar right off and give him hopes of more.

113 Nicia: Take it, that doesn't trouble me; I'll make provision elsewhere.

Ligurio: These friars are a shrewd lot; and no wonder, since they know our sins and their own too. Anyone who didn't know his way about with them might find himself outwitted. However I would not have you spoil everything by talking, because the likes of you, who are buried all day in their studies and learn all they know from books, don't understand worldly things. (This one is so dull I fear he'll spoil everything.)

Nicia: Tell me what you want me to do.

Ligurio: You leave the talking to me, and don't say a word unless I give you the sign.

Nicia: I'm agreed. What sign will you make?

Ligurio: I'll shut an eye, will bite my lip. Let's do nothing else. How long is it since you talked to the friar?

Nicia: More than ten years.

Ligurio: That's all right. I'll tell him that you are deaf; don't you answer, and never say anything unless we speak very loud.

Nicia: Very good, agreed.

Ligurio: Don't be bothered if I say something that seems to cut across our plans, for all will come out right.

Nicia: In God's good time.

SCENE III—Timoteo and a Lady

Timoteo: If you want to confess I will do what you want.

The Lady: Not to-day: some one is waiting for me and I'm quite out of breath with hurrying so. Have you said those masses of our lady?

Timoteo: Yes, madam.

The Lady: Take this florin now and say every Monday for two months the mass of the dead for my husband's soul. Though he was a brute of a man and lived only in the flesh, I cannot resent it when I think of it. But you think he is in purgatory?

Timoteo: Undoubtedly.

The Lady: I'm not so sure of that. If you only knew how he treated me sometimes. Oh, how miserable I was with him! I put him off as much as I could but he was so importunate. Ugh, Good Lord!

Timoteo: Have no fear; the clemency of God is great: if a man doesn't lack the will he'll never lack the time to repent.

The Lady: Do you think the Turk will go through Italy this year?

Timoteo: If you don't pray, yes.

The Lady: Alas! God help us! What with their devilish ways I'm so afraid of that impaling of theirs. But I see here in the church a lady who has a scarf of mine, I must go have it of her. I bid you good day.

Timoteo: Keep well.

SCENE IV—Timoteo, Ligurio and Nicia

Timoteo: The most charitable people are the women and the most
boring. Whoever repels them escapes both the boring and the
useful: whoever takes them to his bosom has the useful and the
boring together. It's true, there's never an apple without the
flies. What are you doing, good men, do I not recognize Messer
Nicia?

Ligurio: Speak loud, for he's pretty deaf, he doesn't hear much any
more.

Timoteo: You are welcome.

Ligurio: Louder.

Timoteo: Welcome.

Nicia: Glad to see you, father.

Timoteo: What have you on hand?

Nicia: Something good.

Ligurio: Address yourself to me, father, for if you made him hear
you'd have to rouse the whole square.

Timoteo: What can I do for you?

Ligurio: Messer Nicia here and another worthy man whom you will
meet later, want to distribute two thousand ducats in charitable
works.

Nicia: A pox on it!

Ligurio: (Be quiet, curse you, it won't be that much.) Don't be surprised, father, at what he says; for he doesn't hear and sometimes
he thinks he does hear and answers off the point.

Timoteo: Just go right ahead, and let him say what he pleases.

Ligurio: Of such a sum I have a part with me, and have planned
that you be the one to distribute it.

Timoteo: Willingly.

Ligurio: But before this charity is given you must help us with a
strange case that has come up for Messer Nicia; and only you
can help us in this matter; the honor of his house is concerned.

Timoteo: What is it?

Ligurio: I don't know if you are acquainted with Camillo Calfucci,
the nephew of Messer Nicia here.

Timoteo: Yes, I know him.

Ligurio: That gentleman went on some business or other to France
a year ago; and not having a wife, for she was dead, left his
marriageable daughter in the protection of a convent, whose
name we need not mention just yet.

115   Timoteo: And then?

Ligurio: And then either because the sisters were negligent or the girl scatter-brained, she found herself four months gone with child: so that if this mishap is not taken care of properly, the doctor, the sisters, the girl, Camillo, the house of Calfucci are put to shame: and the doctor is so much concerned about this shame that he has vowed, if the tale does not get about, to give three hundred ducats for the love of God.

Nicia: What the devil!

Ligurio: Be quiet. And he will give this into your hands, for only you and the abbess can help us.

Timoteo: How?

Ligurio: Persuade the abbess to give a potion to the girl that will make her miscarry.

Timoteo: That's something to think twice about.

Ligurio: Consider if you do it how many good things will be the result. You preserve the honor of the convent, of the girl, of the family; you restore a daughter to her father; you satisfy Messer Nicia here and all those kin of his; you do the vast amount of charity that these three hundred ducats will make possible; and on the other hand you harm nothing but a piece of flesh unborn, without senses, which in a thousand ways might miscarry anyhow. And I think that that is best that does most good and makes the most people a little happy.

Timoteo: So be it in God's name, I'll do what you ask; for God and for charity all shall be done. Tell me the convent, give me the potion, and, if it's agreeable to you, give me money, so that I can begin to do good.

Ligurio: Now you seem the holy man I thought you were. Take this part of the money. The convent is— But wait: there's a lady there in the church beckoning to me: I'll be straight back. Don't go, Messer Nicia, I'd like two words with you.

SCENE v—Timoteo and Nicia

Timoteo: This girl, how old is she?

Nicia: I'm amazed.

Timoteo: I say how old is this girl?

Nicia: May God curse her!

Timoteo: Why?

Nicia: So she will be cursed.

Timoteo: I'm in a hole, trying to work with a fool, and a deaf man. One runs away, the other can't hear. But if these pieces are not merely brass checks, I'll get on better with them. Here's Ligurio coming back.

SCENE VI—Ligurio, Timoteo and Nicia

Ligurio: Be quiet, Messer Nicia; I have great news, father.

Timoteo: What?

Ligurio: The woman I've just spoken to tells me that the girl has miscarried of herself.

Timoteo: Good! This charity will go into the public moneys.

Ligurio: What are you talking about?

Timoteo: I say that all the more now you ought to make this charity.

Ligurio: The charity will be made when you wish; but you must do something else for the doctor's benefit.

Timoteo: What is it?

Ligurio: Something that's less trouble, less scandal, more acceptable to us, more useful to you.

Timoteo: What is it? I'm on such friendly terms and seem to be so arm in arm with you that there's nothing I wouldn't do.

Ligurio: I'd rather tell you in church, just between ourselves. The doctor don't mind waiting here. We'll be here anon.

Nicia: As the toad said to the harrow.

Timoteo: Come.

SCENE VII—Nicia alone

Nicia: Is this day or night? Am I myself or do I dream? Am I drunk, when I have not taken a drink to-day, to go on with this tomfoolery? We are here to say one thing to the friar and he says another; then he orders me to be deaf. I ought to have stopped my ears with pitch so as not to have heard the crazy things he said; and God knows to what end. I find myself twenty-five ducats short, and nothing yet done about my business, and now I'm stuck here like a simpleton. But here they are coming back; damn them if they haven't settled my business!

SCENE VIII—Timoteo, Ligurio and Nicia

Timoteo: Let the ladies come. I know what I have to do; and if my authority is worth anything we shall settle this parentage business this very evening.

Ligurio: Messer Nicia, Brother Timoteo is going to settle everything. See to it that the ladies come.

Nicia: How you relieve me! Shall it be a boy?

Ligurio: A boy.

Nicia: I weep with tenderness.

117 Timoteo: You two go into the church, I'll await the ladies here.

Keep to the side where they won't see you; and when they are gone I'll tell you what they said.

SCENE IX—Timoteo alone

Timoteo: I don't know which of us has cheated the other. This miserable Ligurio comes to me with that first news just to try me out; if I had not agreed to that he would not have mentioned this last, so as not to have it exposed for nothing; about the first, since it was false anyway, they cared nothing. It's true that I've been deceived, but the deceit can serve my ends very well. Messer Nicia and Callimaco are both rich and each for diverse reasons can be well plucked. The thing must be kept dark, that's as important to them as it is to me. Be it as they wish, I'll not repent me of it. Forsooth I doubt not we shall find it hard, for Donna Lucrezia is sensible and good. But I'll work on her kindness, all women have little brains, and if one of them knows enough to say two words, there must be a sermon about it: for in the realm of the blind the one-eyed is king. And here she is with her mother, who is a very beast and will be of great use in bringing her around to my wishes.

SCENE X—Sostrata and Lucrezia

Sostrata: I'm sure you believe, daughter, that I set as much store by your honor as anybody in the world, and that I should never advise you to do anything that was not good. I have told you and I tell you again that if Brother Timoteo says that there's nothing in it to trouble your conscience, you may do it without another thought.
Lucrezia: I have never had a doubt that the longing Messer Nicia has for children would sooner or later make us do something foolish; and just on this account, whenever he has come to me with some notion, have I been jealous and suspicious of it. But of all the things that we have tried, this last seems to me the strangest; to have to submit my body to this outrage, and to cause a man to die for outraging me; I'd never have believed, no not if I were the last woman left in the world and the human race had to start all over again from me, that such a thing could have fallen to my lot.
Sostrata: I can't explain such matters, daughter; you'll talk to the friar and you'll see what he tells you, and then do as you are advised by him, by us and by those who wish you well.
118 Lucrezia: I'm sweating with rage.

scene xi—Timoteo, Lucrezia and Sostrata

Timoteo: You are welcome both. I know what you wish to know from me, Messer Nicia has told me. Truly I have been in my books more than two hours studying this case; and after much question, I find many things both in general and in particular that are in our favor.

Lucrezia: Are you serious or jesting?

Timoteo: Ah! Donna Lucrezia, are these matters for jesting? Is that what you think of me?

Lucrezia: Father, no; but this seems to me the strangest business I ever heard of.

Timoteo: Madam, I believe you: but I would not have you say any more in this vein. There are many things which seen at a distance appear terrible, unbearable, strange; but when you come nearer to them they prove to be human, bearable, familiar; wherefore is it said that the fear is worse than the evil. And this is one of them.

Lucrezia: It's the will of God.

Timoteo: I'll go back to what I was saying at first. For the sake of your conscience you must go on this general principle: where there is a certain good and an uncertain evil, we must not forsake that good for fear of that evil. Here is a certain good, you will be with child. You will donate a soul to the Lord God. The uncertain evil is that he who lies with you after you've taken the potion, dies: but he will also find himself among those who will never die. But since the thing is dubious, it's right that Messer Nicia should run no risk. And if the act is sinful, it's only in a manner of speaking so after all, for the will is what sins, not the body: it's a sin on the grounds that it displeases your husband, and you please him: it's a sin on the grounds of taking pleasure in it, and you take no pleasure in it. Moreover the end is what you must consider in every case. Your end is to fill a seat in Paradise, to make your husband happy. The Bible says that the daughters of Lot, believing that they alone were left in the world, consorted with their father; and since their intention was good they did not sin.

Lucrezia: What would you persuade me to?

Sostrata: Let yourself be persuaded, daughter. Don't you see that a woman who has no children has no home? When her husband is dead she remains, like a beast, deserted by everyone.

Timoteo: I swear to you, Madam, by the holy sacrament, that your duty in this case is to obey your husband, though it were to eat

119

meat on Wednesdays; which is a sin that no holy water can wash away.

Lucrezia: Where are you pushing me, father?

Timoteo: I'm urging you to things that you'll ask God to bless me for, and that next year you'll value more than now.

Sostrata: She'll do what you wish. I'll put her to bed myself to-night. What are you afraid of, idiot? There are fifty women in this land who would lift their hands to heaven for this that you'll be getting.

Lucrezia: I consent; but I don't expect to be alive to-morrow morning.

Timoteo: Have no fear, my daughter: I will pray God for you; I will say a prayer to the angel Rafael to be at your side. Go quickly and prepare for this mystery that the night will bring.

Sostrata: Rest in peace, father.

Lucrezia: God and Our Lady keep me from harm.

SCENE XII—Timoteo, Ligurio and Nicia

Timoteo: O Ligurio, come here.

Ligurio: How goes it?

Timoteo: Well. They have gone home disposed to do everything, and not to make us any trouble; the mother is going with her and will put her to bed.

Nicia: Are you telling the truth?

Timoteo: Heighho, you are healed of your deafness!

Ligurio: San Chimenti, to whom the sterile ladies pray, has shown him grace.

Timoteo: If you wish to offer an image in order to make a place to do a little business— So that I shall have profit with you.

Nicia: We've got to chattering. Will the lady make any trouble about doing what I want?

Timoteo: No, I tell you.

Nicia: I'm the happiest man in the world.

Timoteo: I believe it. You'll soon be pecking at a baby boy: let him that has not go without.

Ligurio: Go, brother, to your prayers; and if there's more need we'll come find you. You, Messer Nicia, go to her and keep her fast in this opinion; and I'll go find Master Callimaco, to send you the potion; let me see you in an hour and arrange what we are to do when the time comes.

Nicia: Excellent; good-bye.

Timoteo: Keep well.

SONG

So sweet is deceit
Toward some desired, dear end,
That everything is stripped of pain,
And every bitter taste is made sweet.
O remedy high and rare,
Thou showest the narrow path to erring souls:
Thou, too, with thy great power to make
Men happy, makest Love rich and fair;
With holy counsels only thou dost quell
Stone, poison, magic spell.

ACT FOUR

SCENE 1—Callimaco alone

Callimaco: I should like excellent well to hear what they have done.
What can it be that keeps Ligurio away? It's not only eleven, it's
twelve o'clock. In what anguish of soul have I been and am! It's
true indeed that fortune and nature keep the account even: you
won't find a good that some evil will not arise to match it. The
more my hope increases, the more my fear increases. Poor me!
How shall I ever live in the midst of so many ills and wracked
by these hopes and fears? I'm like a ship vexed by two contrary
winds, so that the nearer it is to port the more it is afraid. The
simplicity of Messer Nicia gives me hope; the prudence and firm-
ness of Donna Lucrezia makes me fear. Alas, I find no peace anywhere! Sometimes I try to control myself. I reprove myself for
this frenzy and say to myself: What are you doing? Have you
gone mad? When you possess her, what then? You will know
your error and repent the troubles and worries you've had. You
know, don't you, how little good there is in things that man desires, compared to what man has dreamed of finding? On the
other hand the worst that can happen to you is to die and go to
hell. There are so many others dead and so many worthy men
in hell, are you ashamed to go there? Look fortune in the face,
flee what's ill, and when you cannot flee it, bear it like a man.
Don't be prostrated and disheartened like a woman. Thus I keep
a good heart, but it doesn't get me very far, for all of me burns
with desire to be once with her, I feel excited from the soles of

121

my feet to the top of my head; my legs shake, my bowels rumble, my heart jumps out of my breast, my arms are helpless, my tongue is mute, my eyes dazzle, my brain whirls. If I could only find Ligurio I could let myself off to him. But here he comes hurrying to me: his news will make me either live some little more or die outright.

SCENE II—Ligurio and Callimaco

Ligurio: I could never want more than I do now to find Callimaco, and never be sorrier to find him. If I bore sad news I should have met him at once. I have been at his house, in the square, at the market, on the bench of the Spini, at the loggia of the Torna-quinci; and haven't found him. These lovers have quicksilver under their feet, and can't stop.

Callimaco: I see Ligurio go looking about over there, could he be seeking me perhaps? What's the matter with me that I don't call him? He looks very happy. O Ligurio, O Ligurio!

Ligurio: O Callimaco, where have you been?

Callimaco: What news?

Ligurio: Good.

Callimaco: Truly good?

Ligurio: The best.

Callimaco: Does Lucrezia agree?

Ligurio: Yes.

Callimaco: The friar does what is needed?

Ligurio: He does.

Callimaco: O blessed friar! I'll always pray God for him.

Ligurio: O excellent! As if God's grace should reward for evil as well as good. The friar will want something else besides prayers!

Callimaco: What will he want?

Ligurio: Money.

Callimaco: Give it to him. How much have you promised him?

Ligurio: Three hundred ducats.

Callimaco: You've done well.

Ligurio: The doctor has disgorged twenty-five.

Callimaco: How?

Ligurio: It suffices that he has disgorged it.

Callimaco: Lucrezia's mother, what has she done?

Ligurio: Almost everything. When she learned that her daughter was to have this good night without sin, she never left off begging, commanding, encouraging Lucrezia, and so took her to the friar and there managed in such a way that she consented.

Callimaco: O God! what have I done to deserve such blessings! I shall die with joy.

Ligurio: What sort is this! Now he dies for joy, now for grief, this man is bound to die some way or other. Have you the potion ready?

Callimaco: I have.

Ligurio: What will you send her?

Callimaco: A glass of ipocras which is good to make the stomach stronger and the brain gay. Alas, alas, alas, I'm ruined!

Ligurio: What is it? What will it be now?

Callimaco: There's no remedy for us.

Ligurio: What the devil can it be now?

Callimaco: And nothing is won; I'm walled up in a furnace.

Ligurio: Why, tell me why? Take your hand down off your face.

Callimaco: Oh, don't you know that I have said to Messer Nicia that you, he, Siro and I will catch some one to put to bed with his wife?

Ligurio: How does that matter?

Callimaco: How does it matter? If I'm with you how can I be the one who is caught? If I'm not with you he will see through the trick.

Ligurio: You are right; but is there no remedy?

Callimaco: I don't believe so.

Ligurio: Yes, it will prosper yet.

Callimaco: How?

Ligurio: I must think a little.

Callimaco: You've shown me the light; if you have to think now I'm lost.

Ligurio: I've found it.

Callimaco: What?

Ligurio: I'll have the friar help us in this; he'll do the rest.

Callimaco: In what way, how?

Ligurio: We must all disguise ourselves: I'll make the friar disguise his voice, his face, his clothes, and I'll tell the doctor how that one is you; he'll believe it.

Callimaco: That suits me. But what shall I do?

Ligurio: You'll put on a cloak, and with a lute in your hand you'll come along by the corner of his house singing a little song.

Callimaco: With the face uncovered?

Ligurio: Yes, if you wore a mask he'd be suspicious.

Callimaco: And would he not know me?

Ligurio: He won't, for you must distort your face, you must have your mouth open and twisted around, and one eye shut. Try it a little.

Callimaco: Do it this way?

Ligurio: No.

Callimaco: This way?

Ligurio: Not enough.

Callimaco: This way then?

Ligurio: Yes, yes, remember how you do it. I have a nose at home; you must stick it on.

Callimaco: Very well, what then?

Ligurio: When you appear at the corner, we'll be on hand, snatching the lute, seizing you, surrounding you, taking you into the house, putting you to bed; the rest you must do yourself.

Callimaco: Well and good.

Ligurio: That gets you there; when it comes to going back again that will be your affair not ours.

Callimaco: How?

Ligurio: Win her to-night, and before you depart make yourself known to her; discover the trick, show her the love you bear her, tell her how well you wish her; and how without scandal she may be your friend, and with great scandal your enemy. It's not possible she won't agree with you or that she should wish this night to be the only one.

Callimaco: You believe that?

Ligurio: I'm sure of it. But let us not lose more time; it's already two o'clock. Call Siro, send the potion to Master Nicia, and wait for me in the house. I'll go for the friar; make him disguise himself and bring him here; we'll find the doctor and do what remains to do.

Callimaco: You are right. Go ahead.

SCENE III—Callimaco and Siro

Callimaco: O, Siro.

Siro: Master.

Callimaco: Come here.

Siro: Here I am.

Callimaco: Take the silver goblet that is in the wardrobe of my room and cover it with a piece of cloth and bring it here; and see that you don't spill any on the way.

Siro: It shall be done.

Callimaco: That fellow has been ten years with me and always served me faithfully. I believe I can trust him in this affair as well; and though I have not told him of this plot, he guesses it and how bad it is, and is getting used to the idea.

124 Siro: Here it is.

Callimaco: Good, here, go to Messer Nicia's house and tell him that this is the medicine that the lady has to take right after dinner, and the sooner after dinner the better: and that we'll be there at his corner at the appointed time, and see that you are there. Be off.

Siro: I'm off.

Callimaco: Mind this: if he wants you to wait for him, wait and bring him here with you; if he does not wish it, come back here, after you've given it to him and carried out your mission.

Siro: Yes, sir.

SCENE IV—Callimaco alone

Callimaco: I'm waiting for Ligurio to come back with the friar: and anybody that says waiting is a hard lot tells the truth. I'm losing ten pounds to the minute thinking where I am now and where I might be two hours from now, fearing that something may turn up that will spoil my plot. If it should, this would be the last night of my life, for I would throw myself into the Arno, or hang myself, or throw myself out of that window, or stab myself with this knife on her doorstep: something to end my life. But I see Ligurio. He has some one with him who looks lame, hunchbacked, and must surely be the friar disguised. Oh these friars, you know one and you know all. Who is the other one with them? It looks like Siro, who has finished his mission to the doctor; it is. I will wait here to join them.

SCENE V—Siro, Ligurio, Timoteo, disguised, and Callimaco

Siro: Who's with you, Ligurio?

Ligurio: A worthy man.

Siro: Is he lame or just pretending?

Ligurio: Mind your own business.

Siro: Oh, he's got the face of a great carouser.

Ligurio: Shut up, you've already tired us out! Where's Callimaco?

Callimaco: Here I am. You are happily come.

Ligurio: O Callimaco, look after this fool Siro, he's already said a thousand crazy things.

Callimaco: Siro, look here. This evening you've got to do everything Ligurio tells you; and take account, when I order you, who I am. And what you see, feel, and hear you must keep most secret, as you value property, honor, my life and your own good.

Siro: So I will.

Callimaco: Did you give the goblet to the doctor?

125 Siro: Yes, sir.

Callimaco: What did he say?

Siro: That all will be ready.

Timoteo: Is this Callimaco?

Callimaco: I'm at your service! You may dispose of me and of my goods as if it were yourself.

Timoteo: I have heard so and I believe it; and I am moved to do for you what I would do for no other man in the world.

Callimaco: You will lose nothing by your pains.

Timoteo: Your good will is enough.

Ligurio: Let's leave off ceremony. We'll go disguise ourselves, Siro and I. Callimaco, you come with us and get yourself ready; the friar will wait here: we'll return at once and go find Master Nicia.

Callimaco: Let's go.

Timoteo: I'll wait for you.

SCENE VI—Timoteo alone

Timoteo: They are not without good grounds who say that bad company leads men to the gallows; and many times an evil piece of business may be too easy and too good, just as it may be too wicked. God knows I had no thought of hurting anybody; I was in my cell saying my office, I was making my devotions, and along comes this devil of a Ligurio and makes me stick a finger in a sin, and from that I have put in an arm and then my whole person, and I don't know yet what I'm into. One comfort I have: when anything is important to many people many people look after it. But here are Ligurio and the servant coming back.

SCENE VII—Timoteo, Ligurio and Siro, disguised

Timoteo: You are welcome.

Ligurio: Are we going well?

Timoteo: Very well.

Ligurio: We need the doctor still: let's go toward his house. It's growing late, come.

Siro: Who is it opening his door? Is it the servant?

Ligurio: No, it's he. Ah, ah, ah, ah!

Siro: You are laughing.

Ligurio: Who wouldn't laugh? He has a big cloak on him that doesn't cover his behind. What the devil has he on his head? It looks like a monk's hood; and a small sword somewhere. Ah, ah! He's mumbling I don't know what. Let's step aside, and we'll hear some ill fortune of his wife.

SCENE VIII—Nicia disguised

Nicia: How many grimaces this crazy piece of mine has made!
She has sent the servant to her mother's house and the maid to
the farm. I praise her for that, but I don't praise her for making
so many difficulties before she would go to bed. I don't want to—
how shall I do such—what are you making me do—oh, alas, oh
mamma— If her mother had not scolded her she would not have
gone to bed at all. Plague take her! I like to see a woman modest
but not so modest as this: what is it that's turned her head, this
cat's brain of hers! Well I know what I'm about. I'm in high style.
Who'd know me now? I seem bigger, younger, trimmer; and
there's not a woman in the world would take any money for going
to bed with me. But where shall I find them?

SCENE IX—Ligurio, Nicia, Timoteo and Siro

Ligurio: Good evening, Master Nicia.

Nicia: Oi, oi!

Ligurio: Have no fear, we are we.

Nicia: Oh, you are all here! If I hadn't known you before I'd have
given you a crack with this stick as hard as I could. You are
Ligurio? and you Siro? and the other is the master? Ah!

Ligurio: Yes, sir.

Nicia: Look how well he's disguised, nobody would ever know him.

Ligurio: He has put two nuts in his mouth so that his voice won't
be recognized.

Nicia: You're a numskull.

Ligurio: Why?

Nicia: Why didn't you tell me so at first; I could have put in two
of them also. You know how much it matters that your speech
shouldn't be known.

Ligurio: Here, put this in your mouth.

Nicia: What is it?

Ligurio: A ball of wax.

Nicia: Give it here. Ca, pu, ca, co, co, cu, cu, spu! What's this, you
fool?

Ligurio: Oh, pardon me, please do, I've exchanged them without
noticing it.

Nicia: Ca, ca, pu, pu. What—what, what, was it?

Ligurio: Aloes.

Nicia: Curse you! spu, spu! Master, you say nothing.

Timoteo: Ligurio has angered me.

127 Nicia: Oh, how well you disguise your voice!

Ligurio: Let's not lose more time here. I'll be the captain and give the army orders for the day. At the right corner Callimaco will be stationed; at the left I; between the two corners will be the doctor here; Siro will be the rear guard, to succor any band that weakens. The password will be San Cucu.

Nicia: Who is San Cucu?

Ligurio: The most honored saint to be found in France. Come, let's put the ambush at this corner. Listen, I hear a lute.

Nicia: It is one. What are we going to do?

Ligurio: First send a scout to see who it is; and when he brings word, act accordingly.

Nicia: Who'll go?

Ligurio: You go, Siro. You know what you must do, observe, examine, come back quickly, bring news.

Siro: I'm off.

Nicia: I don't want to catch a crab who might be some old man weak and puny; so that we'd have to play this game all over again to-morrow night.

Ligurio: Don't worry, Siro has a head on him. Here he is back. What did you find, Siro?

Siro: It's the finest lad you ever saw. He is not twenty-five, and he comes along alone in a cloak, playing his lute.

Nicia: He's the one surely, if you are telling the truth. But look out that your soup is not thrown in your face.

Siro: He's just what I told you.

Ligurio: Let's wait till he has finished his song, and suddenly be on his back.

Nicia: See here, master, you are like a dumb statue. There he is.

Callimaco: "May the devil come to bed with you
      Since there may not come I."

Ligurio: Halt! Give over the lute.

Callimaco: Alas! What have I done?

Nicia: You'll see. Cover his head, gag him.

Ligurio: Surround him.

Nicia: Hit him again, hit him again, put him in the house.

Timoteo: Master Nicia, I'm going to bed, I've such a headache, that I'm about to die. And if you don't need me I'll not return to-morrow morning.

Nicia: Yes, Master, don't come back; we can manage among ourselves.

SCENE x—Timoteo alone

Timoteo: They are shut up in the house and I'll go to the convent. And you, spectators, don't wait, because to-night nobody will sleep; so that these deeds be not disturbed. I'll say the office. Ligurio and Siro will sup, for they have not eaten to-day. The doctor will go from room to room to see that all is tidy. Callimaco and Donna Lucrezia will not sleep; for I know if I were he and you were she that we should not sleep.

SONG

O sweet night, O blessed and silent hours of night,
Be with desirous lovers;
In you is such delight
You are the source the happy soul discovers;
You give a just reward
To the amorous hosts
For trials long and hard;
You light, O happy hours, and move
In every frozen breast the flame of love.

ACT FIVE

SCENE I—Timoteo alone

Timoteo: All night I couldn't close my eyes, so great was my desire to hear how Callimaco and the rest have come out; I tried to pass the time with other matters. I said matins, read a life of the blessed fathers; went to church and lit a lamp that had gone out; put a veil on a miraculous Madonna. How many times have I said to these friars to keep her clean. It's no wonder there's little devotion. I can remember when she had five hundred images, wax, silver and what not, at her feet and all around, and what have we to-day? about twenty. We are to blame for it for not keeping up her reputation. Every evening after benediction we used to make a procession and every Saturday sing in praise of her. People were always making us offerings here because they saw fresh images; and in confession we prevailed on many men and women to make offerings. Now there's nothing like that, and is it any wonder that things get cold? Oh, how little sense these friars of mine have! But I hear a hubbub in Master Nicia's house. Faith, there he is, and they are bringing out the prisoner. I'll go join them. They're taking a long time about it and day is break-ing. I'd like to hear what they say without their seeing me.

SCENE II—Nicia, Callimaco, Ligurio and Siro

Nicia: You hold him there and I'll hold him here, and, Siro, you catch him by the seat behind.

Callimaco: Don't hurt me.

Ligurio: Don't be afraid, run for it.

Nicia: Let's go no farther.

Ligurio: That's right. Let him go here. Turn him round twice, so that he won't know where he comes from. Turn him, Siro.

Siro: There.

Nicia: Turn him once again.

Siro: There.

Callimaco: My lute.

Ligurio: Go, you rake, if I hear you speak I'll cut your throat.

Nicia: He's fled. Let's go take off this stuff, and it would be a good thing too to be abroad early, so that we won't seem to have been up all night.

Ligurio: That's right.

Nicia: Go, Siro, and find Master Callimaco, and tell him that the plot carried well.

Ligurio: What can we say to him? We know nothing. You know that once inside the house, we went in the pantry to have a drink. You and the mother-in-law had him on your hands, and we never saw you again until now, when you called us to help you put him out.

Nicia: That's true. Oh! I've fine things to tell you. My wife was in bed in the dark. Sostrata waited for me at the fire. I went on with our fine lad, and so as to leave nothing overlooked, I took him into a pantry that I have in the hall, where there was a dim light, so that he couldn't see my face.

Ligurio: Quite rightly.

Nicia: I made him strip. He was whining, I snarling at him like a dog. He is ugly in the face. He had a big nose, a twisted mouth; but you never saw such beautiful flesh! White, soft, smooth, and about the rest don't ask me.

Ligurio: That's not the way to talk, you ought to have seen everything.

Nicia: You're pulling my leg. Since I'd put my hand in the dish I wanted to go to the bottom of it: I wanted to see if he was healthy. If he'd had some disease, where would I have been? What would have happened to me?

Ligurio: You are right.

Nicia: When I had seen that he was all right, I put him behind me and in the dark I led him into the room. I put him to bed and then left, feeling my way along the wall with my hands, for I'm not used to having lightning bugs for lanterns.

Ligurio: With what prudence you've managed everything!

Nicia: I groped along and then left the room, shut the door, and went to my mother-in-law, who was in the kitchen; and we have waited all night talking.

Ligurio: What did you talk about?

Nicia: About the stupidity of Lucrezia and how much better it would have been if without so much winding about she had yielded at first. Then we talked of the baby till I seemed to have the little boy in my arms. As soon as I heard it strike one, and fearing daylight might overtake us, I went into the room. And would you believe it I couldn't make that clown get up.

Ligurio: I believe it.

Nicia: He liked his medicine. However, he got up; I called you and we brought him out.

Ligurio: It has all gone well.

Nicia: Should I be sorry do you think?

Ligurio: Of what?

Nicia: Because that poor young fellow has to die so soon and this night cost him so dear.

Ligurio: Oh! you needn't trouble your thoughts with that; that's his affair.

Nicia: But I seem to be a thousand years finding Master Callimaco, so as to rejoice with him.

Ligurio: He'll be abroad in an hour. But the day is beginning to break. We are going to strip these off, what are you going to do?

Nicia: I'm going into the house too and put on my good clothes. I'll make my wife get up and bathe and make her come to church to be shriven. I'd like you and Callimaco to be there so that we can speak to the friar and thank him and reward him for the good turn he's done us.

Ligurio: Good, it shall be done.

SCENE III—Timoteo alone

Timoteo: I've heard what they said and am pleased, considering what a fool this doctor is. But his last decision most of all has delighted me; they ought to be coming by now; I'd rather not wait any longer here but in the church where my merchandise is of more worth. But who's coming out of that house? It looks to me like Ligurio and with him that must be Callimaco. I don't want them to see me for reasons said. However, if they don't come to find me I'll always be ready to go find them.

SCENE IV—Callimaco and Ligurio

Callimaco: When I made myself known to her and had given her to understand how much I loved her, and how easily through the simplicity of her husband we could live happily and without scandal; promising her that whenever it should please God to remove him, I would take her for my wife; and she having tasted what a difference there is between my company and that of Master Nicia and between the kisses of a young lover and those of an old husband; she with a sigh said: "Since through your shrewdness and the folly of my husband, the simplicity of my mother and the baseness of my confessor, I have been led to do what of myself I should never have done, I shall judge that it comes through the will of heaven, which would have it so; and it is not for me to refuse what heaven wills me to accept. Therefore I take you for lord, master and guide. You shall be my father, my defender, my every good; and what my husband has wished for an evening I wish him to have always. Make a friend of him then and come to dine with us; to go or stay as you like; and we can always and without suspicion be together." I could have died of the sweetness of these words. I could not answer her a hundredth of what I should have liked to say. So that I am the happiest and most contented man that was ever in the world; and if this happiness does not fail me through death or through time I shall be more blessed than the blest, more holy than the saints.

Ligurio: I take great pleasure in any good fortune of yours; and exactly what I said has happened to you. But what shall we do now?

Callimaco: Let's go on toward the church, for I've promised to be there and you will see her, her mother and the doctor.

Ligurio: I hear his door opening: it's they and they are coming out with the doctor behind them.

Callimaco: Let's go into the church and wait for them there.

SCENE V—Nicia, Lucrezia and Sostrata

Nicia: Lucrezia, I believe it's well to do things with the fear of God and not wildly.

Lucrezia: What must we do now?

Nicia: Look how she answers! Like the cock of the roost.

Sostrata: Don't be surprised, she's a little upset.

Lucrezia. What do you want to say?

132 Nicia: I say it's well that I'm going ahead to speak to the friar and

to tell him that you will meet him at the church door to be blessed; for this morning it's just as if you had been born again.

Lucrezia: Why don't you go?

Nicia: You are very bold this morning. Last night she seemed quite dead.

Lucrezia: It's thanks to you.

Sostrata: Go find the friar. But there's no need, he's coming out of the church.

Nicia: So he is.

SCENE VI—Timoteo, Nicia, Lucrezia, Callimaco, Ligurio and Sostrata

Timoteo: I'm coming out because Callimaco and Ligurio have told me that the doctor and the ladies are coming to church.

Nicia: Bona dies, father.

Timoteo: You are welcome; and may God bless you, my lady, and give you a fine boy.

Lucrezia: May God grant—

Timoteo: He will grant it by all means.

Nicia: I see Ligurio and Master Callimaco in the church.

Timoteo: Yes, Messer Nicia.

Nicia: Beckon to them.

Timoteo: They are coming.

Callimaco: God save you.

Nicia: Master, put your hand here on my wife.

Callimaco: Willingly.

Nicia: Lucrezia, this is he who will be the cause of our having a staff to prop our old age.

Lucrezia: I hold him very dear and should like him to be our friend.

Nicia: Now bless you! And I want him and Ligurio to come and dine with us this morning.

Lucrezia: By all means.

Nicia: I'm going to give them the key to the ground room on to the loggia, that they may make themselves at home there as suits their convenience, for they have no woman at home and live like the beasts.

Callimaco: I accept it and will use it when I have need of it.

Timoteo: I must have money for charity!

Nicia: Be sure, domine, it will be sent you to-day.

Ligurio: And Siro, shall he not be remembered?

Nicia: Let him but ask, what I have is his. You, Lucrezia, how many groats must you give the friar to be purified?

133 Lucrezia: Give him ten.

Nicia: Smotheration!

Timoteo: You, Donna Sostrata, as for you, it seems to me, you've
put new sprouts on your old stem.

Sostrata: Who wouldn't be happy?

Timoteo: All of you go in the church and we'll say there the usual
prayer: then after the office you go home to dinner. You, spectators, don't wait for us to come out: the office is long, and I shall
remain in church; and they'll go home by the side entrance. Farewell.

The Prince

Translated by Ninian Hill Thomson

Chapter *Of those who by crime come to be Princes.*   But since from privacy
Eight a man may also rise to be a Prince in one or other of two ways,
neither of which can be ascribed wholly either to valour or to fortune, it is fit that I notice them here, though one of them may fall to
be discussed more fully in treating of Republics.

The ways I speak of are, first, when the ascent to power is made
by paths of wickedness and crime, and second, when a private
person becomes ruler of his country by the favour of his fellow-
citizens. The former method I shall make clear by two examples, one
ancient, the other modern, without entering further into the merits
of the matter, for these, I think, should be enough for any one who
is constrained to follow them.

Agathocles the Sicilian came, not merely from a private station,
but from the very dregs of the people, to be a King of Syracuse.
Son of a potter, through all the stages of his career he led an evil
life. His vices, however, were conjoined with so much vigour both
of mind and body, that enlisting as a common soldier, he rose
through the various grades of the service to be Praetor of Syracuse.
Established in that post, he resolved to make himself Prince, and
to hold by violence and without obligation to others the authority
which had been by consent entrusted to him. Accordingly, after
imparting his design to Hamilcar, who with the Carthaginian armies
was at that time waging war in Sicily, he one morning assembled
the people and senate of Syracuse as though to consult with them
on matters of public moment, and on a preconcerted signal caused
his soldiers to put to death all the senators, and the wealthiest of
134 the commons. These being thus disposed of, he seized and retained

the sovereignty of the city without opposition from the people; and though twice defeated by the Carthaginians, and afterwards besieged, he was able not only to defend his city, but leaving a part of his forces for its protection, to invade Africa with the remainder, and so in a short time to raise the siege of Syracuse, reducing the Carthaginians to the utmost extremities, and compelling them to make terms whereby they resigned Sicily to him and confined themselves to Africa.

Whoever examines this man's actions and achievements will discover little or nothing in them that can be ascribed to Fortune, seeing, as has already been said, that it was not through the favour of any one, but by the regular steps of the military service, gained at the cost of a thousand hardships and hazards, he reached the Princedom which he afterwards maintained by so many daring and dangerous exploits. Still, to slaughter fellow-citizens, to betray friends, to be devoid of honour, pity, and religion, cannot be counted as merits, for these are means that may lead to power, but confer no glory. Wherefore, if in respect of the valour wherewith he encountered and extricated himself from dangers, and the constancy of his spirit in supporting and conquering adverse fortune, there seems no reason to judge him inferior to the greatest captains that have ever lived, his unbridled cruelty and inhumanity, together with his countless other crimes, forbid us to number him with the greatest men; but, at any rate, we cannot attribute to Fortune or to merit what he accomplished without either.

In our own times, during the papacy of Alexander VI, Oliverotto of Fermo, who, left an orphan some years before, had been brought up by his maternal uncle Giovanni Fogliani, was sent while still a lad to serve under Paolo Vitelli, in order that a thorough training under that commander might qualify him for high rank as a soldier. After the death of Paolo, he served under his brother Vitellozzo, and in a very short time, being of a quick wit, hardy and resolute, he became one of the first soldiers of his company. But thinking it beneath him to serve under others, with the countenance of the Vitelleschi and the connivance of certain citizens of Fermo who preferred the slavery to the freedom of their country, he formed the design to seize on that town.

He accordingly wrote to Giovanni Fogliani that after many years of absence from home, he desired to see him and his native city once more, and to look a little into the condition of his patrimony; and as his one endeavour had been to make himself a name, in order that his fellow-citizens might see his time had not been mis-spent, he proposed to return honourably attended by a hundred horsemen from among his own friends and followers; and he begged Giovanni

135

graciously to arrange for his reception by the citizens of Fermo with corresponding marks of distinction, as this would be creditable not only to himself, but also to the uncle who had brought him up.

Giovanni, accordingly, did not fail in any proper attention to his nephew, but caused him to be splendidly received by his fellow-citizens, and lodged him in his house; where Oliverotto having passed some days, and made the necessary arrangements for carrying out his wickedness, gave a sumptuous banquet, to which he invited his uncle and all the first men of Fermo. When the repast and other entertainment proper to such an occasion had come to an end, Oliverotto artfully turned the conversation to matters of grave interest, by speaking of the greatness of Pope Alexander and Cesare his son, and of their enterprises; and when Giovanni and the others were replying to what he said, he suddenly rose, observing that these were matters to be discussed in a more private place, and so withdrew to another chamber; whither his uncle and the other citizens followed him, and where they no sooner seated themselves, than soldiers rushing out from places of concealment slew Giovanni and all the others.

After this butchery, Oliverotto mounting his horse, rode through the streets, and besieged the chief magistrate in the palace, so that all were constrained by fear to yield obedience and accept a government of which he had made himself the head. And all who from being disaffected were likely to stand in his way, he put to death, while he strengthened himself with new ordinances, civil and military, to such purpose, that for the space of a year during which he retained the Princedom, he not merely remained safe in Fermo, but grew formidable to all his neighbours. And it would have been as difficult to unseat him as to unseat Agathocles, had he not let himself be overreached by Cesare Borgia on the occasion when, as has already been told, the Orsini and Vitelli were entrapped at Sinigaglia; where he too being taken, one year after the commission of his parricidal crime, was strangled along with Vitellozzo, who had been his master in villainy as in valour.

It may be asked how it came that Agathocles and some like him, after numberless acts of treachery and cruelty, were able to live long in their own country in safety, and defend themselves from foreign enemies, without being conspired against by their fellow-citizens, whereas, many others, by reason of their cruelty, have failed to maintain their position even in peaceful times, not to speak of the perilous times of war. I believe that this results from cruelty being well or ill employed. Those cruelties we may say are well employed, if it be permitted to speak well of things evil, which are
136 done once for all as necessary for your security, and are not after-

wards persisted in, but so far as possible modified to the advantage of the governed. Ill-employed cruelties, on the other hand, are those which from small beginnings increase rather than diminish with time. They who follow the first of these methods, may, by the grace of God and man, find, as did Agathocles, that their condition is not desperate; but by no possibility can the others maintain themselves.

Hence we may learn the lesson that on seizing a State, the usurper should bethink him of all the injuries he must inflict, and inflict them all at a stroke, that he may not have to renew them daily, but be enabled by their discontinuance to reassure men's minds, and win them by benefits. Whosoever, either through timidity or from follow-ing bad counsels, acts otherwise, must keep the sword always drawn, and can put no trust in his subjects, who suffering from continued and constantly renewed severities, can never feel sure of him. Injuries, therefore, should be inflicted all at once, that their ill savour being less lasting may less offend; whereas, benefits should be conferred little by little, that so they may be more fully relished.

But, before all things, a Prince should so live with his subjects that no vicissitude for better or worse shall cause him to alter his behaviour; for if the need to change come through adversity, it is too late to resort to severity; and any leniency you may then use will be thrown away, since it will be seen to be compulsory and bring you no thanks.

Chapter *How many different kinds of soldiers there are, and of mercenaries.*
Twelve I have already said that a Prince must lay solid foundations, since otherwise he will inevitably be destroyed. Now the main foundations of all States, whether new, old, or mixed, are good laws and good arms. But since you cannot have the former without the latter, and where you have the latter, are likely to have the former, I shall here omit all discussion concerning laws, and speak only of arms.

I say then that the arms wherewith a Prince defends his State are either his own subjects, or they are mercenaries, or they are auxiliaries, or they are partly one and partly another. Mercenaries and auxiliaries are at once useless and dangerous, and he who holds his State by means of mercenary troops can never be solidly or securely seated. For these troops are disunited, ambitious, in-subordinate, treacherous, insolent among friends, cowardly before foes, without fear of God or faith with man. No sooner are you attacked than they fail you; so that in peace you are plundered by them, in war by your enemies. And this because they have no tie or incitement to keep them in the field beyond the pittance you pay them, in return for which it would be too much to expect them
137 to give their lives. They are willing enough, therefore, to be your

soldiers while you are at peace, but when war is declared they make off and disappear. I ought to have little difficulty in getting this believed, for the present ruin of Italy is due to no other cause than her having for many years relied on mercenaries, who though heretofore they may have helped the fortunes of some one man, and made a brave show when matched one against another, have always revealed themselves in their true colours so soon as a foreign enemy appeared. Hence it came that Charles of France was suffered to conquer Italy with chalk; and he who said our sins were the cause, said truly, though it was not the sins he meant, but those that I have noticed. And as these were the sins of Princes, it is they who have paid the penalty.

Chapter *Of Cruelty and Clemency, and whether it is better to be Loved or* Seven- *Feared.* Passing to the other qualities above mentioned, I say that teen every Prince should desire to be accounted merciful and not cruel. Nevertheless, he should be careful not to abuse this quality of mercy. Cesare Borgia was reputed cruel, yet his cruelty restored Romagna, united it, and brought it to order and obedience: so that if we look at things in their true light, it will be seen that he was in reality far more merciful than the people of Florence, who, to avoid the imputation of cruelty, suffered Pistoja to be destroyed by factions.

A Prince should therefore disregard the reproach of cruelty where it enables him to keep his subjects united and faithful. For he who quells disorder by a very few signal examples will in the end be more merciful than he who from excessive leniency suffers things to take their course and so result in rapine and bloodshed; for these hurt the entire State, whereas the severities of the Prince injure individuals only.

And for a new Prince, above all others, it is impossible to escape a name for cruelty, since new States are full of dangers. Wherefore Virgil, by the mouth of Dido:—

'Res dura et regni novitas me talia cogunt
Moliri, et late fines custode tueri.'[1]

Nevertheless, the new Prince should not be too ready of belief, nor too easily set in motion; nor should he himself be the first to raise alarms; but should so temper prudence with kindliness that too great confidence in others shall not throw him off his guard, nor groundless distrust render him insupportable.

And here comes in the question whether it is better to be loved

[1]'A fate unkind, and newness in my reign
Compell me thus to guard a wide domain.'

rather than feared, or feared rather than loved. It might be answered that we should wish to be both; but since love and fear can hardly exist together, if we must choose between them, it is far safer to be feared than loved. For of men it may generally be affirmed that they are thankless, fickle, false, studious to avoid danger, greedy of gain, devoted to you while you confer benefits upon them, and ready, as I said before, while the need is remote, to shed their blood, and sacrifice their property, their lives, and their children for you; but when it comes near they turn against you. The Prince, therefore, who without otherwise securing himself builds wholly on their professions is undone. For the friendships we buy with a price, and do not gain by greatness and nobility of character, though fairly earned are not made good, but fail us when we need them most.

Moreover, men are less careful how they offend him who makes himself loved than him who makes himself feared. For love is held by the tie of obligation, which, because men are a sorry breed, is broken on every prompting of self-interest; but fear is bound by the apprehension of punishment which never loosens its grasp.

Nevertheless a Prince should inspire fear in suchwise that if he do not win love he may escape hate. For a man may very well be feared and yet not hated, as will always be the case so long as he does not intermeddle with the property or with the women of his citizens and subjects. And if constrained to put any one to death, he should do so only when there is manifest cause or reasonable justification. But, above all, he must abstain from the property of others. For men will sooner forget the death of their father than the loss of their patrimony. Moreover, pretexts for confiscation are never to seek, and he who has once begun to live by rapine always finds reasons for taking what is not his; whereas reasons for shedding blood are fewer, and sooner exhausted.

But when a Prince is with his army, and has many soldiers under his command, he must entirely disregard the reproach of cruelty, for without such a reputation in its Captain, no army can be held together or kept ready for every emergency. Among other things remarkable in Hannibal this has been noted, that having a very great army, made up of men of many different nations and brought to serve in a foreign country, no dissension ever arose among the soldiers themselves, nor any mutiny against their leader, either in his good or in his evil fortunes. This we can only ascribe to the transcendent cruelty, which, joined with numberless great qualities, rendered him at once venerable and terrible in the eyes of his soldiers; for without this reputation for cruelty his other virtues would not have effected the like results.

139   Unreflecting writers, indeed, while praising his achievements,

have condemned the chief cause of them; but that his other merits would not by themselves have been so efficacious we may see from the case of Scipio, one of the greatest Captains, not of his own time only but of all times whereof we have record, whose armies rose against him in Spain from no other cause than his excessive leniency in allowing them freedoms inconsistent with military discipline. With which weakness Fabius Maximus taxed him in the Senate House, calling him the corrupter of the Roman soldiery. Again, when the Locrians were shamefully outraged by one of his lieutenants, he neither avenged them, nor punished the insolence of his officer; and this from the natural easiness of his disposition. So that it was said in the Senate by one who sought to excuse him, that there were many who knew better how to refrain from doing wrong themselves than how to correct the wrong-doing of others. This temper, however, must in time have marred the name and fame even of Scipio, had he continued in it, and retained his command. But living as he did under the control of the Senate, this hurtful quality was not merely veiled, but came to be regarded as a glory.

Returning to the question of being loved or feared, I sum up by saying, that since his being loved depends upon his subjects, while his being feared depends upon himself, a wise Prince should build on what is his own, and not on what rests with others. Only, as I have said, he must do his best to escape hatred.

Chapter Eight-een *How Princes should keep faith.* Every one recognises how praise-worthy it is in a Prince to keep faith, and to act uprightly and not craftily. Nevertheless, we see from what has happened in our own days that Princes who have set little store by their word, but have known how to over-reach others by their cunning, have accomplished great things, and in the end had the better of those who trusted to honest dealing.

Be it known, then, that there are two ways of contending, one in accordance with the laws, the other by force; the first of which is proper to men, the second to beasts. But since the first method is often ineffectual, it becomes necessary to resort to the second. A Prince should, therefore, understand how to use well both the man and the beast. And this lesson has been covertly taught by the ancient writers, who relate how Achilles and many others of these old Princes were given over to be brought up and trained by Chiron the Centaur; since the only meaning of their having for teacher one who was half man and half beast is, that it is necessary for a Prince to know how to use both natures, and that the one without the other has no stability.

But since a Prince should know how to use the beast's nature wisely, he ought of beasts to use both the lion and the fox; for the lion cannot guard himself from the toils, nor the fox from wolves. He must therefore be a fox to discern toils, and a lion to drive off wolves.

To rely wholly on the lion is unwise; and for this reason a prudent Prince neither can nor ought to keep his word when to keep it is hurtful to him and the causes which led him to pledge it are removed. If all men were good, this would not be good advice, but since they are dishonest and do not keep faith with you, you, in return, need not keep faith with them; and no Prince was ever at a loss for plausible reasons to cloak a breach of faith. Of this numberless recent instances could be given, and it might be shown how many solemn treaties and engagements have been rendered inoperative and idle through want of faith in Princes, and that he who has best known to play the fox has had the best success.

It is necessary, indeed, to put a good colour on this nature, and to be skilful in feigning and dissembling. But men are so simple, and governed so absolutely by their present needs, that he who wishes to deceive will never fail in finding willing dupes. One recent example I will not omit. Pope Alexander VI had no care or thought but how to deceive, and always found material to work on. No man ever had a more effective manner of asseverating, or made promises with more solemn protestations, or observed them less. And yet, because he understood this side of human nature, his frauds always succeeded.

It is not essential, then, that a Prince should have all the good qualities I have enumerated above, but it is most essential that he should seem to have them. Nay, I will venture to affirm that if he has and invariably practises them all, they are hurtful, whereas the appearance of having them is useful. Thus, it is well to seem merciful, faithful, humane, religious, and upright, and also to be so; but the mind should remain so balanced that were it needful not to be so, you should be able and know how to change to the contrary.

And you are to understand that a Prince, and most of all a new Prince, cannot observe all those rules of conduct in respect whereof men are accounted good, being often forced, in order to preserve his Princedom, to act in opposition to good faith, charity, humanity, and religion. He must therefore keep his mind ready to shift as the winds and tides of Fortune turn, and, as I have already said, ought not to quit good courses if he can help it, but should know how to follow evil if he must.

A Prince should therefore be very careful that nothing ever escapes his lips which is not replete with the five qualities above named, so that to see and hear him, one would think him the embodiment of mercy, good faith, integrity, kindliness, and religion. And there is no virtue which it is more necessary for him to seem to possess than this last; because men in general judge rather by the eye than by the hand, for all can see but few can touch. Every one sees what you seem, but few know what you are, and these few dare not oppose themselves to the opinion of the many who have the majesty of the State to back them up.

Moreover, in the actions of all men, and most of all of Princes, where there is no tribunal to which we can appeal, we look to results. Wherefore if a Prince succeeds in establishing and maintaining his authority, the means will always be judged honourable and be approved by every one. For the vulgar are always taken by appearances and by results, and the world is made up of the vulgar, the few only finding room when the many have no longer ground to stand on.

A certain Prince of our own days, whom it is as well not to name, is always preaching peace and good faith, although the mortal enemy of both; and both, had he practised as he preaches, would, oftener than once, have lost him his kingdom and authority.

Discourses on the First Decade of Titus Livius
Translated by Ninian Hill Thomson

Preface Albeit the jealous temper of mankind, ever more disposed to censure than to praise the work of others, has constantly made the pursuit of new methods and systems no less perilous than the search after unknown lands and seas; nevertheless, prompted by that desire which nature has implanted in me, fearlessly to undertake whatsoever I think offers a common benefit to all, I enter on a path which, being hitherto untrodden by any, though it involve me in trouble and fatigue, may yet win me thanks from those who judge my efforts in a friendly spirit. And although my feeble discernment, my slender experience of current affairs, and imperfect knowledge of ancient events, render these efforts of mine defective and of no great utility, they may at least open the way to some other, who, with better parts and sounder reasoning and judgment, shall carry out my design; whereby, if I gain no credit, at all events I ought to incur no blame.

142   When I see antiquity held in such reverence, that, to omit other

instances, the mere fragment of some ancient statue is often bought at a great price, in order that the purchaser may keep it by him to adorn his house, or to have it copied by those who take delight in this art; and how these, again, strive with all their skill to imitate it in their various works; and when, on the other hand, I find those noble labours which history shows to have been wrought on behalf of the monarchies and republics of old times, by kings, captains, citizens, lawgivers, and others who have toiled for the good of their country, rather admired than followed, nay, so absolutely renounced by every one that not a trace of that antique worth is now left among us, I cannot but at once marvel and grieve at this incon- sistency; and all the more because I perceive that, in civil disputes between citizens, and in the bodily disorders into which men fall, recourse is always had to the decisions and remedies, pronounced or prescribed by the ancients.

For the civil law is no more than the opinions delivered by the ancient jurisconsults, which, being reduced to system, teach the jurisconsults of our own times how to determine; while the healing art is simply the recorded experience of the old physicians, on which our modern physicians found their practice. And yet, in giving laws to a commonwealth, in maintaining States and governing kingdoms, in organizing armies and conducting wars, in dealing with subject nations, and in extending a State's dominions, we find no prince, no republic, no captain, and no citizen who resorts to the example of the ancients.

This I persuade myself is due, not so much to the feebleness to which the present methods of education have brought the world, or to the injury which a pervading apathy has wrought in many provinces and cities of Christendom, as to the want of a right in- telligence of History, which renders men incapable in reading it to extract its true meaning or to relish its flavour. Whence it happens that by far the greater number of those who read History, take pleasure in following the variety of incidents which it presents, without a thought to imitate them; judging such imitation to be not only difficult but impossible; as though the heavens, the sun, the elements, and man himself were no longer the same as they formerly were as regards motion, order, and power.

Desiring to rescue men from this error, I have thought fit to note down with respect to all those books of Titus Livius which have escaped the malignity of Time, whatever seems to me essential to a right understanding of ancient and modern affairs; so that any who shall read these remarks of mine, may reap from them that profit for the sake of which a knowledge of History is to be sought. And although the task be arduous, still, with the help of those

143

at whose instance I assumed the burthen, I hope to carry it forward so far, that another shall have no long way to go to bring it to its destination.

Of the various kinds of Government; and to which of them the Roman Commonwealth belonged. I forego all discussion concerning those cities which at the outset have been dependent upon others, and shall speak only of those which from their earliest beginnings have stood entirely clear of all foreign control, being governed from the first as pleased themselves, whether as republics or as princedoms.

These as they have had different origins, so likewise have had different laws and institutions. For to some at their very first commencement, or not long after, laws have been given by a single legislator, and all at one time; like those given by Lycurgus to the Spartans, while to others they have been given at different times, as need rose or accident determined; as in the case of Rome. That republic, indeed, may be called happy, whose lot has been to have a founder so prudent as to provide for it laws under which it can continue to live securely, without need to amend them; as we find Sparta preserving hers for eight hundred years, without deterioration and without any dangerous disturbance. On the other hand, some measure of unhappiness attaches to the State which, not having yielded itself once for all into the hands of a single wise legislator, is obliged to recast its institutions for itself; and of such States, by far the most unhappy is that which is furthest removed from a sound system of government, by which I mean that its institutions lie wholly outside the path which might lead it to a true and perfect end. For it is scarcely possible that a State in this position can ever, by any chance, set itself to rights; whereas another whose institutions are imperfect, if it have made a good beginning and such as admits of its amendment, may in the course of events arrive at perfection. It is certain, however, that such States can never be reformed without great risk; for, as a rule, men will accept no new law altering the institutions of their State, unless the necessity for such a change be demonstrated; and since this necessity cannot arise without danger, the State may easily be overthrown before the new order of things is established. In proof whereof we may instance the republic of Florence, which was reformed in the year 1502, in consequence of the affair of Arezzo, but was ruined in 1512, in consequence of the affair of Prato.

144   Desiring, therefore, to discuss the nature of the government of

Rome, and to ascertain the accidental circumstances which brought it to its perfection, I say, as has been said before by many who have written of Governments, that of these there are three forms, known by the names Monarchy, Aristocracy, and Democracy, and that those who give its institutions to a State have recourse to one or other of these three, according as it suits their purpose. Other, and, as many have thought, wiser teachers, will have it, that there are altogether six forms of Government, three of them utterly bad, the other three good in themselves, but so readily corrupted that they too are apt to become hurtful. The good are the three above named; the bad, three others dependent upon these, and each so like that to which it is related, that it is easy to pass imperceptibly from the one to the other. For a Monarchy readily becomes a Tyranny, an Aristocracy an Oligarchy, while a Democracy tends to degenerate into Anarchy. So that if the founder of a State should establish any one of these three forms of Government, he establishes it for a short time only, since no precaution he may take can prevent it from sliding into its contrary, by reason of the close resemblance which, in this case, the virtue bears to the vice.

These diversities in the form of Government spring up among men by chance. For in the beginning of the world, its inhabitants, being few in number, for a time lived scattered after the fashion of beasts; but afterwards, as they increased and multiplied, gathered themselves into societies, and, the better to protect themselves, began to seek who among them was the strongest and of the highest courage, to whom, making him their head, they rendered obedience. Next arose the knowledge of such things as are honourable and good, as opposed to those which are bad and shameful. For observing that when a man wronged his benefactor, hatred was universally felt for the one and sympathy for the other, and that the ungrateful were blamed, while those who showed gratitude were honoured, and reflecting that the wrongs they saw done to others might be done to themselves, to escape these they resorted to making laws and fixing punishments against any who should transgress them; and in this way grew the recognition of Justice. Whence it came that afterwards, in choosing their rulers, men no longer looked about for the strongest, but for him who was the most prudent and the most just.

But, presently, when sovereignty grew to be hereditary, and no longer elective, hereditary sovereigns began to degenerate from their ancestors, and, quitting worthy courses, took up the notion that princes had nothing to do but to surpass the rest of the world in sumptuous display, and wantonness, and whatever else ministers to pleasure; so that the prince coming to be hated, and therefore to feel fear, and passing from fear to infliction of injuries, a tyranny soon sprang up. Forthwith there began movements to overthrow the prince, and plots and conspiracies against him, undertaken not by those who were weak, or afraid for themselves, but by such as being conspicuous for their birth, courage, wealth, and station, could not tolerate the shameful life of the tyrant. The multitude, following the lead of these powerful men, took up arms against the prince, and, he being got rid of, obeyed these others as their liberators; who, on their part, holding in hatred the name of sole ruler, formed themselves into a government; and at first, while the recollection of past tyranny was still fresh, observed the laws they themselves made, and postponing personal advantage to the common welfare, administered affairs both publicly and privately with the utmost diligence and zeal. But this government passing, afterwards, to their descendants who, never having been taught in the school of Adversity, knew nothing of the vicissitudes of Fortune, these not choosing to rest content with mere civil equality, but abandoning themselves to avarice, ambition, and lust, converted, without respect to civil rights, what had been a government of the best into a government of the few; and so very soon met with the same fate as the tyrant.

For the multitude loathing its rulers, lent itself to any who ventured, in whatever way, to attack them; when some one man speedily arose who with the aid of the people overthrew them. But the recollection of the tyrant and of the wrongs suffered at his hands being still fresh in the minds of the people, who therefore felt no desire to restore the monarchy, they had recourse to a popular government, which they established on such a footing that neither king nor nobles had any place in it. And because all governments inspire respect at the first, this government also lasted for a while, but not for long, and seldom after the generation which brought it into existence had died out. For, suddenly, liberty passed into license, wherein neither private worth nor public authority was respected, but, every one living as he liked, a thousand wrongs were done daily. Whereupon, whether driven by necessity, or on the suggestion of some wiser man among them and to escape anarchy, the people reverted to a monarchy, from which, step by step, in the manner and for the causes already assigned, they came round once more to license. For this is the circle revolving within which all States are and have been governed; although in the same State the same forms of Government rarely repeat themselves, because hardly any State can have such vitality as to pass through such a cycle more than once, and still hold together. For it may be expected that in

some season of disaster, when a State must always be wanting in prudent counsels and in strength, it will become subject to some neighbouring and better governed State; though assuming this not to happen, it might well pass for an indefinite period from one of these forms of government to another.

I say, then, that all these six forms of government are pernicious —the three good kinds, from their brief duration; the three bad, from their inherent badness. Wise legislators, therefore, knowing these defects, and avoiding each of these forms in its simplicity, have made choice of a form which shares in the qualities of all the first three, and which they judge to be more stable and lasting than any of them separately. For where we have a monarchy, an aristocracy, and a democracy existing together in the same city, each of the three serves as a check upon the other.

Among those who have earned special praise by devising a constitution of this nature, was Lycurgus, who so framed the laws of Sparta as to assign their proper functions to kings, nobles and commons; and in this way established a government, which, to his great glory and to the peace and tranquillity of his country, lasted for more than eight hundred years. The contrary, however, happened in the case of Solon; who by the turn he gave to the institutions of Athens, created there a purely democratic government, of such brief duration, that he himself lived to witness the beginning of the despotism of Pisistratus. And although, forty years later, the heirs of Pisistratus were driven out, and Athens recovered her freedom, nevertheless because she reverted to the same form of government as had been established by Solon, she could maintain it for only a hundred years more; for though to preserve it, many ordinances were passed for repressing the ambition of the great and the turbulence of the people, against which Solon had not provided, still, since neither the monarchic nor the aristocratic element was given a place in her constitution, Athens, as compared with Sparta, had but a short life.

But let us now turn to Rome, which city, although she had no Lycurgus to give her from the first such a constitution as would preserve her long in freedom, through a series of accidents, caused by the contests between the commons and the senate, obtained by chance what the foresight of her founders failed to provide. So that Fortune, if she bestowed not her first favours on Rome, bestowed her second; because, although the original institutions of this city were defective, still they lay not outside the true path which could bring them to perfection. For Romulus and the other kings made many and good laws, and such as were not incompatible with freedom; but because they sought to found a kingdom and not a commonwealth, when the city became free many things were found wanting which in the interest of liberty it was necessary to supply, since these kings had not supplied them. And although the kings of Rome lost their sovereignty, in the manner and for the causes mentioned above, nevertheless those who drove them out, by at once creating two consuls to take their place, preserved in Rome the regal authority while banishing from it the regal name; so that as both senate and consuls were included in that republic, it in fact possessed two of the three elements above enumerated, to wit, the monarchic and the aristocratic.

It then only remained to assign its place to the popular element, and the Roman nobles growing insolent from causes which shall be noticed hereafter, the commons rose against them, when, not to lose the whole of their power, they were forced to concede a share to the people; while with the share which remained, the senate and consuls retained so much authority that they still held their own place in the republic. In this way the tribunes of the people came to be created, after whose creation the stability of the State was much augmented, since each of the three forms of government had now its due influence allowed it. And such was the good fortune of Rome that although her government passed from the kings to the nobles, and from these to the people, by the steps and for the reasons noticed above, still the entire authority of the kingly element was not sacrificed to strengthen the authority of the nobles, nor were the nobles divested of their authority to bestow it on the commons; but all three, blending together, made up a perfect State; which perfection, as shall be fully shown in the next two Chapters, was reached through the dissensions of the commons and the senate.

PIETRO POMPONAZZI

On the Immortality of the Soul
Translated by William Henry Hay II, revised by John Herman
Randall, Jr.

Chapter *In which it is shown that man is a twofold ("ancipitis") nature*
One *and a mean between mortal and immortal things.* Now, I hold
that the beginning of our consideration should be made at this point.
Man is clearly not of simple but of multiple, not of certain but of
ambiguous (*ancipitis*) nature, and he is to be placed as a mean between mortal and immortal things. This is plain to see if we examine
his essential operations, as it is from such operations that essences
are made known. For in performing the functions of the vegetative
and of the sensitive soul, which, as is said in *De anima*, Book ii,
and in *De generatione animalium*, Book ii, chapter 3, cannot be performed without a bodily and perishable instrument, man assumes
mortality. However, in knowing and willing, operations which
throughout the whole *De anima* and in *De partibus animalium*,
Book i, chapter 1, and in *De generatione animalium*, Book ii,
chapter 3, are held to be performed without any bodily instrument,
since they prove separability and immateriality, and these in turn
prove immortality, man is to be numbered among the immortal
things. From these facts the whole conclusion can be drawn, that
man is clearly not of a simple nature, since he includes three souls,
so to speak—the vegetative, the sensitive, and the intellective—and
that he claims a twofold nature for himself, since he exists neither
unqualifiedly (*simpliciter*) mortal nor unqualifiedly immortal but
embraces both natures.

Therefore the ancients spoke well when they established man
between eternal and temporal things for the reason that he is
neither purely eternal nor purely temporal, since he partakes of
149 both natures. And to man, who thus exists as a mean between the

two, power is given to assume whichever nature he wishes. Hence there are three kinds of men to be found. Some are numbered with the gods, although such are but few. And these are the men who, having subjugated the vegetative and the sensitive, have become almost completely rational. Some from total neglect of the intellect and from occupying themselves with the vegetative and the sensitive alone, have changed, as it were, into beasts. And perhaps this is what the Pythagorean fable means when it says that men's souls pass into different beasts. Some are called normal men; and these are the ones who have lived tolerably according to the moral virtues. They have not, however, devoted themselves entirely to the intellect or held entirely aloof from the bodily powers. Each of these two latter sorts has a wide range, as is plain to see. With this agrees what is said in the Psalm: "Thou hast made him but a little lower than the angels," etc.

Chapter
Nine
In which is set forth a fifth way, namely, that the same essence of the soul is mortal and immortal but unqualifiedly mortal and relatively immortal. Since therefore the first way, asserting that the intellective soul is distinct in existence from the sensitive in mortals, has been refuted in all its modes; and the second, asserting that intellective and sensitive are the same in existence, and that this soul is unqualifiedly immortal and relatively mortal, is exceedingly doubtful and does not seem to agree with Aristotle, it remains to assert the last way, which, holding that the sensitive in man is identified with the intellective, maintains that this soul is essentially and truly mortal but relatively immortal.

And that we may proceed in due order, we shall speak according to those five propositions in the previous chapter. And the first we concede unqualifiedly, that the intellective and the sensitive in man are identified in existence. But we are at variance on the second, because we assert that such a soul is truly and unqualifiedly mortal, but relatively and improperly speaking immortal. For evidence of this it must be known and thoroughly committed to memory in this matter, that all cognition in some fashion abstracts from matter. For, as the Commentator says, *De anima* iii, comment 5, matter hinders cognition; and this is to be seen in the senses, which do not know according to real qualities but according to their intentions; whence in *De anima* ii it is said that the property of each sense is to be receptive of species without matter. Therefore, three modes of cognition are found in the universe, corresponding to three
150 modes of separation from matter. For there are some things which

are totally separated from matter and hence in their knowing neither need a body as subject nor as object. For their knowing is not received in any body, since they are not in a body, nor are they moved by any body, since they are unmoved movers. And these are the separated substances which we call Intellects or Intelligences, in which is discovered neither discursive thought, nor composition, nor any motion. But there are some things which, although they know not through sensible qualities but through their species, which assume some manner of immateriality, for they are both said to be without matter and are spiritual; yet because they are the lowest in the genus of knowing things and are exceedingly material, they hence need the body for their operations both as subject and as object. For such cognitions are both received in an organ, whence also they represent only singulars, and are moved by some corporeal thing. And these are all the sensitive powers, although some of them are more spiritual and some less, as the Commentator says (*De anima* iii, comment 6, and *De sunsu et sensato*).

Now since nature proceeds in orderly fashion, as is said in *Physica* viii, between these two extremes, of not needing a body as subject or as object, and of needing a body as subject and object, there is a mean, which is neither totally abstracted nor totally immersed. Whence, since it is impossible for anything to need a body as subject and not as object, as is obvious, it remains that such an intermediary does not need the body as subject but as object. Now this is the human intellect, which by all the ancients and moderns or almost all is held to be halfway between things abstract and things not abstract, that is, between the Intelligences and the sensitive level, below the Intelligences and above the sensitive. Whence it is said also in the Psalm, "Thou hast made him a little less than the angels." And a little further on, "Thou hast established him above the works of thy hands, the sheep and the oxen," etc. And this way of knowing is that of which Aristotle spoke, in *De anima* i, text 12: "If knowing is either imagination or not without imagination, it is impossible for it to exist without a body." And when in *De anima* iii he declared that knowing is not imagination, since it is not through an organ, and it cannot be without imagination; and in the same book, text 29 and 39: "The soul does not know at all without some phantasm." Hence the human soul does not need an organ as subject but as object.

Now, according to Aristotle and Plato, it is fitting that there be souls corresponding to all these levels of cognition. Hence, at least according to Aristotle, any knowing thing is the act of a physical and organic body, though each kind in a different way. For Intelli-
151 gences are not the acts of bodies as Intelligences, since in their

knowing and desiring they in no wise need a body. But in so far as they actuate and move the heavenly bodies, they are souls and are the acts of a physical and organic body. For a star is an organ of the heavens, in *De caelo* ii; and in *Metaphysica* xii, text 48, the whole sphere exists for the sake of the star. Hence the Intelligences actuate a physical and organic body; and, as such, they need the body as object. But, in thus actuating and moving, they receive nothing from the body but only give to it. The sensitive soul, moreover, is unqualifiedly the act of a physical and organic body, because it both needs the body as subject, since it performs its office only in an organ, and needs the body as object. But the mean, which is the human intellect, is in none of its operations wholly freed from the body or wholly immersed in it, whence it will not need the body as subject but will as object. And thus in a fashion halfway between abstract things and things not abstract it will be the act of an organic body. For Intelligences as Intelligences are not souls, because as such they are no wise dependent on a body but in so far as they move the heavenly bodies. But the human intellect in all its operations is the act of an organic body, since it always depends on the body as object.

There is also a difference in the way an Intelligence and a human intellect depend on an organ, because the human soul receives and is completed by a bodily object when it is moved by it, but an Intelligence receives nothing from a heavenly body but only gives. Moreover, the human intellect differs from the sensitive power in its way of depending on the body, because the sensitive depends subjectively and objectively, but the human intellect objectively only. And thus in a fashion halfway between the material and the immaterial the human intellect is the act of an organic body.

Wherefore heavenly things, men and beasts are not animated in the same way, since their souls are not in the same way the acts of a physical and organic body, as has been seen. Hence Alexander in his *Paraphrase of the De anima* said that an Intelligence is rather equivocally called the soul of a heaven, and the heaven an animated being. With this, Averroes seems also to agree in *De substantia orbis*. But beasts are properly called animals, as is the common usage. But men are called animals in an intermediate manner.

Nor is it to be pretended that, with Aristotle, this way of knowing of the human intellect is accidental to it, that is, being moved by an object and not needing a subject; not only because a single thing has but a single essential way of operating but also because just as the way of the sensitive is never transformed into the way of the Intelligence or of the human intellect, nor the way of the Intelligence into the way of the human intellect or of the sensitive; so equally the

human way of understanding does not seem capable of transforma-
tion into the way of the Intelligence. This would be the case if it
knew without needing the body as subject and object. This is also
confirmed, because then a nature would be transformed into another
nature, since its essential operations would also be transformed.

Further, by no natural mark can the human intellect be known to
have any other way of knowing, as we understand from experience,
because we always need some phantasm. Whence it is concluded
that this way of knowing by phantasms is essential to man.

From these considerations we must now syllogize the principal
conclusion we are seeking—that the human soul is unqualifiedly
material and relatively immaterial. And, first, the prosyllogism is
divided as follows: The human intellect is immaterial and material,
as is shown by the above reasons. But it does not partake of these
equally, nor is it more immaterial than material, as has been proved
in the preceding chapter. Hence it is more material than immaterial
and will thus be unqualifiedly material and relatively immaterial.

Secondly, it is essential to the intellect to know by means of
phantasms, as has been demonstrated, and is clear from the definition of the soul, as the act of a physical and organic body; whence
in all its operations it needs an organ. But what knows in this way is
necessarily inseparable; hence the human intellect is mortal. The
minor is evident not only from Aristotle's words: "If knowing is
imagination or not without imagination, it is impossible for it to be
separated"; but also, if it were separable, it would either not have
any operation, and would thus be functionless, or it would have one
and would operate without phantasms, which is contrary to the
demonstrated major.

And again this is confirmed as follows: Since Aristotle did not
posit any Intelligence without a body, as in *Metaphysica* xii, he
maintains that the number of Intelligences corresponds to the number of spheres; much less, therefore, can he posit the human intellect
without a body, since it is far less abstracted than an Intelligence.
Indeed, if the world is eternal, as Aristotle believed, infinitely
infinite forms exist actually without a body. This seems ridiculous
according to Aristotle. Whence the human soul, according to Aristotle, must be declared to be absolutely mortal. But since it is halfway between what is unqualifiedly abstracted and what is immersed in matter, it partakes in some fashion of immortality, which
its essential operation also shows. For it does not depend on the
body as subject, in which it agrees with the Intelligences and differs
from the beasts; and it needs the body as object, in which it agrees
with the beasts. Whence it is mortal. . . .

In which is affirmed the final conclusion in this matter, which in my opinion must be maintained as beyond doubt. Now since these things are so, it seems to me that in this matter, keeping the saner view, we must say that the question of the immortality of the soul is a neutral problem, like that of the eternity of the world. For it seems to me that no natural reasons can be brought forth proving that the soul is immortal, and still less any proving that the soul is mortal, as very many scholars who hold it immortal declare. Wherefore I do not want to make answer to the other side, since others do so, St. Thomas in particular, clearly, fully, and weightily. Wherefore we shall say, as Plato said in the *Laws* i, that to be certain of anything, when men disagree with each other, I think that this can be made certain only through God.

But it does not seem to be fitting or expedient for man to lack such certainty. For if he were in doubt on this matter, he would have actions uncertain and without any end; since if the end be unknown, the means thereto would also be necessarily unknown. Whence if the soul is immortal, earthly things are to be despised, and eternal things to be pursued; but if its existence is mortal, a contrary way is to be pursued. But if other things besides man have their own determinate ends, how much more man himself, since man is the most perfect of mortals, and the only one, as Plato says in the *Republic*, who worships God and justice! Wherefore I say, that before the gift or advent of grace "in many places and in many ways by the prophets" and by supernatural signs God himself settled this question, as is plain to see in the Old Testament. But "most recently by the Son whom he made the heir of all, through whom he also made the ages," he has made clear this question, as the Apostle says in the *Epistle to the Hebrews.* That he is truly the Son of God, true God and true man, most fittingly and without doubt, the light of the Christian name, St. Thomas Aquinas, declares in *Contra Gentiles* i, chapter 6. Which points John Scotus, in my opinion most subtle of all and a man above all most religious, reducing them to the number of eight enumerates in the prologue to the *Sentences.* And indeed so clearly do these eight points set it forth that unless demented or stubborn no one could deny it. Since therefore he is the true God, he alone is truly that light by which all things are seen, as in *John* i, and he alone also is the truth by which other things are true, as in *John* xiv: "I am the way, the truth and the life." But since he himself has made manifest in word and deed that the soul is immortal, in word when he threatens the evil with eternal fire, but to the good

promises eternal life; for he says, "Come, blessed of my Father, etc.,"
and it follows, "Go, accursed ones, into eternal fires, etc."; in deed,
when he rose on the third day from the dead. But as far as the light
differs from the lucid and truth from the true, and as much as the
infinite cause is more powerful than the finite effect, the more
efficaciously does this demonstrate the immortality of the soul.

Wherefore, if any arguments seem to prove the mortality of the
soul, they are false and merely seeming, since the first light and the
first truth show the opposite. But if any seem to prove its immortality, they are true and clear, but not light and truth. Wherefore
this way alone is most firm, unshaken, and lasting; the rest are un-
trustworthy.

Moreover, every art ought to proceed by things proper and fitting
to that art; for otherwise it errs and does not proceed according to
the rule of art, as Aristotle says in *Posteriora* and *Ethica* i. But that
the soul is immortal is an article of faith, as appears from the
Apostles' Creed and the Athanasian Creed; hence it ought to be
proved by what is proper to faith. But the means on which faith
relies is revelation and canonical Scripture. Hence it is proved truly
and properly only by them; but other reasons are foreign, and rely
on a means that does not prove what is intended. Hence it is not
surprising if philosophers disagree among themselves about the
immortality of the soul, when they rely on arguments foreign to the
conclusion and fallacious; but all followers of Christ agree, since
they proceed by what is proper and infallible, since matters cannot
be except in one way.

Further, he who is ill is concerned for health. Yet let no one be
physician to himself, since it is said in *Politics* iii: "In his own affairs
no one judges rightly, since he is in a state of passion." Let him
therefore ask another. But the good physician ought to be skilled in
his art, and of good character, since neither the first without the
second nor the second without the first suffices. But as Plato says,
just as distemper in the humors is sickness of the body, so ignorance
is sickness of the soul. Therefore not knowing whether the soul is
immortal or not, let him seek a man well informed and good. Yet
two classes of men profess to know this: infidels and Christians.
Now there have been many very learned men among the infidels,
but almost all of spotted life. Not to speak of other things, at least of
empty glory, they have understood only natural things, which produce an obscure and infirm knowledge. But many Christians, unless
I am mistaken, have known no less than they in natural philosophy:
like Paul, Dionysius, Basil, Athanasius, Origen, the two Gregories, of
Nazianzus and of Nyssa, Augustine, Jerome, Ambrose, Gregory and
155   countless others; and besides a knowledge of natural things they

have also had a knowledge of divinity. Which things, as Jerome says, "learned Plato did not know, and eloquent Demosthenes was ignorant of," and they led most spotless lives. But who except a madman would rather believe infidels thus ignorant than Christians so well endowed? And to me it makes faith firm that Augustine, in my opinion second to none in learning (for I do not judge him less than Plato or Aristotle), first hostile to the Christian name, having become so virtuous of life, writes in the end of the *City of God* that he had seen made visible by faith so many miracles, which shows a faith unlimited, inviolable, and most firm. And Pope Gregory also, comparable in learning and holiness with any man, adduces so many and such great things in his Dialogues, that all doubt is completely removed.

Wherefore we must assert that beyond doubt the soul is immortal. But we must not go the way the wise men of this age have gone, who, when they call themselves wise, have become fools. For whoever goes this way, I think, will waver always uncertain and wandering. Wherefore I believe that even though Plato wrote so many and such great things about the immortality of the soul, yet I think that he did not possess certainty. This I conjecture from the end of the *Apology,* for there it seems to be left in doubt. In the *Timaeus* also, when he was about to discuss the matter, he said that for him it would be enough if in so difficult a matter he should speak in probabilities. Wherefore, comparing everything he says, he seems to me to speak more as in opinion than in assertion. And it is his endeavor to make good citizens but not learned ones. Indeed, as says St. Thomas, in *Summa* ii a ii ae, question I, article 3, the act remains moral even with a false opinion. But those that go the way of the faithful remain firm and unshaken. This their contempt of riches, honors, pleasures, and all things worldly makes clear, and finally the martyr's crown, which they ardently strove after, and when striven for attained with the highest joy.

And therefore these are the things that seem to me must be said in this matter, yet always submitting myself in this and in other matters to the Apostolic See. Wherefore, etc.

The end has been put to this treatise by me, Peter, son of John Nicholas Pomponazzi of Mantua, the twenty-fourth day of the month of September, 1516.

At Bologna, in the fourth year of the Pontificate of Leo X. To the praise of the indivisible Trinity, etc.

FRANCESCO GUICCIARDINI

Counsels and Reflections
Translated by Ninian Hill Thomson

For eleven successive years I was engaged in governing for the Church, and so much to the satisfaction both of my employers and of those over whom I ruled, that had it not been for the events which took place in Rome and Florence in the year 1527, I might have continued to govern for a great while longer. During all this time I found that nothing strengthened me so much in my position as to seem indifferent whether I was employed or no. For on this footing, without fear or favour, I did whatever was suitable to the office I held; and this gave me such a reputation as of itself helped me more, and more honourably, than any blandishments, interest, or address I could have used.

Let no one trust so entirely to natural prudence as to persuade himself that it will suffice to guide him without help from experience. For there is no man, however prudent, who has been employed in affairs, but has had cause to know that experience leads us to many results we never could have reached by the force of natural intelligence only.

Whoso well considers it will scarce deny that in human affairs Fortune rules supreme. For every hour we find the most momentous results springing from such fortuitous causes as it was not within the power of man either to foresee or to escape. And though discernment and vigilance may temper many things, they cannot do so unhelped, but stand always in need of favourable Fortune.

What a mistake is theirs who cite on all occasions the example of the Romans! To do as the Romans did, we would need to have a city circumstanced like theirs. To attempt it with means so inferior as ours is to require of the ass the fleetness of the horse.

All men are by nature more inclined to good than to evil; nor is there any one who, when other considerations do not move him to the contrary, would not more willingly do you a benefit than an injury. But human nature is so frail, and open to so many temptations, that men easily allow themselves to deviate from their natural goodness. For which reason wise lawgivers have had recourse to rewards and punishments. And this is merely an endeavour to keep men fixed in their natural inclinations by the help of hope and fear.

To pronounce absolutely, categorically, and, as it were, by the card, concerning the things of this world, were a great mistake; for nearly all of them are marked by some singularity or exceptional quality due to difference in their circumstances, making it impossible to refer them all to the same standard. These differences and distinctions will not be found set forth in books, but must be taught by discretion.

If princes, when all goes well with them, make little account of their servants, and slight them or set them aside out of the merest caprice, how can they be displeased or complain if their servants, so long as they fail not in any duty of fidelity or honour, leave them, and accept other more profitable employment?

It is a great matter to be in authority over others; for authority, if it be rightly used, will make you feared beyond your actual resources. Because your subjects, not knowing how far these reach, will be more disposed to give way than to make trial whether or no you can do what you threaten.

States cannot be established or maintained by conforming to the moral law. For if you look to their beginnings, all will be seen to have had their origin in violence; save only the authority of commonwealths within the limits of their own territory, and not beyond. Nor do I except the Emperor himself from this rule, and still less the priests, which last use a twofold violence against us, constraining us at once with weapons spiritual and temporal.

The very same things which, when undertaken at the proper moment, readily, succeed, and, so to speak, accomplish themselves, will, if attempted prematurely, not merely fail then, but will often also lose their aptitude for succeeding at their own time. Accordingly, you are not to rush hastily on any enterprise, nor to precipitate events, but to await their season and maturity.

Small and almost imperceptible beginnings are often the occasion of great disasters or of great prosperity. The highest prudence therefore lies in noting and weighing well all circumstances, even the most trifling.

In narrating current events, some writers will enter on a discussion of what is likely to happen hereafter; and such forecasts, when made by men who are well informed, seem very admirable to him who reads them. Nevertheless they are extremely misleading. For as these reasonings, like the links of a chain, depend one upon another, if any one of them fail, all the others deduced from it fall to the ground, and the most trifling variation in the circumstances suffices to cause an error in the conclusion. It is impossible, therefore, to form a judgment as to the course of events while they are yet remote; our opinions must be formed and modified from day to day.

Those who govern states must not be daunted by seeming dangers, however great, near, and imminent they look. For the Devil, as the proverb says, is never so black as he is painted. Many things may come about that will cause dangers to disappear of themselves; and even when they do arrive, some unthought of remedy or alleviation will be found to accompany them. This is a hint to which you should give heed; for every day you will have occasion to act upon it.

The science of the law stands now on this footing, that if in the trial of a cause there be urged on one side some forcible argument, and on the other the authority of a doctor who has written on the subject, the latter will weigh more with the judge. Whence it follows that practising lawyers must acquaint themselves with all that every one has written, and in consequence that the time which should be devoted to searching into the reason of the thing is wasted in perusing books; and this with such fatigue and weariness both of mind and body, that the profession of the law has come more to resemble the labour of the mechanic than the deliberation of the sage.

Great defects and inconveniences are inseparable from a free government. And yet the wise and good of our city approve it as a less evil.

What the devout tell us of him that hath faith accomplishing great things, and, in the words of Scripture, removing mountains, rests upon this, that faith breeds obstinacy. For faith is no more than to believe firmly and almost with certainty things not in themselves reasonable; or if reasonable, to believe them more implicitly than reason warrants. He therefore that has faith becomes stubborn in his belief, and goes on his way resolute and intrepid, contemning difficulties and dangers, and ready to suffer every extremity. Whence it happens that as the things of this world are subject to infinite changes and chances, in the course of events unlooked-for help may come in many ways to him who has obstinately persevered; which
159 perseverance being the result of faith, it may well be said that whoso

hath faith will accomplish great things. Whereof we have at the present hour signal instance in this stubbornness of the Florentines; who having, contrary to all human reason, set themselves to await the joint attack of Pope and Emperor, without hope of aid from others, disunited among themselves, and encompassed by difficulties on every side, have for seven months withstood behind their walls the assaults of armies against whom it seemed impossible they could hold out for as many days; nay, have brought things to such a point that whereas at first all deemed them lost, were they now to conquer, none would be surprised. And this stubbornness of theirs is mainly due to the belief that, as Friar Girolamo of Ferrara told them in his sermons, they cannot be destroyed.

Though many prove thankless, be not therefore deterred from conferring benefits. For not only is beneficence in itself a noble quality, and almost divine, but it may likewise happen that while you practise it you shall meet with some one so grateful that he atones for all the ingratitude of others.

The same or similar proverbs, though differently expressed, are found among all nations. And this because these spring from experience or from the observation of things, which are everywhere the same or similar.

Since there is nothing so well worth having as friends, never lose a chance to make them. For men are brought into constant contact with one another, and friends help and foes hinder at times and in places where you least expect it.

I know no man who feels deeper disgust than I do at the ambition, avarice, and profligacy of the priesthood, as well because every one of these vices is odious in itself, as because each of them separately and all of them together are utterly abhorrent in men making profession of a life dedicated to God. Besides which, these vices are by nature so contrary to one another, that they can coexist only in some monstrous subject. And yet the position I have filled under several Popes has obliged me for personal reasons to desire their greatness. But for this I should have loved Martin Luther as myself: not that I would be loosed from the laws prescribed by the Christian religion as commonly interpreted and understood, but because I long to see this pack of scoundrels brought within due bounds, that is to say, purged of their vices or stripped of their authority.

Always deny boldly what you would not have known, and affirm what you would have believed. For even though there be many 160 proofs and almost a certainty to the contrary, a confident assertion or denial will often perplex and puzzle the brains of him who hears you.

Since a name for goodness will help you in numberless ways, do all you can to seem good. But since false appearances are never lasting, you can hardly succeed in seeming good for long, unless you be so in reality. I had this admonition from my father.

Learning grafted on a weak intellect, if it does not injure, will certainly not improve it; superadded to natural parts, it makes men perfect and almost divine.

Most truly has the wise man said that of things future and contingent we can have no certain knowledge. Turn this over in your mind as you will, the longer you turn it the more you will be satisfied of its truth.

Whatsoever has been in the past or is now will repeat itself in the future; but the names and surfaces of things will be so altered, that he who has not a quick eye will not recognise them, or know to guide himself accordingly, or to form a judgment on what he sees.

Frank sincerity is a quality much extolled among men and pleasing to every one, while simulation, on the contrary, is detested and condemned. Yet for a man's self, simulation is of the two by far the more useful; sincerity tending rather to the interest of others. But since it cannot be denied that it is not a fine thing to deceive, I would commend him whose conduct is as a rule open and straightforward, and who uses simulation only in matters of the gravest importance and such as very seldom occur; for in this way he will gain a name for honesty and sincerity, and with it the advantages attaching to these qualities. At the same time, when, in any extreme emergency, he resorts to simulation, he will draw all the greater advantage from it, because from his reputation for plain dealing his artifice will blind men more.

Nothing in our republican way of living gives us more trouble than to bestow our daughters suitably in marriage. And this because all men having a higher opinion of themselves than others entertain of them, think at first that they can secure alliances in quarters where they are not to be had. Accordingly, I have seen fathers decline proposals which, after many fruitless attempts in other directions, they would gladly have accepted. You must, therefore, measure fairly your own position with that of others, and not let yourself be carried away by an undue estimate of your own importance. Of this I am convinced; but am not so sure that I should know to put what I say into practice, or avoid the common error of valuing myself more than I ought. This warning, however, is not meant to make us think so meanly of ourselves, that, like Francesco Vettori, we should give our daughters away to the first who asks for them.

Though human life be short, rest assured that he will find it long enough who knows to make wise use of his time, and does not unprofitably waste it. For man's nature fits him for great efforts, and any one who is diligent and resolute will get through an incredible amount of work.

In my youth I made light of such superficial accomplishments as dancing, singing, and playing, nay, even of writing a fair hand, knowing how to ride, how to dress becomingly, and all other like arts, which savour more of show than substance. Since then, however, I have seen reason to change my mind. For though it were doubtless a mistake to waste too much time in cultivating these graces, or to make a lad's entire training consist in acquiring them to perfection, still I have found by experience that these gifts and the knack of doing everything well confer honour and reputation even upon men of good birth; and that too in so marked a degree that we may say he lacks something who is without them. Moreover, excellence in matters of this sort opens the way to the favour of princes, and offers a beginning or occasion to him who is proficient therein to obtain high and lucrative preferment. For the world and its rulers are what they are, and not what they should be.

That spirits do exist may, I believe, be affirmed. I mean what we call spirits, that is to say, certain airy beings conversing familiarly with men. For I myself have had such proof of their existence as makes it seem to me past a doubt. But what they really are, and what their nature is, I take to be as little understood by him who persuades himself he knows, as by him who has never given the subject a thought. These manifestations, as well as the faculty of foretelling the future, which we sometimes see exercised as an art, and sometimes inspired under a divine frenzy, are secret powers of Nature, or rather of that higher agent by whom all things are set in motion, revealed to him, but hidden from us, and so hidden that the minds of men cannot attain to them.

Three things I would willingly see before I die. And yet, though I were to live to a great age, I fear I shall see none of them. I desire to see a well-ordered republic established in Florence; Italy free from all her barbarian invaders; and the world delivered from the tyranny of these rascally priests.

A good name is more to be desired than riches; but since without riches a good name can now-a-days hardly be preserved, worthy men should seek them, not in excess, but so far as may be needed for acquiring and maintaining credit and influence.

Never contend against religion or against aught else that seems to have dependence upon God. For these are matters concerning which the minds of fools are too much made up to be open to argument.

The longing to have children cannot be blamed, since it is natural. Yet I say boldly that it is a kind of happiness not to have them. For even he whose children are good and sensible has undoubtedly more anxiety from them than comfort. This I have seen to be the case with my own father, who in his day was cited in Florence as an example of a sire blessed with good sons. Think then how it must fare with him who has worthless offspring.

Doubtless the man of ordinary parts has more enjoyment in this world, and lives a longer, and in some sort a happier life, than he who is of a loftier intellect. For a noble mind is likely enough to fret and torment its owner. But the first partakes more of the brute than of the man. The other transcends human nature and approaches the divine.

TORQUATO TASSO

Aminta[1]
Translated by Oldmixon

ACT ONE

SCENE I—Daphne, Sylvia

Daphne: Sylvia, will you still persist
   In this strange disgust of Love?
   Will you still refuse to hear
   Our Shepherds sighs, and scorn their tears?
   But if sighs and tears in vain
   Attempt to move your cruel heart,
   Methinks the hopes that you might have
   To see a lovely Infant smile,
   And call you Mother, should succeed:
   Change, foolish Creature, change your thoughts,
   And be not constant to a Crime.
Sylvia: Let others, if they please, be mov'd
   With sighs and tears, and take delight
   To play with Love: I'll never quit
   The Forests, never leave the Chace,
   Whilst Beasts of prey are to be found.
   I'll range the Woods, I'll scour the Plains,
   And with my Bow and Quiver find
   A better way to nobler sport.
Daphne: Dull sport, and an insipid life!
   You Sylvia, stubborn as thou art,
   Will think so too, when you begin
   To taste the sweets of Love.
   So the first people, who possest

164 [1]Amintas is the Anglicized name of the title character Aminta

In Innocence the Infant World,
Fed on Acorns, and when dry
Drank the Waters of the Brook:
Beasts only now on Acorns feed,
And drink the Waters of the Brook:
And thus when you at last shall feel
How pleasant 'tis beneath a shade,
To sit and talk with one you love:
Then, Sylvia, you'll repent and cry,
Ah, fool! I never lov'd till now.
You'll throw away your Arrows, break your Bow,
And curse the minutes you have lost.
Change, foolish Creature, change your thoughts,
And be not constant to a Crime.

Sylvia: When I sit and talk of Love,
    Dogs shall be afraid of Hares,
    Wolves of Lambs, and Streams return
    To the Fountains whence they rose;
    Bears shall then the Forests leave,
    And Dolphins dance about the Plains.

Daphne: I know your pride, for I was once
    Wild and obstinate, like you.
    I was then as fair, my Locks
    As white as yours, my Lips as red:
    Such Roses and such Lillies grac'd
    My Cheeks, as flourish now on yours.
    'Twas then (so stupid was my taste)
    The darling pleasure of my life,
    To set my Lime-twigs, lay my Nets,
    And laugh as often as I saw
    The Birds entangled in my Snares.
    I then delighted in the Chace,
    And scorn'd, with savage modesty,
    The Shepherds whom my Charms had conquer'd.
    I was then so far unjust,
    As once to think it cause enough
    To hate 'em for their loving me;
    And pleasing them displeas'd my self:
    But oh! what will not time effect;
    What will not services and sighs,
    Desert, entreaties, truth and tears?
    What, Sylvia, will not all these do?

Sylvia: Nothing with a mind resolv'd
165   Against their flatteries, like mine.

Daphne: Mistaken Maid!
    They'll master every stubborn thought,
    And force our hearts to think of Love.
    I know it by myself, for I have felt,
    And must confess their power.
    They tempted me to tear my Nets,
    Neglect my Lime-twigs, break my Bow,
    And fling my Arrows in the Air.
    I cry'd there, there, Diana, take
    These useless Weapons, I renounce
    The Woods and all thy sports for Love.
Sylvia: Renounce 'em by yourself and as for me—
Daphne: Who knows, Amintas may in time
    Convert even thee to do as much:
    Is he not handsome? Can you see
    A comelier youth in all the plain?
    If you're related to the Gods,
    Amintas is deriv'd from Pan:
    You oft have Amirillis seen,
    And in some Fountain may compare
    Her beauties with your own.
    The difference, Sylvia, is not great,
    Yet poor Amintas shuns her smiles,
    To follow your contempt and you;
    And for your hate despises Love.
    But think it may not still be thus,
    Think when her Beauties or her smiles
    Have toucht his heart, they'll laugh at yours,
    And make a jest of thy disdain.
Sylvia: Where e're he pleases let him love,
    And Court what Maid he will but me:
    I'll ne're be troubled with his heart,
    Nor give him any hopes of mine.
Daphne: What makes you hate him thus?
Sylvia: His love.
Daphne: Ah cruelty! we might expect
    That Ravens would be born of Swans,
    Of Tygers Lambs, as well as thou
    From tender Parents be deriv'd.
Sylvia: I hate his Love because he hates
    What I love most, a Maiden life.
    While friendship only warm'd his Soul,
    None could esteem him more than I.
166 Daphne: You'd have him then confine his wishes,

To as narrow bounds as yours.
He less deserves to be condemn'd
For wishing much,
Than you do for not wishing more.
Syliva: Daphne, Peace, or if you'll talk,
Prithee talk of something else.
We fool away the day
In idle talk; 'tis time for me
To be provided for my Sport.
First then I'll to the lonely Brook,
Which glides thro yon delicious Wood,
And bathe me in the Crystal stream;
There playing with the waves a while,
I grow refresh'd, and with new life,
Rise from the Waters to the Chace.
Daphne: 'Tis early, I must first go home,
I'll meet you after at the Brook,
And bathe me with you, if you please.
But, Sylvia, think on what I've said,
'Tis of more consequence than Brooks,
Or Dogs, or Forests, or your Game;
And if you know not yet what 'tis
To love, ah! learn of those that do:
Love of all pleasures is the best,
And none can be without it blest.   Exeunt.

SCENE II—Amintas, Thyrsis

Amintas: I've often found that Rocks and Waves
Have answer'd my complaint: But oh!
I never found, nor hope to find
The Nymph, whom I've so long ador'd,
As gentle ev'n as Rocks and Waves.
Is she a Woman? One may well suspect
If she's of humane race, and yet I see
Her beautiful and young, her form
Of such a mould, so soft, so sweet,
That 'twere impossible to think
It lodg'd a Soul averse to Love,
If to my cost I had not found
That things inanimate are less
Insensible of pity than her heart.
167 Thyrsis: Lambs feed on Grass, and Wolves on Lambs,

They're satisfy'd in time; but Love,
Who feeds on Tears, is never satisfy'd.
Amintas: If Tears cou'd glut his appetite,
  He had been surfeited e're this:
  Or if the Virgin cou'd be mov'd
  With Seas of Tears I had been blest:
  No, they both hunger after Blood,
  And I resolve to give 'em mine.
Thyrsis: Ah! why, Amintas, will you talk
  Of Blood? If she is so severe,
  Are there not other Maids as young,
  As fair as she? Look out and try,
  Another Beauty may be kind.
Amintas: Where shall I look, or how expect to find?
  A Maid to please me, when I've lost my self.
Thyrsis: Don't flatter your despair, but hope
  This cruel fair may yield at last:
  Lyons and Tygers may be tam'd,
  And she you Love with Love be overcome.
Amintas: But who so wretched, who so near
  To death as I am, can be pleas'd
  With Life, or bear the torment long?
Thyrsis: The torment will not be so long
  As you suspect, for Womens minds
  Are movable, like Aspin leaves;
  And what they may this minute hate,
  They'll love the next. But say, my friend,
  Where lives? and who's this haughty Maid,
  That treats Amintas with such scorn?
  You've told me often that you love,
  But never told me whom: be free,
  And open all your heart, without reserve.   —
Amintas: Well, you shall hear what every Wood,
  What all our Hills and Streams have heard,
  But no Man ever knew before;
  'Tis fit now I'm so near the Grave,
  Some friend should know the fatal cause,
  And write my sorrows on the Tomb,
  Where my pale body shall be laid,
  That every passenger may read
  My fate, and she for whom I dye
  Be pleas'd to triumph o're my dust:
  It may be when she sees how far

Despair has carry'd me, the thought

(And yet I fear I hope too much)
Will fetch a sigh, or force a tear;
And make her pity me, and wish
That poor Amintas were alive.
Hear then—
Thyrsis: I hearken: and perhaps
For better ends than you suppose.
Amintas: While I was yet a little Boy,
Scarce tall enough to reach a Bough,
Or pluck an Apple from a Tree,
I felt my heart engag'd to love
The fairest Creature ever liv'd;
Sylvia, the glory of the Woods,
Montano's and Cydippe's Daughter:
Sylvia, whose beauty, mien and youth,
Charm every heart as well as mine;
Our Houses joyn'd, but were not half
So close united as our Hearts:
Two Friends ne're lov'd as we did then;
Two Turtles ne're so fondly sought
Each others company, as we did;
Our pleasures with our years agreed,
The same diversions suited both;
We sometimes Hunted, sometimes Fish'd;
Sometimes we laid our Nets for Birds,
And always shar'd the Game we caught.
But while we pleasantly pursu'd
Our mutual sports, alas! I felt
Strange wishes growing in my heart:
Like Flow'rs that on a sudden spring
From beds where they were never set:
When're we parted now I wept
For grief, and when we met, for joy
I suckt in poison from her eyes,
Which seem'd delicious to the taste,
But left a bitter smart behind.
I saw her now with new delight;
I found new Graces in her face;
I often sigh'd, but knew not why;
I lov'd, but did not know 'twas love,
Till chance discover'd it.
Thyrsis: Pray how?
Amintas: Sylvia, Phillis, and myself,
169   Sitting underneath a Shade,

Saw a Bee fly round the bank,
Gathering Honey from the Flow'rs
Which adorn'd our happy seat:
Weary'd there, he fled to us,
Pitcht on Phillis, who has Cheeks
Fairer, sweeter than the Rose,
Fancying every Grace a Flow'r,
There he hung a while and suckt
Sweets much richer than his own!
Phillis wept to feel the smart;
Sylvia bid her weep no more,
I, she crys, can say a Charm,
That will quickly give you ease:
'Tis a Secret which I learnt
Of wise Aricia, to whom
For her Art I gave my Horn,
Tipt with Ivory and Gold.
Then she put her fragrant Lips
To the Cheek the Bee had stung,
Said some Verses o're the Wound,
And as soon as Sylvia spoke,
Phillis felt the pain no more.
See the wonderful effects,
See the force of Magic words,
Or, what I would rather think,
See what Sylvia's Lips can do,
Every thing they touch they heal.
Thyrsis: How, Amintas, could you find
Love had wounded you by this?
Amintas: I till this desir'd no more
Than to see her radiant Eyes,
Or to listen to her Voice,
Soft as Rivulets that glide
Murmuring thro our smiling Vales;
Soft as Zephyr's evening breath,
Playing with the Leaves of Trees:
But as soon as I observ'd
What her Lips had lately done,
Then I wish'd 'em close to mine,
And, I know not how, contriv'd
Ways to taste of what I wish'd.
Thyrsis: None want artifice to gain
What they covet to possess;
All are cunning when in love.

170

Amintas: I, to touch her rosy mouth,
  Feign'd a Bee had stung me too;
  And complain'd with such an air,
  That it seem'd to beg the Cure,
  Which my tongue cou'd ne'r have askt.
  Sylvia kindly did to me
  What she had to Phillis done,
  And her Lips thus fix'd to mine,
  Cur'd the counterfeited smart,
  But encreast my real pain.
  Bees sure never from their Flow'rs
  Drew such Honey as I suckt
  From my Sylvia's humid kisses.
  Sure no Roses but what grow
  On her Lips can yield such sweets.
  Tho my pleasure was disturb'd
  By my shame, and guilty fears:
  Yet I counterfeited still,
  And by this deceit prevail'd
  O're her to repeat the Charm.
  Something sweet from ev'ry kiss,
  Mixt with poyson, struck my heart,
  Which at last grew so inflam'd,
  That when once we met to play,
  With some other Nymphs and Swains,
  I, just dying with my fears,
  Softly whisper'd her, *I Love.*
Thyrsis: How did Sylvia take the news?
  That you seem so much concern'd.
Amintas: Soon her fiery blushes shew'd
  Both her anger and her shame;
  She stood silent, but I read
  By her silence what she meant,
  That she never wou'd forgive me.
  Now she flies me, and will since
  Not so much as hear me speak.
  Thrice our Golden Fields have bent
  Under their rich loads, and thrice
  Winter has with nipping frosts
  Made our Groves and Forests bare,
  Since I've try'd a thousand ways
  To appease her, but I find
  Death can only calm her rage.
  Death shall calm her then, my blood

Shall appease her for my fault.
I cou'd dye, methinks, with joy,
Were I sure my Death would make her
Either sorrowful or glad;
And I know not which to wish·
Yes, her Pity would reward
All my sufferings, and shew
What my Constancy deserv'd.
Yet, ah! why should I desire
That her beauteous Eyes should weep,
Or her Rest be lost for me?

CHORUS

Ah! the Golden Age is past,
  Which our happy Fathers blest;
When whate're they long'd to taste,
  They but wisht for, and possest.

The Meads were painted still with Flow'rs,
  The Birds ne'r ceas'd to sing;
And then, without the help of show'rs,
  They saw eternal Spring.

Rivers then with Milk were fill'd,
Honey from their Woods distill'd;
None attempted then the Main,
Nor expos'd their Lives for gain:
Free from danger, want or care;
Free from tumult, noise and war·
They a thousand Joys possest,
Peace and Plenty were the least.

Ah! the Golden, &c.

Honour, whose Laws are so severe,
  So hard to be obey'd;
Who reigns with so much rigor here,
  Ne're o're their pleasures sway'd.

The only maxim which they knew
  They were by Nature taught,
That what they had a mind to do,
  They might, without a fau't.

The Virgin never blush'd to shew
  By day her naked Charms;
And when she lov'd a Swain, would go
  With freedom to his arms.

By Woods, on Greens they danc'd and play'd,
In Fountains kist and toy'd;
The youth then boldly took his Maid,
And what he lik'd enjoy'd.

But now when men the blessing want,
They long must court the fair in vain;
For Honor will not let 'em grant
The pleasure they deny with pain.
'Twas honour that first swell'd their hearts,
That taught 'em shame, and to be coy;
To frown, and use those little arts,
Which only cheat 'em of their joy.

Hence thou Idol Honour, hence;
Leave us to our humble sports;
Reign in Cities and in Courts;
Honor is the child of Pride:
Here let Nature be our Guide:
Hence thou Idol Honour, hence.

ACT TWO

SCENE 1—Daphne, Thyrsis

Daphne: I knew long since Amintas lov'd
  The haughty Sylvia, and Heaven knows
  Have oft endeavour'd to dispose
  Her heart to be as much concern'd
  As he deserves, and I could wish:
  But all that I can say's in vain,
  For Bears and Tygers may be tam'd
  Sooner than such a simple Maid,
  As proud and silly as she's fair:
  Who, ignorant of what she does,
  Or that her Eyes are arm'd with death,
  Commits new Murders every hour
  And kills when she has no design to wound.
173 Thrysis: Where, Daphne, can you find a Maid

So weak, so innocent, so young,
As to be ign'rant of her Charms?
They early deck themselves with smiles,
They know the wounds their Eyes have made,
They know too what will cure those wounds,
And raise their Slaves from misery to bliss.
Daphne: Who teaches 'em all this?
Thyrsis: The same
   That teaches Nightingales to sing,
   The Peacock how to spread his Plumes,
   That teaches Bulls to use their Horns,
   The Ram to push, and Fish to swim:
   Nature instructs 'em what to do,
   Without the Mother or the Nurses help.
Daphne: Nay Thyrsis, now I plainly see
   Thou'rt both malicious and a fool;
   But to speak truth, I don't believe
   That Sylvia is as ignorant
   As she pretends; for t'other day
   I found her in the little Isle
   That stands in yonder spacious Meads,
   Encompast with a Crystal Lake;
   In whose clear Waters she beheld
   Her Beauties; ravish'd with the sight,
   She seem'd to ask 'em how to place
   Her hair, and put her Garland on;
   She often with her Cheeks compar'd
   A Rose, and Lillies with her Neck;
   On Rose and Lilly then she look'd
   With scorn, as if she said, O Flow'rs,
   Yield, yield to me; I wear ye now
   That you may blush to be outdone,
   And not for ornament, for see
   I've better Graces of my own.
   While thus she with the Waters play'd
   She look'd around, and spy'd me out,
   She drest herself in haste, and dropt
   Her Flow'rs, asham'd to be perceiv'd.
   I laugh'd aloud, and she I saw
   Was more asham'd to see me laugh:
   Yet did not dress her in such haste,
   But to the Fountain once or twice
   She ran, to see her hair was set
174 In order, and with pleasure saw

Those locks in sweet confusion flow,
Which haste had forc'd her to neglect:
I look'd and laugh'd, and said no more.
Thyrsis: I ever did believe as much,
Tho I could never prove it true.
Daphne: Sylvia and myself anon
Are to bathe us in the Brook
Which is from Diana call'd;
Where the Nymphs that love the Chace
Play beneath the Plantain shade,
In the fiercest heats of noon:
There I tell you Sylvia bathes,
And leaves naked all her Charms.
Thyrsis: What then?
Daphne: What then? Why thou'rt a fool,
Can't you guess my meaning then?
Thyrsis: I guess your meaning, tho I fear
Amintas will not dare to do't.
Daphne: Not dare! then truly he may stay
Till she seeks him.

scene ii—Amintas, Thyrsis

Amintas: I fain, methinks, before I dye,
Would know how Thyrsis has succeeded:
If he can do more than I
Have done, and Sylvia will not hear
With patience any one that speaks for me,
Here on this spot of Earth I'll end my pains,
And in her presence finish with my breath,
The tortures of my Soul.
The wounds which in my breast my hands shall make
Will certainly transport her, since
With so much pleasure she beholds
The wounds which in my heart her eyes have made.
Thyrsis: Courage, Amintas, I have news
To tell thee that will bring thee hope.
Amintas: Ah, Thyrsis, is it Life or Death?
Thyrsis: 'Tis Life and Joy, if thou art bold enough
To meet 'em where they're to be found:
But then, Amintas, 'tis requir'd
That thou shouldst shew thyself a Man;
A Man that dares do any thing for Love.
175 Amintas: What must I dare? and whom encounter?

Thyrsis: Suppose your Mistress, in a Wood,
    Encompast with high Rocks, where Wolves,
    Where Lyons, Bears and Tygers lurk,
    Would you to get her venture there?
Amintas: I'd run as joyfully as e're I went
    To Dance and Revel at our rural Feasts.
Thyrsis: Suppose her in the hands of Thieves,
    Amidst arm'd Robbers, would you venture there?
Amintas: Swift as parcht Stags to cooling Waters run.
Thyrsis: Something more daring, something yet more bold
    Than this, is to be done to make thee blest.
Amintas: I'd leap into the Ocean, when the Waves
    By ruffling Winds are mingled with the Clouds:
    I'd walk thro Fire, or else, as I've been told
    Orpheus once did, descend to Hell
    To find my Sylv'a out, but sure
    'Twould not be Hell if she were there.
    Tell me then where I am to go?
    And what I am to do?
Thyrsis: Sylvia, naked and alone,
    Attends thee at Diana's Brook:
    Amintas durst thou venture there?
Amintas: What dost thou tell me? Sylvia wait
    Naked and alone for me?
Thyrsis: Alone, if Daphne is not there.
    And if she is, you're safe in her.
Amintas: Wait for me, and naked!
Thyrsis: Naked—But—
Amintas: But what? Speak out, thy silence kills me.
Thyrsis: But 'tis not certain that she waits for thee.
Amintas: This ruins what you said before:
    Ah! if you were not sure of that,
    Why, Thyrsis, did you say so much?
    Why did you shew me joy so near,
    And fling me from my hopes so soon!
    Sure 'tis not friendly to insult
    O're one in misery, like me:
    Did you believe my griefs too light,
    That you encrease their weight?
Thyrsis: Be rul'd
    By me, you shall be happy still.
Amintas: What would ye have me do?
Thyrsis: Go seize

The Maid, while Fortune is your Friend.

Amintas: Ah! Heaven forbid that I should think
    Of any thing that would displease her,
    Whom I will ne're offend but by my Love;
    And if my Love offends her,
    'Tis her Beauty's fault, not mine:
    In all my actions I resolve
    More to consult her pleasure than my own.
Thyrsis: Then you resolve you will not go?
Amintas: Yes, I will go, but not where you
    Advise.
Thyrsis: Where then?
Amintas: To Death, if you
    Can tell me of no other way
    To life; if this is all the good
    That you can do me by your help.
Thyrsis: Is this so little then? And canst
    Thou fancy, foolish as thou art,
    That Daphne would have bid us come,
    If she, who knows what Sylvia thinks,
    Believ'd 'twould give her such offence?
    She thought perhaps that 'twas not fit
    For you and me to know as much
    As she of Sylvia's Soul: Besides,
    Enquiring farther in so nice a case,
    Instead of pleasing will displease.
    You often wisht that you knew how
    To please her, you may do it now:
    No matter if you take by theft
    The joys you covet, or by gift;
    When once they're tasted she'll forget
    The Crime, the sin will be so sweet.
    Proceed.
Amintas: Ah, stay a little.
Thyrsis: Stay! You know
    Time flys us.
Amintas: Prithee let us think
    A little more of what we have to do.
Thyrsis: We'll think a little more then as we go.
    Come, you may alter if you tarry,
    Things too much thought on frequently miscarry.

ACT THREE

SCENE 1—Thyrsis, Chorus

Thyrsis: O Cruelty extream! ungrateful Maid!
   Oh most ungrateful Sex! and thou
   Oh Nature, careless of thy Sons,
   Why hast thou plac'd in Womens eyes
   All that is amiable and kind?
   And hast forgot to mould their Hearts as soft,
   Or make 'em with their Eyes agree.
   Ah, poor Amintas! miserable Youth,
   Where hast thou hid thyself from human sight?
   I've sought thee everywhere in vain;
   I fear the transports of thy rage
   Have hurry'd thee to do a thing
   For which we all must mourn: But see,
   Perhaps those Swains can tell me where
   Thou art. Ah Shepherds have ye seen
   Amintas?
Chorus: You seem concern'd:
   What reason have ye for these tears?
Thyrsis: Amintas, poor Amintas, is the cause:
   Have ye not seen him lately?
Chorus: No;
   We have not seen him since he went
   With you towards yonder Wood; but why
   D'ye ask so earnestly?
Thyrsis: I fear
   H' has kill'd himself since that.
Chorus: Amintas kill'd himself! For what?
Thyrsis: Anothers hatred, and his love.
Chorus: When two such Enemies unite
   What can they not effect? Explain
   Yourself more clearly: what d'ye mean?
Thyrsis: He lov'd a Nymph too much, and she
   Too much despis'd him for his love.
Chorus: Ah tell me all, while you relate
   The story, some may come this way,
   And bring us news of him you seek:
   Perhaps Amintas will himself

Before you've finish'd it, arrive.
Thyrsis: Yes, you shall know it, for 'tis but just
    That such ingratitude should be
    As infamous as 'tis extream.
    Amintas heard (I told him where,
    Alas! and brought him to the place)
    That Sylvia was with Daphne gone
    To bathe 'em in a neighb'ring Brook,
    Fearful and dubious there he went,
    His heart still bidding him to stay,
    As I perswaded him to go;
    And thus as he inclin'd to stop,
    I push'd him on, and forc'd him to proceed.
    As we approach'd the Brook, we heard
    A woman's lamentable cryes,
    And Daphne presently appear'd,
    Beating her Breasts, and looking wild,
    As if some horrid thing was done;
    But when she spy'd us, she cry'd out,
    Help, fly, or Sylvia's ravish'd, fly.
    Swifter than Leopards on their prey
    The amorous Amintas flew,
    I follow'd, and behind the Boughs
    Saw the young Maid, all naked bound,
    Her hair, which in bright tresses us'd to flow,
    Now ty'd her to a Tree: What once preserv'd
    Her Virgin Bosom from lascivious looks,
    Was now the fatal Instrument
    To hurt her Modesty, and bind
    Her arms about the rugged Bark:
    Her tender feet were ty'd with twigs:
    And o're against her I perceiv'd
    A wicked Satyr, who had then
    Just fasten'd her for his design:
    Sylvia, as well she could, strove
    To hinder his attempts.
Chorus: But what
    Could she have done at last?
Thyrsis: Amintas like a Lyon fierce
    Rusht on the Satyr with his Dart,
    I pick'd up Stones, and was prepar'd
    To help him, when the Monster fled
    Far from revenge, and left our friend
    Behind, who now had time to gaze

On all the Beauties he ador'd:
He saw a thousand hidden Charms,
Which set afresh his heart on fire,
And easily one in his looks
Might read his wonder and delight,
Who mingling with his Love Respect,
Thus in submissive accents spoke:
Forgive, fair Maid, forgive these hands,
If they with too much boldness touch
Your heavenly body, thus expos'd.
Oh! Sylvia, murmur not at fate,
Who sent me here to set you free.
Chorus: Such words would soften Rocks,
    And melt the most obdurate heart.
    What said she now?
Thyrsis: Nothing; but lookt
    On him who sav'd her, with disdain;
    Asham'd to be thus found, and loth
    To be by one she hated, freed.
    She strove with all her art to hide
    Her Breasts, and keep 'em from his sight.
    Amintas coming up with fear,
    Unbound her Hair, and as he touch'd
    Her Locks thus said. Oh barbarous Tree,
    Unworthy of these sacred knots,
    With which we Lovers only should be bound:
    Ah how couldst thou such Beauty wrong!
    Then trembling he unty'd her arms,
    Whiter than Ivory or Snow,
    And bending to the ground, began
    To break the twigs which bound her feet;
    But Sylvia rudely push'd him off,
    And spite of his respect, commanded
    Him proudly not to touch her feet.
    Hence Shepherd, touch me not, she cry'd,
    For I'm Diana's, and can loose
    My feet without your help.
Chorus: Oh! how
    Could she with so much pride reward
    Such services, and such respect.
Thyrsis: Amintas modestly withdrew,
    And durst not look on her again,
    But what he long'd so much to see,
180   With pain deny'd himself, afraid

To be by her he lov'd, deny'd.
I, who behind the Covert stood,
And saw and heard what he had said and done,
Was oft by just resentment mov'd,
And hardly kept from crying out,
To see how haughtily she us'd
The man to whom she ow'd her Life,
Or what is dearer than her Life,
Her Honour, by his means preserv'd.
And yet, oh strange ingratitude!
When with much trouble she had unty'd
Her Feet, away she ran, and scorn'd
To bid the Swain adieu: She flew
Fast as a Stag, but had no cause
To fear Amintas, who had shewn
Such proofs of wonderful respect.
Chorus: What made her fly?
Thyrsis: She rather chose
To owe her safety to her flight,
Than to Amintas love.
Chorus: She shew'd in this
That she delights to be ingrate:
Where went the Shepherd then?
Thyrsis: I know not.
Justly provok'd, I ran to stop
The Nymph, but she was gone too far:
When to the Fountain I return'd,
In hopes to find Amintas there,
I found him not, and fear he's gone
To end his troubles with his Life.

SCENE II—Amintas, Daphne, Nerina

Amintas: Oh! Pityless pity, cruel friend!
To snatch away my Dart, with which
I might have ended all my woes:
The longer I retard my death
'Twill be the sharper when it comes.
Ah! Daphne, why wouldst thou perswade
A wretch to live in misery?
Daphne: Despair no more, for if I know
Sylvia's mind, 'twas more her shame,
Than fear or scorn that made her fly.
Nerina: Why, like the Raven, must I be

181

The omen of bad news? Ah poor
Montano! how wilt thou survive
Thy Daughter's loss, thy Sylvia's death,
The death of one thou lov'dst so well?
No more a Father now, at least
Without a Child.
Daphne: I hear the voice
Of one that talks of death.
Amintas: I hear
My Sylvia nam'd, it strikes my heart:
Who calls on Sylvia?
Nerina: Why have I liv'd, oh Heaven! to be
The messenger of these sad tydings.
Sylvia came naked to our house,
(You know perhaps the fatal cause)
Where being cloath'd she fain would go,
And forc'd me with her to the Chace.
We went, and in the Forest found
The Nymphs, who by appointment met,
Were ready to begin the sport,
When from the Thicket I perceiv'd
A Wolf of monstrous size rush forth,
Licking his bloody Lips, whose foam
Reeking and Crimson, made us shake with fear;
But Sylvia from her Quiver took
An Arrow, put it to the Bow
I gave her, which she nimbly bent,
And taking at the Beast just aim,
She shot him near the Head; the Wolf enrag'd
Fled to the Thicket: Sylvia drew,
And brandishing her Dart, pursu'd
Him in the Woods.
Amintas: Oh doleful story!
Of which, if 'tis so sad to hear
So much, what must it be to know the rest.
Nerina: I, with another Dart,
Follow'd 'em by the blood the Wolf had spilt,
But could not reach 'em, they were gone too far.
I lost her in the Woods, yet still
Kept on alone, and wander'd thro'
The frightful Thicket, till I came
To its most unfrequented tracts,
Where Sylvia's Dart lay on the ground,
And at a little distance thence

Her veil; and while I gaz'd on these,
I spy'd seven Wolves around a Corps,
Who tore it with their bloody Teeth.
So eager on their Prey,
I saw the woful sight unseen by them;
With fear and pity mov'd, I turn'd
My steps, and got in safety home.
This, this is all that I can tell: (Shews the Veil.)
This all of Sylvia which remains.
Amintas: Ah! thou hast told too much.
  Oh! Dear Remains: Oh! precious Blood,
  Oh Sylvia! now alas no more.
Daphne: Ah! What, Nerina, hast thou said?
  It strikes his Soul: he swoons, he dyes!
Nerina: Perhaps 'tis but a Lovers fit;
  He breathes still; see, he comes to life.
Amintas: Ah! Grief too mighty to be born,
  And yet too weak to be my death;
  This office for my hand's reserv'd,
  And by my hand shall be perform'd.
  If my misfortunes are so sure,
  If Sylvia's dead, oh Daphne, why,
  Why didst thou renew my pain,
  By bringing me to life again?
  How good, how pleasant had it been,
  If in an extasie of woe
  Thou hadst permitted me to dye:
  The Gods, who knew I should by this
  Prevent the torments they've prepar'd
  For me to feel, inspir'd your hearts
  With pity, that being forc'd to live
  I might endure 'em all; and all
  I have endur'd, for Sylvia's dead:
  Nor is it possible for me
  To be more wretched than I am:
  And now methinks 'tis just that Heav'n and you
  And all should suffer me to dye.

ACT FOUR

SCENE 1—Daphne, Sylvia, Chorus

183 Daphne: Thanks to the Gods, that all our tears

Were needless, all our plaints and fears
In vain, since she for whom we mourn'd
Is living, and in health return'd.
Tell me the risque you ran, and how
You scap't the danger.
Sylvia: You shall know.
    Too day I as the Chace pursu'd
    A Wolf so far into the Wood
    I lost my Game, I lost the track,
    And turn'd on purpose to come back,
    When with seven other Wolves I found
    The Beast, and knew him by his wound:
    Round some dead Animal they stood,
    And tore its flesh, and lickt its blood:
    The Wolf I shot soon spy'd me out,
    And left his prey to meet his foe.
    I with my Dart oppos'd his way,
    Tho, mistress of my art, you know
    I very seldom miss my blow,
    Yet by bad luck I mist it now,
    And my Dart rested in a Bough:
    The Wolf at this more furious grew,
    And got so near me, that I knew
    My Bow would stand in little stead;
    So to preserve myself I fled:
    And as I fled I was methought
    By something which oppos'd me, caught.
    The Veil I wore hitcht in a Tree,
    And with my hair entangled me.
    I pull'd my Veil, I tore my hair,
    And yet was forc'd to leave it there.
    Wing'd by my fright away I flew
    Like air, and so got safe to you.
    Why, Daphne, are you now so sad:
    What, can't my safety make you glad?
Daphne: You live, I'm glad to find it true,
    And wish another was as safe as you.
Sylvia: Perhaps you hate me, you appear
    No more concern'd to see me here.
Daphne: I hate you not, I joy in your return,
    But for anothers death must mourn.
Sylvia: Whose?
Daphne: Poor Amintas.
184 Sylvia: What hast thou said!

Daphne: We met the Nymph, who by mistake
  Inform'd us you were slain; the youth,
  Without examining the truth,
  Believ'd, despair'd, and in the heat
  Of grief, fell breathless at our feet.
  We took him up, he breath'd again,
  We strove to comfort him in vain;
  For all the reasons we could give,
  Could not prevail on him to live:
  But rushing forth, away he fled
  To death, I believe is dead.
Sylvia: D'ye really believe it?
Daphne: Yes.
Sylvia: Daphne, it torments my mind
  When I consider how unkind,
  How cruel I have been:
  Pride I call'd Honour once, perhaps
  'Twas Honour, but 'twas too severe;
  And such as will, if he is dead,
  Sharpen my grief, my cruelty reprove,
  And force me to repent I wrong'd his Love.
Daphne: Oh Heaven! She's pitiful, repents,
  Her heart grows tender, she relents;
  She weeps—
  Is thy pride humbled then? O strange!
  Whence, Sylvia, comes this mighty change?
  Whence all these tears, from Pity or from Love?
Sylvia: Pity, not Love, attracts my tears.
Daphne: Pity's Love's Messenger, and shews,
  As Lightning before Thunder goes,
  Love is not far.
Chorus: When he'd surprize a Maid
  Who of his Empire is afraid,
  Who by false honour would defend her heart,
  And be secure against his Dart,
  He takes his Servant Pity's shape,
  And in that figure few escape
  His snares, he slily wins on every heart,
  And beaten off by force, prevails by art.
Daphne: Love at first in storms appears,
  Waited on by sighs and tears:
  Love has touch'd thee, tho too late,
  Into fondness turn'd thy hate.
  Ah Amintas, Sylvia's chang'd,

Weeps for Love, and thou'rt reveng'd.
Now thou mayst the Conquest boast,
Which if living thou hadst lost.
Thou hast Dying left behind
Such a sting in Sylvia's mind,
As will work more mischief there,
Than thou ever feltst for her.
Bees thus can't their Stings outlive,
But perish with the wounds they give.
If thou'rt, as I believe, a Spirit, fled
From the bright mansions of the dead;
From heavenly Groves, and sacred streams,
To play unseen about her Limbs,
See, Sylvia weeps, behold how much she's mov'd,
You lov'd alive, and are when dead belov'd.
If Destiny had so decreed,
That thou shouldst for thy Mistress bleed;
If in her thoughts she had resolv'd that this,
Whene're she sold her Love, should be the price,
'Tis thine, now thou hast done thy part,
And with thy Life hast bought her heart.
Chorus: Too vainly sold, and bought too dear;
   For him too hard, too infamous for her.
Sylvia: Oh that my Love could fetch again his breath,
   Or my heart purchase him of Death.
   Oh that my Life could be the price,
   I'd gladly part with it for his.
Daphne: Too late you're pitiful and wise,
   Your tears are useless, and in vain your sighs.

SCENE II—Ergastus, Chorus, Sylvia, Daphne

Ergastus: Pity and horror have so far
   Possest my Soul, I know not what
   I hear or see, but every thing
   I meet, amazes and afflicts me.
Chorus: What tydings hast thou brought, which make
   Thy looks thus troubled, and thy words
   Confus'd?
Ergastus: I bring the bitter news
   Of poor Amintas death.
Sylvia: What is't he says?
Ergastus: The noblest Shepherd of these Woods,
186   The kind, the gay, the gentle Swain,

Our Virgins and the Muses darling,
Young as he was, is dead; but how;
Oh! who can tell, or hear it told?
Chorus: Tell all, that we may mourn with thee
His sad misfortunes and our own.
Sylvia: Oh! how can I stay to hear
This most horrid story out?
Where is all my fierceness now?
Oh! my heart, so haughty once,
Shew thy Pride, and if thou canst
Stay and hear it all unmov'd:
Speak then what thou hast to say.
Shepherd, let me know the worst,
Tell it me, I'm most concern'd;
Speak. I'm ready for thy news.
Ergastus: Nymph, I know thou art concern'd,
Dying, the Despairing wretch
Call'd on thee, and with thy name
Finish'd his unhappy Life.
Daphne: Prithee begin the dismal tale.
Ergastus: Sitting on yonder Hill, where I
Had laid some Nets, I saw but now
Amintas run that way; his looks
Distracted, and his carriage wild;
His eyes, his mein so chang'd, I thought
That something strange might happen since
I left the Vale: he spy'd and shunn'd me;
Fearing the worst, I then pursu'd,
O'retook and stopp'd him; he grew calm,
Begg'd me to go and see him do
A thing which he pretended then
He was oblig'd to do, but first
Forc'd me to swear I would not stir,
Beyond the bounds he set, nor lift
My hands to hinder him. I swore
By Pan, by Pallas, by Pomona,
And all our Sylvan Deities,
(Alas! not thinking what he meant.)
I would not stir nor lift my hands,
Unless he gave me leave. This done,
He led me to a Precipice,
Where, from the margent of the Hill
Directly down the pathless dale,
Between high Rocks appears, my head

Grew giddy, I stepp'd back, afraid
To view the depth: Amintas smil'd
And look'd serenely, which deceiv'd
My fears, and made me more assur'd.
Thus then he said—
Ergastus, tell
The Nymphs and Swains what thou shalt see,
Since, since he cry'd, and then look'd down,
The Gods will not permit my end
To be the same with Sylvia's, since
My Limbs must not be torn like hers,
And I'm deny'd the Paws and Teeth
Of Wolves to use, as they serv'd
Her lovely Body: I must take
Whatever death they please to send.
These Rocks direct the way, I wish
I had deserv'd the same with hers.
But this is sure and short. Oh see!
I follow thee, my Sylvia, don't
Disdain my Company in death.
I'd dye contented, were I sure
'Twould not displease thee, I should then,
Oh Sylvia, follow thee with joy.
I come, I follow thee, I come:
And saying this,
He threw him headlong down,
While my heart chill'd to see him fall.
Daphne: Oh miserable youth!
Sylvia: Oh Heavens!
   I should, I own I should have been
   Amintas kind Companion here;
   But since I can't be so, I will,
   By thy assistance quickly follow him,
   And bear him company in Death.
Chorus: Comfort thyself, poor Virgin, 'tis
   The hand of Fate, and not thy fault.
Sylvia: Why weepst thou Swain? if 'tis for me,
   Weep not, for I deserve no tears,
   No pity. Hitherto I've only liv'd
   For myself, the little time
   That's now left me, I'll devote
   To Amintas, if I can't
   Live for him, I'll live at least

   For his pale unhappy Body.

I must put off death a while,
Till I've seen it, and then end
With his Funeral my Life.
Shepherd, lead us to the Vale,
To the fatal Precipice.

ACT FIVE

SCENE I—Elpinus, Chorus

Elpinus: Rejoyce, my friends, rejoice, the news
　　You heard is false; Amintas lives.
Chorus: Ah! what, Elpinus, dost thou say?
　　How dost thou comfort us? Is't false?
Elpinus: Hear then what I shall say, no more
　　Than I have with these eyes beheld.
　　I've in the Desart Vale a Cave,
　　Where Thyrsis came to me to day,
　　Where, while we talkt of that proud Nymph
　　Whose Fetters formerly he wore,
　　And I at present wear, we heard
　　A voice, and lookt up tow'rds the hill;
　　Whence, down the Precipice, we saw
　　A Body tumble on a Bush.
　　Just by my Cave, and near the Mount,
　　A few tall Bushes rise from Box
　　And other Trees, which all unite
　　In one; on these we saw him fall:
　　But, carry'd by the Body's weight,
　　He rowl'd off thence, and at our feet
　　Fell next; the Bushes sav'd the blow
　　So much, we took him up alive.
　　He was yet speechless, and 'twas long
　　E're we had any other signs
　　Of Life, besides his sighs and groans, which shew'd
　　Us that he breath'd: But, oh!
　　When we perceiv'd who 'twas, what tongue
　　Can tell the fright which we were in?
　　Pity and wonder struck us dumb:
　　Yet thinking by his breath, he might
　　Still live, we were a little calm'd.
189　Chorus: Oh wonderful Escape!

SCENE II—Elpinus, Thyrsis, Alfibeus, Chorus, Daphne, Sylvia, Amintas lying on a couch

Sylvia: See, Daphne, how these Shepherds smile
    At my Despair, how unconcern'd
    They hearken to my griefs; ev'n I,
    As savage as I was, scarce saw
    Amintas mourn with so much ease.
Daphne: Hence, Shepherds hence, and don't disturb
    The wretched with untimely joy.
Sylvia: Not that I court your pity, or
    Expect compassion, but methinks
    Amintas death should touch your hearts;
    And you should still consider me
    As one Amintas lov'd. But oh!
    You look on me as one that hated him,
    You see his murderer in me, and set
    Your souls against the cause of so much woe.
    Oh! that you all could in this minute lose
    Your native tenderness, and that your rage
    Were equal to your hate, that I might soon
    Be sent to meet him in those blissful plains,
    Where he himself will treat me with more love.
Alfibeus: Sylvia forbear these sad complaints,
    And don't afflict yourself for things
    Which heaven has wonderfully made
    The subject of our joy, Amintas lives.
Sylvia: Ha, Daphne, whither are we got?
    I heard a voice, which said Amintas lives;
    And in the midst of grief invites to joy.
    Ha! see what heavenly vision strikes my eyes,
    Behold it well, my Friend, and tell me then
    If anything but my Amintas self
    Could look more lovely. 'Tis Amintas self,
    I know him now: I feel him at my heart,
    It dances in my breast, and bids me do
    What Love commands and you must all excuse.

                               (Falls on Amintas.)

    Where, where is he who said Amintas lives?
    Let him come here, and tell me if he can,
    Why his eyes languish, why he looks so pale?
    Why lifeless, when his Sylvia clasps him thus,
    And deaf to all she says? Ah speak, my Love,
    Inform me if my glances hurt thy eyes,

And drive away thy Soul from what it loaths.
Whoe're thou art that said Amintas lives,
'Twas falsely said, and with a vile intent
To shew me hope, and leave me in despair.
He lives indeed, but in a better world,
Whence now methinks I hear him call on me,
And Sylvia's name is in Elysium sung.
Amintas: Where am I? on what happy Region thrown?
What Musick wakes me from the arms of death,
And charms me with the name of my belov'd?
Oh! all ye Glorious Spirits, who in peace
And perfect bliss possess these sacred Groves,
Direct me to the Bow'r, where Sylvia waits
For me, whom now she can no longer hate,
Since all Paradice are friends.
Sylvia: He speaks, he lives, and injur'd as he was,
Talks kindly of me still. Look up Amintas,
Look on thy Sylvia with thy usual joy,
And let thy Eyes speak kindly, like thy Tongue.
Amintas: Who breathes new life into me with her kisses,
And quickens me with her embraces? Ha! my Love,
My Sylvia winding in my arms! I can scarce
Spare time to ask the meaning of these things.
Have not I seen you all, and been your friend?
And is not this the darling of my Soul?
Yes, yes, 'tis she; her Beauty shews 'tis she,
Nor could I feel such Transports with another.
Sylvia: When he reflects how barb'rous I have been
He'll loath me for my Cruelty, and hate
A Maid who so unjustly hated him.
Amintas: Oh Sylvia! we'll not think of what is past,
I'll not enquire how I became so blest,
But thank the Gods and thee for what I know.
As for the rest, thou could'st not but be just,
And love decreed the troubles we have known,
To shew his Pow'r, and make our bliss the greater.
Elpinus: There's nothing wanting but Montano's word,
To make 'em both as happy as they wish.
Chorus: They need not question his consent,
He longs to see his Daughters Sons,
To sport about him and revive
His Age, and soon will grant what they desire.
Alfibeus: Then let us to her Father's house repair
And see him join their hands and share his joy.

Amintas: You all may by my fate perceive
　　The Laws which Love prescribes Mankind,
　　By which Eternally he rules
　　His Empire here,
　　Are not fantastical and hard,
　　As sometimes we suppose his works,
　　Tho they're mysterious, are wise
　　And such as we should ne're condemn.
　　With how much art, thro hidden ways,
　　And paths unknown, he leads to bliss.
　　And when we think him ready to destroy,
　　He opens Paradice, and leaves our Souls injoy.

BALDASSARE CASTIGLIONE

The Book of the Courtier
Translated by Sir Thomas Hoby, Modernized

Second
Book

For so much as therefore the Count yesterday night entreated upon Courtiership so copiously and in so good a manner, he has made me (truly) conceive no small fear and doubt that I shall not so thoroughly satisfy this noble audience in the matter that lies upon me to discourse in, as he has done in that was his charge. Yet to make myself partner in what I may of his praise, and to be sure not to err (at the least in this part) I will not contrary him in any point.

Wherefore agreeing to his opinions, and beside the rest, as touching nobleness of birth, wit and disposition of person, and grace of countenance, I say unto you that to get him worthy praise and a good estimation with all men, and favour with such great men as he shall attend upon, methinks it is behoveful he have the understanding to frame all his life and to set forth his good qualities generally in company with all men without purchasing himself envy.

The which how hard a matter it is of itself, a man may consider by the seldomness of such as are seen to attain to that point: because we are all the sort of us in very deed more inclined of nature to dispraise faults, than to commend things well done. And a man would think that many by a certain rooted malice, although they manifestly discern the goodness, enforce themselves with all study and diligence to find in things either a fault, or at the least the likeness of a fault.

Therefore it behoves our Courtier in all his doings to be chary and heedful, and what so he says or does to accompany it with wisdom, and not only to set his delight to have in himself parts and excellent qualities, but also to order the tenor of his life after such a trade, that the whole may be answerable unto these parts, and see the selfsame to be always and in everything such, that it disagree not from itself, but make one body of these good qualities, so that every deed of his may be compact and framed of all the virtues, as the Stoics say the duty of a wise man is: although notwithstanding always one virtue is the principal, but all are so knit and linked one to another, that they tend to one end, and all may be applied and serve to every purpose.

Therefore it behoves he have the understanding to set them forth, and by comparison, and (as it were) contrariety of the one, sometime to make the other better known: as the good painters with a shadow make the lights of high places to appear, and so with light make low the shadows of plains, and meddle diverse colours together, so that through that diversity both the one and the other are more sightly to behold, and the placing of the figures contrary the one to the other is a help to them to do the feat that the painter's mind is to bring to pass.

So that lowliness is much to be commended in a gentleman that is of prowess and well seen in arms: and as that fierceness seems the greater when it is accompanied with sober mood, even so does sober mood increase and show itself the more through fierceness.

Therefore little speaking, much doing, and not praising a man's own self in commendable deeds, dissembling them after an honest sort, does increase both the one virtue and the other in a person that can discreetly use this trade: and the like is to be said in all the other good qualities.

Therefore will I have our Courtier in that he does or says to use certain general rules, the which (in my mind) contain briefly as much as belongs to me to speak.

And for the first and chief let him avoid (as the Count said well in that behalf yesternight) above all things curiosity.

Afterward let him consider well what the thing is he does or speaks, the place where it is done, in presence of whom, in what time, the cause why he does it, his age, his profession, the end whereto it tends, and the means that may bring him to it: and so let him apply himself discreetly with these advertisements to whatsoever he minds to do or speak.

After Sir Frederick had thus said, he seemed to stay a while. Then said M. Morello of Ortona: methinks these your rules teach but little. And I for my part am as skillful now as I was before you spoke them, although I remember I have heard them at other times also of the Friars with whom I have been in confession, and I ween they term them circumstances.

Then laughed Sir Frederick and said: if you do well bear in mind,
194 the Count willed yesternight that the chief profession of the Courtier

should be in arms, and spoke very largely in what sort he should do it, therefore will we make no more rehearsal thereof.

Yet by our rule it may be also understood, that where the Courtier is at skirmish, or assault, or battle upon the land, or in such other places of enterprise, he ought to work the matter wisely in separating himself from the multitude, and undertake notable and bold feats which he has to do, with as little company as he can, and in the sight of noble men that be of most estimation in the camp, and especially in the presence and (if it were possible) before the very eyes of his king or great personage he is in service withal: for indeed it is meet to set forth to the show things well done.

And I believe even as it is an evil matter to seek a false renown, and in the thing he deserves no praise at all, so is it also an ill matter to defraud a man's self of his due estimation, and not to seek that praise, which alone is the true reward of virtuous enterprises.

And I have known of them in my time, that for all they were of prowess, yet in this point they have showed themselves but grossheaded, and put their life in as great hazard to go take a flock of sheep, as in being the foremost to scale the walls of a battered town, the which our Courtier will not do if he bear in mind the cause that brings him to war, which ought to be only his estimation.

And if he happen moreover to be one to show feats of Chivalry in open sights, at tilt, tourney, or *Joco di canne*, or in any other exercise of the person, remembering the place where he is, and in presence of whom, he shall provide beforehand to be in his armour no less handsome and sightly than sure, and feed the eyes of the lookers on with all things that he shall think may give a good grace, and shall do his best to get him a horse set out with fair harness and sightly trappings, and to have proper devices, apt poses, and witty inventions that may draw unto him the eyes of the lookers on as the adamant stone doth iron.

He shall never be among the last that come forth into the lists to show themselves, considering the people, and especially women take much more heed to the first than to the last: because the eyes and minds that at the beginning are greedy of that novelty, note every light matter, and print it: afterward by continuance they are not only full, but weary of it.

Therefore was there a noble stageplayer in old time that for this respect would always be the first to come forth to play his part.

In like manner also if our Courtier do but talk of arms, he shall have an eye to the profession of them he talks withal, and according to that frame himself, and use one manner of talk with men, and another with women: and in case he will touch anything sounding to his own praise, he shall do it so dissemblingly as it were a chance and by the way, and with the discretion and wariness that Count Lewis showed us yesterday.

Do you not now think (M. Morello) that our rules can teach somewhat? Trow you not that that friend of ours I told you of a few days ago had clean forgotten with whom he spoke, and why? When to entertain a gentlewoman whom he never saw before, at his first entering in talk with her, he began to tell how many men he had slain, and what a hardy fellow he was, and how he could play at two hand sword.

And had never done until he had taught her how to defend certain strokes with a pollaxe being armed, and how unarmed, and to show how (in a man's defence) to lay hand upon a dagger, so that the poor gentlewoman stood upon thorns, and thought an hour a thousand years till she were got from him, for fear lest he would go nigh to kill her as he had done those other.

Into these errors run they that have not an eye to the circumstances which you say you have heard of Friars.

Some there be that knowing themselves to have an excellency in one thing, make their principal profession in another, in which notwithstanding they are not ignorant, but when time serves to show themselves in that they are most skillful in, they do it always very perfectly: and otherwhile it comes to pass, that the company perceiving them so cunning in that which is not their profession, they imagine them to be much better in that they profess indeed.

This art in case it be coupled with a good judgment, discontents me nothing at all.

Then answered the Lord Gasper Pallavicin. I think not this an art, but a very deceit, and I believe it is not meet for him that will be an honest man to deceive at any time.

This quoth Sir Frederick, is rather an ornament that accompanies the thing he does, than a deceit: and though it be a deceit, yet it is not to be disallowed.

Will you not say also, that he that beats his fellow, where there be two playing at fence together, beguiles him, and that is because he has more art than the other?

And where you have a jewel that unset seems fair, afterward when it comes to a goldsmith's hands that in well setting it makes it appear much more fair, will you not say that the goldsmith deceives the eyes of them that look on it? And yet for that deceit, deserves he praise, for with judgment and art a cunning hand does many times add a grace and ornament to ivory, or to silver, or to a stone that is

fair in sight, setting it in gold.

BALDASSARE CASTIGLIONE, 1478–1529

We say not then that this art or deceit (in case you will so term it) deserves any manner blame.

Also it is not ill for a man that knows himself skillful in a matter, to seek occasion after a comely sort to show his feat therein, and in like case to cover the parts he thinks scant worthy praise, yet notwithstanding after a certain wary dissimulation.

Do you not remember how king Ferdinand without making any show to seek it, took occasion very well to strip himself sometime into his doublet? and that because he knew he was very well made and nimble withal. And because his hands were not all of the fairest, he seldom plucked off his gloves, and (in manner) never. And few there were that took heed to this wariness of his.

Methinks also I have read, that Julius Cæsar wore for the nonce a garland of laurel, to hide his baldness withal. But in these matters a man must be very circumspect and of a good judgment, lest he pass his bounds: for to avoid one error oftentimes a man falls into another, and to get him praise, purchases blame.

Therefore the surest way in the world, is, for a man in his living and conversation to govern himself always with a certain honest mean, which (no doubt) is a great and most sure shield against envy, the which a man ought to avoid in what he is able.

I will have our Courtier also to take heed he purchases not the name of a liar, nor of a vain person, which happens many times, and to them also that deserve it not. Therefore in his communication let him be always heedful not to go out of the likelihood of truth, yea and not to speak too often those truths that have the face of a lie, as many do that never speak, but of wonders, and will be of such authority, that every incredible matter must be believed at their mouth.

Other, at the first entering into friendship with a new friend, to get favor with him, the first thing that they speak, swear that there is not a person in the world whom they love better, and they are willing to jeopard their life for his sake, and such other matters out of reason, and when they part from him, make wise to weep, and not to speak a word for sorrow. Thus because they would be counted to be loving worms, they make men count them liars, and fond flatterers.

But it were too long a matter and tedious to reckon up all vices that may happen in conversation. Therefore, for that I desire in the Courtier, it suffices to say (beside the matters rehearsed) that he be such a one than shall never want good communication and fit for them he talks withal, and have a good understanding with a certain
197 sweetness to refresh the hearers' minds, and with merry conceits and

jests to provoke them to solace and laughter, so that without being at any time loathsome or satiate, he may evermore delight.

Bembo notwithstanding sought to make an end of reasoning, but the Duchess desired him to say on, and he began thus afresh.

Too unlucky were the nature of man, if our soul (in the which this so fervent coveting may lightly arise) should be driven to nourish it with that only, which is common to her with beasts, and could not turn it to the other noble part, which is proper to her.

Therefore since it is so your pleasure: I will not refuse to reason upon this noble matter. And because I know myself unworthy to talk of the most holy mysteries of love, I beseech him to lead my thought and my tongue so, that I may show this excellent Courtier how to love contrary to the wonted manner of the common ignorant sort.

And even as from my childhood I have dedicated all my whole life unto him, so also now that my words may be answerable to the same intent, and to the praise of him.

I say therefore, that since the nature of man in youthful age is so much inclined to sense, it may be granted the Courtier, while he is young, to love sensually. But in case afterward also in his ripe years, he chance to be set on fire with this coveting of love, he ought to be good and circumspect and heedful, that he beguile not himself, to be led willfully into the wretchedness, that in young men deserves more to be pitied than blamed: and contrariwise in old men, more to be blamed than pitied.

Therefore when an amiable countenance of a beautiful woman comes in his sight, that is accompanied with noble conditions and honest behaviours, so that as one practised in love, he wotes well that his hew has an agreement with hers, as soon as he is aware that his eyes snatch that image and carry it to the heart, and that the soul begins to behold it with pleasure, and feels within herself the influence that stirs her, and by little and little sets her in heat, and that those lively spirits, that twinkle out through the eyes, put continual fresh nourishment to the fire: he ought in this beginning to seek a speedy remedy and to raise up reason, and with her to sense the fortress of his heart, and to shut in such wise the passages against sense and appetites, that they may enter neither with force nor subtle practice.

Thus if the flame be quenched, the jeopardy is also quenched. But in case it continue or increase, then must the Courtier determine
(when he perceives he is taken) to shun thoroughly all filthiness of

common love, and so enter into the holy way of love, with the guide of reason.

And first consider that the body, where that beauty shines, is not the fountain from whence beauty springs, but rather because beauty is bodiless, and (as we have said) an heavenly shining beam, she loses much of her honour when she is coupled with that vile subject and full of corruption, because the less she is partner thereof, the more perfect she is, and clean sundered from it, is most perfect.

And as a man heareth not with his mouth, nor smelleth with his ears: no more can he also in any manner wise enjoy beauty, nor satisfy the desire that she stirs up in our minds, with feeling, but with the sense, unto whom beauty is the very butt to level at: namely, the virtue of seeing.

Let him lay aside therefore the blind judgment of the sense, and enjoy with his eyes the brightness, the comeliness, the loving sparkles, laughters, gestures, and all the other pleasant furnitures of beauty: especially with hearing the sweetness of her voice, the tunableness of her words, the melody of her singing and playing on instruments (in case the woman beloved be a musician) and so shall he with most dainty food feed the soul through the means of these two senses, which have little bodily substance in them, and be the ministers of reason, without entering farther toward the body, with coveting unto any longing otherwise than honest.

Afterward let him obey, please, and honour with all reverence his woman, and reckon her more dear to him than his own life, and prefer all her commodities and pleasures before his own, and love no less in her the beauty of mind, than of the body.

Therefore let him have a care not to suffer her to run into an error, but with lessons and good exhortations seek always to frame her to modesty, to temperance, to true honesty, and so to work that there may never take place in her other than pure thoughts, and far wide from all filthiness of vices. And thus in sowing of virtue in the garden of that mind, he shall also gather the fruits of most beautiful conditions, and savour them with a marvellous good relish.

And this shall be the right engendering and imprinting of beauty in beauty, the which some hold opinion to be the end of love. In this manner shall our Courtier be most acceptable to his Lady, and she will always show herself toward him tractable, lowly and sweet in language, and as willing to please him, as to be beloved of him: and the wills of them both shall be most honest and agreeable, and they consequently shall be most happy.

Here Master Morello. The engendering (quoth he) of beauty in beauty aright, were the engendering of a beautiful child in a beautiful woman, and I would think it a more manifest token a great deal that she loved her lover, if she pleased him with this, than with the sweetness of language that you speak of.

Master Peter Bembo laughed, and said: You must not (Master Morello) pass your bounds. I may tell you, it is not a small token that a woman loves, when she gives unto her lover her beauty, which is so precious a matter: and by the ways that be a passage to the soul, that is to say, the sight and the hearing, sends the looks of her eyes, the image of her countenance, and the voice of her words, that pierce into the lover's heart, and give a witness of her love.

Master Morello said: Looks and words may be, and oftentimes are false witnesses. Therefore who so has not a better pledge of love (in my judgment) he is in an ill assurance. And surely I looked still that you would have made this woman of yours somewhat more courteous and free toward the Courtier, than my Lord Julian has made his: but (me seems) you be both of the property of those judges, that (to appear wise) give sentence against their own.

Bembo said: I am well pleased to have this woman much more courteous toward my Courtier not young, than the Lord Julian's is to the young: and that with good reason, because mine covets but honest matters, and therefore may the woman grant him them all without blame. But my Lord Julian's woman that is not so assured of the modesty of the young man, ought to grant him the honest matters only, and deny him the dishonest.

Therefore more happy is mine, that has granted him whatsoever he requires, than the other, that has part granted, and part denied.

And because you may moreover the better understand, that reasonable love is more happy than sensual, I say unto you that selfsame things in sensual ought to be denied otherwhile, and in reasonable, granted: because in the one, they be honest, and in the other dishonest.

Therefore the woman to please her good lover, beside the granting him merry countenances, familiar and secret talk, jesting, dallying, hand in hand, may also lawfully and without blame come to kissing: which in sensual love according to the Lord Julian's rules, is not lawful. For since a kiss is a knitting together both of body and soul, it is to be feared, lest the sensual lover will be more inclined to the part of the body, than of the soul: but the reasonable lover wotes well, that although the mouth be a parcel of the body, yet is it an issue for the words, that be the interpreters of the soul, and for the inward breath, which is also called the soul.

And therefore hath a delight to join his mouth with the woman's beloved with a kiss: not to stir him to any dishonest desire, but because he feels that that bond is the opening of an entry to the
souls, which drawn with a coveting the one of the other, pour them-

selves by turn the one into the other's body, and be so mingled together, that each of them has two souls.

And one alone so framed of them both rules (in a manner) two bodies. Whereupon, a kiss may be said to be rather a coupling together of the soul, than of the body, because it has such force in her, that it draws her unto it, and (as it were) separates her from the body.

For this do all chaste lovers covet a kiss, as a coupling of souls together. And therefore Plato the divine lover says, that in kissing, his soul came as far as his lips to depart out of the body.

And because the separating of the soul from the matters of the sense, and the thorough coupling her with matters of understanding may be betokened by a kiss, Solomon says in his heavenly book of ballads, O that he would kiss me with a kiss of his mouth, to express the desire he had, that his soul might be ravished through heavenly love to the beholding of heavenly beauty, in such manner, that coupling herself inwardly with it, she might forsake the body.

They stood all harkening heedfully to Bembo, reasoning, and after he had stayed a while, and saw that none spoke, he said: Since you have made me to begin to show our not young Courtier this happy love, I will lead him yet somewhat farther forwards, because to stand still at this stay were somewhat perillous for him, considering (as we have oftentimes said) the soul is most inclined to the senses.

And for all reason with discourse chooseth well, and knoweth that beauty not to spring of the body, and therefore sets a bridle to the unhonest desires, yet to behold it always in that body, does oftentimes corrupt the right judgment. And where no other inconvenience ensues upon it, once absence from the wight beloved carries a great passion with it.

Because the influence of that beauty when it is present, gives a wonderous delight to the lover, and setting his heart on fire, quickens and melts certain virtues in a trance and congealed in the soul, the which nourished with the heat of love, flow about and go bubbling nigh the heart, and thrust out through the eyes those spirits which be most fine vapours made of the purest and clearest part of the blood, which receive the image of beauty, and deck it with a thousand sundry furnitures.

Whereupon the soul takes a delight, and with a certain wonder is aghast, and yet enjoys she it, and (as it were) astonished together with the pleasure, feels the fear and reverence that men accustomably have toward holy matters and thinks herself to be in Paradise.

The lover therefore that considers only the beauty in the body,
201 loses this treasure and happiness, as soon as the woman beloved with

her departure leaves the eyes without their brightness, and consequently the soul as a widow without her joy. For since beauty is far off, that influence of love sets not the heart on fire, as it did in presence.

Whereupon the pores be dried up and withered, and yet does the remembrance of beauty somewhat stir those virtues of the soul in such wise, that they seek to scatter abroad the spirits, and they finding the ways closed up, have no issue, and still they seek to get out, and so with those shootings inclosed, prick the soul, and torment her bitterly, as young children, when in their tender gums they begin to breed teeth.

And hence come the tears, sighs, vexations and torments of lovers: because the soul is always in affliction and travail and (in a manner) waxes wood, until the beloved beauty comes before her once again, and then is she immediately pacified and takes breath, and thoroughly bent to it, is nourished with most dainty food, and by her will, would never depart from so sweet a sight.

To avoid therefore the torment of his absence, and to enjoy beauty without passion, the Courtier by the help of reason must full and wholly call back again the coveting of the body to beauty alone, and (in what he can) behold it in itself simple and pure, and frame it within in his imagination sundered from all matter, and so make it friendly and loving to his soul, and there enjoy it, and have it with him day and night, in every time and place, without mistrust ever to lose it: keeping always fast in mind, that the body is a most diverse thing from beauty, and not only not increases, but diminishes the perfection of it.

In this wise shall our not young Courtier be out of all bitterness and wretchedness that young men feel (in a manner) continually, as jealousies, suspicions, disdains, angers, desperations and certain rages full of madness, whereby many times they be led into so great error, that some do not only beat the woman whom they love, but rid themselves out of their life.

He shall do no wrong to the husband, father, brethren or kinsfolk of the woman beloved. He shall not bring her in slander. He shall not be in case, with much ado otherwhile to refrain his eyes and tongue from discovering his desires to others. He shall not take thought at departure or in absence, because he shall evermore carry his precious treasure about with him shut fast within his heart.

And beside, through the virtue of imagination, he shall fashion with himself that beauty much more fair than it is indeed. But among these commodities, the lover shall find another yet far
202 greater, in case he will take this love for a stair (as it were) to climb

up to another far higher than it. The which he shall bring to pass, if
he will go and consider with himself, what a straight bond it is to
be always in the trouble to behold the beauty of one body alone.
And therefore to come out of this so narrow a room, he shall gather
in his thought by little and little so many ornaments, that meddling
all beauty together, he shall make an universal conceit, and bring
the multitude of them to the unity of one alone, that is generally
spread over all the nature of man. And thus shall he behold no more
the particular beauty of one woman, but an universal, that decks out
all bodies.

Whereupon being made dim with this greater light, he shall not
pass upon the lesser, and burning in a more excellent flame, he shall
little esteem it, that he set great store by at the first.

This stair of love, though it be very noble and such as few arrive
at it, yet is it not in this sort to be called perfect, forsomuch as
where the imagination is of force to make conveyance, and has no
knowledge, but through those beginnings that the senses help her
withal, she is not clean purged from gross darkness: and therefore though she do consider that universal beauty in sunder and in
itself alone, yet does she not well and clearly discern it, nor without
some doubtfulness, by reason of the agreement that the fancies have
with the body.

Wherefore such as come to this love, are like to young birds
almost flush, which for all they flitter a little their tender wings, yet
dare they not stray far from the nest, nor commit themselves to the
wind and open weather.

When our Courtier therefore shall be come to this point, although
he may be called a good and happy lover, in respect of them that be
drowned in the misery of sensual love, yet will I not have him to set
his heart at rest, but boldly proceed farther, following the high way
after his guide, that leads him to the point of true happiness. And
thus instead of going out of his wit with thought, as he must do that
will consider the bodily beauty, he may come into his wit, to behold
the beauty that is seen with the eyes of the mind, which then begin
to be sharp and thoroughly seeing, when the eyes of the body lose
the flower of their sightliness.

Therefore the soul rid of vices, purged with the studies of true
Philosophy, occupied in spiritual, and exercised in matters of understanding, turning her to the beholding of her own substance, as it
were raised out of a most deep sleep, opens the eyes that all men
have, and few occupy, and sees in herself a shining beam of that
light, which is the true image of the Angel-like beauty partened with
her, whereof she also partens with the body a feeble shadow.

203   Therefore waxed blind about earthly matters, is made most quick

of sight about heavenly. And otherwhile when the stirring virtues of the body are withdrawn alone through earnest beholding either fast bound through sleep, when she is not hindered by them, she feels a certain privy smell of the right Angel-like beauty, and ravished with the shining of that light, begins to be inflamed, and so greedily follows after, that (in a manner) she waxeth drunken and beside herself, for coveting to couple herself with it, having found (to her weening) the footsteps of God, in the beholding of whom (as in her happy end) she seeks to settle herself.

And therefore burning in this most happy flame, she arises to the noblest part of her which is the understanding, and there no more shadowed with the dark night of earthly matters, sees the heavenly beauty: but yet does she not for all that enjoy it altogether perfectly, because she beholdeth it only in her particular understanding, which can not conceive the passing great universal beauty.

Whereupon not thoroughly satisfied with this benefit, love gives unto the soul a greater happiness. For like as through the particular beauty of one body he guides her to the universal beauty of all bodies: Even so in the least degree of perfection through particular understanding he guides her to the universal understanding.

Thus the soul kindled in the most holy fire of true heavenly love, flees to couple herself with the nature of Angels, and not only clean forsakes sense, but has no more need of the discourse of reason, for being changed into an Angel, she understands all things that may be understood: and without any veil or cloud, she sees the main sea of the pure heavenly beauty and receives it into her, and enjoys the sovereign happiness, that can not be comprehended of the senses.

Since therefore the beauties, which we daily see with these our dim eyes in bodies subject to corruption, that nevertheless be nothing else but dreams and most thin shadows of beauty, seem unto us so well favored and comely, that oftentimes they kindle in us a most burning fire, and with such delight, that we reckon no happiness may be compared to it, that we feel otherwhile through the only love which the beloved countenance of a woman casts at us.

What happy wonder, what blessed abashment may we reckon that to be, that takes the souls, which come to have a sight of the heavenly beauty? what sweet flame? What sweet incense may a man believe that to be, which arises of the fountain of the sovereign and right beauty? Which is the original of all other beauty which never increases nor diminishes, always beautiful, and of itself, as well on the one part as on the other, most simply, only like itself, and partner of none other, but in such wise beautiful, that all other beautiful things be beautiful, because they be partners of the beauty of it.

204

This is the beauty unseparable from the high bounty, which with her voice calls and draws to her all things: and not only to the endowed with understanding gives understanding, to the reasonable reason, to the sensual sense and appetite to live, but also partakes with plants and stones (as a print of herself) stirring, and the natural provocation of their properties.

So much therefore is this love greater and happier than others, as the cause that stirs it, is more excellent. And therefore, as common fire tries gold and makes it fine, so this most holy fire in souls destroys and consumes whatsoever there is mortal in them, and relieves and makes beautiful the heavenly part, which at the first by reason of the sense was dead and buried in them.

This is the great fire in the which (the Poets write) that Hercules was buried on the top of the mountain Oeta: and through that consuming with fire, after his death was holy and immortal.

This is the fiery bush of Moses: The divided tongues of fire: the inflamed Chariot of Helias: which doubles grace and happiness in their souls that be worthy to see it, when they forsake this earthly baseness, and flee up unto heaven.

Let us therefore bend all our force and thoughts of soul to this most holy light, that shows us the way which leads to heaven: and after it, putting off the affections we were clad at our coming down, let us climb up the stairs, which at the lowermost step have the shadow of sensual beauty, to the high mansion place where the heavenly, amiable and right beauty dwells, which lies hidden in the innermost secrets of God, lest unhallowed eyes should come to the sight of it: and there shall we find a most happy end for our desires, true rest for our travels, certain remedy for miseries, a most healthful medicine for sickness, a most sure haven in the troublesome storms of the tempestuous sea of this life.

What tongue mortal is there then (O most holy love) that can sufficiently praise thy worthiness? Thou most beautiful, most good, most wise, art derived of the unity of the heavenly beauty, goodness and wisdom, and therein dost thou abide, and unto it through it, (as in a circle) turnest about.

Thou the most sweet bond of the world, a mean betwixt heavenly and earthly things, with a bountiful temper bendest the high virtues to the government of the lower, and turning back the minds of mortal men to their beginning, couplest them with it.

Thou with agreement bringest the Elements in one, stirrest nature to bring forth, and that which arises and is born for the succession of the life. Thou bringest severed matters into one, to the unperfect givest perfection, to the unlike likeness, to enmity amity, to the earth fruits, to the sea calmness, to the heaven, lively light.

Thou art the father of true pleasures, of grace, peace, lowliness, and good will, enemy to rude wildness, and sluggishness: to be short, the beginning, and end of all goodness.

And forsomuch as thou delightest to dwell in the flower of beautiful bodies and beautiful souls, I suppose that thy abiding place is now here among us, and from above otherwhile showest thyself a little to the eyes and minds of them that be not worthy to see thee.

Therefore vouchsafe (Lord) to harken to our prayers, pour thyself into our hearts, and with the brightness of thy most holy fire lighten our darkness, and like a trusty guide in this blind maze show us the right way: correct the falsehood of the senses, and after long wandering in vanity, give us the right and sound joy. Make us to smell those spiritual savours that relieve the virtues of the understanding, and to hear the heavenly harmony so tunable, that no discord of passion take place any more in us. Make us drunken with the bottomless fountain of contentation, that always does delight, and never gives fill, and that gives a smack of the right bliss unto whoso drinks of the renewing and clear water thereof. Purge with the shining beams of thy light our eyes from misty ignorance, that they may no more set by mortal beauty, and well perceive that the things which at the first they thought themselves to see, be not in deed, and those that they saw not, to be in effect. Accept our souls, that be offered unto thee for a sacrifice. Burn them in the lively flame that wastes all gross filthiness, that after they be clean sundered from the body, they may be coupled with an everlasting and most sweet bond to the heavenly beauty. And we severed from ourselves, may be changed like right lovers into the beloved, and after we be drawn from the earth, admitted to the feast of the angels, where fed with immortal ambrosia and nectar, in the end we may die a most happy and lively death, as in times past died the fathers of old time, whose souls with most fervent zeal of beholding, thou didst hale from the body, and coupledst them with God.

When Bembo had hitherto spoken with such vehemency, that a man would have thought him (as it were) ravished and beside himself, he stood still without once moving, holding his eyes toward heaven as astonied: when the Lady Emilia, which together with the rest gave most diligent ear to this talk, took him by the plait of his garment, and plucking him a little said:

Take heed (Master Peter) that these thoughts make not your soul also to forsake the body.

Madam, answered Master Peter, it should not be the first miracle that love has wrought in me. Then the Duchess and all the rest
began afresh to be instant upon Master Bembo that he would

proceed once more in his talk, and every one thought he felt in his mind (as it were) a certain sparkle of that godly love that pricked him, and they all coveted to hear farther: but Master Bembo,

My Lords (quoth he) I have spoken what the holy fury of love has (unsought for) indited to me: now that (it seems) he inspires me no more, I wot not what to say. And I think verily that love will not have his secrets discovered any farther, nor that the Courtier should pass the degree that his pleasure is I should show him, and therefore it is not perhaps lawful to speak any more of this matter.

GIORDANO BRUNO

The Mercurial Ass
Translated by John Charles Nelson

CHARACTERS

The Ass, Micco the Pythagorean, Mercury

Ass: Now why should I abuse your high, rare and excellent gift, o thundering Juppiter? Why should I hide under the black and gloomy ground of most ungrateful silence such talent as you conferred upon me *(indicante fato)* with your so partial glance? Shall I still bide exhortations to speak, so as not to let that extraordinary bellow escape from my mouth, which your generosity, in this most confused world, has sown in my interior spirit? Let then the asinine palate be opened by the key of this occasion, let my tongue be freed by the industry of the aforesaid palate, let the hand of attention guided by the arm of understanding pick the fruits of the trees and the flowers of the herbs that are in the garden of asinine memory.

Micco: O strange portent, o stupendous prodigy, o incredible marvel, o miraculous event! May the gods avoid some disaster! Is the ass speaking? The ass? O Muses, O Apollo, O Hercules, can articulate sounds come from such a head? Hush, Micco, maybe you are being fooled; maybe some man is disguised under this hide, to make fun of you.

Ass: Think that there is nothing sophistical about me, Micco, but that I am a completely natural speaking ass; and I remember other times having had human limbs as I now have bestial parts.

Micco: Next, you demon incarnate, I'll ask you who, what and how you are? Now, first of all, I would like to know what you want here? What augury, what order from the gods, do you bring us? Where is this scene going to end? For what purpose have you put your feet in this portico of ours to precisely show that you can speak?

Ass: First of all I want you to know that I am trying to be declared a member and doctor of some school or academy, in order that my ability may be authenticated, so that my concepts will be heard, my words pondered, and my learning esteemed with the same faith as—

Micco: O Juppiter! Is it possible that *ab aeterno* there has ever been recorded a fact, an event or a case like this one?

Ass: Forget your astonishment for now; and answer me quickly, you or one of these other amazed fellows who are running here to listen to me. O didactic masters with your caps and gowns and rings, arch-didactic and wise as heroes and demigods: do you wish, would it please you, and do you strongly desire to accept in your company, society, and fellowship and under the emblem and standard of your communion this ass which you see and hear? For among you some laughing are amazed, others amazed are laughing, and others (who are the majority) are biting their lips. And no one answers?

Micco: You see that for astonishment they don't speak, and by turning to me they all indicate that I should answer you; as president, it is my business to give you a solution; from me, as from all, you must await the decision.

Ass: What academy is this, which has the inscription over the door, *Lineam ne pertransito?*

Micco: There is a school of Pythagoreans there.

Ass: May one enter?

Micco: As an academician not without many and difficult conditions.

Ass: Now what are these conditions?

Micco: They are really very many.

Ass: I asked what, not how many.

Micco: I shall answer you the best I can, giving you the main ones. First, that when someone applies for admission, before he can be accepted he must be examined as to the disposition of his body, physiognomy and wit, because of the great relative consequence which we know that the body has with and from the soul.

Ass: "Let the song begin with Juppiter," if he wishes to marry.

Micco: Second, having been admitted, he is given a term of not under two years during which he must be silent, and he is not permitted to dare ask about any point, even about things he doesn't understand, let alone to argue and examine aims; and in that period he is called a listener. Third, after this period he is permitted to speak, ask, write the things he has heard, and

209

explain his own opinions; and in this interval he is said to be a mathematician or Chaldean. Fourth, informed of such things and adorned by those studies, he turns to the consideration of the works of the world and principles of nature; and here he halts his stride, and is called a physicist.

Ass: Doesn't he proceed further?

Micco: He cannot be more than a physicist; because there can be no knowledge of supernatural things, except in so far as they shine in natural things; for only the purged and superior intellect can consider them in themselves.

Ass: Have you no metaphysics?

Micco: No; and that which others boast as metaphysics is simply part of logic. But let's leave this; it's not to the point. Such, in conclusion, are the conditions and rules of our academy.

Ass: These?

Micco: Yes sir.

Ass: O honored school, distinguished university, beautiful sect, venerable college, most illustrious seminary, unsurpassed institution and chiefest among the chief academies! The wandering ass, like a thirsty deer, comes to you as to clearest cool waters; humble and suppliant, the ass presents himself to you, most kind receivers of pilgrims, eager to be registered in your society.

Micco: In our society, huh?

Ass: Yes, yes, yes sir, in your society.

Micco: Go through that other door, sir, because asses are banned from this one.

Ass: Tell me, brother; through which door did you enter?

Micco: Heaven can make asses talk, but it can never let them enter a Pythagorean school.

Ass: Don't be so haughty, Micco, and remember that your Pythagoras teaches not to despise anything that is found in the bosom of nature. Although at present I am in the form of an ass, I may have been and may soon be in the form of a great man; and although you are a man, you may have been and may soon be a great ass, according to what appears expedient to the dispensator of habits and places and administrator of transmigrating souls.

Micco: Tell me, brother, did you understand the covenants and conditions of the academy?

Ass: Very well.

Micco: Have you considered your being, and whether for some defect your entry might be impeded?

Ass: A great deal, in my judgment.

210   Micco: Now explain yourself.

Ass: The main condition which made me doubt was the first. It's quite true that I don't have that disposition, that tender flesh, that delicate, clear and gentle skin, which the physiognomists say are most fit for the reception of doctrine; because their coarseness is contrary to the agility of the intellect. But it seems to me that the principal should be able to dispense with such a condition; because he should not exclude anyone when many other qualities make up for such a defect, like sincerity of manners, sharpness of wit, efficacy of intelligence, and other accompanying conditions deriving from these. I pass over the fact that souls do not universally take after the complexion of the body; because some more efficacious spiritual principle may defeat and overcome the outrage done him by that crassness or other bodily defect. Apropos of which I give you the example of Socrates, whom the physiognomist Zopiro judged an intemperate man, stupid, dull, effeminate, inclined to become enamored of boys, and fickle; all of which was conceded by the philosopher, but not that the act of such inclinations were realized: since he became temperate by the continual study of philosophy, which had placed the tiller firmly in his hand against the fury of the waves of natural indispositions, for there is nothing that cannot be overcome by study. As for the other main physiognomical part, which consists not in the complexion of temperaments, but in the harmonious proportion of members, I tell you that it is impossible to find any defect in me, when you consider thoroughly. You know that a pig is not supposed to be a fine horse, nor the ass a handsome man; but an ass should be a beautiful ass, the pig a beautiful pig, a man a beautiful man. For if, reversing the judgment, the horse does not seem beautiful to the pig, neither does the pig appear beautiful to the horse; if man does not think the ass beautiful, and does not fall in love with the ass, neither on the contrary does man seem beautiful to the ass nor enamor him. So with regard to this law, when things are examined and weighed with reason, one will concede to the other according to their respective affections, that the kinds of beauty vary according to different proportionalities; and nothing is truly and absolutely beautiful, except beauty itself, or that which is beautiful in essence and not by participation. I omit that in the human species itself that which is said of the flesh must be considered *respectu habito* according to twenty-five circumstances and glosses, which adapt it; because otherwise that physiognomical rule of soft flesh is false; since children are not more able in science than men: unless the possibility which is further from the act were called greater ability.

211 Micco: Up to the present this ass seems to know a very great deal.

Go ahead, Mister Ass, and make your cause as strong as you please; because

You're plowing in the wave, and sow in sand,
And with a net you hope to catch the wind,
And place your hopes upon a woman's heart,

if you hope that entry into this or any other sect can or should be conceded to you by the academicians. But if you are learned, be content with remaining alone with your doctrine.

Ass: O senseless people, do you think that I am telling you my reasons so that you can validate them for me? Do you think I have done this for another end than to accuse you and render you inexcusable before Juppiter? When Juppiter made me learned he made me "Doctor." I was just waiting for you to spit forth this sentence from the fine judgment of your sufficiency: "It is not proper for asses to enter an academy together with us men." This, if it can be said by a scholar of any other sect whatever, cannot be reasonably said by you Pythagoreans, because in the act of denying me entry, you destroy the principles, foundations and body of your philosophy. Now what difference do you find between us asses and you men, not judging things by their surface, aspect and appearance? Besides that, inept judges: how many of you wander in the academy of asses? How many learn in the academy of asses? How many take their degrees, rot and die in the academy of asses? How many are favored, elevated, magnified, canonized, glorified and deified in the academy of asses?—who, if they had not been and were not still asses, I don't know, I don't know how the affair would have gone and would go now for them. Are there not so many highly honored and most splendid studies, where lessons are given in becoming an ass, to have not only the good of temporal life, but of eternal life as well? Tell me, what and how many faculties and honors are entered through the door of asininity? Tell me, how many are impeded, excluded, rejected and placed in infamy, for not participating in the asinine faculty and perfection? Now why shall it not be proper for a few asses, or at least one ass to enter the academy of men? Why should I not be accepted by having the majority of the voices and votes in my favor in any academy whatever, being that, if not all, at least the larger and greatest part is written and sculptured in our own so universal academy? Now if we asses are so liberal and unstinted in receiving everybody, why must you be so reluctant to accept at least one of us?

Micco: Greater difficulty is made in more worthy and important things: and so much importance is not given and eyes are not opened so wide in things of little consequence. Therefore all are received without repugnance or much scruple of conscience in the academy of asses, and it must not be so in the academy of men.

Ass: But, dear sir, tell me if you can, and resolve somewhat for me, which of the two is more worthy, for a man to become an ass, or for an ass to become human? But here in truth is my Mercury: I know him by his staff and wings.—Welcome to the handsome winged messenger of Juppiter, trusty interpretor of the will of all the gods, liberal giver of sciences, corrector of the arts, continual oracle of mathematicians, admirable bookkeeper, elegant speaker, fine countenance, charming appearance, eloquent aspect, pleasant personage, man among men, among women woman, wretch among wretches, blessed among the blessed, all among all; you enjoy with those who enjoy, with those who cry you cry; therefore everywhere you go and stay you are well liked and accepted. What do you bring that is good?

Mercury: Because, Ass, you wish to call yourself and be an academician, I, as the one who has given you other gifts and favors, again at present with plenary authority order, constitute and confirm you an academician and general dogmatist, so that you may enter and live everywhere, without anyone being able to stop you or work any kind of outrage or impediment, *quibuscumque in oppositum non obstantibus*. Enter, then, wherever you like and please. Neither do we wish you to be obligated by the requirement of biennial silence which is found in the Pythagorean order, or by any other ordinary laws whatsoever: because, when new cases arise, new laws must be written, and for the same reasons established laws do not apply: and meanwhile the decision must be referred to the judgment of the best judge, whose concern it is to provide for what is necessary and fitting. Speak then among the listeners; consider and contemplate among the mathematicians; discuss, ask, teach, declare and determine among the physicists; be found with everyone, discuss with everyone, fraternize, unite yourself and identify yourself with all, be all.

Ass: Did you hear him?

Micco: I'm not deaf.

SPAIN

ANONYMOUS

JUAN LUIS VIVES

ST. IGNATIUS LOYOLA

MIGUEL DE CERVANTES SAAVEDRA

LOPE DE VEGA

ANONYMOUS

The Life of Lazarillo de Tormes
Translated by Thomas Roscoe

You must know, then, in the first place, that my name is Lázaro de Tormes, and that I am the son of Thomas Gonzalez and Antonia Perez, natives of Tejares, a village of Salamanca. My surname was acquired by the singular circumstance of my birth, which happened in the river Tormes, and in the following manner. My father (to whom God be merciful) was employed to superintend the operations of a water-mill which was worked by the course of the above river (a situation that he held above fifteen years), and my mother at that time being *enceinte* with me, while staying one night at the mill was suddenly seized with the pains of labour, which terminating happily, it may with truth be said, that my surname, borrowed from the river, was not inaptly bestowed.

I had only reached my ninth year, when my unfortunate father was charged with administering certain copious but injudicious bleedings to the sacks of customers to the mill; a lowering system which was voted by them to be neither salutary nor profitable. He was forthwith taken into custody; when, not being about to deny the indiscreet application of his professional ability, he experienced the usual penalty of the law. It is, however, to be hoped that he is now reaping the reward which has been faithfully promised by the Evangelist to all those who have suffered persecution for justice' sake; for they are declared to be in the highest degree fortunate in such their tribulations. By this disaster, my poor father being thrown out of employment, joined an armament then preparing against the Moors, in the quality of mule-driver to a gentleman; and in that expedition, like a loyal servant, he, along with his master, finished his life and services together.

My widowed mother, thus bereft of husband and of home, determined, in order to acquire a reputation, to associate herself with people of character; she therefore hired a small place in the city, and opened an eating-house for the accommodation of the students, adding likewise to her gains, by washing linen for the
217 servants of his Excellency, the Comendador of the order of Mag-

dalena. It was in the exercise of the duties of this latter branch of industry that she became acquainted with a groom of the stables, a man of colour rather than of character or fortune. Under the pretence of buying eggs he would continually come to our house, and at last obtained an intimate footing therein. At first, in consequence of his colour and the roughness of his manners, I was frightened by him; but when I found that our scanty fare was changed by his visits into abundance, for he always brought bread and meat, and in winter wood for our fire, I not only conquered my repugnance, but even hailed his approach with pleasure. One unpleasantness attended this intimacy, which was that my mother presented me with a little brother, very pretty, though of a darkish complexion, and whom I was obliged to assist in nursing and bringing up.

Matters were not carried on so secretly, however, but that some intelligence of Zayde's gallantry reached the ears of the Comendador's majordomo, who, on enquiry, found a terrible deficiency in the barley, to say nothing of currycombs, brushes, and such like moveables which had been unaccountably lost; and it was found also, that when nothing better offered itself, even the horses were unshod for the sake of the iron, and all was unluckily traced to my mother for the support of my little brother.

One can hardly wonder at a priest or a friar, the one robbing the poor, the other his convent for the sake of their fair and devout believers, when love can stimulate a poor slave to do the like. All this was fully proved; for when they came to me, like a child as I was, and fearful of the threats of punishment, I discovered to them all I knew of the matter, even to the very horse-shoes which my mother had directed me to sell to the farrier. My poor father-in-law was soundly flogged, and his flesh tickled with drops of scalding fat; while my mother was forbidden the house of the Comendador, and was commanded, under the severest penalties, never to receive Zayde into her presence again. Not to make matters worse, my mother fulfilled the obligation of the sentence, and to avoid danger, as well as to escape further scandal, she engaged herself to serve the guests at the inn of the Solana, where, notwithstanding she suffered a thousand inconveniences, she managed to rear my little brother. As to myself, I went on errands, and endeavoured to make myself as useful as possible.

About this time a blind man came to lodge at the house, and thinking that I should do very well to lead him about, asked my mother to part with me for that purpose. My mother recommended me strongly, stating that I was the son of an excellent man who died

in battle against the enemies of our faith, and "I trust in God," added she, "that he will never make a worse man than was his father." She confided me to his care as an orphan boy, and entreated him to use me with kindness. The old man promised to receive me, not as a servant, but as a son; and thus I commenced service with my new though blind and aged master. We remained in Salamanca some few days, but my master finding his gains in that city to be very inconsiderable, determined to seek greater profits elsewhere. When we were ready to depart, I went to take leave of my mother, who, with an abundance of tears, from which I, too, could not refrain, gave me her blessing and said, "My son, this may probably be the last time I shall ever see you; endeavour then for my sake to be good, and may the Almighty assist you. I have reared you from childhood, and now provide you with a kind master; look to yourself for the future, and farewell." I then went to rejoin my master, who was waiting for me at a short distance.

We left Salamanca, and having arrived at the bridge, my master directed my attention to an animal carved in stone in the form of a bull, and desired me to take him near it. When I had placed him close to it, he said, "Lázaro, if you put your ear close to this bull, you will hear an extraordinary noise within." In the simplicity of my heart, believing it to be as he said, I put my ear to the stone, when the old man gave my head such a violent thump against it, that I was almost bereft of sense, and for three days after I did not lose the pain I suffered from the blow. My old master laughed heartily at the joke: "You rogue," said he, "you ought to know that a blind man's boy should have more cunning than the very devil himself."

It seemed to me as though that moment had awakened me from the simplicity of childhood, and I said to myself, "The old man says truly. I am now alone, and if I do not keep a sharp look out for myself, I shall find none to assist me."

Notwithstanding all my master's astuteness and cunning, I contrived so to outwit him, that generally the best half came to my share. Whenever we ate, the old man took care to keep a small jar of wine near him, which was reserved for his own especial service; but I very soon adopted the practice of bestowing on this favourite jar sundry loving though stolen embraces. Such pleasures were but short-lived, for the fervency of my attachment was soon discovered in the deficiency of the wine; and the old man afterwards, to secure his draught, never let the jar go without tying it to him by the handle. But I was a match for him even there; for I procured a large straw, and dipping it into the mouth of the jar, renewed my intimacy with such effect, that but a small share was his who came after me. The old traitor was not long in finding me out; I think he must have heard me drink, for he quickly changed his plan, and placed the jar between his knees, keeping the mouth closed with his hand, and in this manner considered himself secure from my depredations.

Being thus deprived of my customary allowance from the jar, I was ready to die with longing; and finding my plan of the straw no longer available, I took an opportunity of boring a very small hole in the bottom of the jar, which I closed very delicately with wax. At dinnertime, when the poor old man sat over the fire, with the jar between his knees, the heat, slight as it was, melted the little piece of wax with which I closed the hole, and I, feigning to be cold, drew close to the fire, and placed my mouth under the little fountain in such a manner, that the whole contents of the jar came to my share. When the old boy had finished his meal, and thought to regale himself with his draught of wine, the deuce a drop did he find, which so enraged and surprised him, that he thought the devil himself had been at work; nor could he conceive how it could be. "Now, uncle," said I, "don't say that I drank your wine, seeing that you have had your hand on it the whole time." But he was not satisfied with my declaration of innocence, so turning and twisting the jar about in every direction, he at last discovered the hole, which at once let him into the secret of my ingenious contrivance. He concealed his discovery so well, that I had not the slightest suspicion that my ruse was detected; so the next day, having prepared my jar as before, little foreseeing the consequences, nor dreaming of the wicked thoughts which were passing in the old man's mind, I placed myself under the jar, which presently began to distil its delicious contents, my face turned towards heaven, and my eyes partly closed, the better to enjoy the delightful draught. The evil-minded old man, judging this to be the time to take his vengeance, raised with both hands the sweet, though alas, to me, bitter jar, and let it fall directly on my mouth, adding to its weight by giving all the impetus in his power. The poor unhappy Lázaro, who little reckoned on such a disaster, but had quietly resigned himself to the delicious enjoyment of the moment, verily believed in the crash which succeeded, that the heavens with all they contained had fallen upon him. The blow was so tremendous that my senses fairly left me, and the jar breaking, cut my face in many places, several pieces remaining in the wounds, besides breaking nearly all my teeth, the loss of which I feel to this very day.

From that hour I bore an inveterate grudge against my old rogue of a master, for though he attended to me, and cured me of my wounds, I could plainly see that he enjoyed my cruel chastisement. 220 He washed the wounds with wine which the broken jar had made in my face; and would say smiling, "Lázaro, my boy, what is that which makes you ill, cures you, and gives you strength?" with other little witticisms, which he would repeat, not by any means to my taste.

When I was nearly cured of my wounds and bruises, considering that by a few more such pleasantries the old man would effectually get rid of me, I began to think how I might in the best manner get rid of him; however, I resolved to wait until an opportunity should offer of effecting my purpose with safety to myself, and more to my satisfaction with regard to the past proceedings of my master.

Although I might in time have pardoned the jar adventure, yet the continual ill-treatment to which I was henceforward subjected, kept alive the vindictive feeling which it originally occasioned; for now, upon the slightest occasion, and even without cause, he would beat and flog me without any mercy. If any humane person interfered, he immediately recounted the history of the jar, prefacing it with some such expression as, "Don't believe the young rogue is quite so innocent as he looks; just listen, and then say whether the devil himself would ever have had the cunning to do the like." Those who listened would reply, "Who could have thought that so much wickedness could be packed in such a small compass?" and they would laugh heartily at my exploit, and say, "Thrash him well, good man; thrash him well; he deserves it richly!" With such encouraging advice he persevered to the very letter, and I can say to my cost, that in his leisure hours he did little else; in return I took him over the worst roads I could find, and led him wherever there was the slightest chance of his hurting himself. If stones were near, over the very sharpest; if mud through the deepest; and although this mode of travelling was not the pleasantest, yet if I inconvenienced myself, I annoyed the old man still more, which was all I desired to do. It is true that my head and shoulders were subjected in consequence to the angry visitations of his staff; and though I continually assured him that his uneasy travelling was not the result of my ill-will, but for want of better roads, yet the old traitor had too much cunning to believe a word I said.

That I may not be tiresome, I shall omit many curious anecdotes of this my first service, and will only relate the following, and then say how I at last took my leave of my blind master. We were in Escalona, a place belonging to the Duke of that name, when one day he gave me a piece of a large sausage to cook. While the sausage was in the roaster before the fire, he regaled himself with the dripping; and then taking out his purse, gave me a halfpenny to fetch him some wine. I don't know how it was, unless the devil placed the means before my eyes, but I was tempted to play the thief; for on looking round I saw a turnip, not unlike the shape of a sausage, which had been thrown away as unfit for use. There was nobody near us, and I, with a raging appetite, still further stimulated by the savoury smell of the sausage, which I knew full well was all the old man intended for my share, without a thought for the consequences, snatched the sausage from the roaster while the old man was fumbling for his money, and in a twinkling supplied its place with the turnip.

As I started for the wine, my master began to blow up the fire, thinking the more speedily to cook, what his miserable parsimony, and my urgent appetite, had caused to vanish. On my road for the wine, I was not long in dispatching the sausage; and when I returned, I found the miserable old sinner with the turnip stuck between two slices of bread, preparing, as he thought, to make a most delicious repast. As he bit through the bread, however, thinking to take part of the sausage, his teeth encountered the cold hard turnip, when the truth flashing on his mind, he exclaimed in an altered tone, "Lazarillo, how is this?" "Mercy on me," said I, "do you suspect me? Have I not this instant returned with your wine? Somebody has been here and played this trick upon you." "No, no," said he, "my hand has been on the roaster all the time, that is impossible." I turned to swear and forswear myself as being innocent of this fraud, but little did the old man credit me. He arose, and seizing me by the head, as he possessed as keen a scent as a spaniel, determined to satisfy himself of the truth; so opening my mouth by main force, he thrust therein his ugly nose, which was long and pointed, and at that time had increased considerably in length from spite and anger. With this, and the excessive fear which came over me, added to the shortness of time allowed for my stomach to settle, and more than all, the tickling of that immense proboscis, so unpleasant a feeling began to manifest itself, that hardly had the old man withdrawn his trunk, than the whole contents of my stomach followed, and with such force as entirely to cover his face. Had he not been blind before, his eyesight could hardly have escaped such an explosion. Oh! heavens! what were my feelings at that unhappy moment! never shall I forget it! Such was the rage of that diabolical old man, that had not my screams attracted some people, I verily believe I should never have escaped with life.

I escaped from his hands in the best way I could, leaving the few hairs that remained to me in his grasp, my face, neck, and throat bearing the marks of his vindictive talons. Lest the bystanders should compassionate me, the old man recounted my exploits to them, which set them into such a roar of laughter, that the place soon became thronged like a fair. And with such humour did the old rogue varnish my misdeeds, that, weeping and wounded as I was, I could easily forgive their mirth.

Considering the injuries I had sustained, in addition to the ridicule to which I was continually exposed, I determined at all hazards to leave the old tyrant to his fate, and chose the following opportunity of doing so. The next day we went about the town to ask alms; but as the weather turned out very wet, we did not stir from beneath the arcades, with which this place is provided. As the night approached, and the rain had not ceased, the old man said, "Lázaro, this wet weather is very unwholesome, and as night comes on it will be still more so, let us therefore get home in good time."

On our return we had to pass a small stream of water, which with the day's rain had considerably increased. I therefore said, "Uncle, the brook is very much swollen; but I see a place a little higher, where, by giving a little jump, we may pass almost dry shod." "Thou art a good lad," said the old man; "I like you for your carefulness. Take me to the narrowest part, for at this time of the year to get one's feet wet would be dangerous." Delighted that my plot seemed to succeed so well, I led him from beneath the arcades, and took him directly opposite to a pillar, or rather a large stone post, which I observed in the square. "Now, uncle," said I, "this is the place where the brook is the narrowest." The rain was pouring down, and the old man was getting very wet; and whether it was by haste he made to avoid it, or, what was more probable, Providence had at that moment beguiled him of his usual cunning, that he might the more readily fall into the snare, and give me my revenge; so it was, that for once he believed me, and said, "Now place me directly opposite the spot, and then jump yourself." I placed him exactly opposite the pillar, so that he could not miss it, and leaping myself, I took my position immediately behind it, crying out, "Now, master, jump with all your force, and you will clear the water." I had hardly said the words, when the poor old rogue jumped up as nimbly as a goat, giving all his strength to the leap, and taking a step or two backwards by way of impetus, which lent him such force, that instead of alighting on soft ground, as he supposed, he gave his poor bald pate such a smash against the pillar, that he fell on the pavement without sense or motion.

"Take that, you unhappy old thief," said I, "and remember the sausage;" then leaving him to the care of the people who began to gather around, I took to my heels as swiftly as possible through the town gates, and before night reached Torrijos. What became of the old man afterwards I don't know, and neither did I ever give myself any pains to enquire.

223

JUAN LUIS VIVES

A Fable about Man
Translated by Nancy Lenkeith

I should like to begin this essay of mine on man by some fables and plays, since man is himself a fable and a play. Once upon a time, after a certain lavish and sumptuous feast given by Juno on her birthday for all the gods, they, feeling carefree and elated by the nectar, asked whether she had prepared some plays which they might watch after the banquet. Thus nothing would be lacking to complete their happiness on this august occasion.

To gratify this wish of the immortal gods, Juno earnestly asked her brother and husband Jupiter, since he was all-powerful, to improvise an amphitheater and to bring forth new characters, after the manner of regular plays, lest in this respect a day which she wanted most distinguished seem deficient to the gods. Thereupon, all of a sudden, at a command of almighty Jupiter, by whom alone all things are done, this whole world appeared, so large, so elaborate, so diversified, and beautiful in places, just as you see it. This was the amphitheater: uppermost, to wit in the skies, were the stalls and seats of the divine spectators; nethermost—some say in the middle— the earth was placed as a stage for the appearance of the actors, along with all the animals and everything else.

When everything was ready and the banquet tables carried away, Mercurius Braubeta announced that the players were already on the stage. Joyfully the spectators went forth and were seated, each according to his rank. The great Jupiter was director of the plays, and when he saw that all were there, he gave the signal. Since he was the maker, he ordered everything and explained it to all that they might understand. Lest something be done differently from what he himself liked, he prescribed to the company of actors the entire arrangement and sequence of the plays, from which not even by the breadth of a finger, as they say, should they depart.

Indeed, as soon as the voice and signal of the great Jupiter reached the actors, each in their turn they came onto the stage, and there with such skill and poise, and so much in the manner of Roscius, did they perform tragedies, comedies, satires, mimes, farces, and other things of the sort that the gods swore that a more beautiful spectacle they had never beheld. Overjoyed at the delight and satisfaction of the gods, and quite elated herself, Juno kept asking them, one by one, how they liked the games. All agreed wholeheartedly that there had never been a more admirable spectacle, nothing worthier of Juno herself and of the birthday which they were celebrating.

This greatest spouse of the greatest god could not contain her excitement; briskly she would skip among the stalls of the immortal gods and, besides other things, repeatedly asked everyone which of the actors they considered the greatest. The wisest of the gods answered that none was more praiseworthy than man, and the father of the gods himself nodded his assent. Indeed, the more intently they watched the gestures, the words, and all the actions of this character, the greater was the astonishment that struck them. It pleased Jupiter to see so much admiration and praise given to man, his own offspring, by all the gods.

Those who sat at Jupiter's side, seeing how much pleasure he took in this human archmime, easily understood that he himself had made this personage; nay, looking more carefully, they recognized in man himself a great resemblance to Jupiter, so that even the dullest of gods might have known that man was born of Jupiter. Verily, man, peering oft through the mask which hides him, almost ready to burst forth and revealing himself distinctly in many things, is divine and Jupiter-like, participating in the immortality of Jupiter himself, in his wisdom, prudence, memory, sharing so many of his talents that it was easy to know that these great gifts had been bestowed upon him by Jupiter from out of his treasury and even from his own person.

Then, as he of gods the greatest, embracing all things in his might, is all things, they saw man, Jupiter's mime, be all things also. He would change himself so as to appear under the mask of a plant, acting a simple life without any power of sensation. Soon after, he withdrew and returned on the stage as a moral satirist, brought into the shapes of a thousand wild beasts: namely, the angry and raging lion, the rapacious and devouring wolf, the fierce and wild boar, the cunning little fox, the lustful and filthy sow, the timid hare, the envious dog, the stupid donkey. After doing this, he was out of sight for a short time; then the curtain was drawn back and he returned a man, prudent, just, faithful, human, kindly, and friendly, who went about the cities with the others, held the authority and obeyed in turn, cared for the public interest and welfare, and was finally in every way a political and social being.

The gods were not expecting to see him in more shapes when, behold, he was remade into one of their own race, surpassing the nature of man and relying entirely upon a very wise mind. O great Jupiter, what a spectacle for them! At first they were astonished that they, too, should be brought to the stage and impersonated by such a convincing mime, whom they said to be that multiform Proteus, the son of the Ocean. Thereupon there was an unbelievable outburst of applause, and they prevented that great player from acting any longer. They begged Juno to let him into the stalls of the gods, unmasked, and to make of him a spectator rather than an actor. She was already eagerly going about obtaining this of her husband, when, at that very moment, man came out upholding the great Jupiter, the worthiest of gods, and with marvelous and indescribable gestures impersonating his father. He had transcended the characters of the lower gods and was piercing into that inaccessible light surrounded by darkness where Jupiter dwells, of kings and gods the king.

When the gods first saw him, they were roused and upset at the thought that their master and father had stooped to the stage. Soon, however, with composed minds, they glanced repeatedly at Jupiter's stall wondering whether he himself was sitting there or whether he had appeared masked to play a part. Seeing him there, they gazed back again at man and then at Jupiter. With such skill and propriety did he play Jupiter's part that, up and down, from Jupiter's stall to the stage, they kept glancing, lest they be misled by a likeness or the accurate mimic of an actor. Among the other players there were some who swore that this was not man but Jupiter himself, and they underwent severe punishment for their error.

Yet the gods, out of respect for this image of the father of all gods, and by their own suffrage, unanimously decreed that divine honors be granted to man. They prevailed upon Jupiter, through Juno's intercession, that man, who had so rightly played the parts of Jupiter and the gods, put off his mask and be seated among the gods. Jupiter complied with the gods, granting them what he himself, long before, had decided to bestow gratuitously upon man. Thus man was recalled from the stage, seated by Mercury among the gods, and proclaimed victor. There were no cheers to greet him but a silence of wonder. The whole man lay bare, showing the immortal gods his nature akin to theirs, this nature which, covered with mask and body, had made of him an animal so diverse, so desultory, so changing like a polypus and a chameleon, as they had seen him on the stage. Jupiter was then declared and proclaimed the father not only of the gods but also of men. With a gentle and mild countenance, he took delight in both, and was hailed and adored as a parent by both. With pleasure he received this august double name; and now, using also this favored title, we proclaim him of gods and men the father.

Now, when Mercury first came into the stalls of the gods, carrying in his arms the stage costumes, the gods looked at them with great interest; having examined them attentively, a long while, they praised Jupiter's wisdom and skill and adored him, for the costumes which he had made were no less appropriate than useful for all the acts. There was the lofty head, stronghold and court of the divine mind; in it the five senses arranged and placed ornately and usefully. The ears, accordingly, did not droop with soft skin, nor were they firmly fixed with a hard bone, but both were rounded by a sinuous cartilage. Thus they could receive sounds from all directions, and the dust, straw, fluff, gnats which might be flying around would not penetrate into the head but be caught in the folds. The eyes in equal number, two indeed, were high up so that they could observe all things and protected by a fine wall of lashes and eyelids against the same bits of straw and fluff, dust and tiny insects. They were the gauge of the soul and the noblest part of the human face. Then came the very attire of the mask or the mask itself, so handsomely shaped, divided into arms and legs which were long and ending with fingers, so good-looking and useful for all purposes. As there is no time to go through all that which others have related at great length, I shall add this conclusion. All is so well fitted and interrelated that if one were to withdraw or change or add something, all that harmony and beauty and the whole effi- cacy would be immediately lost. By no ingenuity could a more appropriate mask be conceived for a man, unless someone perhaps wish for the impossible.

When the gods saw man and embraced their brother, they deemed it unworthy of him to appear on a stage and practice the disreputable art of the theater, and they could not find enough praise for their own likeness and that of their father. They investi- gated one by one and examined the many hidden secrets of man and derived more pleasure from this than from the spectacle of all the plays, "Nor having seen him once are they content; they wish to linger on." There indeed was a mind full of wisdom, prudence, knowledge, reason, so fertile that by itself it brought forth extraor- dinary things. Its inventions are: towns and houses, the use of herbs, stones and metals, the designations and names of all things, which foremost among his other inventions have especially caused

227

wise men to wonder. Next and no less important, with a few letters he was able to comprise the immense variety of the sounds of the human voice. With these letters so many doctrines were fixed in writing and transmitted, including religion itself and the knowledge and cult of Jupiter the father and of the other brother gods. This one thing, which is found in no other animal but man, shows his relationship to the gods. Of little good would all these inventions have been if there had not been added, as the treasury of all things and for the safekeeping of these divine riches, a memory, the storehouse of all that we have enumerated. From religion and memory, foreknowledge is almost obtained, with the prophecy of the future, evidently a spark of that divine and immense science which perceives all future events as if they were present.

The gods were gazing at these and other things, as yet sateless; just as those who contemplate their beautiful reflection in a mirror take delight in these things and willingly tarry on, so the gods, seeing themselves and Jupiter their father so well portrayed in man, wished to look more and more at what they had already beheld, inquiring about one thing after another. How did he act plants, herbs, even wild animals, man, gods, the god king Jupiter, by what craft and gesture?

While man explained all this calmly and clearly, Jupiter ordered that ambrosia and nectar from the remains of the feast be placed before him. Cheerfully neglecting the plays, many of the gods had their afternoon refreshment with him. They were charmed by their brotherly guest or fellow-citizen, who, refreshed by heavenly victuals after the toil of the plays, wrapped like the other gods in the purple *praetexta* and bearing the crown, went forth to watch the spectacle. Many of the gods stood up for him, many gave up their seats. In different directions they pulled his cloak and retarded his progress that he might stay next to them, until the great Jupiter nodded to Mercury, who led him, that he was to be received in the orchestra among the gods of the first rank, who considered this a great honor. Far was it from those gods of the highest order to despise man, who had been an actor a short time before. He was received by them with respect and invited to the front seats. He sat in their company and watched the games which proceeded without interruption, until Apollo himself reduced the light at Juno's request (for the masters of the feast and other servants, warned by the cooks, announced that supper was more than ready), and night fell upon them. Chandeliers, torches, wax tapers, candlesticks, and oil lamps brought by the stars were lighted, and they were entertained at supper with the same pomp as they had been at

228   dinner. Juno also invited man, and Jupiter the father "assented and

with a nod made all Olympus tremble."

Man, just as he had watched the plays with the highest gods, now reclined with them at the banquet. He put on his mask, which he had meanwhile laid aside, for this stage costume was so greatly honored. Since it had so well met the needs of man, it was deemed worthy of the most sumptuous feast and of the table of the gods. Thus it was given the power of perception and enjoyed the eternal bliss of the banquet.

ST. IGNATIUS
LOYOLA

Spiritual Exercises
Translated by John Charles Nelson

Preface In order that both he who gives the Spiritual Exercises and he who receives them may be helped and profit more, it must be presupposed that every good Christian should be more eager to save his neighbor's proposition than to condemn it. And if he cannot save it, let him inquire how he understands it; and if he understands it wrong, let him correct his neighbor with love, and if that is not enough, let him search all proper means by which, understanding it correctly, he may be saved.

Principle and Foundation   Man was created to praise, revere and serve our Lord God, and thereby to save his soul: and the other things over the face of the earth were created for man, so that they might help him in the realization of the end for which he was created. Whence it follows that man must use them in so far as they help him toward his end; and must leave them aside where they impede him. Consequently it is necessary to be indifferent to all created things in all that is conceded to our free will, and is not barred from it, in such wise that we do not for our part seek health rather than sickness, riches rather than poverty, honor rather than dishonor, a long life rather than a short one, and so in all else; desiring and choosing only that which best leads us toward the end for which we were created.

First Week   *The First Exercise is a meditation with the three powers upon the first, second and third sin. It contains in itself, after a preparatory*

230

prayer and two preambles, three principal points and one colloquy.
The preparatory prayer is to ask grace from our Lord God that
all my intentions, actions and operations may be purely ordered in
service and praise of his Divine Majesty.

The first preamble is a composition, seeing the place. Here it
should be noted that in contemplation, or visible meditation, such
as contemplating Christ our Lord, who is visible, the composition
will be to see with the eye of the imagination the corporeal place
where the thing which I wish to contemplate is found. I say the
corporeal place, such as a temple or mountain, where Jesus Christ or
our Lady is found, accordingly as I wish to contemplate. In invisible
matters, as in this case of the sins, the composition will be to see
with imaginative sight and to consider that my soul is imprisoned
in this corruptible body, and that the whole compound of body and
soul in this valley is like an exile among brute animals.

The second is to ask of our Lord God that which I wish and
desire. The request must be according to the subject matter; that is,
if the contemplation is of the Resurrection, to ask for joy with the
joyful Christ; if it is of the Passion, to ask for pains, tears, and
torment with the tormented Christ. Here shame and confusion
should be asked for myself, seeing how many have been damned for
a single mortal sin, and how many times I should merit eternal
damnation for so many sins of mine.

Before each contemplation or meditation one should always make
the preparatory prayer without change, and the two aforesaid
preambles, changing them sometimes according to the subject
matter.

The first point will be to recall the first sin, which was of the
Angels; and then with the intellect to discourse about the same; then
with the will to try to remember and understand all this, to my
greater shame and dismay, comparing so many sins of mine to the
one sin of the Angels; and whereas they for one sin went to hell,
how many times I have deserved it for so many sins. I say to remember the Angels' sin; that is, how they being created in grace but
not wishing to help themselves by their liberty to revere and obey
their Creator and Lord, coming to pride they were changed from
grace to malice, and hurled from heaven to hell: and so consequently
to discourse in greater detail with the intellect, and so move the
affections more vigorously with the will.

The second, to do the same, that is to bring the three powers over
the sin of Adam and Eve, bringing to memory how for such a sin
they did penance so long, and how much corruption came into mankind, with so many people going to hell. I say to remember the
second sin of our Parents; how after Adam was created in the

Damascene field, and placed in the Terrestrial Paradise, and Eve created from his rib; and it being prohibited to eat of the tree of knowledge, they ate and thereby sinned; and afterwards dressed in tunics of hide and driven out of Paradise they lived all their life in many labors and great penitence, without the original justice which they had lost; and consequently to discourse more particularly with the intellect, and using the will as has been said.

The third, to do likewise the same about the third particular sin of each one who for a mortal sin has gone to hell; and countless others for fewer sins than I have committed. I say to do likewise about the third particular sin, bringing to memory the gravity and malice of the sin against one's Creator and Lord; to discourse with the intellect, how in sinning and acting against infinite goodness, the sinner has been justly condemned forever; and conclude with the will, as has been said.

Colloquy. Imagining Christ our Lord before us on the cross, to make a colloquy, how from Creator he came to be a man, and from life eternal to temporal death, and so to die for my sins. Likewise looking at myself, what I have done for Christ, what I am doing for Christ, what I should do for Christ, and so seeing him in such manner suspended on the cross, to discourse as I may be inspired.

Properly speaking, the colloquy is held just as one friend speaks to another, or a servant to his master, now asking some favor, now blaming himself for some wrong deed, now communicating his affairs, and seeking counsel in them. And say a *Pater noster*.

The Second Exercise is a meditation upon sins; and contains in itself, after the preparatory prayer and two preambles, five points and one colloquy. Let the preparatory prayer be the same.

The first preamble will be the same composition.

The second is to ask what I wish: here it will be to ask increased and intense pain and tears for my sins.

The first point is the procession of sins; that is, to recall all the sins of my life, looking year by year, or period by period. Here three things will be of help: first, to look at the place and house where I have lived; second, at the intercourse which I have held with others; third, at the station in which I have lived.

The second, to ponder my sins, looking at the ugliness and malice which each mortal sin committed contains in itself, even if it were not forbidden.

The third, to examine who I am, depreciating myself by examples: (1) Who am I in comparison to all men? (2) What are men in comparison to all the Angels and Saints of Paradise? (3) Consider what all creation is in comparison to God. Then what can I alone be? (4) Look at all my bodily ugliness and corruption. (5) Look upon myself as a sore and abscess, whence so many sins and so many evils, and such a filthy venom have issued forth.

The fourth, to consider who God is, against whom I have sinned, according to his attributes, comparing them to their contraries in me: his wisdom to my ignorance, his omnipotence to my faintness, his justice to my iniquity, his goodness to my malice.

The fifth, an admiring exclamation with great affection, discoursing through all creatures, how they have left me in life and sustained me: how the Angels are the sword of divine justice, how they have borne with me and guarded me and prayed for me; how the Saints have interceded and prayed for me; and the heavens, sun, moon, stars and elements, fruits, birds, fish and animals; and how the earth has not opened to swallow me, creating new hells in which to make me forever agonize.

Finish with a colloquy of mercy, reasoning and thanking our Lord God that he has given me life until now, proposing emendation for the future with his grace. *Pater noster.*

MIGUEL
DE CERVANTES
SAAVEDRA

Don Quixote de la Mancha
Translated by Peter Motteux

Part
One
Book
One
Chapter
Eight *Of the good success which the valorous Don Quixote had in the most terrifying and never-to-be-imagined adventure of the wind- mills.* As they were thus discoursing, they discovered some thirty or forty windmills that are in that plain; and, as soon as the knight had spied them, "Fortune," cried he, "directs our affairs better than we ourselves could have wished: look yonder, friend Sancho, there are at least thirty outrageous giants, whom I entend to encounter; and, having deprived them of life, we will begin to enrich ourselves with their spoils: for they are lawful prize; and the extirpation of that cursed brood will be an acceptable service to Heaven."

"What giants?" quoth Sancho Pança.

"Those whom thou seest yonder," answered Don Quixote, "with their long-extended arms; some of that detested race have arms of so immense a size, that sometimes they reach two leagues in length."

"Pray, look better, sir," quoth Sancho; "those things yonder are no giants, but windmills, and the arms you fancy, are their sails, which, being whirled about by the wind, make the mill go."

"It is a sign," cried Don Quixote, "thou art but little acquainted with adventures. I tell thee they are giants; and therefore, if thou art afraid, go aside and say thy prayers, for I am resolved to engage in a dreadful, unequal combat against them all." This said, he clapped spurs to his horse Rozinante, without giving ear to his squire Sancho, who bawled out to him, and assured him that they were windmills, and no giants. But he was so fully possessed with a strong conceit of the contrary, that he did not so much as hear his squire's outcry, nor was he sensible of what they were, although he was already very

234

near them; far from that. "Stand, cowards," cried he as loud as he could; "stand your ground, ignoble creatures, and fly not basely from a single knight, who dares encounter you all."

At the same time the wind rising, the mill-sails began to move, which, when Don Quixote spied, "Base miscreants," cried he, "though you move more arms than the giant Briareus, you shall pay for your arrogance." He most devoutly recommended himself to his lady Dulcinea, imploring her assistance in this perilous adventure; and so, covering himself with his shield, and couching his lance, he rushed with Rozinante's utmost speed upon the first windmill he could come at, and, running his lance into the sail, the wind whirled about with such swiftness, that the rapidity of the motion presently broke the lance into shivers, and hurled away both knight and horse along with it, till down he fell, rolling a good way off in the field. Sancho Pança ran as fast as his ass could drive to help his master, whom he found lying, and not able to stir, such a blow he and Rozinante had received. "Mercy on me!" cried Sancho, "did I not give your worship fair warning? did not I tell you they were windmills, and that nobody could think otherwise, unless he had also windmills in his head?"

"Peace, friend Sancho," replied Don Quixote: "there is nothing so subject to the inconstancy of fortune as war. I am verily persuaded, that cursed necromancer Freston, who carried away my study and books, has transformed these giants into windmills, to deprive me of the honour of the victory; such is his inveterate malice against me; but, in the end, all his pernicious wiles and stratagems shall prove ineffectual against the prevailing edge of my sword."

"Amen, say I," replied Sancho; and so heaving him up again upon his legs, once more the knight mounted poor Rozinante, that was half shoulder-slipped with his fall.

Part *How Don Quixote set free many miserable creatures, who were*
One *carrying, much against their wills, to a place they did not like*
Book Cid Hamet Benengeli, an Arabian and Manchegan author, related
Three in this most grave, high-sounding, minute, soft, and humorous
Chapter history, that after this discourse between the renowned Don Quixote
Eight and his squire, Sancho Pança, which we laid down at the end of
the seventh chapter, the knight lifting up his eyes, saw about twelve men a-foot, trudging in the road, all in a row, one behind another, like beads upon a string, being linked together by the neck to a huge iron chain, and manacled besides. They were guarded by two horsemen, armed with carbines, and two men a-foot, with swords and javelins. As soon as Sancho spied them, "Look ye, sir," cried he,

"here is a gang of wretches hurried away by main force to serve the king in the galleys."

"How!" replied Don Quixote, "is it possible the king will force anybody?"

"I do not say so," answered Sancho; "I mean these are rogues whom the law has sentenced for their misdeeds, to row in the king's galleys."

"However," replied Don Quixote, "they are forced, because they do not go of their own free will."

"Sure enough," quoth Sancho.

"If it be so," said Don Quixote, "they come within the verge of my office, which is to hinder violence and oppression, and succour all people in misery."

"Ay, sir," quoth Sancho, "but neither the king nor law offer any violence to such wicked wretches, they have but their deserts."

By this the chain of slaves came up, when Don Quixote, in very civil terms, desired the guards to inform him why these poor people were led along in that manner? "Sir," answered one of the horsemen, "they are criminals condemned to serve the king in his galleys. That is all that I have to say to you, and you need inquire no further."

"Nevertheless, sir," replied Don Quixote, "I have a great desire to know in few words the cause of their misfortune, and I will esteem it an extraordinary favour, if you will let me have that satisfaction."

"We have here the copies and certificates of their several sentences," said the other horseman, "but we cannot stand to pull them out and read them now; you may draw near and examine the men yourself: I suppose they themselves will tell you why they are condemned; for they are such honest people, they are not ashamed to boast of their rogueries."

With this permission, which Don Quixote would have taken of himself had they denied it him, he rode up to the chain, and asked the first, for what crimes he was in these miserable circumstances? The galley-slave answered him, that it was for being in love. "What, only for being in love!" cried Don Quixote; "were all those that are in love to be thus used, I myself might have been long since in the galleys."

"Ay, but," replied the slave, "my love was not of that sort which you conjecture: I was so desperately in love with a basket of linen, and embraced it so close, that had not the judge taken it from me by force, I would not have parted with it willingly. In short, I was taken in the fact, and so there was no need to put me to the rack, it was proved so plain upon me. So I was committed, tried, condemned, had the gentle lash; and besides that, was sent, for three years, to be an element-dasher, and there is an end of the business."

"An element-dasher!" cried Don Quixote, "what do you mean by that?"

"A galley-slave," answered the criminal, who was a young fellow, about four-and-twenty years old, and said he was born at Piedra-Hita.

Then Don Quixote examined the second, but he was so sad and desponding, that he would make no answer; however, the first rogue informed the knight of his affairs. "Sir," said he, "this canary-bird keeps us company for having sung too much."

"Is it possible!" cried Don Quixote; "are men sent to the galleys for singing?"

"Ay, Mary are they," quoth the arch rogue; "for there is nothing worse than to sing in anguish."

"How!" cried Don Quixote, "that contradicts the saying, 'Sing away sorrow, cast away care.'"

"Ay, but with us the case is different," replied the slave, "'he that sings in disaster, weeps all his life after.'"

"This is a riddle which I cannot unfold," cried Don Quixote.

"Sir," said one of the guards, "singing in anguish, among these jail-birds, means to confess upon the rack: this fellow was put to the torture, and confessed his crime, which was stealing of cattle; and because he squeaked, or sung, as they call it, he was condemned to the galleys for six years, besides an hundred jerks with a cat-o'-nine-tails that have whisked and powdered his shoulders already. Now the reason why he goes thus mopish and out of sorts, is only because his comrogues jeer and laugh at him continually for not having had the courage to deny: as if it had not been as easy for him to say No as Yes; or, as if a fellow, taken up on suspicion, were not a lucky rogue, when there is no positive evidence can come in against him but his own tongue; and in my opinion they are somewhat in the right."

"I think so too," said Don Quixote.

Thence addressing himself to the third, "And you," said he, "what have you done?"

"Sir," answered the fellow, readily and pleasantly enough, "I must mow the great meadow for five years together, for want of twice five ducats."

"I will give twenty with all my heart," said Don Quixote, "to deliver thee from that misery."

"Thank you for nothing," quoth the slave; "it is just like the proverb, 'After meat comes mustard'; or, like money to a starving man at sea, when there are no victuals to be bought with it. Had

I had the twenty ducats you offer me before I was tried, to have greased the clerk's fist, and have whetted my lawyer's wit, I might have been now at Toledo in the market-place of Zocodover, and not have been thus led along like a dog in a string. But Heaven is powerful, Basta; I say no more."

Then passing to the fourth, who was a venerable old Don, with a grey beard that reached to his bosom, he put the same question to him; whereupon the poor creature fell a-weeping, and was not able to give him an answer. So the next behind him lent him a tongue. "Sir," said he, "this honest person goes to the galleys for four years, having taken his progress through the town in state, and rested at the usual stations."

"That is," quoth Sancho, "as I take it, after he had been exposed to public shame."

"Right," replied the slave; "and all this he is condemned to for being a broker of human flesh: for, to tell the truth, the gentleman is a pimp, and, besides that, he has a smack of conjuring."

"If it were not for that addition of conjuring," cried Don Quixote, "he ought not to have been sent to the galleys, purely for being a pimp, unless it were to be general of the galleys; for, the profession of a bawd, pimp, or messenger of love, is not like other common employments, but an office that requires a great deal of prudence and sagacity; an office of trust and weight, and most highly necessary in a well-regulated commonwealth; nor should it be executed but by civil well-descended persons of good natural parts, and of a liberal education. Nay, it were requisite there should be a comptroller and surveyor of the profession, as there are of others; and a certain and settled number of them, as there are of exchange-brokers. This would be a means to prevent an infinite number of mischiefs that happen every day, because the trade or profession is followed by poor ignorant pretenders, silly waiting women, young giddy-brained pages, shallow footmen, and such raw inexperienced sort of people, who in unexpected turns and emergencies stand with their fingers in their mouths, know not their right hand from their left, but suffer themselves to be surprised, and spoil all for want of quickness of invention either to conceal, carry on, or bring off a thing artificially. Had I but time I would point out what sort of persons are best qualified to be chosen professors of this most necessary employment in the commonwealth; however, at some fitter season I will inform those of it who may remedy this disorder.

"All I have to say now, is, that the grief I had to see those venerable grey hairs in such distress, for having followed that no less useful than ingenious vocation of pimping, is now lost in my abhorrence of his additional character of a conjurer; though I very well know that no sorcery in the world can affect or force the will, as some ignorant credulous persons fondly imagine: for our will is a free faculty, and no herb nor charms can constrain it. As for philtres and such-like compositions which some silly women and designing pretenders make, they are nothing but certain mixtures and poisonous preparations, that make those who take them run mad; though the deceivers labour to persuade us they can make one person love another; which, as I have said, is an impossible thing, our will being a free, uncontrollable power."

"You say very well, sir," cried the old coupler; "and, upon my honour, I protest I am wholly innocent as to the imputation of witchcraft. As for the business of pimping, I cannot deny it, but I never took it to be a criminal function; for my intention was, that all the world should taste the sweets of love, and enjoy each other's society, living together in friendship and in peace, free from those griefs and jars that unpeople the earth. But my harmless design has not been so happy as to prevent my being sent now to a place whence I never expect to return, stooping as I do under the heavy burden of old age, and being grievously afflicted with the strangury, which scarce affords me a moment's respite from pain." This said, the reverend procurer burst out afresh into tears and lamentations, which melted Sancho's heart so much, that he pulled a piece of money out of his bosom and gave it to him as an alms.

Then Don Quixote turned to the fifth, who seemed to be nothing at all concerned. "I go to serve his majesty," said he, "for having been somewhat too familiar with two of my cousin-germans, and two other kind-hearted virgins that were sisters; by which means I have multiplied my kind, and begot so odd and intricate a medley of kindred, that it would puzzle a convocation of casuists to resolve their degrees of consanguinity. All this was proved upon me. I had no friends, and what was worse, no money, and so was like to have hung for it: however, I was only condemned to the galleys for six years, and patiently submitted to it. I feel myself yet young, to my comfort; so if my life but does hold out, all will be well in time. If you will be pleased to bestow something upon poor sinners, Heaven will reward you; and when we pray, we will be sure to remember you, that your life may be as long and prosperous, as your presence is goodly and noble." This brisk spark appeared to be a student by his habit, and some of the guards said he was a fine speaker, and a good Latinist.

After him came a man about thirty years old, a clever, well-set, handsome fellow, only he squinted horribly with one eye: he was strangely loaded with irons; a heavy chain clogged his leg, and was 239 so long, that he twisted it about his waist like a girdle: he had a couple of collars about his neck, the one to link him to the rest of the slaves, and the other, one of those iron-ruffs which they call a keep-friend, or a friend's foot; from whence two irons went down to his middle, and to their two bars were riveted a pair of manacles that gripped him by the fists, and were secured with a large padlock; so that he could neither lift his hands to his mouth, nor bend down his head towards his hands. Don Quixote inquiring why he was worse hampered with irons than the rest, "Because he alone has done more rogueries than all the rest," answered one of the guards. "This is such a reprobate, such a devil of a fellow, that no gaol nor fetters will hold him; we are not sure he is fast enough, for all he is chained so."

"What sort of crimes then has he been guilty of," asked Don Quixote, "that he is only sent to the galleys?"

"Why," answered the keeper, "he is condemned to ten years' slavery, which is no better than a civil death: but I need not stand to tell you any more of him, but that he is that notorious rogue Gines de Passamonte, alias Ginesillo de Parapilla."

"Hark you, sir," cried the slave, fair and softly; "what a pox makes you give a gentleman more names than he has? Gines is my Christian name, and Passamonte my surname, and not Ginesillo, nor Parapilla, as you say. Blood! let every man mind what he says, or it may prove the worse for him."

"Do not you be so saucy, Mr. Crack-rope," cried the officer to him, "or I may chance to make you keep a better tongue in your head."

"It is a sign," cried the slave, "that a man is fast, and under the lash; but one day or other somebody shall know whether I am called Parapilla or no."

"Why, Mr. Slip-string," replied the officer, "do not people call you by that name?"

"They do," answered Gines, "but I will make them call me otherwise, or I will fleece and bite them worse than I care to tell you now. But you, sir, who are so inquisitive," added he, turning to Don Quixote, "if you have a mind to give us anything, pray do it quickly, and go your ways; for I do not like to stand here answering questions; broil me! I am Gines de Passamonte, I am not ashamed of my name. As for my life and conversation, there is an account of them in black and white, written with this numerical hand of mine."

"There he tells you true," said the officer, "for he has written his own history himself, without omitting a tittle of his roguish pranks; and he has left the manuscript in pawn in the prison for two hundred reals."

"Ay," said Gines, "and will redeem it, burn me! though it lay
there for as many ducats."

"Then it must be an extraordinary piece," cried Don Quixote.

"So extraordinary," replied Gines, "that it far outdoes not only Lazarillo de Tormes, but whatever has been, and shall be written in that kind: for mine is true every word, and no invented stories can compare with it for variety of tricks and accidents."

"What is the title of the book?" asked Don Quixote.

" 'The Life of Gines de Passamonte,' " answered the other.

"Is it quite finished?" asked the knight.

"How the devil can it be finished and I yet living?" replied the slave. "There is in it every material point from my cradle, to this my last going to the galleys."

"Then it seems you have been there before," said Don Quixote.

"To serve God and the king, I was some four years there once before," replied Gines: "I already know how the biscuit and the bull's-pizzle agree with my carcase: it does not grieve me much to go there again, for there I shall have leisure to give a finishing stroke to my book. I have the devil knows what to add; and in our Spanish galleys there is always leisure and idle time enough in conscience: neither shall I want so much for what I have to insert, for I know it all by heart."

"Thou seemest to be a witty fellow," said Don Quixote.

"You should have said unfortunate too," replied the slave; "for the bitch fortune is still unkind to men of wit."

"You mean to such wicked wretches as yourself," cried the officer.

"Look you, Mr. Commissary," said Gines, "I have already desired you to use good language; the law did not give us to your keeping for you to abuse us, but only to conduct us where the king has occasion for us. Let every man mind his own business, and give good words, or hold his tongue: for by the blood—I will say no more, murder will out; there will be a time when some people's rogueries may come to light, as well as those of other folks." With that the officer, provoked by the slave's threats, held up his staff to strike him; but Don Quixote stepped between them, and desired him not to do it, and to consider, that the slave was the more to be excused for being too free of his tongue, since he had never another member at liberty.

Then addressing himself to all the slaves, "My dearest brethren," cried he, "I find, by what I gather from your own words, that though you deserve punishment for the several crimes of which you stand convicted, yet you suffer execution of the sentence by constraint, and merely because you cannot help it. Besides, it is not unlikely but that this man's want of resolution upon the rack, the other's want of money, the third's want of friends and favour, and, in short, the judges' perverting and wresting the law to your great prejudice, may have been the cause of your misery. Now, as Heaven has sent me into the world to relieve the distressed, and free suffering weakness from the tyranny of oppression, according to the duty of my profession of knight-errantry, these considerations induce me to take you under my protection—but, because it is part of a prudent man not to use violence where fair means may be effectual, I desire you, gentlemen of the guard, to release these poor men, there being people enough to serve his majesty in their places; for it is a hard case to make slaves of men whom God and nature made free; and you have the less reason to use these wretches with severity, seeing they never did you any wrong. Let them answer for their sins in the other world: Heaven is just, you know, and will be sure to punish the wicked, as it will certainly reward the good. Consider besides, gentlemen, that it is neither a Christian-like, nor an honourable action, for men to be the butchers and tormentors of one another; particularly, when no advantage can arise from it. I choose to desire this of you, with so much mildness, and in so peaceable a manner, gentlemen, that I may have occasion to pay you a thankful acknowledgment, if you will be pleased to grant so reasonable a request: but, if you provoke me by refusal, I must be obliged to tell ye, that this lance, and this sword, guided by this invincible arm, shall force you to yield that to my valour which you deny to my civil entreaties."

"A very good jest indeed," cried the officer, "what a devil makes you dote at such a rate? Would you have us set at liberty the king's prisoners, as if we had authority to do it, or you to command it? Go, go about your business, good Sir Errant, and set your basin right upon your empty pate; and pray do not meddle any further in what does not concern you, for those who will play with cats must expect to be scratched."

"Thou art a cat, and rat, and a coward also," cried Don Quixote; and with that he attacked the officer with such a sudden and surprising fury, that before he had any time to put himself into a posture of defence, he struck him down dangerously wounded with his lance, and as fortune had ordered it, this happened to be the horseman who was armed with a carbine. His companions stood astonished at such a bold action, but at last fell upon the champion with their swords and darts, which might have proved fatal to him, had not the slaves laid hold of this opportunity to break the chain, in order to regain their liberty: for, the guards perceiving their endeavours to get loose, thought it more material to prevent them, than to be fighting a madman. But as he pressed them vigorously on one side, and the slaves were opposing them and freeing themselves on the other, the hurly-burly was so great, and the guards so perplexed, that they did nothing to the purpose. In the mean time Sancho was helping Gines de Passamonte to get off his chain, which he did sooner than can be imagined; and then that active desperado having seized the wounded officer's sword and carbine, he joined with Don Quixote, and sometimes aiming at one, and sometimes at the other, as if he had been ready to shoot them, yet still without letting off the piece, the other slaves at the same time pouring volleys of stone-shot at the guards, they betook themselves to their heels, leaving Don Quixote and the criminals masters of the field. Sancho, who was always for taking care of the main chance, was not at all pleased with this victory; for he guessed that the guards who were fled would raise a hue and cry, and soon be at their heels with the whole posse of the holy brotherhood, and lay them up for a rescue and rebellion. This made him advise his master to get out of the way as fast as he could, and hide himself in the neighbouring mountains.

"I hear you," answered Don Quixote to this motion of his squire, "and I know what I have to do." Then calling to him all the slaves, who by this time had uncased the keeper to his skin, they gathered about him to know his pleasure, and he spoke to them in this manner. "It is the part of generous spirits to have a grateful sense of the benefits they receive, no crime being more odious than ingratitude. You see, gentlemen, what I have done for your sakes, and you cannot but be sensible how highly you are obliged to me. Now all the recompense I require is only, that every one of you, loaded with that chain from which I have freed your necks, do instantly repair to the city of Toboso; and there, presenting yourselves before the Lady Dulcinea del Toboso, tell her, that her faithful votary, the Knight of the Woeful Countenance, commanded you to wait on her, and assure her of his profound veneration. Then you shall give her an exact account of every particular relating to this famous achievement, by which you once more taste the sweets of liberty; which done, I give you leave to seek your fortunes where you please."

To this the ringleader and master-thief, Gines de Passamonte, made answer for all the rest. "What you would have us do," said he, "our noble deliverer, is absolutely impracticable and impossible; for we dare not be seen all together for the world. We must rather part, and skulk some one way, some another, and lie snug in creeks and corners underground, for fear of those damned manhounds that will be after us with a hue and cry; therefore all we can, and ought to do in this case, is to change this compliment and homage which you would have us pay to the Lady Dulcinea del Toboso, into a certain number of Ave Marias and Creeds, which we will say for your worship's benefit; and this may be done by night or by day, walking or standing, and in war as well as in peace: but to imagine we will return to our flesh-pots of Egypt; that is to say, take up our chains again, and lug them the Devil knows where, is as unreasonable as to think it is night now at ten o'clock in the morning. 'Sdeath, to expect this from us, is to expect pears from an elm-tree."

"Now, by my sword," replied Don Quixote, "Sir son of a whore, Sir Ginesello de Parapilla, or whatever be your name, you yourself, alone, shall go to Toboso, like a dog that has scalded his tail, with the whole chain about your shoulders."

Gines, who was naturally very choleric, judging, by Don Quixote's extravagance in freeing them, that he was not very wise, winked on his companions, who, like men that understood signs, presently fell back to the right and left, and pelted Don Quixote with such a shower of stones, that all his dexterity to cover himself with his shield was now ineffectual, and poor Rozinante no more obeyed the spur, than if he had been only the statue of a horse. As for Sancho, he got behind his ass, and there sheltered himself from the volleys of flints that threatened his bones, while his master was so battered, that in a little time he was thrown out of his saddle to the ground. He was no sooner down, but the student leaped on him, took off his basin from his head, gave him three or four thumps on the shoulders with it, and then gave it so many knocks against the stones, that he almost broke it to pieces. After this, they stripped him of his upper coat, and had robbed him of his hose too, but that his greaves hindered them. They also eased Sancho of his upper coat, and left him in his doublet: then, having divided the spoils, they shifted every one for himself, thinking more how to avoid being taken up, and linked again in the chain, than of trudging with it to my Lady Dulcinea del Toboso. Thus the ass, Rozinante, Sancho, and Don Quixote remained indeed masters of the field, but in an ill condition: the ass hanging his head, and pensive, shaking his ears now and then, as if the volleys of stones had still whizzed about them; Rozinante lying in a desponding manner, for he had been knocked down as well as his unhappy rider; Sancho uncased to his doublet, and trembling for fear of the holy brotherhood; and Don Quixote filled with sullen regret, to find himself so barbarously used by those whom he had so highly obliged.

LOPE
DE VEGA

The History of Mireno
from Book One of THE PILGRIM
Anonymous translation

At a small town, not far distant from this famous city, lived a gentleman, whose name was Telemachus, who had married a lady not
quite so chaste as the Roman Lucretia, though she bore her name;
this fair one affected a deep melancholy, a careless air, and negligent
dress, as if some secret grief reigned over her heart. Telemachus
took all the pains imaginable to divert her, that he might avoid the
accustomed censure of the world, which frequently attributes the
faults of a woman, to the ill humour of her husband. He caused
her to dress richly, take the air by the sea side, to walk in his fine
garden, and all this availing nothing, he kept a kind of open house,
that her grief might be drown'd in company.

Among the rest of the young gentlemen who frequented the villa
of Telemachus, there was one whose name was Mireno, a man so
much my friend, that I have scarce thought myself living since he
has been dead; after frequent visits, it fell out that Mireno felt
himself enamoured of the lovely spouse of Telemachus, whose in-
clination had hitherto been turned another way. Time as is usual
in such cases, encreased the mischief, till from liking, he fell to
languishing for the fair Lucretia. To me, as to another self, he
confided the story of his fortune, shall I call it, or his folly, which
had he taken my advice, should never have proved fatal to him.
But alas! it is the mode of lovers, always to seek advice and never
to pursue it. Though he consulted as a lover, I answered as a friend,
I shewed him from reason the madness of his proceedings, and I
quoted him from sacred and profane history all the examples I could
remember of men undone in the same way; but it was like music
to the adder, or the breath of Zephyr, when the rest of the winds
are let loose, it made no impression, nay, it was scarce perceived.

One effect it had, indeed, which was a very bad one, that it diminished our friendship; he seldom visited me after, forbore to converse with me in publick places; in a word, estranged himself as much from me as from wisdom: for such, dear Sir, is the hard lot of man, that he either mistakes a flatterer for a friend, or forsakes his friend, because he is no flatterer.

There was a third friend, to whom Mireno and I went, when we found not each other; to him, the young man had recourse. He was less considerate than I, being one who placed the essence of friendship in running any risque in any cause for the man he called his friend: people of this cast fare like gunpowder on a holiday, they consume themselves that they may please others. They consulted together without speaking to me, which when I perceived, I used to disguise myself, and follow them of a night. For some time I made no discoveries, but one evening tarrying abroad later than usual, I perceived at the back gate of Telemachus's garden, which looked to the sea, a ladder of ropes; my heart immediately smote me, and would not permit me to retire, not that I wanted to satisfy my curiosity, but that I thought it would be acting like a friend to remain on the spot, and to assist if any ill accident happened; about midnight, I saw what I expected; for after a little noise, I saw Mireno descend, and his friend Aurelius slip from behind a corner, and receive him in his arms, and after whispering a little, persuaded him to get away with all speed. They were scarce withdrawn, before a servant unhooked the ladder, and let it fall, I immediately took it up, and withdrew into a corner; presently afterwards, Telemachus came to the window in his shirt, with his sword in one hand, and a flaming torch in the other, looking strictly about, to see if he could observe anything of those whose noise he had heard. A little after, I went to the gate, when I heard all the family in an uproar, but at the same time, learned, to my no small satisfaction, that this was taken for an attempt of thieves, and that Telemachus had not the least suspicion that they came for somewhat more valuable than riches, and instead of purloining his wealth, sought to injure his honour. In the morning I sent for Mireno and found him out with much ado. When he came, we talked of many things, and at last, when I found he was unwilling to speak to me, I asked him of a sudden, what was become of his amour; instead of answering me, he desired we might talk no more on that subject, since, said he, all evil secrets should be kept from friends. I told him, it was to no purpose to conceal them, since Telemachus had been with me, and told me, that he had observed him descending a ladder in his garden, to which allude those mighty lines.

Love, mighty love, eludes observing spies.
Love can evade ev'n Argus' hundred eyes.

I thought it my duty not to let Mireno go away in an error, I therefore told him how things really stood; that Telemachus suspected nothing of his amour, though he had been alarmed by the fall of the ladder, and had miss'd his wife out of bed. I informed him likewise of the small service I had done him, and renewed my intreaties that he would desist while he was yet safe, from a business, which if pursued, would certainly be attended with the worst consequences imaginable to his person, and to his reputation. I likewise repeated again and again, my earnest exhortations to him, not to trifle, or to resolve that this or that visit should be the last, but break off this iniquitous correspondence immediately. Mireno not only heard me with patience, but also promised to follow my advice, and in order to do it effectually, to quit Barcelona, to which proposition I readily assented, knowing that there is no better remedy for love, than putting the persons at a very great distance from each other. It will certainly seem strange to you that I affirm Mireno perform'd all he promised, and that quitting sight of Lucretia, he lost also all thoughts of her, betaking himself again to his old affection for Erephila, the lady I hinted at before, and loving her with greater warmth and sincerity for this short interruption of his passion. Mireno was in every respect amiable in his person; his behaviour, his address, his air, his reputation as a soldier, his skill in languages, and in all polite literature. The remembrance I have of him is so strong that with ease I drew that representation of him which you see, and which I can assure you does not flatter him; and to mark the concern with which his image fills me, I have borrowed that line from the Aeneid.

The shade of hapless Hector seem'd to rise.

After this eclaircisement, we returned to our former familiarity, we conversed together, walked together, and in short did all things together as we were wont, and I conceived my friend perfectly safe, because Telemachus had retired to his country seat, and carried his wife and family with him. But our quiet, like all the pleasures of this world, was of no long continuance; Lucretia was so uneasy in her country obscurity, that she never suffered her husband to have rest till he brought her back to Barcelona. The sight of Mireno rekindled all her former flames, for smothered love, like smothered fire, is never safe, the least vent sets all again in a blaze, and the last mischief is frequently worse than the first; it was likely to prove so in this case, which Mireno himself perceived, and therefore talk'd 247 of marrying to prevent it; I was entirely for this measure, and in consequence thereof, he fixed on me a very troublesome office, that of looking out for him a proper wife. True friendship refuses nothing that is honourable, and I therefore fatigued myself exceedingly to bring this matter to bear; I proposed several ladies to him, all of whom, in my opinion, might have been proper companions for him for life; but it was all in vain, he had objections to them all; this was of too great a family, that of too mean a one; one was not handsome, another not rich; at length I found the source of all these dislikes; his old flame began to revive, and Lucretia became once more the object of his desires, the sovereign of his heart, and the bane of his fortunes.

Erephila, who passionately loved Mireno, began to find out from his short visits, his coldness, and seldom writing to her, that he had affairs somewhere else, which took up his time; she set all her wits to work, in order to discover her rival, and a woman's are seldom misemployed on such occasions; in a short time, therefore, if she did not discover all that passed between her lover and his new mistress, she at least discovered who that new mistress was.

When Erephila had proceeded thus far, she framed in her own mind a scheme the most extraordinary that ever was heard of, and which may serve as an instance of the genius and spirit of the sex; she found a way to be in a place where Telemachus some times came, and she took all imaginable pains to make him admire her: the thing had its effect, Telemachus could not avoid the bait, she struck him with such art, fell in with his humour, without seeming to observe it, and met his eyes with such soft engaging glances, that in spite of his love for Lucretia, he was smitten. He visited Erephila often, for which Mireno gave him all the opportunity imaginable, seldom coming near her; and as our passions are generally quickest at their beginnings, things were shortly at that ripeness which Erephila desired and expected. One day, when Telemachus came to visit her, she appeared to be much out of humour, and pretending to know nothing of his being a married man, she reproached him with going to the house of one Lucretia. Telemachus excused himself as having business at that house, but she continuing still to look sad, and proceeding at last to shed tears; Telemachus assured her that Lucretia was a woman of the greatest virtue, commended her fine qualities, her prudence, good sense, and unaffected chastity, concluding with an account of her husband's care, and representing him to her as a person of merit and worth. Erephila, who had now a very good opportunity for performing her very bad intent, answered in a few words, that it might be very possible Lucretia's husband was a very worthy gentleman, but that as to Lucretia, there was somewhat between her and a certain young gentleman in the city.

248

Here she stopped short, Telemachus immediately turned pale, trembled, and shewed evident signs how nearly this matter touched his heart; he conjured however Erephila to inform him who this chevalier might be, but that was not so easily to be known; Erephila pretended to lapse into her former jealousy, and taking notice of his uneasiness and confusion, upbraided him with his falsehood and dissimulation towards her; Telemachus, who was in no humour to be trifled with, forgot in an instant all his tenderness for Erephila, and even the respect due to her sex, for finding it impossible by fair means to extract from her the secret, he of a sudden drew his dagger, and clapping it to her throat, forced her to acknowledge it was Mireno, whom he knew as well as she. Afterwards, he sought again to appease her, telling her when he went away, that it was true he had loved Lucretia, but that since she assured him that the lady had another lover, he would withdraw his affections, hate her for the future, and settle his love entirely upon her; as a testimony of which, he presented her with a fine gold chain curiously wrought, and having a rich diamond cross hanging thereto.

Thus ended an interview strange in itself, and managed with much much artifice on both sides. Erephila pretended to testify a passion she never felt, and Telemachus to smother one that could not be concealed.

Erephila flattered herself that by this means she should prevent Mireno from visiting Lucretia any more, being confident that Telemachus would be so alarmed, that he would not fail to keep a very strict eye over his wife; but in this she was quite mistaken, he judged it in vain to watch over what was already lost, and bent therefore all his thoughts, not on securing his honour, but on revenging the loss of it, which he conceived could be in no way done, but by destroying the person who had dishonoured him. Full of these sanguine thoughts which so tormented his mind, that the effects of his inward agitation were visible enough to an intelligent eye in his countenance; he began to frame a thousand plots for the fulfilling of his design. At last, he pitched on one which he thought more feasible than the rest; he pretended that he was obliged to make a journey to Montferrat. Lovers are not always without suspicions, and besides, I who was now in the secret, presently conceived that this might be a contrivance.

We resolved, therefore, to send Aurelius to watch him, but Telemachus knew well enough he had not to do with fools; he therefore defeated all our contrivance, by going to the place and returning from it exactly at the times prefixed. This, as he rightly judged, took away all suspicion; so that when he sometime after gave out that business called him to Valencia, there was not the least question made of it, yet he returned when he was got half way thither, and concealed himself privately in Barcelona.

Mireno and Lucretia did not sleep together so improvidently, as to have nobody to watch; I performed that office, till my friend earnestly desired me to spare myself the trouble, yet I could not help attending near the garden door, which care, notwithstanding, proved vain; for on the third night Telemachus, attended by one servant, returned and entered the garden by a private gate, which none in his family knew anything of.

He went with a harquebuss in his hand to the bed-chamber door, and finding the hapless couple yet asleep, he dispatched Mireno before he could have any apprehension of his danger: the discharge of the piece struck me almost as dead as my friend; I ran to the gate, but found no entrance, yet this impediment did not continue long, the neighbourhood was all in arms, the door presently forced, and there we saw the dreadful effects of outrageous jealousy, Mireno dead, and Lucretia breathing her last in a short prayer to God for forgiveness, the sword reaking by her body which had forced her soul from thence. To this wretched and deplorable spectacle those lines at the bottom of the picture refer.

Oh! was it not a deep and dreadful stain,
That hitherto by thee men had been slain.

Hitherto I had not seen the body of my deceased friend, the dying Lucretia having fixed my attention for a few moments; but when I beheld him, my soul was so transported with rage, that forgetting the injury he had offered Telemachus, and having the author of his death before my eyes, in the first fury of my resentment, struck him to the heart, and sent him to receive sentence at that bar, whither in the midst of their sins he had sent these unfortunate lovers; by this time the house was surrounded by the officers of justice, who finding there no criminal but myself, hurried me hither, where I have endured life now five years. To this lamentable spectacle of my departed friend, refers that picture, and those lines addressed as it were to Aurelius.

To thee, alas! with aking heart my friend
The breathless Pallas bleeding corpse I send.

My labours and my grief are depicted in the representation of Sisipheus and Titius, and in some measure expressed in words by those lines of Ovid.

Oh! how wretched 'tis to live,
When from us all comforts fly,
And when death would comfort give,
250 Oh! how wretched not to die.

I have endeavoured also to mark the universal grief of all degrees of people, for Mireno by the story of Orpheus, thus interpreted in words.

His hapless fate, now welt'ring in his gore,
The senseless woods and savage beasts deplore.

Here with incessant tears let me put an end to this melancholy story, to which I have nothing to add, unless you will please to hear the lines I made for the tomb of Lucretia.

Lucretia lovely luckless Dame lies here,
Than Rome's less chaste, but oh! how much more fair?
No brutal Tarquin in her fall had part,
But love! almighty love! subdu'd her heart.
Love caus'd her death, oh! do not then refuse,
To let that death her lawless love excuse.

FRANCE

PIERRE DE RONSARD

FRANÇOIS RABELAIS

JOACHIM DU BELLAY

MARGARET QUEEN OF NAVARRE

MICHEL DE MONTAIGNE

JEAN BODIN

BONAVENTURE DES PÉRIERS

PIERRE CHARRON

PIERRE
DE RONSARD

Songs and Sonnets
Translated by Curtis Hidden Page

EVEN UNTO DEATH

To think one thought a hundred hundred ways,
'Neath two loved eyes to lay your heart quite bare,
To drink the bitter liquor of despair
And eat forever ashes of lost days—

In spirit and flesh to know youth's bloom decays,
To die of pain, yet sweet no pain is there,
The more you sue, to move the less your fair;
Yet make her wish, the law your life obeys—

Anger that passes, faith that cannot move,
Far dearer than yourself your foe to love,
To build a thousand vain imaginings,

To long to plead, yet fear to voice a breath,—
In ruin of all hope to love all things—
These are the signs of love—love even to death.

LOVE'S COMPARINGS

Carnations and lilies are loseless
When set by the face of my fair,
And fine-woven gold is but worthless
If weighed with the wealth of her hair;
Through arches of coral passes
Her laughter that banisheth care,
And flowers spring fresh 'mongst the grasses
Where'er her feet may fare.

PIERRE
DE RONSARD

Songs and Sonnets
Translated by Curtis Hidden Page

EVEN UNTO DEATH

To think one thought a hundred hundred ways,
   'Neath two loved eyes to lay your heart quite bare,
   To drink the bitter liquor of despair
And eat forever ashes of lost days—

In spirit and flesh to know youth's bloom decays,
   To die of pain, yet swear no pain is there,
   The more you sue, to move the less your fair,
Yet make her wish, the law your life obeys—

Anger that passes, faith that cannot move;
   Far dearer than yourself your foe to love;
   To build a thousand vain imaginings,

To long to plead, yet fear to voice a breath,
   In ruin of all hope to love all things—
   These are the signs of love—love even to death.

LOVE'S COMPARINGS

Carnations and lilies are hueless
   When set by the face of my fair,
And fine-woven gold is but worthless
   If weighed with the wealth of her hair;
     Through arches of coral passes
   Her laughter that banisheth care,
     And flowers spring fresh 'mongst the grasses
   Wherever her feet may fare.

MADRIGAL

Take my heart, Lady, take my heart—
   Take it, for it is yours, my sweet,
So yours it is, that 'twere not meet
Another shared its slightest part.

So yours, if yours it pine and die,
   Then yours, all yours, shall be the blame,
   And there below, your soul in shame
Shall rue such bitter cruelty.

Were you a savage Scythian's child,
Yet love, that turns the tigers mild,
   Would melt you at my sighing.

But you, more cruel-fierce than they,
Have set your will my heart to slay,
   And live but through my dying.

TO HIS VALET

I want three days to read the Iliad through!
   So, Corydon, close fast my chamber door.
   If anything should bother me before
I've done, I swear you'll have somewhat to rue!

No! not the servant, nor your mate, nor you
   Shall come to make the bed or clean the floor.
   I must have three good quiet days—or four.
Then I'll make merry for a week or two.

Ah! but—if any one should come from HER,
   Admit him quickly! Be no loiterer,
   But come and make me brave for his receiving.

But no one else!—not friends or nearest kin!
   Though an Olympian God should seek me, leaving
   His Heaven, shut fast the door! Don't let him in!

"MARIE, ARISE!"

Marie, arise, my indolent sweet saint!
   Long since the skylark sang his morning stave,
   Long since the nightingale, love's gentle slave,
Carolled upon the thorn his love-complaint.

Arise! come see the tender grass besprent
   With dew-pearls, and your rose with blossoms brave.
   Come see the dainty pinks to which you gave
Last eve their water with a care so quaint.

Last eve you swore and pledged your shining eyes
   Sooner than I this morning you would rise,
   But dawn's soft beauty-sleep, with sweet disguising,

Still gently seals those eyes—that now I kiss
   And now again—and now this breast, and this,
   A hundred times, to teach you early rising!

CARPE DIEM

Were I to meet thee 'mongst the dead
   I'd pass by, and disdain thee,
     Thee, once my lover!

Thy skull shall know nor hair nor skin,
   Thy jowl the worms shall fatten,
     Erstwhile so winning;
Thou'lt have no other teeth within
   Thy jaws, but such as batten
     In death's-heads grinning. . . .

Sweet, while we live, oh! seize to-day,
   And every respite using,
     Spare not thy kisses!
Soon, soon, Death comes, and then for aye
   Thou'lt rue thy cold refusing
257   And mourn lost blisses.

TRANSIT MUNDUS

Another Winter comes. The last comes soon, I know.
For six and fifty years have blanched my head with snow.
The time is here to say, Farewell, to love and song,
And take my leave of life's best days, for oh! how long! . . .

Yet I have lived. So much stands safe beyond recall.
I grudge not life its joys. I have tasted one and all,
Nor e'er refrained my hand from pleasures within reach,
Save but as Reason set due measure unto each.
The part assigned me I have played on this life's stage
In costume fitted to the times and to my age.

I've seen the morning dawn, and evening come again.
I've seen the storm, the lightning-flash, the hail, the rain.
Peoples I've seen, and kings!—For twenty years now past
I've seen each day rise upon France as though her last.

Wars I have seen, and strife of words, and terms of truce
First made and then unmade again, then made by ruse
To break and make again! . . . I've seen that neath the moon
All was but change and chance, and danced to Fortune's tune.
Though man seek Prudence out for guide, it boots him naught;
Fate ineluctable doth hold him chained and caught,
Bound hand and foot, in prison; and all he may propose
Fortune and Fate, wisely mayhap, themselves dispose.

Full-feasted of the world, even as a wedding-guest
Goes from the banquet-hall, I go to my long rest;
As from a king's great feast, I go not with ill grace
Though after me one come, and take the abandoned place.

Sonnets for Helen
Translated by Humbert Wolfe

So oft to quarrel, so often to agree,
  so oft to end the pact, so oft remake it,
  so oft curse passion, and so often slake it,
258 so often seek what we so often flee,

so oft in ambush, so oft openly,
   so oft embrace the yoke, so often shake it,
   so often breathe a vow, so often break it:
all these are signs that love has you and me.
Inconstant love is the true lover's token,
   and since we pity what our hate discovers,
   swear and forswear, take oaths and perjure these,
hope without hope, find comfort in hearts broken,
   we give the final proof that we are lovers
   for ever bound in equal war and peace.

By too long gazing on your flawless face
   my heart took fire, which such a heat dispersed
   that with a drought my lips were like to burst,
and speech itself was banished from its place.
You bad them bring well-water of your grace
   in a bejewelled vase, but, in my thirst,
      I brushed the spot which drinking you brushed first
still royal with your aromatic trace.
And well I knew the moment that I smutched it
   with mine, the vase, enamoured with your kiss,
and to the flame subdued whose splendour touched it,
   as in a furnace, was consumed with this.
How could I hope to rule my own desire,
when on the instant water changed to fire?

When the sun yoked his horses of the air
   Helen one summer morning took the breeze,
while love, with empty quiver, did repair
   for arrows to his lucid armouries.
I saw the apples of her breast as fair
   as orchard fruit of the Hesperides
outshining what the Cnidian laid bare,
   or hers who suckled Mars upon her knees.
The swelling ivories in their rounded arches
   were such as Pheidiias fashioned in relief
   for his Andromeda, when her young Greek
found her rock-fastened by the sea's cold marches,
   her breasts by mortal terror changed and grief
   into the marbled globe of Verd Antique.

When you are old, at evening candle-lit
   beside the fire bending to your wool,
read out my verse and murmur, "Ronsard writ
   this praise for me when I was beautiful."
And not a maid but, at the sound of it,
   though nodding at the stitch on broidered stool,
will start awake, and bless love's benefit
   whose long fidelities bring Time to school.
I shall be thin and ghost beneath the earth
   by myrtle shade in quiet after pain,
but you, a crone, will crouch beside the hearth
   mourning my love and all your proud disdain.
And since what comes to-morrow who can say?
Live, pluck the roses of the world to-day.

Wish thee good-morrow, sweet my life, as merry
   as must farewell at parting sorrowful be,
and tell me of thy mercy doth't miscarry
   the captive heart I must return to thee?
Have the long days and miles that bade us tarry
   alone divided cooled in its degree
the fire I thought began thy soul to harry?
   For strange, were it not so, it seemeth me,
I know by proof how with a keener dart
   love from afar wounds than in neighbourhood,
   when absence lends a double edge to sorrow.
But let me live unaltered in my heart
   that cannot further walk in love, nor should,
   lest I grow mad and will not, Sweet, good-morrow.

I am your spoil, and therefore I am bold
   to bring this ivy that in sliding laces
by wall and tree, fold upon rising fold,
   coil upon coil, clips, smothers and embraces.
The crown of ivy, sweet, is yours to hold.
   God! that I might about your pillared graces
myself ecstatic exquisitely mould
   both day and night in love's unspoken phrases.
Will the time never come when sleeping under
   branches as morning, with her bright alarms,
   the world awakes to bird-song in the closes,
I kiss your mouth that opens to love's wonder,
   and tell my pain while softly in my arms
   you lie, all waiting, ivory and roses?

My lady drank to me and bad me sip,
    passing the cup, her soul within the wine,
and as I drank I felt her spirit slip—
    a heavenly boatman—from her lips to mine.
My blood assumed in that companionship,
    where heart and heart did with the draught combine,
so great a burden as was like to trip
    the soul outwearied by its weight divine.
But who could tipple beauty in the cup
    where love for ever swims, and not be drowned?
    Not I, who was upon the instant sunk.
Yes, from that day my soul was swallowed up,
    not in the wine I supped, but, as I found,
    with a sweet flame, and sweeter poison drunk.

FRANÇOIS RABELAIS

GARGANTUA AND PANTAGRUEL

The First Book of Rabelais,
Treating of the Inestimable Life of the Great Gargantua

How a Monk of Sevillé Saved the Close of the Abbey from Being Ravaged by the Enemy. So much they did, and so far they went pillaging and stealing, that at last they came to Sevillé, where they robbed both men and women, and took all they could catch: Nothing was either too hot or too heavy for them. Although the plague was there in the most part of all the houses, they nevertheless entered everywhere; then plundered and carried away all that was within, and yet, for all this, not one of them took any hurt, which is a most wonderful case. For the curates, vicars, preachers, physicians, chirurgeons, and apothecaries, who went to visit, to dress, to cure, to heal, to preach unto, and admonish those that were sick, were all dead of the infection; and these devilish robbers and murderers caught never any harm at all. Whence comes this to pass (my masters), I beseech you think upon it?

The town being thus pillaged, they went unto the abbey with a horrible noise and tumult, but they found it shut and made fast against them; whereupon, the body of the army marched forward towards a ford, called Sue (Gue) de Vede, except seven companies of foot, and two hundred lanciers, who, staying there, broke down the walls of the close to waste, spoil and make havock of all the vines and vintage within that place. The monks (poor devils) knew not in that extremity, to which of all their sancts they should vow themselves; nevertheless, at all adventures they rang the bells *ad capitulum capitulantes*. There it was decreed, that they should make a fair procession, stuffed with good lectures, prayers, and litanies, *contra hostium insidias*, and jolly responses *pro pace*.

There was then in the abbey, a claustral monk, called Friar John
de Entoumeures, young, gallant, frisky, lusty, nimble, quick, active,

bold, adventurous, resolute, tall, lean, wide-mouthed, long-nosed, a rare mumbler of mattins, unbridler of masses, and runner over of vigils: and to conclude summarily, in a word, a right monk, if ever there were any, since the monking world monked a monkery. For the rest a clerk, even to the teeth, in matter of breviary. This monk, hearing the noise that the enemy made within the inclosure of the vineyard, went out to see what they were doing, and perceiving that they were cutting and gathering the grapes, whereon was grounded the foundation of all their next year's wine, returned unto their choir of the church where the other monks were, all amazed and astonished like so many bell-melters, whom, when he heard sing, *im, nim, pe, ne, ne, ne, ne, nede, tum, ne, num, num, ini, i, mi, co, o, no, o, o, neno ne, no, no, no, rum, nenum, num:* "This is," said he, "bien chié chanté, well shit, well sung. By the virtue of God; why do you not sing paniers farewell, vintage is done. The devil snatch me if they be not already within the middle of our close and cut so well both vines and grapes, that by Cods Body, there will not be found for these four years to come so much as a gleaning in it. By the belly of Sanct James, what shall we (poor devils) drink the while? Lord God! *da mihi potum.*" Then said the prior of the convent, "What should this drunken fellow do here, let him be carried to prison for troubling the divine service?" "Nay," said the monk, "the wine service? let us behave ourselves so that it be not troubled; for you yourself, my lord prior, love to drink of the best, and so doth every honest man. Never yet did a man of worth dislike good wine; it is a monastical apophthegm: But these responses that you chaunt here, by G—, are not in season. Wherefore is it, that our devotions were instituted to be short in the time of harvest and vintage, and long in the advent and all the winter?

"The late friar Messepelosse, of good memory, a true zealous man (or the devil take me) of our religion, told me, and I remember it well, how the reason was, that in this season we might press and make the wine, and in the winter whiff it up. Hark you, my masters, you that love the wine, Cops Body, follow me, for Sanct Anthony burn me as freely as a faggot, if they taste one drop of the liquor, that will not now come and fight in defence of the vine. Hog's belly the goods of the church! Ha, no, no: What the devil would have Sanct Thomas of England died for them; If I die, shall not I be a Sanct likewise? Yet will not I die for all this, but send others a packing."

As he spake this, he threw off his great monk's habit, and laid hold upon the staff of the cross, which was made of the heart of a sorb-apple-tree, it being of the length of a lance, round, of a full
263 gripe, and a little powdered with flower de luces, almost all defaced

and worn out. Thus went he out in a fair long-skirted jacket, putting his frock scarfways athwart his breast, and with his staff of the cross laid on so lustily upon his enemies, who without any order, or ensign, or trumpet, or drum, were busied in gathering the grapes of the vineyard; for the cornets, guidons, and ensign-bearers had lain down their standards, banners, and colours by the wall-sides: The drummers had knocked out the heads of their drums on one end, to fill them with grapes: The trumpeters were loaded with great bundles of bunches, and huge knots of clusters: In sum, every one of them was out of array, and all in disorder. He hurried therefore upon them so rudely, without crying *gare,* or beware, that he overthrew them like hogs, tumbled them over like swine, striking athwart and amongst, and by one means or other laid so about him, after the old fashion of fencing, that to some he beat out their brains, to others he crushed their arms, battered their legs, and bethwacked their sides till their ribs cracked with it; to others again, he unjointed the spondyles of the neck, disfigured their chaps, gashed their faces, made their cheeks hang flapping over their chin, and so swinged and belamed them, that they fell down before him like hay before a mower: to some others he spoiled the frame of their kidnies, marred their backs, broke their thigh bones, pushed in their noses, poached out their eyes, cleft their mandibules, tore their jaws, dashed their teeth into their throat, shook asunder their *omoplates,* or shoulder-blade, *sphacelated* their shins, mortified their shanks, inflamed their ancles, heaved off of the hinges their ishies, their *sciatica* or hip-gout, dislocated the joints of their knees, squattered into pieces the boughs or pestles of their thighs, and so thumped, mauled, and belaboured them everywhere, that never was corn so thick and threefold threshed upon by ploughmen's flails, as were the pitifully disjointed members of their mangled bodies, under the merciless baton of the cross.

If any offered to hide himself amongst the thickest of the vines, he laid him squat as a flounder, bruised the ridge of his back, and dashed his reins like a dog. If any thought by his flight to escape, he made his head to fly in pieces by the *lamboidal commissure.* If anyone did scramble up into a tree, thinking there to be safe, he rent up his perinee, and impaled him in at the fundament. If any one of his old acquaintance happened to cry out, "Ha, Friar John, my friend; Friar John, quarter, quarter, I yield myself to you; to you I render myself." "So thou shalt," said he, "*per* force, and thy soul to all the devils in hell;" then suddenly gave him *dronos.* If any was so rash and full of temerity as to resist him to his face, then was it he did shew the strength of his muscles; for without more ado he did transpierce him, by running him at the breast through the *mediatestine* and the heart. Others again he so quashed and bebumped, that with a sound bounce under the hollow of their short ribs, he overturned their stomachs, so that they died immediately. To some, with a smart souse on the *epigaster,* he would make their midriff swag; then redoubling the blow, gave them such a home push on the navel, that he made their puddings gush out. To others, through their ballocks he pierced their bumgut, and left not bowel, tripe, nor entrail in their body, that had not felt the impetuosity, fierceness, and fury of his violence. Believe, that it was the most horrible spectacle that ever one saw: Some cried unto Sanct Barbe, others to St. George; "O, the holy Lady Nytouch," said one, "the good sanctess;" "O, *our lady of succours,*" said another, "help, help!" Others cried, "Our lady of Cunaut, of Loretta, of *good tidings,* on the other side of the water St. Mary-over:" Some vowed a pilgrimage to St. James, and others to the holy handkerchief at Chamberry, which three months after that burnt so well in the fire, that they could not get one thread of it saved: others sent up their vows to St. Cadouin, others to St. John d'Angelie, and to St. Eutropius of Xantes: Others again invoked St. Mesmes of Chinon, St. Martin of Candes, St. Cloud of Sinays, the holy relics of Laurezay, with a thousand other jolly little sancts and santrels. Some died without speaking, others spoke without dying; some died in speaking, others spoke in dying. Others shouted aloud, *"Confession, confession, confiteor, miserere, in manus."* So great was the cry of the wounded, that the prior of the abbey with all his monks came forth; who, when they saw these poor wretches so slain amongst the vines, and wounded to death, confessed some of them. But whilst the priests were busy in confessing them, the little monkies ran all to the place where Friar John was, and asked him wherein he would be pleased to require their assistance.

To which he answered, that they should cut the throats of those he had thrown down upon the ground. They, presently leaving their outer habits and cowls upon the rails, began to throttle and make an end of those whom he had already crushed. Can you tell with what instruments they did it? With fair *gullicks,* which are little hulched-backed demi-knives, wherewith the little boys in our country cut ripe walnuts in two.

In the meantime, Friar John, with his formidable baton (staff) of the cross, got to the breach which the enemies had made, and there stood to snatch up those that endeavoured to escape. Some of the monkitos carried the standards, banners, ensigns, guidons, and colours into their cells and chambers, to make garters of them, but when those that had been shriven would have gone out at the gap of the said breach, the sturdy monk quashed and felled them down

with blows, saying, "These men have had confession and are peni-
tent souls, they have got their absolution, and gained the pardons:
they go into Paradise as straight as a sickle, or as the way is to Faye
(*like Crooked-lane at Eastcheap*).

Thus by his prowess and valour were discomfited all those of the
army that entered into the close of the abbey, unto the number of
thirteen thousand six hundred twenty and two, besides the women
and little children, which is always to be understood. Never did
Maugis the hermit bear himself more valiantly with his *pilgrim's*
staff against the Saracens, of whom it is written in the Acts of the
four sons of Haymon, than did this *monk* against his *enemies with
the staff of the cross.*

Chapter *How Gargantua Did Eat up Six Pilgrims in a Sallad.* The story
Thirty- requireth, that we relate what happened unto six pilgrims, who
Eight came from Sebastian near to Nantes; and who for shelter that night,
being afraid of the enemy, had hid themselves in the garden upon
the chicheling pease, among the cabbages and lettices. Gargantua,
finding himself somewhat dry, asked whether they could get any
lettice to make him a sallad; and hearing that there were the greatest and fairest in the country (for they were as great as plum-trees,
or as walnut-trees) he would go thither himself, and brought thence
in his hand what he thought good, and withal carried away the six
pilgrims, who were in so great fear, they did not dare to speak nor
cough.

Washing them, therefore, first at the fountain, the pilgrims said
one to another softly, "*What shall we do? we are almost drowned
here amongst these lettices, shall we speak? but if we speak he will
kill us for spies.*" As they were thus deliberating what to do, Gargantua put them with the lettice into a platter of the house as large
as the huge tun of the Cistertians, which done, with oil, vinegar, and
salt, he eat them up, to refresh himself a little before supper, and
had already swallowed up five of the pilgrims, the sixth being in
the platter, totally hid under a lettice, except his staff that appeared,
and nothing else; which Grangousier seeing, said to Gargantua, "I
think that is the horn of a shell snail, do not eat it." "Why not?" said
Gargantua; "they are good all this month," which he no sooner said,
but drawing up the staff, and therewith taking up the pilgrim, he
eat him very well, then drank a terrible draught of excellent white-
wine, and expected supper to be brought up.

The pilgrims, thus devoured, made shift to save themselves as
266 well as they could, by withdrawing their bodies out of the reach

of the grinders of his teeth, but could not escape from thinking they had been put in the lowest dungeon of a prison. And when Gargantua whiffed the great draught, they thought to have been drowned in his mouth, and the flood of wine had almost carried them away in the gulph of his stomach. Nevertheless, skipping with their staves, as St. Michael's palmers used to do, they sheltered themselves from the danger of that inundation, under the banks of his teeth. But one of them by chance, groping or sounding the country with his staff to try whether they were in safety or no, struck hard against the cleft of a hollow tooth, and hit the *mandibulary* sinew or nerve of the jaw, which put Gargantua to very great pain, so that he began to cry for the rage that he felt. To ease himself therefore of his smarting ach, he called for his tooth-picker, and rubbing towards a young walnut-tree, unnestled you my gentlemen pilgrims.

For he caught one by the legs, another by the scrip, another by the pocket, another by the scarf, another by the band of the breeches, and the poor fellow that had hurt him with the staff, him he hooked to him by the codpiece, which snatch nevertheless did him a great deal of good, for it broke upon him a pocky botch he had in the groin, which grievously tormented him ever since they were past Ancenis. The pilgrims, thus dislodged, ran athwart the plain a pretty fast pace, and the pain ceased, even just at the time when by Eudemon he was called to supper, for all was ready. "I will go then," said he, "and piss away my misfortune," which he did do in such a copious measure, that, the urine taking away the feet from the pilgrims, they were carried along with the stream unto the bank of a tuft of trees: upon which, as soon as they had taken footing, and that for their self-preservation they had run a little out of the road, they on a sudden fell all six, except Fourniller, into a trap that had been made to take wolves by a train; out of which they escaped nevertheless by the industry of the said Fourniller, who broke all the snares and ropes. Being gone from thence, they lay all the rest of that night in a lodge near unto Coudry, where they were comforted in their miseries, by the gracious words of one of their company, called Sweertogo, who shewed them that this adventure had been foretold by the prophet David in the Psalms. "*Quum exurgerent homines in nos, forte vivos deglutissent nos;* when we were eaten in the sallad, with salt, oil, and vinegar. *Quum irasceretur furor eorum in nos, forsitan aqua absorbuisset nos;* when he drank the great draught. *Torrentem pertransivit anima nostra;* when the stream of his water carried us to the thicket. *Forsitan pertransisset anima nostra aquam intolerabilem;* that is, the water of his urine, the flood whereof, cutting our way, took our feet from us.

Benedictus dominus qui non dedit nos in captionem dentibus eorum: anima nostra sicut passer erepta est de laqueo venantiam; when we fell in the trap. *Laqueus contritus est,* by Fourniller. *Et nos liberati sumus. Adjutorium nostrum, &c.*"

Chapter Fifty-two

How Gargantua Caused to Be Built for the Monk the Abbey of Theleme. There was left only the monk to provide for, whom Gargantua would have made abbot of Sevillé, but he refused it. He would have given him the abbey of Bourgueil, or of Sanct Florent, which was better, or both if it pleased him. But the monk gave him a very peremptory answer, that he would never take upon him the charge nor government of monks. "For how shall I be able," said he, "to rule over others, that have not power and command over myself? If you think I have done you, or may hereafter do you any acceptable service, give me leave to found an abbey after my own mind and fancy." The notion pleased Gargantua very well, who thereupon offered him all the country of Theleme by the river of Loire, till within two leagues of the great forest of Porthuaut. The monk then requested Gargantua to institute his religious order *contrary* to all others. "First then," said Gargantua, "you must not build a wall about your convent, for all other abbeys are strongly walled and mured about." "See," said the monk, "and without cause, where there is *mur* before and *mur* behind, there is a store of *murmur,* envy, and mutual conspiracy."

Moreover, seeing there are certain convents in the world, whereof the custom is, if any woman come (I mean chaste and honest women) they immediately sweep the ground which they have trod upon. Therefore was it ordained, that if any man or woman, entered into religious orders, should by chance come within this new abbey, all the *rooms* should be thoroughly *washed* and cleansed, through which they had passed. And because in all other monasteries and nunneries all is compassed, limited, and regulated by *hours,* it was decreed, that in this new structure there should be neither clock nor dial, but that, according to the opportunities and incident occasions, all *their hours* should be disposed of. "For," said Gargantua, "the greatest loss of time that I know, is, to count the *hours.* What good comes of it? Nor can there be any greater dotage in the world, than for one to guide and direct his courses by the sound of a bell, and not by his own judgment and discretion."

Item, because at that time they put no *women* into nunneries, but such as were either purblind, blinkards, lame, crooked, ill-favoured, mis-shapen, fools, senseless, spoiled, or corrupt; nor encloistered *any men,* but those that were either sickly, subject to defluxions, ill-bred louts, simple sots, or peevish trouble-houses. "But to the purpose," said the monk: "a woman that is neither fair nor good, to what use serves she?" "To make a *nun* of," said Gargantua. "Yea," said the monk, "and to make shirts and smocks." Therefore was it ordained, that *into this religious* order should be admitted *no women* that were not fair, well featured, and of a sweet disposition; nor *men that* were not comely, personable, and well-conditioned.

Item, because in the convents of women, men come not but underhand, privily, and by stealth; it was therefore enacted, that in this house there shall be no women in case there be not men, nor men in case there be not women.

Item, because both men and women that are received into religious orders, after the expiring of their *novitiat,* or probation year, were constrained and forced perpetually to stay there all the days of their life; it was therefore ordered, that all whatever, men or women, admitted within this abbey, should have full leave to depart with peace and contentment, whensoever it should seem good to them so to do.

Item, for that the religious men and women did ordinarily make three vows, to wit, those of *chastity, poverty,* and *obedience;* it was therefore constituted and appointed, that in this convent they might be honourably *married,* that they might be *rich,* and live at *liberty.* In regard of the legitimate time of the persons to be initiated, and years under and above which they were not capable of reception, the women were to be admitted from *ten till fifteen,* and the men from *twelve to eighteen.*

Chapter Fifty-four **The Inscription Set upon the Great Gate of Theleme.**

"Here enter not, religious boobies, sots,
Impostors, sniveling hypocrites, bigots:
Dark-brain distorted owls, worse than the Huns
Or Ostrogots; fore-runners of baboons:
Curs'd snakes, dissembling varlets, seeming sancts,
Slipshop caffards, beggars pretending wants;
Fomentors of divisions and debates,
Elsewhere, not here, make sale of your deceits.
    Your filthy trumperies,
    Stuff'd with pernicious lies.
        (Not worth a bubble)
        Would only trouble

269

Our earthly Paradise.
Your filthy trumperies.

"Here enter not attorneys, barraters,
Nor bridle-champion-law practitioners:
Clerks, commissaries, scribes, nor pharisees,
Wilful disturbers of the people's ease,
Judges, destroyers, with an unjust breath,
That, like dogs, worry honest men to death.
We want not your *demurrers*, nor your *pleas;*
So at the gibbet go and seek your fees.
We are not for attendance or delays;
But would with ease and quiet pass our days,
   Law-suits, debates, and wrangling
   Hence are exil'd, and jangling.
    Here we are very
    Frolic and merry,
   And free from all intangling
   Law-suits, debates, and wrangling.

"Here enter not base pinching usurers,
Pelf-lickers, everlasting gatherers;
Gold-graspers, coin-gripers, gulpers of mists,
With harpy-griping claws, who, tho' your chests
Vast sums of money should to you afford,
Would nevertheless be adding to the hoard:
And yet not be content; ye cluntch-fist dastards,
Insatiable friends, and Pluto's bastards;
Greedy devourers, chichy, sneak-bill rogues;
Hell-mastiff's gnaw your bones, you rav'nous dogs.
   You beastly looking fellows,
   Reason doth plainly tell us,
    That we should not
    To you allot
   Room here, but at the gallows;
   You beastly looking fellows.

"Here enter not, unsociable wight,
Humoursome churl, by day, nor yet by night.
No grumbling awf, none of the sharping trade,
No huff-cap squire, or brother of the blade.
A Tartar bred, or in Alsatia wars,
The ruffian comes not hither with his bears.
Elsewhere for shelter scour, ye bully-rocks,
And rogues, that rot with infamy and pox.
   Grace, honour, praise, delight,
   Here sojourn day and night,

Sound bodies, lin'd
With a good mind,
Do here pursue with might
Grace, honour, praise, delight.

"Here enter you, and welcome from our hearts,
All noble sparks, endow'd with gallant parts.
This is the glorious place which nobly shall
Afford sufficient to content you all;
Were you a thousand, here you shall not want
For anything; for what you ask, we grant.
The brave, the witty, here we entertain,
And, in a word, all worthy gentlemen,
  Men of heroic breasts
  Shall taste here of the feasts,
    Both privily
    And civilly
  All you are welcome guests,
  Men of heroic breasts.

"Here enter you, pure, honest, faithful, true,
Expounders of the *Scriptures,* old and new;
Whose glosses do not the plain truth disguise,
And with false light distract or blind our eyes.
Here shall we find a safe and warm retreat,
When Error beats about and spreads her net.
Strange doctrines here must neither reap nor sow,
But Faith and Charity together grow.
In short, confounded be their first device
Who are the holy *Scriptures'* enemies.
  Here in the *holy word*
  Trust all, with one accord;
    It will some help afford:
    Tho' you be knight or lord,
  You may find shield and sword,
  Here in the *holy word*.

"Here enter ladies all, of high degree,
Of goodly shape, of humour gay and free;
Of lovely looks, of sprightly flesh and blood:
Here take, here chuse, here settle your abode.
The gent, the brisk, the fair, whoever comes,
With eyes that sparkle, or whose beauty blooms.
This *bower* is fashion'd by a gentle knight,
Ladies, for you, and innocent delight.
  This is design'd a place
  For every charming grace;

"The witty and the fair
Hither may all repair;
For every lovely face
This is design'd a place."

*How the Thelemites Were Governed, and of Their Manner of
Living.* All their life was spent not in laws, statutes, or rules, but
according to their own free will and pleasure. They rose out of their
beds when they thought good; they did eat, drink, labour, sleep,
when they had a mind to it, and were disposed for it. None did
awake them, none did offer to constrain them to eat, drink, nor do
any other thing; for so had Gargantua established it. In all their rule
and strictest tie of their order, there was but this one clause to be
observed:

DO WHAT THOU WILT.

Because men that are free, well-born, well-bred, and conversant
in honest companies, have naturally an *instinct* and spur that
prompteth them unto virtuous actions, and withdraws them from
vice, which is called *honour*. Those same men, when by base subjection and constraint they are brought under and kept down, turn
aside from that noble disposition, by which they formerly were
inclined to *virtue,* to shake off that bond of servitude, wherein they
are so tyrannously inslaved; for it is agreeable to the nature of man
to long after things forbidden, and to desire what is denied us. By
this liberty they entered into a very laudable emulation, to do all of
them what they saw did please one. If any of the gallants or ladies
should say, "Let us drink," they would all drink. If any one of them
said, "Let us play," they all played. If one said, "Let us go a walking
into the fields," they went all. If it were to go a hawking, or a hunting, the ladies mounted upon dainty well-paced nags, seated in a
stately palfrey saddle, carried on their lovely fists *miniardly be-
gloved* every one of them, either a sparhawk, or a laneret, or a
marlin, and the young gallants carried the other kinds of hawks. So
nobly were they taught, that there was neither he nor she amongst
them, but could read, write, sing, play upon several musical instruments, speak five or six several languages, and compose in them
all very quaintly, both in verse and prose. Never were seen so valiant
knights, so noble and worthy, so dexterous and skilful both on foot
and horseback, more brisk and lively, more nimble and quick, or
better handling all manner of weapons, than were there. Never
were seen *ladies* so proper and handsome, so miniard and dainty,
272 less froward, or more ready with their hand, and with their needle,

in every honest and free action belonging to that sex, than were there. For this reason, when the time came that any *man* of the *abbey*, either at the request of his parents, or for some other cause, had a mind to go out of it, he carried along with him one of the *ladies*, namely, her, whom he had before that chosen for his *mistress*, and they were married together. And if they had formerly in Theleme lived in good devotion and amity, they did continue therein, and increase it to a greater height in their state of matrimony; and did entertain that mutual love till the very last day of their life, in no less vigour and fervency than at the very day of their wedding.

The Second Book of Rabelais,
Treating of the Heroic Deeds and Sayings of the Good Pantagruel.

Chapter *Of the Nativity of the Most Dread and Redoubted Pantagruel.*
Two Gargantua, at the age of four hundred fourscore forty and four years, begat his son Pantagruel, upon his wife named Badebec, daughter to the king of the Amaurots in Utopia, who died in child-birth; for he was so wonderfully great and lumpish, that he could not possibly come forth into the light of the world, without thus suffocating his mother. But that we may fully understand the cause and reason of the name of Pantagruel, which, at his baptism, was given him, you are to remark, that in that year there was so great a drought over all the country of Afric, that there past thirty and six months, three weeks, four days, thirteen hours, and a little more, without rain, but with a heat so vehement, that the whole earth was parched and withered by it; neither was it more scorched and dried up with heat in the days of Elijah, than it was at that time; for there was not a tree to be seen that had either leaf or bloom upon it: the grass was without verdure or greenness, the rivers were drained, the fountains dried up, the poor fishes abandoned and forsaken by their proper element, wandering and crying upon the ground most horribly: the birds did fall down from the air, for want of moisture and dew wherewith to refresh them: the wolves, foxes, harts, wild-boars, fallow-deer, hares, conies, weesils, brocks, badgers, and other such beasts were found dead in the fields, with their mouths open. In respect of men, there was the pity, you should have seen them
273 lay out their tongues like greyhounds that had run six hours; many

did throw themselves into the wells; others entered within a cow's belly to be in the shade; those Homer calls the Alibants: all the country was at a stand, and nothing could be done; it was a most lamentable case, to have seen the labour of mortals in defending themselves from the vehemency of this horrific drought; for they had work enough to do to save the holy water in the churches from being wasted: but there was such order taken by the counsel of my lords the cardinals, and of our holy father, that none did dare to take above one lick; yet when any one came into the church, you should have seen above twenty poor thirsty fellows hang upon him that was the distributor of the water, and that with a wide open throat, gaping for some little drop, like the rich glutton in St. Luke, that might fall by, lest anything should be lost. O how happy was he that year who had a cool cellar under ground, well plenished with fresh wine!

The philosopher reports in moving the question, *wherefore is it that the sea-water is salt?* that at the time when Phœbus gave the government of his resplendent chariot to his son Phæton, the said Phæton, unskilful in the art, and not knowing how to keep the *ecliptic* line betwixt the two *tropics* of the *latitude* of the sun's course, strayed out of his way, and came so near the earth, that he dried up all the countries that were under it, burning a great part of the heaven, which the *philosophers* call *Via lactea,* and the huff-snuffs, St. James's way; although the most lofty and high-crested poets affirm that to be the place where Juno's milk fell when she gave suck to Hercules.

The earth at that time was so excessively heated, that it fell into an enormous sweat, yea, such an one that made it sweat out the sea, which is therefore *salt,* because all *sweat* is *salt;* and this you cannot but confess to be true, if you will taste of your own, or of those that have the pox, when they are put into a *sweating;* it is all one to me. Just such another case fell out this same year; for on a certain Friday, when the whole people were bent upon their devotions, and had made goodly *processions,* with store of *litanies,* and fair *preachings,* and beseechings of God Almighty to look down with his eye of mercy upon their miserable and disconsolate condition, there was even then visibly seen issue out of the ground great drops of water, such as fall from a man in a top *sweat;* and the poor hoydons began to rejoice, as if it had been a thing very profitable unto them; for some said, that there was not one drop of moisture in the air, whence they might have any rain, and that the earth did supply the default of that. Other learned men said, that it was a shower of the *antipodes,* as Seneca saith, in his fourth book

274 *Quæstionum Naturalium,* speaking of the source and spring of Nilus;

but they were deceived; for the procession being ended, when every one went about to gather of this dew, and to drink of it with full bowls, they found it was nothing but *pickle,* and the very *brine* of salt, more brackish in taste than the saltest water of the sea: and because in that very day Pantagruel was born, his father gave him that name; for *Panta* in Greek is as much as to say *all,* and *Gruel* in the Hagarene language doth signify *thirsty;* inferring hereby, that *at his birth the whole world was a-dry and thirsty;* as likewise fore-seeing that he would be some day supreme lord and sovereign of the thirsty companions, which was shewn to him at that very same hour, by a more evident sign; for when his mother Badebec was in the bringing of him forth, and that the midwives did wait to receive him, there came first out of her belly threescore and eight *sellers* of *salt,* every one of them leading in a halter a *mule,* heavy loaded with *salt;* after whom issued forth nine *dromedaries,* with great loads of gammons of bacon, and dried neat's-tongues on their backs; then followed seven *camels* loaded with links and chitterlings, hog's pudding, and sausages; after them came out twenty-five great wains full of leeks, garlic, onions, and chibals. At the sight hereof the midwives were much amazed; yet some of them said, "Lo, here is *good provision, and indeed we need it, for we drink but lazily, as if our tongues walked on crutches: truly this is a good sign, there is nothing here but what is fit for us, these are the spurs of wine that set it going."* As they were tattling thus together, after their own manner of chat, behold! out comes Pantagruel, all hairy like a bear; whereupon one of them, inspired with a prophetical spirit, said, *"This will be a terrible fellow; he is born with all his hair, he is undoubtedly to do wonderful things; and, if he live, he will be of age."*

Chapter *Of the Infancy of Pantagruel.* I find, by the ancient historiogra-
Four phers and poets, that divers have been born in this world after very strange manners, which would be too long to repeat; read therefore the seventh book of Pliny, if you have so much leisure: yet have you never heard of any so wonderful as that of Pantagruel; for it is a very difficult matter to believe how, in the little time he was in his mother's belly, he grew both in body and strength. That which Hercules did was nothing, when in his cradle he slew two serpents; for those serpents were but little and weak: but Pantagruel, being yet in his cradle, did far more admirable things, and more to be amazed at. I pass by here the relation of how at every one of his
275 meals he supped up the milk of four thousand six hundred cows;

and how to make him a skillet to boil his milk in, there were set a-work all the braziers of Saumure in Anjou, of Villedieu in Normandy, and of Bramont in Lorrain: and they served meat to him in a huge great bell, which is yet to be seen in the city of Bourges in Berry, near the palace; but his teeth were already so well grown, and so strengthened in vigour, that of the said bell he bit off a great morsel, as very plainly doth appear till this hour.

One day in the morning, when they would have made him suck one of his cows—for he never had any other nurse, as the history tells us—he got one of his arms loose from the swaddling bands, wherewith he was kept fast in the cradly, laid hold on the said cow under the left fore-ham, and grasping her to him, ate up her udder, and half her paunch, with the liver and the kidnies, and had devoured all up, if she had not cried out most horribly, as if the wolves had held her by the legs; at which noise company came in, and took away the said cow from Pantagruel: yet could they not so well do it, but that the quarter whereby he caught her was left in his hand, of which quarter he gulped up the flesh in a trice, even with as much ease as you would eat a sausage; and that so greedily, with desire of more, that when they would have taken away the bone from him, he swallowed it down whole, as a cormorant would do a little fish, and afterwards began fumblingly to say, "*Good, good, good!*" for he could not yet speak plain; giving them to understand thereby that he had found it very good, and that he did lack but so much more: which when they saw that attended him, they bound him with great cable-ropes, like those that are made at Tain for the carriage of salt to Lyons, or such as those are whereby the great French ship rides at anchor in the road of Newhaven in Normandy. But on a certain time a great bear, which his father had bred, got loose, came towards him, began to lick his face, for his nurses had not thoroughly wiped his chaps: at which unexpected approach, being on a sudden offended, he as lightly rid himself of those great cables as Sampson did of the hauser ropes wherewith the Philistines had tied him, and, by your leave, takes up monsieur the bear, and tears him in pieces like a pullet, which served him for a gorge full, or good warm bit for that meal.

Whereupon Gargantua, fearing lest the child should hurt himself, caused four great chains of iron to be made to bind him, and so many strong wooden arches unto his cradle, most firmly stocked and mortised in huge frames: of those chains you have one at Rochel, which they draw up at night betwixt the two great towers of the haven; another is at Lyons; a third at Angiers; and the fourth was carried away by the devils, to bind Lucifer, who broke his chains at that time by reason of a cholic that did extraordinarily torment him, taken with eating a serjeant's soul fricasseed for his breakfast; and therefore you may believe that which Nicolas de Lyre saith upon that place of the psalter, where it is written, *"Et Og regem Basan;"* that the said Og, being yet little, was so strong and robustious, that they were fain to bind him with chains of iron in his cradle. Thus continued Pantagruel for awhile very calm and quiet, for he was not able so easily to break those chains, especially having no room in the cradle to give a swing with his arms. But see what happened; once upon a great holiday, that his father Gargantua made a sumptuous banquet to all the princes of his court: I am apt to believe that the menial officers of the house were so imbusied in waiting each on his proper service at the feast, that nobody took care of poor Pantagruel, who was left *à reculorum*, behindhand all alone, and as forsaken. What did he? Hark what he did, good people: he strove and essayed to break the chains of the cradle with his arms, but could not, for they were too strong for him; then did he keep with his feet such a stamping stir, and so long, that at last he beat out the lower end of his cradle, which notwithstanding was made of a great beam five foot in square; and as soon as he had gotten out his feet, he slid down as well as he could, till he had got his soles to the ground; and then, with a mighty force, he rose up, carrying this cradle upon his back, bound to him like a tortoise that crawls up against a wall; and to have seen him, you would have thought it had been a great carrick of five hundred tun upon one end. In this manner he entered into the great hall, where they were banquetting, and that very boldly, which did much affright the company: yet because his arms were tied in, he could not reach anything to eat, but, with great pain, stooped now and then a little, to take, with the whole flat of his tongue, some lick, good bit, or morsel.

Which when his father saw, he knew well enough that they had left him without giving him anything to eat, and therefore commanded that he should be loosed from the said chains, by the counsel of the princes and lords there present: besides that, also the physicians of Gargantua said, that if they did thus keep him in the cradly, he would be all his liftetime subject to the stone. When he was unchained, they made him to sit down, where, after he had fed very well, he took his cradle, and broke it into more than five hundred thousand pieces, with one blow of his fist that he struck in the midst of it, swearing that he would never come into it again.

Of the Acts of the Noble Pantagruel in His Youthful Age. Thus
grew Pantagruel from day to day, and, to every one's eye, waxed
more and more in all his dimensions, which made his father to rejoice by a natural affection; therefore caused he to be made for him,
whilst he was yet little, a pretty cross-bow, wherewith to shoot at
small birds, which now they call the great crossbow at Chantelle.
Then he sent him to school to learn, and to spend his youth in
virtue: in the prosecution of which design he came first to Poiters,
where, as he studied and profited very much, he saw that the
scholars were oftentimes idle, and knew not how to bestow their
time, which moved him to take such compassion on them, that one
day he took from a long ledge of rocks (called there Passelourdin) a
huge great stone, of about twelve fathom square and fourteen
handfuls thick, and with great ease set it upon four pillars, in the
midst of a field, to no other end, but that the said scholars, when
they had nothing else to do, might pass their time in getting up on
that stone, and feast it with store of gammons, pasties, and flaggons,
and carve their names upon it with a knife; in token of which deed,
till this hour, the stone is called the *lifted stone:* and in remembrance
hereof, there is none entered into the register and matricular book
of the said university of Poitiers, till he have first drunk in the cabal-
line fountain of Croustelles, passed at Passelourdin, and got up upon
the *lifted stone.*

Afterwards reading the delectable chronicles of his ancestors, he
found that Jeffrey of Lusinian, called *Jeffrey with the great tooth,*
grandfather to the cousin-in-law of the eldest sister of the aunt of
the son-in-law of the uncle of the good daughter of his step-mother,
was interred at Maillezais; therefore he took a *play-day* to pay his
respects to him in a visit; and going from Poitiers with some of his
companions, they passed by Legugé, visiting the noble Abbot
Ardillon: then by Lusinian, by Sansay, by Celles, by Colonges, by
Fontenay le Comte, saluting the learned Tiraqueau, and from thence
arrived at Maillezais, where he went to see the sepulchre of the said
Jeffrey with the great tooth; which made him somewhat afraid, looking upon the portraiture, representing a man in an extreme fury,
drawing his great malchus faulchion half-way out of his scabbard.
When the reason hereof was demanded, the canons of the said place
told him, that there was no other cause of it, but that *pictoribus
atque poetis,* &c., that is to say, that painters and poets have liberty
to paint and devise what they list after their own fancy: but he
was not satisfied with their answer, and said, "He is not thus painted

without a cause; and I suspect that at his death there was some wrong done him, whereof he requireth his kindred to take revenge: I will inquire further into it, and then do what shall be reasonable." Then he returned not to Poitiers, but would take a view of the other universities of France: therefore going to Rochel, he took shipping, and arrived at Bourdeaux, where he found no great diversion, only now and then he would see some mariners and lightermen a wrestling on the key, or strand, by the river-side. From thence he came to Thoulouse, where he learned to *dance* very well, and to play with the *two-handed sword*, as the fashion of the scholars of the said university is. But he staid not long there, when he saw that they stuck not to burn their regents alive, like red-herrings, saying, "Now, God forbid that I should die this death, for I am by nature sufficiently dry already, without being *heated* any further."

He went then to Montpellier, where he met with the good wives of Mirevaux, and good jovial company withal, and thought to have set himself to the study of *physic;* but he considered that that calling was too troublesome and melancholy, and that *physicians* did smell of *glisters* like old devils; therefore he resolved he would study the laws; but seeing that there were but three scalled, and one bald-pated legist in that place, he departed from thence, and in his way made the bridge of Guard, and the amphitheatre of Nemes, in less than three hours, which nevertheless seems to be more than mortal man could do. After that he came to Avignon, where he was not above three days before he fell in love; for the women there take great delight in playing at the close buttock-game, because it is papal ground; which his tutor Epistemon perceiving, he drew him out of that place, and brought him to Valence in the Dauphiny, where he saw no great matter of recreation, only that the lubbards of the town did beat the scholars; which so incensed him with anger that when, upon a certain very fair Sunday, the people being at their public dancing in the streets, and one of the *scholars* offering to put himself into the ring, the bumkins would not let him; where-upon Pantagruel taking the scholar's part, so belaboured them with blows, and laid such load upon them, that he drove them all before him, even to the brink of the river Rhosne, and would have there drowned them, but that they did squat into the ground like moles, and there lay close a full half league under the river. The hole is to be seen there yet.

After that, he departed from thence, and in three strides and a leap came to Angiers, where he found himself very well, and would have continued there some space, but that the plague drove them away. So from thence he came to Bourges, where he studied a good

long time, and profited very much in the faculty of the laws; and would sometimes say that *law books* were like a wonderful rich cloth of gold, edged with sirreverence; for in the world are no goodlier books to be seen, more ornate, nor more eloquent than the texts of the pandects; but the *bordering* of them, that is to say, the *gloss* of Accursius, is so vile, mean, and scandalous, that it is nothing but dirt and excrement.

Going from Bourges he came to Orleans, where he found store of sparkish *scholars* that made him great entertainment at his coming, and with whom he learned to play at *tennis* so well, that he was a master at that game: for the students there are excellent at it. And sometimes they carried him unto Cupid's gardens, there to re-create his person at the poussevant, or in and in. As for breaking his head with over-much study, he had an especial care not to do it in any case, for *fear of spoiling his eyes;* which he the rather observed, for that one of the *regents* there had often in his *lectures* maintained, that *nothing could be so hurtful to the sight as to have sore eyes.* So one day, when a scholar of his acquaintance (who had of learn-ing not much more than his brethren, though, instead of that, he could *dance* very well, and play at *tennis*) was made a licentiate in law, he blazoned the licentiates of that university in this maner:

"In his hand is always a racket,
Or his tennis-ball in a placket:
In a dance he neatly can trip it;
And for law, it is all in his tippet."

Chapter **How Panurge Related the Manner How He Escaped out of the**
Fourteen **Hands of the Turks.** The great wit and judgment of Pantagruel was immediately after this made known to all the world, by setting forth his praises in print, and putting upon record this late won-derful proof he had given thereof amongst the rolls of the crown, and registers of the palace; in such sort, that everybody began to say that Solomon, who by a probable guess only, without any further certainty, caused the child to be delivered to his own mother, shewed never in his time such a masterpiece of wisdom, as the good Pantagruel had done: happy are we therefore that have him in our country. And indeed they would have made him thereupon master of the requests, and president in the court; but he refused all, very graciously thanking them for their offer; "for," said he, "there is too much slavery in these offices, and very hardly can they be saved that do exercise them, considering the great corruption that is amongst men; which makes me believe, if the empty seats

of angels be not filled with other kind of people than those, we shall not have the final judgment these seven thousand sixty and seven jubilees yet to come: and so Cusanus will be deceived in his conjecture. Remember that I have told you of it, and given you fair advertisement in time and place convenient. But if you have any hogsheads of good wine, I willingly will accept of a present of that." Which they very heartily did do, in sending him of the best that was in the city; and he drank reasonably well. But poor Panurge bibbed and bowsed of it most villainously: for he was as dry as a red-herring, as lean as a rake, and like a poor lank slender cat, walked gingerly as if he had trod upon eggs; so that by some one being admonished, in the midst of his draught of a large deep bowl, full of excellent claret, with these words: "Fair and softly, gossip, you suck up as if you were mad;" "I give thee to the devil," said he; "thou hast not found here thy little tippling sippers of Paris, that drink no more than the chaffinch, and never take in their beak full of liquor, till they be bobbed on the tails after the manner of the sparrows. O companion, if I could mount up as well as I can get down, I had been long ere this above the sphere of the moon with Empedocles. But I cannot tell what a devil this means. This wine is so good and delicious, that the more I drink thereof, the more I am athirst. I believe the shadow of my master Pantagruel maketh men a-thirsty, as the moon makes the catarrhs and defluxions." At which word the company began to laugh; which Pantagruel perceiving, said: "Panurge, what is that which moves you to laugh so?" "Sir," said he, "I was telling them that those devilish Turks are very unhappy, in that they never drink one drop of wine; and that though there were no other harm in all Mahomet's alcoran, yet for this one base point of abstinence from wine, which therein is commanded, I would not submit myself unto their law." "But now tell me," said Pantagruel, "how you escaped out of their hands." "By G—, sir," said Panurge, "I will not lie to you in one word."

"The rascally Turks had broached me upon a spit, all larded like a rabbit: for I was so dry and meagre, that otherwise of my flesh they would have made but very bad meat: and in this manner began to roast me alive. As they were thus roasting me, I recommended myself unto the divine grace, having in my mind that the good St. Lawrence, and always hoped in God that he would deliver me out of this torment; which came to pass, and that very strangely; for as I did commit myself with all my heart to God, crying, 'Lord God, help me! Lord God, save me! Lord God, take me out of this pain and hellish torture, wherein these traitorous dogs detain me for my sincerity in the maintenance of thy law!' the turnspit fell asleep by the divine will, or else by the virtue of some good Mercury, who cunningly brought Argus into a sleep for all his hundred eyes. When I saw that he did no longer turn me in roasting, I looked upon him, and perceived that he was fast asleep: then took I up in my teeth a firebrand, by the end where it was not burnt, and cast it into the lap of my roaster, and another did I throw as well as I could under a field bed, that was placed near to the chimney, wherein was the straw-bed of my master turnspit. Presently the fire took hold in the straw, and from the straw to the bed, and from the bed to the loft, which was planked and ceiled with fir, after the fashion of the foot of a lamp. But the best was that the fire, which I had cast into the lap of my paltry roaster, burnt all his groin, and was beginning to seize upon his cullions, when he became sensible of the danger: for his smelling was not so bad, but that he felt it sooner than he could have seen daylight. Then suddenly getting up, and in great amazement running to the window, he cried out to the streets as high as he could, 'Dal-baroth! dal-baroth! dal-baroth!' which is as much as to say, fire! fire! fire! Incontinently turning about, he came straight towards me, to throw me quite into the fire; and, to that effect, had already cut the ropes wherewith my hands were tied, and was undoing the cords from off my feet, when the master of the house hearing him cry fire, and smelling the smoke from the very street where he was walking with some other bashaws and mustaphas, ran with all the speed he had to save what he could, and to carry away his jewels; yet such was his rage, before he could well resolve how to go about it, that he caught the broach whereon I was spitted, and therewith killed my roaster stark dead, of which wound he died there for want of regimen, or otherwise: for he ran him in with the spit a little above the navel, towards the right flank, till he pierced the third lappet of his liver, and the blow slanting upwards from the diaphragm, through which it had made penetration, the spit pass'd athwart the pericardium, and came out above at his shoulders, betwixt the spondyls and the left homoplat.

"True it is, for I will not lie, that in drawing the spit out of my body, I fell to the ground near unto the andirons, and so by the fall took some hurt; which indeed had been greater, but that the lardons, or little slices of bacon wherewith I was stuck, kept off the blow. My bashaw then seeing the case to be desperate, his house burnt without remission, and all his goods lost, gave himself over unto all the devils in hell, calling upon some of them by their names, Grilgoth, Astarot, Rappalus, and Gribouillis, nine several times, which when I saw, I had above five pennyworth of fear, dreading that the devils would come even then to carry away this fool, and seeing me so near him would perhaps snatch me up too. I am ready, thought I, half roasted, and my lardons will be the cause of my mischief; for these devils are very lickorous of lardons, according to the authority which you have of the philosopher Jamblicus and Murmault, in the apology of Bossutis, adulterated *pro magistros nostros:* but for my better security I made the sign of the cross; crying, 'Hagios, *athanatos ho theos!*' and none came. At which, my rogue bashaw, being very much aggrieved, would in transpiercing his heart with my spit have killed himself; and to that purpose had set it against his breast, but it could not enter, because it was not sharp enough. Whereupon I, perceiving that he was not like to work upon his body the effect which he intended, although he did not spare all the force he had to thrust it forward, came up to him, and said, 'Master Bugrino, thou dost here but trifle away thy time, for thou wilt never kill thyself thus as thou doest. Well, thou may'st hurt or bruise somewhat within thee, so as to make thee languish all thy life time most pitifully amongst the hands of the chirurgeons: but if thou wilt be counselled by me, I will kill thee clear outright, so that thou shalt not so much as feel it; and trust me, for I have killed a great many others, who never have complained afterwards.' 'Ha, my friend,' said he, 'I prythee do so, and for thy pains I will give thee my codpiece: take, here it is, there are six hundred seraphs in it, and some fine diamonds, and most excellent rubies.'" "And where are they?" said Epistemon. "By St. John!" said Panurge, "they are a good way hence, if they always keep going: but where is the last year's snow? This was the greatest care that Villon the Parisian poet took." "Make an end," said Pantagruel, "that we may know how thou didst dress thy bashaw." "By the faith of an honest man," said Panurge, "I do not lie in one word; I swaddled him in a scurvy swathel-binding, which I found lying there half-burnt, and with my cords tied him royster-like both hand and foot, in such sort that he was not able to wince; then past my spit through his throat, and hanged him thereon, fastening the end thereof at two great hooked or cramp-irons, upon which they did hang their halberds; and then, kindling a fire under him, did flame you up my milourt, as they use to dry herrings in a chimney: with this, taking his budget, and a little javelin that was upon the foresaid hooks, I ran away a fair gallop-rake, and God he knows how I did smell my shoulder of mutton.

"When I was come down into the street, I found everybody come to put out the fire with store of water, and seeing me so half-roasted, they did naturally pity my case, and threw all their water upon me, which by a most joyful refreshing of me, did me very much good. Then did they present me with some victuals; but I could not eat much, because they gave me nothing to drink but water, after their fashion. Other hurt they did me none; only one little villainous

Turkey knob-breasted rogue came to snatch away some of my lardons; but I gave him such a sturdy thump, and sound rap on the fingers, with all the weight of my javelin, that he came no more the second time. Shortly after this, there came towards me a pretty young Corinthian wench, who brought me a box full of conserves, of round Myrabolan plums, called emblicks, and looked upon my poor Roger with an eye of great compassion, as it was flea-bitten and pinked with the sparkles of the fire from whence it came; for it reached no further in length, believe me, than my knees. But note, that this roasting cured me entirely of a sciatica, whereunto I had been subject above seven years before, upon that side which my roaster, by falling asleep, suffered to be burnt.

"Now whilst they were thus busy about me, the fire triumphed; never ask, how? for it took hold on above two thousand houses; which one of them espying, cried out, saying, 'By Mahoom's belly all the city is on fire, and we do nevertheless stand gazing here, without offering to bring any relief.' Upon this, every one ran to save his own. For my part, I took my way towards the gate. When I was got upon the nap of a little hillock, not far off, I turned me about as did Lot's wife, and looking back, saw all the city burning in a fair fire: whereat I was so glad, that I had almost beshit myself for joy; but God punished me well for it." "How?" said Pantagruel. "Thus," said Panurge; "for when with pleasure I beheld this jolly fire, jesting with myself, and saying, 'Ha poor fleas, ha poor mice, you will have a bad winter of it this year; the fire is in your reeks, it is in your bedstraw:' out came more than six, yea more than thirteen hundred and eleven dogs, great and small, all together out of the town, flying away from the fire. At the first approach they ran all upon me, being carried on by the scent of my leacherous half-roasted flesh, and had even then devoured me in a trice, if my good angel had not then inspired me with the instruction of a remedy, very sovereign against the pain of the teeth." "And wherefore," said Pantagruel, "wert thou afraid of the pain of the teeth? wert thou not cured of thy rheums?" "By Palm-Sunday," said Panurge, "is there any greater pain of the teeth than when the dogs have you by the legs? But on a sudden, as my good angel directed me, I thought upon my lardons, and threw them into the midst of the field amongst them: then did the dogs run, and fight with one another at fair teeth, which should have the lardons; by this means they left me, and I left them also bustling with, and haring one another. Thus did I escape frolic and lively, grammercy roast-meat and cookery."

Chapter *How Pantagruel with his Tongue Covered a Whole Army, and*
Thirty- *What the Author Saw in His Mouth.* Thus as Pantagruel with
two all his army had entered into the country of the Dipsodes, every
one was glad of it, and incontinently rendered themselves unto
him, bringing him out of their own good wills the keys of all the
cities where he went, the Almirods only excepted; who, being resolved to hold out against him, made answer to his heralds, that they
would not yield but upon very honourable and good conditions.

"What!" said Pantagruel, "do they ask any better terms than the
hand at the pot, and the glass in their fist? Come, let us go sack
them, and put them all to the sword." Then did they put themselves
in good order, as being fully determined to give an assault. But by
the way, passing through a large field, they were overtaken by a
great shower of rain, whereat they began to shiver and tremble,
to crowd, press, and thrust close to one another. When Pantagruel
saw that, he made their captains tell them that it was nothing, and
that he saw well above the clouds, that it would be nothing but a
little dew; but howsoever, that they should put themselves in order,
and he would cover them. Then did they put themselves in a close
order, and stood as near to each other as they could; and Pantagruel
drew out his tongue only half way, and covered them all, as a hen
doth her chickens.

In the meantime I, who relate to you these so veritable stories,
hid myself under a burdock-leaf, which was not much less in large-
ness than the arch of the bridge of Montrible; but when I saw them
thus covered, I went towards them, to shelter myself likewise, which
I could not do; for that (as the saying is) at the yard's end there is
no cloth left. Then, as well as I could, I got upon it, and went
forwards full two leagues upon his tongue; and so long marched,
that at last I came into his mouth. But O gods and goddesses, what
did I see there! Jupiter confound me with his trisulk lightning if I
lie. I walked there as they do in Sophie at Constantinople, and saw
there great rocks, like the mountains in Denmark; I believe that
those were his teeth: I saw also fair meadows, large forests, great
and strong cities, not a jot less than Lyons or Poitiers. The first
Man I met with there was a good honest fellow planting colworts;
whereat being very much amazed, I asked him, "My friend, what
art thou doing here?" "I am planting colworts," said he. "But how,
and wherewith?" said I. "Ha, sir," said he, "every one cannot have
his baws as heavy as a mortar; neither can we be all rich. Thus do
285 I get my poor living, and carry them to the market to sell in the

city, which is here behind." "Jesus!" said I, "is there here a new world?" "Sure," said he, "it is never a jot new: but it is commonly reported, that without this there is an earth, whereof the inhabitants enjoy the light of a sun and moon; and that it is full of, and replenished with, very good commodities; but yet, this is more ancient than that." "Yea, but," said I, "my friend, what is the name of that city whither thou carriest thy colworts to sell?" "It is called Alpharage," said he, "and all the indwellers are Christians, very honest men, and will make you good cheer." To be brief, I resolved to go thither. Now, in my way, I met with a fellow that was lying in wait to catch pigeons, of whom I asked, "My friend, from whence come these pigeons?" "Sir," said he, "they come from the other world." Then I thought, that when Pantagruel yawned the pigeons went into his mouth in whole flocks, thinking that it had been a pigeon house.

Then I went into the city, which I found fair, very strong, and seated in a good air; but, at my entry, the guard demanded of me my pass or ticket; whereat I was much astonished, and asked them, "My masters, is there any danger of the plague here?" "O Lord," said they, "they die hard by here so fast, that the cart runs about the streets." "Good God!" said I, "and where?" Whereunto they answered, that it was in Larinx and Phærinx; which are two great cities, such as Rouen and Nantz, rich, and of great trading; and the cause of the plague was, by a stinking and infectious exhalation which lately vapoured out of the abismes, whereof there have died above two and twenty hundred and threescore thousand and sixteen persons within this sevennight. Then I considered, calculated, and found that it was a rank and unsavoury breathing, which came out of Pantagruel's stomach when he did eat so much garlic, as we have aforesaid.

Parting from thence, I passed amongst the rocks, which were his teeth, and never left walking till I got upon one of them; and there I found the pleasantest places in the world, great large tennis-courts, fair galleries, sweet meadows, store of vines, and an infinite number of banqueting summer out-houses in the fields, after the Italian fashion, full of pleasure and delight; where I staid full four months, and never made better cheer in my life than at that time. After that, I went down by the hinder teeth to come to the chaps; but in the way I was robbed by thieves in a great forest, that is in the territory towards the ears. Then (after a little further travelling) I fell upon a pretty village (truly I have forgot the name of it) where I was yet merrier than ever, and got some certain money to live by. Can you tell how? by sleeping; for there they hire men by the day to sleep, and they get by it sixpence a day; but they that can snore hard, get at least nine-pence. How I had been robbed in the valley I informed the senators, who told me, that in very truth the people of that side were bad livers, and naturally thievish; whereby I perceived well, that as we have with us the countries Cidentine and Tradentine, that is, behither and beyond the teeth; but it is far better living on this side, and the air is purer. There I began to think, that it is very true which is commonly said, that the one half of the world knoweth not how the other half liveth. Seeing none before myself had ever written of that country, wherein are above five and twenty kingdoms inhabited, besides desarts, and a great arm of the sea, I have composed a great book, intituled, "The History of the Gorgians," because they dwell in the gorge of my master Pantagruel.

At last I was willing to return, and, passing by his beard, I cast myself upon his shoulders, and from thence slid down to the ground, and fell before him. As soon as I was perceived by him, he asked me, "Whence comest thou, Alcofribas?" I answered him, "Out of your mouth, my lord." "And how long hast thou been there?" said he. "Since the time," said I, "that you went against the Almirods." "That is about six months ago," said he. "And wherewith didst thou live? What didst thou drink?" I answered, "My lord, of the same that you did, and of the daintiest morsels that passed through your throat I took toll." "Yea, but," said he, "where didst thou shite?" "In your throat, my lord," said I. "Ha, ha! thou art a merry fellow," said he. "We have, with the help of God, conquered all the land of the Dipsodes, I will give thee the Chastelleiny of Salmigondin." "Grammercy, my lord," said I, "you gratify me beyond all that I have deserved of you."

JOACHIM
DU BELLAY

Poems
Translated by William Frederic Giese

THE WINNOWER'S SONG

Ye zephyrs of wing
That musically sing
Down hill and dale,
Or 'mong the flow'rets drift
And tenderly uplift
Their odorous veil,

These purple violets yet
With globèd dewdrops wet,
I offer you;
Lily and rose I bring,
Sweet buds just opening,
And pale pinks too.

Breathe soft, ye fanning airs,
Down these green thoroughfares;
Cool this parched soil,
While in the noonday heat
I winnow my ripe wheat
With weary toil.

ROME

O wanderer that seekest Rome in Rome,
Though naught of Rome in Rome doth now appear,
These crumbling fanes, these ancient piles that rear

So high their heads, were once the Roman's home.
See Rome in ruin, that once like a king
Beheld all lands 'neath its dominion cast,
And, spoiling all, despoiled itself at last,
A prey to Time, who conquers everything.
Rome is of Rome the last sad monument,
And Rome alone wrought Rome's abolishment;
Now Tiber only in his seaward flight
Flows past old Rome. Thus age succeeds our prime:
All that stood firm is levelled by Time's spite,
But that which flows withstands the flight of Time.

TO HIS LADY

For all the griefs, my dear, I have sustained,
For all the love that year on year I lavished,
For all those tears and sighs that passion ravished
From my sad soul, with yet no guerdon gained,
I asked one kiss, such as could never move
Envy or blame, or make the mockers sport,
Favor oft granted to an honest love
Even by the chastest lady of the court.
But you, alas! whether indifference sway
Your heart, or pity, lest a grace like this
Should make my swooning soul die on a kiss,
Deny me still. Oh drive this fear away!
I would adventure all for such fond bliss,
And, dying so, deem death a holiday.

ELEGY ON HIS CAT

I have not lost my rings, my purse,
My gold, my gems—my loss is worse,
One that the stoutest heart must move.
My pet, my joy, my little love,
My tiny kitten, my Belaud,
I lost, alas, three days ago.
O little friend, adieu, adieu!
Would that I too were dead like you!
Dame Nature never shaped a cat
So sleek as you, so soft to pat,
289 So sweetly bred, so midget-sized,

So fit to be immortalized.
     His like in France you will not meet,
But only in a Roman street.
Gray was his coat, yet not all gray,
But streaked with many a silver ray,
All satin-smooth; and down his spine
In little billows argentine
It rose and fell, then vanished quite
Beneath a belly ermine-white.
Tiny his head and small his joints,
And short his ears, with pinkish points;
Under his nostrils coraline
A little muzzle leonine,
And all around it, bristling bright,
Twice seven whiskers, silver white.
Cruel death has struck at him
And has chilled each furry limb.
Death, alas, had never seen
Belaud frolic on the green,
Seen him leap, and run, and scratch
Or with lightning motion catch
Some poor mouse which scurried past,
Catch him, loose him, hold him fast.
Oh, how soft would Belaud climb
On my couch at napping-time,
Or with sudden impulse shrewd
Ravish from my lips the food,
Or with frenzied jerk and bound
Like a wheel spin round and round,
Following the speeding trail
Of his own revolving tail,
Or, displaying all the fur
Of his ermine stomacher,
On his velvet haunches perch
Like some Doctor of the Church.
     Sweet Belaud, you cunning actor,
You were sure no malefactor!
E'en your sins did halfway please.
It was you who stole my cheese,
You, alas, who killed my linnet,
Wrecked the cage with birdie in it,
Feeling sure you did no wrong
Since it irked you with its song.
I forgive you, little pet,
I, too, am not perfect yet.

MARGARET
QUEEN OF NAVARRE

The Heptameron
Translated by George Saintsbury

Novel
Seventy

There was in the duchy of Burgundy a duke who was a very agreeable prince and of very goodly person. He had a wife with whose beauty he was so satisfied that it blinded him to her disposition, and he thought only of pleasing her, whilst she, on her part, made a show of responding only to his affection. This duke had in his household a young gentleman so accomplished in all that can be desired in a man, that he was loved by everybody, and especially by the duke, about whose person he had been brought up from childhood, and who, knowing him to possess so many perfections, had the warmest regard for him, and trusted him in all affairs suitable to his years. The duchess, who was not a virtuous woman, nor satisfied with her husband's love and the kind treatment she received from him, often cast her eyes on this gentleman, and found him so much to her taste, that she loved him beyond measure. She was evermore trying to make this known to him by languishing and tender glances, sighs, and impassioned airs; but the gentleman, who never studied anything but virtue, knew nought of vice in a lady who had so little excuse for it; so that the glances, sighs, and impassioned airs of the poor wanton brought her nothing but bitter disappointment. She carried her extravagance so far, that, forgetting she was a wife who ought, though solicited, to grant no favor, and a princess who was made to be adored, yet disdain such servants, she resolved to act like a man transported with passion, and to discharge her bosom of a burden that was insupportable.

One day then, when the duke went to council, to which the gentleman was not admitted, being too young, she beckoned to him, and he came, thinking she had some order to give him. Leaning then on his arm, like a woman wearied by too much repose, she walked about with him in a gallery, and said, "I am surprised that, being as you are, young, handsome, and full of engaging qualities, you have been able hitherto to live in continual intercourse with so many fair ladies without loving any of them." And then, with one of her most gracious looks, she paused for his answer.

"Madam," he replied, "if I were worthy that your greatness should descend to think of me, you would have more reason for surprise, to see so insignificant a man as I am offer his services only to meet with refusal or mockery."

Upon this discreet reply the duchess loved him more than ever, and vowed that there was not a lady in the court but would be too happy to have a lover of his merit; that he might try, and that she assured him he would succeed without difficulty. The gentleman kept his eyes constantly bent on the ground, not daring to look on the countenance of the duchess, which glowed enough to warm an icicle. Just when he was about to excuse himself, the duke sent for the duchess to come to the council upon an affair in which she was interested. She went with much regret. As for the gentleman, he pretended not to have understood what she said, which vexed and confused her so much that she knew not what to impute it to but the silly fear with which she thought the young man possessed. Seeing, then, that he did not understand her language, she resolved a few days afterwards to overleap fear and shame, and declare her passion to him in plain terms, never doubting but that beauty like hers could not fail to be well received. Nevertheless, she would have been glad to have had the honor to be solicited; but, after all, she preferred pleasure to honor.

After having several times again tried the same means she had first essayed, and always with the same unwelcome result, she plucked him by the sleeve one day, and told him she wanted to speak to him on an affair of importance. With all due respect and humility the gentleman followed her to a window recess, where, finding that she could not be seen from the chamber, she resumed the subject of her past conversation with a trembling voice, indicative alike of desire and fear. She reproached him for not having yet made choice of a lady, and assured him that wherever he fixed his affections she would spare no pains to ensure his success. The gentleman, not less distressed than astonished at such language, replied, "My heart is so tender, madam, that if I were once refused I should never know joy; and I am so well aware of my slender merit, that I am sure there is no lady in the court who would accept my services."

The duchess blushed at these words, and imagining that his
292 heart was lost, protested he had only to wish, and she would an-

swer for it that she knew the fairest lady in the court who would receive him with extreme joy, and make him consummately happy. "I do not believe, madam," he replied, "that there is any woman in this court so unfortunate and so infatuated as to have made me the object of her predilections."

Seeing that he would not understand her, she proceeded to give him a more direct glimpse of her passion; and as the gentleman's virtue gave her cause for fear, she spoke by way of interrogation. "If fortune," she said, "had so favored you that it was myself who was thus well inclined to you, what would you say?"

The gentleman, who thought he was dreaming to hear her speak thus, dropped on one knee on the ground and replied, "When God shall do me the grace, madam, to make me possessor of the good-will of the duke my master, and of yourself, I shall deem myself the happiest of men. It is the sole recompense I crave for my faithful services, bound as I am above all others to sacrifice my life for you both. I am convinced, madam, that the love you have for my lord your spouse is so pure and great, that not even the greatest prince and the most accomplished man in the world, to say nothing of myself, who am but a worm of the earth, could impair the union that subsists between my master and you. As for me, whom he has nurtured from childhood and made what I am, I would not for my life entertain a thought other than that which becomes a faithful servant as regards either his wife, sister, or mother."

The duchess would not suffer him to proceed, but seeing she was in danger of receiving a shameful refusal, she broke in upon him suddenly, "Wicked and arrogant fool! who requires any such thing of you? Because you are good-looking you imagine that the very flies are enamored of you; but if you were presumptuous enough to address yourself to me, I would soon let you know that I love, and will love, none but my husband. I have spoken to you as I have done only for my diversion, to sift you, and make you my laughing-stock, as I do all amorous coxcombs."

"I have all along been assured that it was just as you say, madam," replied the gentleman.

She would hear no more, but turned abruptly from him, and to avoid her ladies who followed her into her chamber, she shut herself up in her closet, where she gave way to an indescribable burst of bitter feeling. On the one hand, the love in which she had failed caused her mortal sadness; and on the other, her despite against herself for entering upon so injudicious a dialogue, and against the gentleman for having answered so prudently, put her into such a fury that at one moment she wished to kill herself, at the next she
would live to be revenged on him she regarded as her deadliest

enemy. After a long fit of tears she feigned indisposition, to avoid appearing at the duke's supper, at which the gentleman was usually in attendance. The duke, who loved his wife more than himself, failed not to go and see her; when, in order to arrive the more easily at her ends, she told him she believed she was pregnant, and that her pregnancy had caused a rheum to fall upon her eyes, which gave her great pain. The duchess kept her bed for two or three hours in so sad and melancholy a mood, that the duke suspected there was something else the matter besides pregnancy. He went to sleep with her that night; but seeing that, in spite of all the caresses he could bestow upon her, she continued to sigh incessantly, he said, "You know, my dear, that I love you as my own life, and that if you die I cannot possibly survive you. If, then, you value my health and life, tell me, I entreat, what makes you sigh thus; for I cannot believe that pregnancy alone can produce that effect."

The duchess, seeing her husband in the very mood she wished, hastened to turn it to her vengeful purpose. "Alas! monsieur," she said, embracing him with tears, "my worst suffering is to see you the dupe of those whose duty it is to preserve your honor and all that is yours." This made the duke wondrously eager to know what she meant, and he begged her to speak openly, without fear or disguise. "I shall never be surprised," she said at last, after repeated refusals, "if strangers make war on princes, since those who are most bound to them undertake to wage such a horrible war against them, that the loss of domains is nothing in comparison with it. I say this, monsieur, with reference to a gentleman" (here she named her enemy) "whom you have fed, reared, treated more like a relation than a domestic, and who, by way of gratitude has had the impudence and the baseness to attempt the honor of your wife, on which depends that of your house and your children. Though he long labored to insinuate to me things that left me no doubt of his black perfidy, yet my heart, which is only for you, and thinks only on you, could not comprehend him; but at last he explained himself, and I replied to him as my rank and my honor required. I hate him, however, so that I cannot bear the sight of him; and this it was, monsieur, which made me keep my room and lose the happiness of your company. I beseech you, monsieur, not to keep such a pestilence near you; for after such a crime, the fear of your being made acquainted with it might very likely induce him to do something worse. You know now, monsieur, the cause of my grief, which seems to me most just and most worthy that you should right it without delay."

The duke, who on the one hand loved his wife and felt himself
294 outraged, and on the other hand loved the gentleman, of whose

fidelity he had often had practical proof, could hardly believe that this lie was truth. He withdrew to his chamber in great perplexity and anger, and sent word to the gentleman that he was not to appear any more in his presence, but was to retire to his own home for some time. The gentleman, ignorant of the cause of an order so peremptory and so unexpected, was the more keenly affected by it, as he thought he had deserved the very opposite treatment. Conscious of his innocence in heart and deed, he got one of his comrades to speak to the duke on his behalf, and deliver him a letter, wherein he most humbly entreated, that if he had the misfortune to be removed from his master's presence, in consequence of some report to his prejudice, the duke would have the goodness to suspend his judgment until he should have inquired into the truth; and then he durst hope it would be found he had in nowise offended. This letter somewhat appeased the duke; he sent for the gentleman to come secretly to his chamber, and said to him with great gravity, "I could never have believed that after having had you nurtured like my own child, I should have cause to repent of having so highly advanced you, forasmuch as you have sought to outrage me in a manner that would have been worse to me than the loss of life and fortune, namely, by attempting the honor of her who is the half of myself, and seeking to cover my house with perpetual infamy. You may believe that I feel this insult so deeply, that if I was quite sure that the fact was true, you would by this time be at the bottom of the water, to punish you secretly for the affront you have secretly sought to put upon me."

The gentleman was not dismayed by this speech; on the contrary, he spoke with the confidence of innocence, and besought the duke to have the goodness to tell him who was his accuser, the accusation being one of those which are better discussed with the lance than with the tongue. "Your accuser," replied the duke, "has no other arms than her chastity. It was my wife, and no one else, who told me this, praying me to take vengeance upon you."

Amazed as the poor gentleman was at the prodigious malice of the duchess, he would not accuse her, but contented himself with saying, "My lady may say what she pleases. You know her, monsieur, better than I; and you know if I have seen her elsewhere than in your company, except once only when she spoke to me a very little. Your judgment is as sound as that of any prince in Christendom. Therefore, my liege, I beseech you to consider if you have ever seen anything in me which can have caused you suspicion. It is a fire which it is impossible long to conceal in such wise that those who labor under the same malady shall not have some inkling of it. I beg, my liege, that you will be graciously pleased to believe two things of me; one is, that I am so true to you, that though my lady your spouse were the finest woman in the world, love would not be capable of making me do anything contrary to my honor and my duty; the other is, that even were she not your spouse, she is, of all the women I have ever seen, the one I should be the least inclined to love; and there are enough of others on whom I should sooner fix my choice."

The duke's anger was somewhat mitigated by these words. "Well," said he, "I did not believe it; so you may go on as usual, with the assurance that if I find that the truth is on your side, I will love you more than ever; but if the contrary appears, your life is in my hand." The gentleman thanked him, and declared his willingness to submit to the severest penalty his master could devise if he were found guilty.

The duchess, seeing the gentleman continue to serve as usual, could not patiently endure it, and said to her husband, "It would be no more than you deserve, monsieur, if you were poisoned, since you have more confidence in your mortal enemies than in your nearest friends."

"Do not make yourself uneasy, my dear," replied the duke; "for if it appears that what you have told me is true, I assure you he has not twenty-four hours to live. But as he has protested the contrary to me on oath, and as, besides, I never perceived anything of the sort, I cannot believe it without good proofs."

"Truly, monsieur," she returned, "your goodness makes my malice greater. What greater proof would you have than that a man like him has never had any amour imputed to him. Be assured, monsieur, that but for the vain and presumptuous idea with which he has flattered himself of becoming my servant, he would not be without a mistress at this time of the day. Never did a young man live so solitary as he in good company; and the reason can only be that his heart is set so high that his vain hope stands him in stead of everything else. If you believe that he conceals nothing from you, swear him as to his amours. If he tells you that he loves another, why then believe him; I am content you should; but if not, be assured that what I say is true."

The duke approved of his wife's suggestion, and taking the gentleman into the country, said to him, "My wife continues still to speak to me of you to the same purpose, and mentions a circumstance which gives me some suspicion. To be plain with you, it excites surprise that you, a young and gallant man, have never been known to be in love; and this very thing makes me fear that you entertain the sentiments you have been charged with, and the hope you cherish is so pleasing to you that you cannot think of any other woman. I pray you then as a friend, and order you as a master, to tell me truly do you pay your court to any lady in this world?"

The poor gentleman, who would fain have concealed his love as carefully as he would have preserved his life, seeing his master's extreme jealousy, was constrained to swear to him that he loved a lady so beautiful that the beauty of the duchess and of all the ladies of her suite was mean in comparison, not to say ugliness and deformity; at the same time he besought the duke not to insist on his naming the lady, because the intimacy between him and his mistress was such that it could only be broken by whichever of the two first disclosed it. The duke promised he would never press him on that point, and was so satisfied with him, that he behaved more graciously to him than ever. The duchess perceived it, and employed her usual artifices to find out the reason; nor did the duke conceal it from her. Strong jealousy was now added to her thirst of vengeance, and she besought the duke to insist that the gentleman should name his mistress, declaring that if he refused to do so, her husband would be the most credulous prince in the world to put faith in so vague a statement.

The poor prince, who was led by his wife as she pleased, went and walked alone with the gentleman, and told him he was in still greater embarrassment than ever, being afraid that what he had told him was only an excuse to hinder him from coming at the truth, which made him more uneasy than before; therefore he besought him most earnestly to tell him the name of her he loved so much. The poor gentleman implored the duke not to constrain him to break the promise he had given to a person he loved as his life, and which he had kept inviolate until that moment. It would be tantamount to requiring him to lose in one day what he had preserved for more than seven years, and he would rather die than do that wrong to a person who was so faithful to him. His refusal threw the duke into such a violent fit of jealousy, that he exclaimed furiously, "Take your choice: either tell me the name of her you love above all others, or quit my dominions on pain of death if you are found in them after eight days."

If ever faithful servant was smitten with keen anguish it was this poor gentleman, who might well say, *Angustiæ sunt mihi undique*. On the one hand, if he told the truth he lost his mistress, should it come to her knowledge that he had broken his word to her; on the other, if he did not tell it, he was exiled from the country where she resided, and could never see her more. Thus pressed on all sides, a cold sweat broke out upon him, as if his anguish had brought him to the brink of the grave. The duke, perceiving his embarrassment, imagined he loved only the duchess, and that his confusion arose from the fact that he could not name any one else. In this belief he said to him sternly, "If you had told me the truth, you would have less difficulty in doing what I desire; but I believe that it is your crime that occasions your embarrassment."

The gentleman, stung by these words, and urged by the love he bore his master, resolved to tell him the truth, assuring himself that the duke was a man of so much honor that he would keep his secret inviolate. He fell on his knees then, and said to him, with his hands pressed together, "My liege, the obligations I am under to you, and the love I bear you, constrain me more than the fear of death. You are possessed with so false a prejudice against me, that, to undeceive you, I am resolved to tell you what no torments could extort from me. The only favor I ask of you, my liege, is, that you will swear, on the faith of a prince and a Christian, never to reveal the secret which you force from me." The duke promised him, with all the oaths he could think of, never to tell his secret to any one, either by word, act, or signs; and the gentleman, relying on the good faith of a prince whom he knew, put the first hand to his own undoing, saying to him, "It is seven years, my lord, since having known your niece, the Lady du Verger, as a widow and disengaged, I tried to acquire her good-will. As I was not of birth to marry her, I contented myself with being received by her as a lover, in which I succeeded. Our intercourse has been conducted hitherto with so much prudence, that no one has come to the knowledge of it except you, my lord, into whose hands I put my life and honor, entreating you to keep the secret, and to have no less esteem for my lady your niece, than whom I do not think there is under a heaven a creature more perfect."

The duke was delighted with this declaration, for knowing the extraordinary beauty of his niece, he doubted not that she was more capable of pleasing than his wife. But not conceiving it possible that such a mystery should have been carried on without adequate means, he begged to know how her lover managed to see her. The gentleman told him that his mistress's chamber opened on a garden, and that on the days when he was to visit her a little gate was left open, through which he entered on foot, and advanced until he heard the barking of a little dog, which the lady let loose in the garden after her women had all retired; that then he went to her, and conversed with her all night, and on his departure appointed the day when he was to come again in which he had never failed, except for indispensable reasons. The duke, who was the most curious of men, and who had been very gallant in his time, begged him, as well to dissipate his suspicions as for the pleasure of hearing so singular an adventure recounted, to take him with him, not as a

298

master, but as a companion, the next time he went thither. The gentleman, having gone so far, assented, and told him his assignation was for that very day. The duke was as glad of this as if he had won a kingdom, and feigning to retire to his *garderobe* to rest, had two horses brought, one for the gentleman and the other for himself, and they travelled all night from Argilly, where the duke resided, to Le Verger, where they left their horses at the entrance of the park.

The gentleman made the duke enter through the little gate, and begged him to place himself behind a large walnut-tree, whence he might see if what he had told him was true or not. They had not been long in the garden before the little dog began to bark, and the gentleman walked towards the tower, whilst the lady advanced to meet him. She saluted him with an embrace, and told him it seemed a thousand years since she had seen him. Then they entered the chamber, the door of which they locked. The duke having seen the whole of this mystery, felt more satisfied; nor had he time to grow weary, for the gentleman told the lady that he was obliged to leave her sooner than usual, because the duke was going to the chase at four o'clock, and he durst not fail to attend him. The lady, who preferred honor to pleasure, did not attempt to hinder him from doing his duty; for what she prized most in their honorable intimacy was that it was a secret for all mankind.

The gentleman quitted the house at one o'clock in the morning, and his lady, in mantle and kerchief, escorted him not so far as she wished, for he made her go back for fear she should meet the duke, with whom he mounted again and returned to the château of Argilly. On the way, the duke never ceased protesting to the gentleman that he would rather die than ever divulge his secret; and his confidence in him was so confirmed, that no one at court stood higher in favor. The duchess was enraged at this. The duke forbade her ever to mention the subject any more to him, saying that he knew the truth, and was satisfied, for the lady whom the gentleman loved was handsomer than herself. Those words so stung the heart of the duchess that they threw her into an illness worse than fever. The duke tried to console her, but nothing would do unless he would tell her who was that fair lady who was so devotedly loved. So much did she importune him, that at last he quitted the chamber, saying to her, "If you speak to me any more of these things, we will part." This made her still more ill, and she pretended to feel her infant move; whereat the duke was so rejoiced that he went to bed to her; but when she saw that his passion for her was at the height, she turned from him, saying, "Since you love neither wife nor child, monsieur, I entreat you let both die." These words she

299

accompanied with so many tears and cries, that the duke was greatly afraid she would miscarry; wherefore, taking her in his arms, he entreated her to tell him what she wanted, protesting he had nothing that was not at her command. "Ah! monsieur," she replied, sobbing and crying, "what hope can I have that you would do a difficult thing for me, since you will not do the easiest and most reasonable thing in the world, which is to tell me the name of the mistress of the worst servant you ever had? I thought that you and I had but one heart, one soul, and one flesh, but I see that you regard me as a stranger, since you conceal your secrets from me as if I were an alien. You have confided to me many important secrets, and have never known that I divulged a tittle of them. You have had such proof that I have no will but yours, that you ought not to doubt but that I am more you than myself. If you have sworn never to tell any one the gentleman's secret, you do not violate your oath in telling it to me, for I neither am nor can be other than yourself. I have you in my heart; I hold you between my arms; I have a child in my womb in whom you live; yet I cannot have your love as you have mine. The more faithful I am to you, the more cruel and austere you are to me. This makes me long a thousand times for the day when a sudden death may deliver your child from such a father, and me from such a spouse. I hope it will soon come, since you prefer a faithless servant to your wife, to the mother of a child which is your own, and which is on the point of perishing because you will not tell me what I have the greatest longing to know."

So saying, she embraced and kissed her husband, watering his face with her tears, and sobbing and crying so violently, that the poor prince, fearing he should lose both mother and child, resolved to tell her the truth; but he swore that if ever she mentioned it to any one in the world she should die by no hand but his own. She accepted the condition; and then the poor abused duke told her all he had seen from beginning to end. She pretended to be satisfied, but in her heart it was quite otherwise. However, as she was afraid of the duke, she dissembled her passion as well as she could.

The duke, holding his court on a great feast-day, had called to it all the ladies of the country, his niece among the rest. After the banquet the dances began, and every one did his devoir; but the duchess was too much vexed by the sight of her niece's beauty and grace to enjoy herself, or hide her spleen. Making all the ladies sit down, she turned the conversation on love; but seeing that Madame du Verger said not a word, she said to her, with a heart rankling with jealousy, "And you, fair niece, is it possible that your beauty is without a lover?"

"Madam," replied the Lady du Verger, "my beauty has not yet

produced that effect; for since my husband's death I have had no lovers but his children; nor do I desire any others."

"Fair niece, fair niece," rejoined the duchess, with execrable spite, "there is no love so secret as not to be known, nor any little dog so well trained as not to be heard to bark."

I leave you to imagine the anguish of poor Madame du Verger at finding that an affair she had thought so secret was published to her shame. The thought of her honor, so carefully guarded, and so unhappily lost, was torture to her; but the worst was her fear that her lover had broken his word to her, which she did not believe he could ever have done unless he loved some fairer lady, and in doting fondness had suffered her to extort the secret from him. However, she had so much self-command that she did not let her emotion be seen, but laughingly replied that she did not understand the language of brutes. But her heart was so wrung with grief that she rose, and, passing through the duchess's chamber, entered a *garderobe* in sight of the duke, who was walking about. Thinking herself alone, she threw herself on a bed. A demoiselle, who had sat down beside it to sleep, roused herself and peeped through the curtains to see who it might be, and perceiving it was the duke's niece, who thought herself alone, she durst not speak, but remained as still as possible to listen, whilst the poor lady in a dying voice thus began her lamentation:

"Alas! what have I heard! What words of death have smitten my ears! O thou who was loved as man was never loved before, is this the reward of my chaste and virtuous love? O my heart! hast thou made so dangerous a choice, and attached thyself to the most faithless, artful, and mischievous-tongued of all men, mistaking him for the most faithful, upright, and secret? Is it possible, alas! that a thing hidden from all the world has been revealed to the duchess? My little dog, so well trained, sole agent of my long and virtuous friendship, it was not you that betrayed my secret: it was a man, with a voice more piercing than a dog's, and a heart more ungrateful than any beast's. It was he who, contrary to his oath and his word, divulged the happy life we long led without injuring any one. O my friend! for whom alone my heart cherished love, a love wherewith my life has been preserved, has the beauty of the duchess metamorphosed you, as that of Circe did her lovers? Has she turned you from virtue to vice, from good to bad, from a man into a savage beast? O my friend! though you have broken your word to me, I will keep mine, and never see you more after having revealed our intimacy. But as I cannot live without seeing you, I willingly yield to the excess of my sorrow, and will never seek any remedy for it either from reason or from medicine. Death alone shall end it, and that death will be more welcome to me than to remain in the world without my lover, without honor, and without contentment. Neither war nor death has taken my lover from me; my sins and transgressions have not deprived me of honor; nor has my bad conduct bereft me of happiness. It is cruel fortune that has made an ingrate of the most favored of all men, and has brought upon me the contrary of what I deserved. O duchess, how delighted you were to make that jeering allusion to my little dog! Revel in a bliss that belongs to me alone. Laugh at her who thought to escape derision whilst loving virtuously and concealing it with care. How that word wrung my heart! How it made me red with shame and pale with jealousy! Heart, heart, I feel thou art undone. Ill-requited love burns thee, jealousy and grief turn thee to ice, and forbid thee all consolation. Through having too much adored the creature, my soul has forgotten the Creator. It must return to Him from whom a vain love detached it. Be assured, my soul, thou wilt find a Father more tender than the friend for whom thou hast often forgotten Him. O God, my creator, who art the true and perfect love, by whose grace the love I have borne my friend has been sullied by no vice, save that of loving too much, be pleased to receive in the greatness of Thy mercy the soul and spirit of her who repents of having broken Thy first and righteous command. Through the merits of Him whose love is incomprehensible, forgive the fault which excess of love made me commit, for my trust is in Thee alone. Farewell, my friend, whose unworthiness of that name breaks my heart." So saying she fell backwards, her face ghastly, her lips blue, and her extremities cold.

At the same moment the gentleman she loved entered the reception-room, where the duchess was dancing with the other ladies. He looked round for his mistress, and not seeing her, went into the duchess's chamber, where he found the duke, who guessing his purpose, whispered him that she was gone into the *garderobe*, and appeared to be unwell. The gentleman asked for leave to follow her, and the duke not only granted it, but urged him to do so. Entering the *garderobe* then, he found her at the last gasp; and, throwing his arms round her, he said, "What is this, my love? Do you want to quit me?" Roused by the well-known voice, the poor lady opened her eyes to look upon him who was the cause of her death; but that look so increased her love and her anguish, that with a piteous sigh she gave up the ghost.

The gentleman, more dead than alive, asked the demoiselle how the lady's illness had begun, and she told him all she had heard. He then knew that the duke had revealed his secret. His grief was so intense, that, embracing the body of his mistress, he wept over it

302

long in silence, and at last exclaimed, "Traitor, villain, wretch that I am! Why has not the penalty for my treachery fallen on me, and not on her who was innocent? Why did not Heaven's lightning blast me the day my tongue revealed our secret and virtuous love? Why did not the earth open to swallow up a wretch who violated his faith? May my tongue be punished as was that of the wicked rich man in hell! O heart, that too much feared death and exile, may eagles tear thee perpetually as they did that of Ixion! Alas, my dear friend! in thinking to hold you fast, I have lost you. I thought to possess you long alive, with virtue and pleasure, and I embrace you dead, and you have been dissatisfied to your last gasp with me, my heart, and my tongue. O most faithful of women! I denounce myself as the most inconstant, faithless, and perfidious of men. I would I could complain of the duke, whose word I trusted, hoping by that means to prolong our agreeable life; but ought I not to have known that no one could keep my secret better than myself? The duke was more justifiable in telling his secret to his wife, than I in telling mine to him. I am the only guilty one, the only one who deserves to be punished for the greatest crime ever committed between friends. I ought to have suffered him to throw me into the river as he threatened. You at least, dear one, would then be alive, and I should have closed my life with the glory of having observed the rule prescribed by true friendship; but having broken it I live still, and you are dead for having perfectly loved. Your pure heart could not know the baseness of mine, and live. O my God, why didst thou create me with a love so frivolous and a heart so ignorant? Why was I not the little dog that faithfully served its mistress? Alas! my little friend, I used to feel joy at the sound of your barking; but that joy is turned into sorrow, for having been the cause of another besides us two hearing your voice. Yet, sweetheart, neither love of the duchess nor of any other woman ever made me vary, though the wicked duchess has often solicited me to love her; but ignorance has undone me, for I thought by what I did to insure our intimacy for ever. But that ignorance does not make me the less guilty. I have revealed my mistress's secret, I have broken my word, and therefore it is that she is dead before me. Alas, sweetheart, will death be less cruel to me than to you, who have died only for having loved? Methinks death would not deign to touch my faithless and miserable heart. The loss of honor, and the memory of her I have lost through my fault, are more insupportable to me than ten thousand deaths. If any one had cut short your days through mischance or malice, I should use my sword to avenge you. It is not reasonable, then, that I should pardon that murderer, who has caused your death by a deed more vile than if he had killed you with a sword.

303

If I knew a more odious executioner than myself, I would entreat him to do justice upon your perfidious lover. O love! I have offended thee from not having known how to love; and therefore thou wilt not succour me as thou hast succoured her who perfectly kept all thy laws. Nor is it just that I should make such a glorious end: it must be by my own hand. I have washed your face with my tears; I have implored your pardon; and it now only remains that my arm make my body like yours, and send my soul whither yours is gone, in the assurance that a virtuous and honorable love ends neither in this world nor in the next."

Starting up then, like a frantic man, from the corpse, he drew his poniard, and stabbed himself to the heart; and then, clasping his mistress in his arms for the second time, he kissed her so fondly, that he seemed more like a blissful lover than a dead man. The demoiselle seeing the deed, ran to the door and screamed for help. The duke, suspecting the disaster of those he loved, was the first to enter the *garderobe*, and on seeing that sad couple he tried to separate them, in order to save the gentleman if it were possible; but he held his mistress so fast, that it was impossible to tear him from her until he had expired. Nevertheless, hearing the duke exclaim, "My God! who has been the cause of this?" "My tongue and yours, monsieur," he replied, with a look of fury. So saying he breathed his last, with his face laid on that of his mistress.

The duke, wishing to know more of the matter, constrained the demoiselle to tell him all she had seen and heard, which she did from beginning to end, without forgetting anything. The duke then, knowing that he was the cause of the whole mischief, threw himself on the bodies of the two lovers, and with cries and tears implored their pardon. He kissed them repeatedly; and then rising furiously, he drew the poniard out of the gentleman's body. As a wild boar wounded by a spear runs impetuously at him who has struck the blow, so ran the duke at her who had wounded him to the soul. He found her still dancing in the reception-room, and gayer than usual, because she thought she had so well revenged herself on the Lady du Verger. Her husband seized her in the midst of the dance, and said, "You took the secret upon your life, and upon your life shall fall the forfeiture." So saying he grasped her by her head-dress, and buried the poniard in her bosom.

The astonished company thought the duke was out of his senses; but he had done the deed advisedly; and assembling all his servants on the spot, he recounted to them the glorious and melancholy story of his niece, and the wicked conduct of his wife: a narrative which drew tears from all his hearers. The duke then ordered that his wife should be buried in an abbey which he founded, partly with a view to atone for the sin he had committed in killing his wife; and then he had a magnificent tomb erected, in which the remains of his niece and of the gentleman were laid side by side, with an epitaph setting forth their tragic history. The duke made an expedition against the Turks, in which God so favored him that he achieved glory and profit. Finding on his return that his eldest son was of age to govern, he became a monk, and retired to the abbey in which his wife and the two lovers were buried, and there he passed his old age happily with God.

MICHEL
DE MONTAIGNE

Essays
Translated by John Florio

The *Of three commerces or societies.* We must not cleave so fast unto
Third our humours and dispositions. Our chiefest sufficiency is, to apply
Book, ourselves to divers fashions. It is a being, but not a life, to be tied
Chapter and bound by necessity to one only course. The goodliest minds are
Three those that have most variety and pliableness in them. Behold an
honourable testimony of old Cato: *Huic versatile ingenium sic
pariter ad omnia fuit, ut natum ad id unum diceres, quodcunque
ageret* (LIV. *Bel. Mac. IX.*). *He had a wit so turnable for all things
alike, as one would say he had been only born for that he went
about to do.* Were I to dress myself after my own manner, there
is no fashion so good, whereto I would be so affected or tied, as
not to know how to leave and lose it. *Life is a motion unequal, irregular and multiform.* It is not to be the friend (less the master)
but the slave of oneself to follow incessantly, and be so addicted
to his inclinations, as he cannot stray from them, nor wrest them.
This I say now, as being extremely pestered with the importunity
of my mind, forsomuch as she cannot amuse herself, but whereon
it is busied; nor employ itself, but bent and whole. How light soever
the subject is one gives it, it willingly amplifieth, and wire-draws
the same, even unto the highest pitch of toil. Its idleness is therefore a painful trade unto me, and offensive to my health. Most
wits have need of extravagant stuff, to un-benumb and exercise
themselves: mine hath need of it, rather to settle and continue
itself: *Vitia otii negotio discutienda sunt* (SEN. *Ep. lvi.*), *The vices
of idleness should be shaken off with business:* For, the most laborious care and principal study of it, is, to study itself. Books are one of
those businesses that seduce it from study. At the first thoughts that
present themselves, it rouseth up and makes proof of all the vigour

306

it hath. It exerciseth its function sometimes toward force, sometimes towards order and comeliness, it rangeth, moderates and
fortifieth. It hath of itself to awaken the faculties of it: Nature
having given it, as unto all other, matter of its own for advantage,
subjects fit enough whereon to devise and determine. Meditation
is a large and powerful study to such as vigorously can taste and
employ themselves therein. I had rather forge than furnish my mind.

There is no office or occupation either weaker or stronger, than
that of entertaining of one's thoughts according to the mind, whatsoever it be. The greatest make it their vocation, *Quibus vivere est
cogitare, to whom it is all one to live and to meditate.* Nature hath
also favoured it with this privilege, that there is nothing we can do
so long: nor action, whereto we give ourselves more ordinarily
and easily. It is the work of Gods (said Aristotle) whence both
their happiness and ours proceedeth. Reading serves me especially,
to awake my conceit by divers objects: to busy my judgment, not
my memory. Few entertainments then, stay me without vigour and
force. 'Tis true that courtesy and beauty possess me, as much or
more, than weight and depth. And because I slumber in all other
communications, and lend but the superficial parts of my attention
unto them, it often befalleth me, in such kind of weak and absurd
discourses, (discourses of countenance) to blurt out and answer
ridiculous toys, and fond absurdities, unworthy a child; or wilfully
to hold my peace; therewithal more foolishly and uncivilly. I have
a kind of raving fanciful behaviour, that retireth me into myself;
and on the other side, a gross and childish ignorance of many ordinary things; by means of which two qualities, I have in my days
committed five or six as sottish tricks, as anyone whosoever; which
to my degradation may be reported. But to follow my purpose, this
harsh complexion of mine makes me nice in conversing with men
(whom I must pick and cull out for the nonce) and unfit for common actions. We live and negotiate with the people: If their behaviour importune us, if we disdain to lend ourselves to base and
vulgar spirits, which often are as regular as those of a finer mould;
and *all wisdom is unsavory, that is not conformed to common in-
sipience.* We are no longer to intermeddle either with our, or other
men's affairs: and both public and private forsake such kind
of people.

The least wrested, and most natural proceedings of our mind, are
the fairest; the best occupations, those which are least forced. Good
God, how good an office doth wisdom unto those, whose desires she
squareth according to their power! There is no science more profitable. *As one may,* was the burden and favoured saying of Socrates:
A sentence of great substance. We must address and stay our de-

sires, to things most easy and nearest. It is not a fond-peevish humour in me, to disagree from a thousand; to whom my fortune joineth me, without whom I cannot live, to adhere unto one or two, that are out of my commerce and conversation; or rather to a fantastical conceit, or fanciful desire, for a thing I cannot obtain? My soft behaviours and mild manners, enemies to all sharpness and foes to all bitterness, may easily have discharged me from envy and contention. To be beloved, I say not, but not to be hated, never did man give more occasion. But the coldness of my conversation, hath with reason robbed me of the good will of many; which may be excused, if they interpret the same to other, or worse sense. I am most capable of getting rare amities, and continuing exquisite acquaintances. For so much as with so greedy hunger I snatch at such acquaintances as answer my taste and square with my humour. I so greedily produce and headlong cast myself upon them, that I do not easily miss to cleave unto them, and where I light on, to make a steady impression; I have often made happy and successful trial of it.

In vulgar worldly friendships, I am somewhat cold and barren: for my proceeding is not natural, if not unresisted and with hoisted-full sails. Moreover, my fortune having enured and allured me, even from my infancy, to one sole singular and perfect amity, hath verily, in some sort, distasted me from others: and over deeply imprinted in my fantasy, that it is a beast sociable and for company, and not of troupe, as said an ancient writer. So that it is naturally a pain unto me, to communicate myself by halves, and with modification: and that servile or suspicious wisdom, which in the conversation of these numerous and imperfect amities, is ordained and proposed unto us: Prescribed in these days especially, *Wherein one cannot speak of the world but dangerously or falsely.* Yet I see, that who (as I do) makes for his end, the commodities of his life (I mean essential commodities) must avoid as a plague, these difficulties and quaintness of humour.

I should commend a high-raised mind, that could both bend and discharge itself: that wherever her fortune might transport her, she might continue constant: that could discourse with her neighbours of all matters, as of her building, of her hunting and of any quarrel; and entertain with delight a Carpenter or a Gardener. I envy those which can be familiar with the meanest of their followers, and vouchsafe to contract friendship, and frame discourse with their own servants. Nor do I like the advice of Plato, ever to speak imperiously unto our attendants, without blitheness and sans any familiarity: be it to men or women servants. For, besides my
reason, it is inhumanity, and injustice, to attribute so much unto

that prerogative of fortune: and the government, where less inequality is permitted between the servant and master, is, in my conceit the more indifferent. Some other study to rouse and raise their mind; but I to abase and prostrate mine: it is not faulty but in extension.

HOR. *Car.* iii. *Od.* xix. 3.

Narras et genus Æaci,
Et pugnata sacro bella sub Ilio.
Quo Chium pretio cadum
Mercemur, quis aquam temperet ignibus
Quo praebente domum, et quota
Pelignis caream frigoribus, taces.

You tell of Æacus the pedigree;
The wars at sacred Troy you do display,
You tell not at what price a hogshead we
May buy of the best Wine; who shall allay
Wine-fire with water, at whose house to hold
At what o'clock, I may be kept from cold.

Even as the Lacedemonian valour had need of moderation, and of sweet and pleasing sounds of Flutes, to flatter and allay it in time of war, lest it should run headlong into rashness and fury: whereas all other nations use commonly piercing sounds and strong shouts, which violently excite, and inflame their soldiers' courage: so think I (against ordinary custom) that in the employment of our spirit, we have for the most part more need of lead than wings; of coldness and quiet, than of heat and agitation. Above all, in my mind, *The only way to play the fool well, is to seem wise among fools:* to speak as though one's tongue were ever bent to *Favelar in punta di forchetta* (Ital. Prov.), *To syllabize or speak mincingly.* One must lend himself unto those he is with, and sometimes affect ignorance: Set force and subtlety aside; In common employments 'tis enough to reserve order; drag yourself even close to the ground, if they will have it so. The learned stumble willingly on this block: making continual muster, and open show of their skill, and dispersing their books abroad: And have in these days so filled the closets, and possessed the ears of Ladies, that if they retain not their substance, at least they have their countenance: using in all sorts of discourse and subject how base or popular soever, a new, an affected and learned fashion of speaking and writing.

JUVEN. *Sat.* vi. 189.

Hoc sermone pavent, hoc iram, gaudia, curas,
Hoc cuncta effundunt animi secreta, quid ultrà?
Concumbunt docte.

They in this language fear, in this they fashion
Their joys, their cares, their rage, their inward passion;
What more? they learned are in copulation.

And allege Plato, and Saint Thomas for things, which the first man they meet would decide as well, and stand for as good a witness. Such learning as could not enter into their mind, hath stayed on their tongues. If the well-born will give any credit unto me, they shall be pleased to make their own and natural riches to prevail and be of worth: They hide and shroud their forms under foreign and borrowed beauties: *It is great simplicity, for anybody to smother and conceal his own brightness, to shine with a borrowed light:* They are buried and entombed under the Art of CAPSULA TOTÆ, It is because they do not sufficiently know themselves: the word contains nothing of more beauty: It is for them to honour Arts, and to beautify embellishment. What need they more than to live beloved and honoured? They have, and know but too much in that matter. There needs but a little rousing and inflaming of the faculties that are in them.

When I see them meddling with Rhetoric, with Law, and with Logic, and such like trash, so vain and unprofitable for their use: I enter into fear, that those who advise them to such things, do it, that they may have more law to govern them under that pretence. For, what other excuse can I devise for them? It is sufficient, that without us, they may frame, or rule the grace of their eyes, unto cheerfulness, unto severity, and unto mildness: and season a *No* with forwardness, with doubt and with favour; and require not an interpretor in discourses made for their service. With this learning they command without control, and over-rule both Regents and Schools. Yet if it offend them to yield us any preëminence and would for curiosity's sake have part in books also: Poesy is a study fit for their purpose: being a wanton, amusing, subtle, disguised, and prattling Art; all in delight, all in show, like to themselves. They may also select divers commodities out of History. In Moral Philosophy, they may take the discourses which enable them to judge of our humours, to censure our conditions, and to avoid our guiles and treacheries; to temper the rashness of their own desires, to husband their liberty: lengthen the delights of life, gently to bear the inconstancy of a servant, the peevishness or rudeness of a husband, the importunity of years, the unwelcomeness of wrinkles, and such like mind-troubling accidents. Lo here the most and greatest share of learning I would assign them. There are some particular, retired and close dispositions.

My essential form is fit for communication, and proper for pro-duction: I am all outward and in appearance; born for society and unto friendship. The solitude I love and commend, is especially but to retire my affections and redeem my thoughts unto myself: to restrain and close up, not my steps, but my desires and my cares, resigning all foreign solicitude and trouble, and mortally shunning all manner of servitude and obligation; and not so much the throng of men as the importunity of affairs. Local solitariness (to say truth) doth rather extend and enlarge me outwardly; I give myself to State-business, and to the world, more willingly when I am all alone. At the court, and in press of people, I close and slink into my own skin. Assemblies thrust me again into myself. And I never entertain myself so fondly, so licentiously, and so particularly, as in places of respect, and ceremonious discretion. Our follies make me not laugh, but our wisdoms do. Of my own complexion, I am no enemy to the agitations and stirrings of our Courts: I have there passed great part of my life: and am inured to be merry in great assemblies; so it be by intermission, and suitable to my humour.

But this tenderness and coyness of judgment (whereof I speak) doth perforce tie me unto solitariness. Yea even in my own house, in the midst of a numerous family and most frequented houses, I see people more than a good many, but seldom such as I love to converse or communicate withal. And there I reserve, both for myself, and others, an unaccustomed liberty; making truce with ceremonies, assistance, and invitings, and such other troublesome ordinances of our courtesies (O servile custom and importunate manner) there every man demeaneth himself as he pleaseth, and entertaineth what his thoughts affect: whereas I keep myself silent, meditating and close, without offence to my guests or friends.

The men whose familiarity and society I hunt after, are those which are called honest, virtuous and sufficient: the image of whom doth distaste and divert me from others. It is (being rightly taken) the rarest of our forms; and a form or fashion chiefly due unto nature.

The end or scope of this commerce, is principally and simply familiarity, conference and frequentation: the exercise of minds, without other fruit. In our discourses, all subjects are alike to me: I care not though they want either weight or depth; grace and pertinency are never wanting; all therein is tainted with a ripe and constant judgment, and commixt with goodness, liberty, cheerfulness, and kindness. It is not only in the subject of Laws and affairs of Princes, that our spirit showeth its beauty, grace and vigor: It showeth them as much in private conferences. I know my people by their very silence and smiling, and peradventure discover them better at a Table, than sitting in serious counsel.

Hippomacus said, he discerned good Wrestlers but by seeing them march through a Street. If learning vouchsafe to step into our talk, she shall not be refused; yet must not she be stern, mastering, imperious and importunate, as commonly she is; but assistant, and docile of herself. Therein we seek for nothing but recreation and pastime: when we shall look to be instructed, taught and resolved, we will go seek and sue to her in her Throne. Let her if she please keep from us at that time; for, as commodious and pleasing as she is: I presume that for a need we could spare her presence, and do our business well enough without her. Wits well born, soundly bred and exercised in the practice and commerce of men, become gracious and plausible of themselves. Art is but the Check-rule, and Register of the Productions uttered, and conceits produced by them.

The company of fair, and society of honest women is likewise a sweet commerce for me: *Nam nos quoque oculos eruditos habemus* (CIC. *Parad.*), *for we also have learned eyes.* If the mind have not so much to solace herself, as in the former; the corporal senses, whose part is more in the second, bring it to a proportion near unto the other; although in my opinion not equal. But it is a society wherein it behooveth a man somewhat to stand upon his guard; and especially those that are of a strong constitution, and whose body can do much, as in me. In my youth I heated myself therein and was very violent: and indured all the rages and furious assaults, which Poets say happen to those who without order or discretion abandon themselves over-loosely and riotously unto it. True it is indeed, that the same lash hath since stood me instead of an instruction.

OVID, *Trist.* i. *El.* i. 83.

Quicunque Argolico de classe Capharea fugit,
Semper ab Euboicis vela retorquet aquis.

Greek Sailors that Capharean Rocks did fly,
From the Eubœan Seas their sails still ply.

It is folly to fasten all one's thoughts upon it, and with a furious and indiscreet affection to engage himself unto it: But on the other side, to meddle with it without love or bond of affection, as Comedians do, to play a common part of age and manners, without ought of their own but bare-conned words, is verily a provision for one's safety: and yet but a cowardly one; as is that of him, who would forgo his honour, his profit or his pleasure for fear of danger; for it is certain that the practisers of such courses, cannot hope for any fruit able to move or satisfy a worthy mind.

312   One must very earnestly have desired that, whereof he would

enjoy an absolute delight: I mean, though fortune should unjustly favour their intention: which often happeneth, because there is no woman, how deformed and unhandsome soever, but thinks herself lovely, amiable and praiseworthy, either for her age, her hair or gait (for there are generally no more fair than foul ones). And the Brachmanian maids wanting other commendations; by Proclamation for that purpose, made show of their matrimonial parts unto the people assembled, to see if thereby at least they might get them husbands. By consequence there is not one of them, but upon the first oath one maketh to serve her, will very easily be persuaded to think well of herself. Now this common treason and ordinary protestations of men in these days, must needs produce the effects, experience already discovereth: which is, that either they join together, and cast away themselves on themselves, to avoid us, or on their side follow also the example we give them; acting their part of the play, without passion; without care, and without love lending themselves to this intercourse: *Neque affectui suo aut alieno obnoxiæ: Neither liable to their own nor other folks' affection.* Thinking, according to Lysias' persuasions in Plato, they may so much the more profitable and commodiously yield unto us; by how much less we love them: Wherein it will happen as in Comedies, the spectators shall have as much or more pleasure, as the Comedians. For my part, I no more acknowledge Venus without Cupid, than a motherhood without an offspring: They are things which interlend and interowe one another their essence. Thus doth this cozening rebound on him that useth it; and as it cost him little, so gets he not much by it. Those which made Venus a goddess, have respected that her principal beauty was incorporeal and spiritual. But she whom this kind of people hunt after, is not so much as human, nor also brutal; but such as wild beasts, would not have her so filthy and terrestrial. We see that imagination inflames them, and desire or lust urgeth them, before the body: We see in one and other sex, even in whole herds, choice and distinctions in their affections, and amongst themselves acquaintances of long continued goodwill and liking. And even those to whom age denieth bodily strength, do yet bray, neigh, roar, skip and wince for love. Before the deed we see them full of hope and heat; and when the body hath played his part, even tickle and tingle themselves with the sweetness of that remembrance: some of them swell with pride at parting from it, others all weary and glutted, ring out songs of glee and triumph. Who makes no more of it but to discharge his body of some natural necessity, hath no cause to trouble others with so curious preparation. *It is no food for a greedy and clownish hunger.* As one that would not be accounted better than I am, thus much I will display

313

of my youth's wanton errors: Not only for the danger of one's health that follows that game (yet could I not avoid two, though light and cursory assaults) but also for contempt, I have not much been given to mercenary and common acquaintances. I have coveted to set an edge on that sensual pleasure by difficulty, by desire, and for some glory. And liked Tiberius' fashions, who in his amours was swayed as much by modesty and nobleness, as by any other quality. And Flora's humour, who would prostitute herself to none worse than Dictators, Consuls, or Censors, and took delight in the dignity and greatness of her lovers, doth somewhat suit with mine. Surely glittering pearls and silken clothes add something unto it, and so do titles, nobility and a worthy train. Besides which, I made high esteem of the mind, yet so as the body might not justly be found fault withal: For, to speak my conscience, if either of the two beauties were necessarily to be wanting, I would rather have chosen to want the mental, whose use is to be employed in better things. But in the subject of love; a subject that chiefly hath reference unto the two senses of seeing and touching, something may be done without the graces of the mind, but little or nothing without the corporal. *Beauty is the true availful advantage of women:* It is so peculiarly theirs, that ours though it require some features and different allurements, is not in her right cue, or true bias, unless confused with theirs; childish and beardless. It is reported, that such as serve the great Turk under the title of beauty (whereof the number is infinite) are dismissed at furthest when they once come to the age of two and twenty years. *Discourse, discretion, together with the offices of true amity, are better found amongst men: and therefore govern they the world's affairs.* These two commerces or societies are accidental, and depending of others; the one is troublesome and tedious for its rarity; the other withers with old age: nor could they have sufficiently provided for my life's necessities. That of books, which is the third, is much more solid-sure and much more ours; some other advantages it yieldeth to the two former: but hath for her share constancy and the facility of her service. This accosteth and secondeth all my course, and everywhere assisteth me: It comforts me in age, and solaceth me in solitariness: It easeth me of the burden of a wearisome sloth: and at all times rids me of tedious companies: it abateth the edge of fretting sorrow, on condition it be not extreme and over insolent. *To divert me from any importunate imagination or insinuating conceit, there is no better way than to have recourse unto books:* with ease they allure me to them, and with facility they remove them all. And though they perceive I neither frequent nor seek them, but wanting other more essential, 314 lively, and more natural commodities, they never mutiny or murmur at me; but still entertain me with one and selfsame visage. *He may well walk afoot, that leads his horse by the bridle,* saith the proverb. And our James king of Naples and Sicily, who being fair, young, healthy and in good plight, caused himself to be carried abroad in a plain wagon or screen, lying upon an homely pillow of coarse feathers, clothed in a suit of home spun gray, and a bonnet of the same, yet royally attended on by a gallant troupe of Nobles, of Litters, Coaches, and of all sorts of choice led horses, a number of gentlemen, and officers, represented a tender and wavering austerity. *The sick man is not to be moaned, that hath his health in his sleeve.* In the experience and use of this sentence, which is most true, consisteth all the commodity I reap of books. In effect I make no other use of them, than those who know them not. I enjoy them, as a miser doth his gold; to know, that I may enjoy them when I list; my mind is settled and satisfied with the right of possession. I never travel without books, nor in peace nor in war; yet do I pass many days and months without using them. It shall be anon, say I or tomorrow, or when I please; in the meanwhile the time runs away, and passeth without hurting me. For it is wonderful, what repose I take, and how I continue in this consideration, that they are at my elbow to delight me when time shall serve; and in acknowledging what assistance they give unto my life. This is the best munition I have found in this human peregrination, and I extremely bewail those other kinds of amusements, how slight so-ever, forsomuch as this cannot fail me. At home I betake me some-what the oftener to my library, whence all at once I command and survey all my household; It is seated in the chief entry of my house, thence I behold under me my garden, my base court, my yard, and look even into most rooms of my house. There without order, with-out method, and by piecemeal I turn over and ransack, now one book and now another. Sometimes I muse and rave; and walking up and down I indite and inregister these my humours, these my conceits. It is placed on the third story of a tower. The lowermost is my Chapel; the second a chamber with other lodgings, where I often lie, because I would be alone. Above it is a great ward-robe. It was in times past the most unprofitable place of all my house. There I pass the greatest part of my life's days, and wear out most hours of the day. I am never there a-nights: Next unto it is a hand-some neat cabinet, able and large enough to receive fire in winter, and very pleasantly windowed. And if I feared not care, more than cost; (care which drives and diverts me from all business) I might easily join a convenient gallery of a hundred paces long, and twelve broad, on each side of it, and upon one floor; having already, for some other purpose, found all the walls raised unto a convenient

315

height. Each retired place requireth a walk. My thoughts are prone
to sleep, if I sit long. My mind goes not alone as if legs did move
it. Those that study without books, are all in the same case. The
form of it is round, and hath no flat side, but what serveth for my
table and chair: In which bending or circling manner, at one look
it offereth me the full sight of all my books, set round about upon
shelves or desks, five ranks one upon another. It hath three bay-
windows, of a far-extending, rich and unresisted prospect, and is in
diameter sixteen paces void. In winter I am less continually there:
for my house (as the name of it importeth) is perched upon an over-
peering hillock; and hath no part more subject to all weathers than
this: which pleaseth me the more, both because the access unto it is
somewhat troublesome and remote, and for the benefit of the
exercise which is to be respected; and that I may the better seclude
myself from company, and keep encroachers from me: There is my
seat, there is my throne. I endeavour to make my rule therein
absolute, and to sequester that only corner from the community
of wife, of children and of acquaintance. Elsewhere I have but a
verbal authority, of confused essence. Miserable, in my mind is he,
who in his own home, hath nowhere to be to himself; where he may
particularly court, and at his pleasure hide or withdraw himself.
Ambition payeth her followers well, to keep them still in open view,
as a statue in some conspicuous place. *Magna servitus est magna
fortuna* (SEN. *Cons. ad Pol.* c. xxvi. p.): *A great fortune is a great
bondage.* They cannot be private so much as at their privy. I have
deemed nothing so rude in the austerity of the life, which our
Churchmen affect, as that in some of their companies they institute
a perpetual society of place, and a numerous assistance amongst
them in anything they do. And deem it somewhat more tolerable
to be ever alone, than never able to be so. If any say to me, It is a
kind of vilifying the Muses, to use them only for sport and recreation, he wots not as I do, what worth, pleasure, sport and pastime is
of: I had well nigh termed all other ends ridiculous. I live from
hand to mouth, and with reverence be it spoken, I live but to myself: there end all my designs. Being young I studied for ostentation;
then a little to enable myself and become wiser; now for delight
and recreation, never for gain. A vain conceit and lavish humour I
had after this kind of stuff; not only to provide for my need, but
somewhat further to adorn and embellish myself withal: I have
since partly left it. *Books have and contain divers pleasing qualities
to those that can duly choose them. But no good without pains;
no Roses without prickles.* It is a pleasure not absolutely pure and
neat, no more than all others; it hath his inconveniences attending
316 on it and sometimes weighty ones: The mind is therein exercised,

but the body (the care whereof I have not yet forgotten) remaineth therewhilst without action, and is wasted, and ensorrowed. I know no excess more hurtful for me, nor more to be avoided by me, in this declining age. Lo here my three most favoured and particular employments. I speak not of those I owe of duty to the world.

Chapter *Of experience* There's more ado to interpret interpretations, than
Thirteen to interpret things: and more books upon books, than upon any other subject. We do but inter-gloss ourselves. All swarmeth with commentaries: Of Authors there is great penury. Is not the chiefest and most famous knowledge of our ages, to know how to understand the wise? Is it not the common and last scope of our study: Our opinions are grafted one upon another. The first serveth as a stock to the second; the second to the third. Thus we ascend from step to step. Whence it followeth, that the highest-mounted hath often more honour, than merit. For, he is got up but one inch above the shoulders of the last save one. How often and peradventure foolishly, have I enlarged my Book to speak of himself? Foolishly if it were but for this reason: That I should have remembered, that what I speak of others, they do the like of me. That those so frequent glances on their works, witness their heart shivereth with their love they bear them; and that the disdainful churlishness wherewith they beat them, are but migniardizes and affectations of a motherly favour. Following Aristotle, in whom, both esteeming and disesteeming himself, arise often of an equal air of arrogance. For my excuse; That in this I ought to have more liberty than others, forsomuch as of purpose, I write both of myself and of my writings, as of my other actions: that my theme doth turn into itself: I wot not whether every man will take it. I have seen in Germany, that Luther hath left as many divisions and altercations, concerning the doubt of his opinions, yea and more, than himself moveth about the Holy Scriptures. Our contestation is verbal. I demand what Nature voluptuousness, circle and substitution is? The question is of words, and with words it is answered. A stone is a body: but he that should insist and urge: And what is a body? A substance: And what a substance? And so go-on: Should at last bring the respondent to his Calepine or wit's end. One word is changed for another word, and often more unknown. I know better what *Homo* is, than I know what *Animal* is, either mortal or reasonable. To answer one doubt, they give me three: It is Hydra's head. Socrates demanded of Memnon what virtue was: There is answered Memnon, the virtue of a Man, of a Woman, of a Magistrate, of a private Man, of a Child, of an old Man: What virtue mean you? Yea marry, this is very well, quoth Socrates; we were in search of one virtue, and thou bringest

me a whole swarm. We propose one question, and we have a whole huddle of them made unto us again. As no event or form doth wholly resemble another, so doth it not altogether differ one from another. Oh ingenious mixture of Nature. *If our faces were not like, we could not discern a man from a beast: if they were not unlike, we could not distinguish one man from another man.* All things hold by some similitude: Every example limpeth. And the relation, which is drawn from experience, is ever defective and imperfect. Comparisons are nevertheless joined together by some end. So serve the Laws, and so are they sorted and fitted to all our suits or affairs; by some wiredrawn, forced and collateral interpretation. Since the moral Laws which respect the particular duty of every man in himself, are so hard to be taught and observed, as we see they are: It is no wonder, if those which govern so many particulars, are more hard. Consider the form of this Law, by which we are ruled: It is a lively testimony of human imbecility; so much contradiction, and so many errors are therein contained. That which we think favour or rigour in Law (wherein is so much of either, that I wot not well whether we shall so often find indifference in them), are crazed-infected parts and unjust members of the very body and essence of Law. Certain poor countrymen came even now to tell me in a great haste, that but now in a forest of mine, they have left a man wounded to death, with a hundred hurts about him, yet breathing, and who for God's sake hath begged a little water and some help to raise himself at their hands. But that they durst not come near him, and ran all away, for fear some officers belonging to the Law should meet and catch them; and as they do with such as they find near unto a murdered body, so they should be compelled to give an account of this mischance, to their utter undoing; having neither friends nor money to defend their innocence. What should I have said unto them? It is most certain, that this Office of humanity had brought them to much trouble. How many innocent and guiltless men have we seen punished? I say without the Judge's fault; and how many more that were never discovered? This hath happened in my time. Certain men are condemned to death for a murder committed; the sentence, if not pronounced, at least concluded and determined. This done, The Judges are advertised by the Officers of a subalternal Court, not far off, that they have certain prisoners in hold, that have directly confessed the foresaid murder, and thereof bring most evident marks and tokens. The question and consultation is now in the former Court, whether for all this, they might interrupt, or should defer the execution of the sentence pronounced against the first. They consider the novelty of the example and consequence thereof, and how to reconcile the judgment. They conclude, that the

condemnation hath passed according unto Law, and therefore the
Judges are not subject to repentance. To be short, these miserable
Wretches are consecrated to the prescriptions of the Law. Philip,
or some other, provided for such an inconvenience, in this manner.
He had by an irrevocable sentence condemned one to pay another
a round sum of money for a fine. A while after, the truth being discovered, it was found, he had wrongfully condemned him. On one
side was the right of the cause, on the other the right of judiciary
forms. He is in some sort to satisfy both parties, suffering the
sentence to stand in full power: and with his own purse recom-
pensed the interest of the condemned. But he was to deal with a
reparable accident, my poor slaves were hanged irreparably. How
many condemnations have I seen more criminal, than the crime
itself? All this put me in mind of those ancient opinions; That *He
who will do right in gross, must needs do wrong by retail; and
injustly in small things, that will come to do justice in great matters;*
That human justice is framed according to the model of physic,
according to which, whatsoever is profitable is also just and honest:
And of that the Stoics hold, that Nature herself in most of her
works, proceedeth against justice: And of that which the Cyreni-
aques hold, that there is nothing just of itself: That customs and
laws frame justice. And the Theodorians, who in a wise man allow
as just, all manner of theft, sacrilege and paillardise, so he think it
profitable for him. There is no remedy: I am in that case, as Alcibiades was, and if I can otherwise choose, will never put myself
unto a man that shall determine of my head; or consent that my
honour or life, shall depend on the industry or care of my attorney,
more than my innocence. I could willingly adventure myself, and
stand to that Law, that should as well recompense me for a good
deed, as punish me for a misdeed: and where I might have a just
cause to hope, as reason to fear. *Indemnity is no sufficient coin for
him, who doth better than not to trespass.* Our Law presents us
but one of her hands, and that is her left hand. *Whosoever goes to
Law, doth in the end but lose by it.* In China, the policy, arts and
government of which kingdom, having neither knowledge or commerce with ours; exceed our examples in divers parts of excellence;
and whose Histories teach me, how much more ample and divers the
World is than either we or our forefathers could ever enter into. The
Officers appointed by the Prince to visit the state of his Provinces,
as they punish such as abuse their charge, so with great liberality
they reward such as have uprightly and honestly behaved themselves in them, or have done anything more than ordinary, and
besides the necessity of their duty: There, all present themselves,
319 not only to warrant themselves, but also to get something: Not

simply to be paid, but liberally to be rewarded. No judge hath yet, God be thanked, spoken to me as a judge in any cause whatsoever, either mine or another man's; criminal or civil. No prison did ever receive me, no not so much as for recreation to walk in. The very imagination of one, maketh the sight of their outside seem irksome and loathsome to me. I am so besotted unto liberty, that should any man forbid me the access unto any one corner of the Indies I should in some sort live much discontented. And so long as I shall find land or open air elsewhere, I shall never lurk in any place, where I must hide myself. Oh God, how hardly could I endure the miserable condition of so many men, confined and immured in some corners of this kingdom, barred from entering the chiefest Cities, from access into Courts; from conversing with men, and interdicted the use of common ways, only because they have offended our laws. If those under which I live, should but threaten my finger's end, I would presently go find out some others, wheresoever it were. All my small wisdom, in these civil and tumultuous wars, wherein we now live, doth wholly employ itself, that they may not interrupt my liberty, to go and come wherever I list. Laws are now maintained in credit, not because they are essentially just, but because they are laws. It is the mystical foundation of their authority; they have none other: which avails them much: They are often made by fools; more often by men, who in hatred of equality, have want of equity; But ever by men, who are vain and irresolute Authors. There is nothing so grossly and largely offending, nor so ordinarily wronging as the Laws. Whosoever obeyeth them because they are just, obeys them not justly the way as he ought. Our French laws do in some sort, by their irregularity and deformity, lend an helping hand unto the disorder and corruption, that is seen in their dispensation and execution. Their behest is so confused, and their command so inconstant, that it in some sort excuseth, both the disobedience and the vice of the interpretation, of the administration and of the observation. Whatsoever then the fruit is we may have of Experience, the same which we draw from foreign examples, will hardly stead our institution much; if we reap so small profit from that we have of ourselves, which is most familiar unto us: and truly sufficient to instruct us of what we want. I study myself more than any other subject. It is my supernatural Metaphysic, it is my natural Philosophy.

PROPERT. iii. *El.* iv. 26.

Qua Deus hanc mundi temperet arte domum,
Qua venit exoriens, qua deficit, unde coactis
Cornibus in plenum menstrua luna redit:

Unde salo superant venti, quid flamine captet
Eurus, et in nubes unde perennis æqua.
Sit ventura dies mundi quæ subruat arces.

This World's great house by what art God doth guide;
From whence the monthly Moon doth rising ride,
How wane, how with closed horns return to pride,
How winds on seas bear sway, what th' Eastern wind
Would have, how still in clouds we water find;
If this world's Towers to raze a day be signed.

Quærite quos agitat mundi labor:

All this do you enquire
Whom this world's travails tire.

In this universality I suffer myself ignorantly and negligently to be managed by the general law of the world. I shall sufficiently know it when I shall feel it. My learning cannot make her change her course: she will not diversify herself for me; it were folly to hope it: And greater folly for a man to trouble himself about it; since it is necessarily semblable, public and common. The governour's capacity and goodness, should thoroughly discharge us of the government's care. Philosophical inquisitions and contemplations serve but as a nourishment unto our curiosity. With great reason do Philosophers address us unto nature's rules: But they have nought to do with so sublime a knowledge: They falsify them, and present her to us with a painted face, too high in colour and overmuch sophisticated; whence arise so many different portraits of so uniform a subject. As she hath given us feet to go withal, so hath she endowed us with wisdom to direct our life. A wisdom not so ingenious, sturdy and pompous, as that of their invention; but yet easy, quiet and salutary. And that in him who hath the hap to know how to employ it orderly and sincerely, effecteth very well what the other saith: that is to say naturally. For a man to commit himself most simply unto nature, is to do it most wisely. *Oh how soft, how gentle, and how sound a pillow is ignorance and incuriosity to rest a well composed head upon.* I had rather understand myself well in myself, than in Cicero. Out of the experience I have of myself, I find sufficient ground to make myself wise, were I but a good proficient scholar. Whosoever shall commit to memory the excess or inconvenience of his rage or anger past, and how far that fit transported him, may see the deformity of that passion, better than in Aristotle, and conceive a more just hatred against it. Whosoever calleth to mind, the dangers he hath escaped, those which have

321

threatened him, and the light occasions that have removed him from one state to another state, doth thereby the better prepare himself to future alterations, and knowledge of his condition. Cæsar's life hath no more examples for us, than our own; Both imperial and popular; it is ever a life that all human accidents regard. Let us but give ear unto it, we record all that to us, that we principally stand in need of. He that shall call to mind how often and how several times he hath been deceived, and misaccounted his own judgment: is he not a simple gull, if he do not forever afterward distrust the same? When by other's reason, I find myself convicted of a false opinion, I learn not so much, what new thing he hath told me; and this particular ignorance; which were but a small purchase; as in general I learn my own imbecility and weakness, and the treason of my understanding: whence I draw the reformation of all the mass. The like I do in all my other errors: by which rule I apprehend and feel great profit for, and unto my life. I regard not the *species* or *individuum*, as a stone whereon I have stumbled. I learn everywhere to fear my going, and endeavour to order the same. To learn that another hath either spoken a foolish jest, or committed a sottish act, is a thing of nothing. A man must learn, that he is but a fool: A much more ample and important instruction. The false steps my memory hath so often put upon me, at what time she stood most upon herself, have not idly been lost: she may swear and warrant me long enough; I shake my ears at her: the first opposition made in witness of her, makes me suspect. And I durst not trust her in a matter of consequence; nor warrant her touching others' affairs. And were it not, that what I do for want of memory, others more often do the same for lack of faith, I would even in a matter of fact rather take the truth from another's mouth, than from my own. Would every man pry truth from another's mouth, than from my own. Would every man pry into the effects and circumstances of the passions that sway him, as I have done of that whereunto I was allotted; he should see them coming; and would somewhat hinder their course and abate their impetuosity: They do not always surprise and take hold of us at the first brunt, there are certain forethreatenings and degrees as forerunners.

The best of my corporal complexions, is, that I am flexible and little opinionative. I have certain inclinations, more proper and ordinary, and more pleasing than others. But with small ado and without compulsion, I can easily leave them and embrace the contrary. A young man should trouble his rules, to stir up his vigor; and take heed he suffer not the same to grow faint, sluggish or resty: For, there is no course of life so weak and sottish, as that which is
managed by Order, Method and Discipline.

JUVEN. *Sat.* vi. 477.

Ad primum lapidem vectari cum placet, hora
Sumitur ex libro, si prurit frictus ocelli
Angubus, inspecta genesi collyria quærit.

List he to ride in coach but to Mile-end,
By th' Almanac he doth the hour attend:
If his eye-corner itch, the remedy,
He fets from calculation of nativity.

If he believe me, he shall often give himself unto all manner of excess: otherwise the least disorder will utterly overthrow him; and so make him unfit and unwelcome in all conversations. *The most contrary quality in an honest man, is nice-delicateness, and to be tied to one certain particular fashion.* It is particular, if it be not supple and pliable. *It is a kind of reproach, through impuissance not to do or not to dare, what one seeth his other companions do or dare.* Let such men keep their kitchen. It is indecent in all other men, but vicious and intolerable in one professing Arms: who (as Philopæmen said) should fashion himself to all manner of inequality and diversity of life. Although I have (as much as might be) been inured to liberty, and fashioned to indifference; yet in growing aged, I have through carelessness relied more upon certain forms (my age is now exempted from institution, and hath not anything else to look unto, but to maintain itself) which custom hath already, without thinking on it, in certain things so well imprinted her character in me, that I deem it a kind of excess to leave them. And without long practice, I can neither sleep by day; nor eat between meals; nor break my fast; nor go to bed without some intermission; (as of three hours after supper) nor get children, but before I fall asleep, and that never standing; nor bear my own sweat; nor quench my thirst, either with clear water or wine alone; nor continue long bareheaded; nor have my hair cut after dinner. And I could as hardly spare my gloves as my shirt: or forbear washing of my hands, both in the morning and rising from the table; or lie in a bed without a tester and curtains about it, as of most necessary things: I could dine without a table-cloth, but hardly without a clean napkin, as Germans commonly do. I foul and sully them more than either they or the Italians: and I seldom use either spoon or fork. I am sorry we follow not a custom, which according to the example of Kings I have seen begun by some; that upon every course or change of dish, as we have shift of clean trenchers, so we might have change of clean napkins. We read that that laborious soldier Marius, growing old, grew more nicely delicate in his drinking, and would taste no
323   drink, except in a peculiar cup of his. As for me, I observe a kind

of like method in glasses, and of one certain form, and drink not willingly in a common-glass, no more than of one ordinary hand: I mislike all manner of metal in regard of a bright transparent matter: let my eyes also have taste of what I drink according to their capacity. I am beholding to custom for many such nicenesses and singularities. Nature hath also on the other side bestowed this upon me, that I cannot well brook two full meals in one day, without surcharging my stomach; nor the mere abstinence of one, without filling myself with wind, drying my mouth and dulling my appetite: And I do find great offence by a long serein or night-calm. For some years since, in the out-roads or night-services that happen in times of wars, which many times continue all night, five or six hours after my stomach begins to qualm, my head feeleth a violent aching, so that I can hardly hold out till morning without vomiting. When others go to breakfast, I go to sleep: and within a while after I shall be as fresh and jolly as before.

There are very few examples of life, absolutely full and pure. And our instruction is greatly wronged, in that it hath certain weak, defective and imperfect forms proposed unto it, scarcely good for any good use, which divert and draw us back; and may rather be termed corrupters than correctors. *Man is easily deceived.* One may more easily go by the sides, where extremity serveth as bound, as a stay and as a guide, than by the midway, which is open and wide: and more according unto art, than according unto nature, but therewithal less nobly and with less commendation. *The greatness of the mind is not so much, to draw up and hale forward, as to know how to range, direct and circumscribe itself.* It holdeth for great whatsoever is sufficient. And showeth her height, in loving mean things better than eminent. *There is nothing so goodly, so fair and so lawful as to play the man well and duly: Nor Science so hard and difficult, as to know how to live this life well.* And of all the infirmities we have, the most savage, is to despise our being. Whoso will sequester or distract his mind, let him hardily do it, if he can, at what time his body is not well at ease, thereby to discharge it from that contagion: And elsewhere contrary: that she may assist and favour him, and not refuse to be partaker of his natural pleasures, and conjugally be pleased with them: adding thereunto, if she be the wiser, moderation, lest through indiscretion, they might be confounded with displeasure. *Intemperance is the plague of sensuality: and temperance is not her scourge, but rather her seasoning.* *Eudoxus*, who thereon established his chief felicity: and his companions, that raised the same to so high a pitch, by means of temperance, which in them was very singular and exemplar, 324 savoured the same in her most gracious sweetness. I enjoin my mind,

with a look equally regular, to behold both sorrow and voluptuousness: *Eodem enim vitio est effusio animi in lætitia, quo in dolore
contractio* (CIC. *Tusc. Qu.* iv.). *As faulty is the enlarging of the
mind in mirth, as the contracting it in grief:* and equally constant:
But the one merrily and the other severely: And according to that
she may bring unto it, to be as careful to extinguish the one, as
diligent to quench the other. *To have a perfect insight into a good,
draws with it an absolute insight into evil.* And sorrow hath in her
tender beginning something that is unavoidable: and voluptuousness in her excessive end, something that is evitable. Plato coupleth
them together, and would have it to be the equal office of fortitude,
to combat against sorrows, and fight against the immoderate and
charming blandishments of sensuality. They are two fountains, at
which whoso draweth, whence, when and as much as he needeth, be
it a city, be it a man, be it a beast, he is very happy. The first must
be taken for physic and necessity, and more sparingly: The second
for thirst but not unto drunkenness. *Pain, voluptuousness, love and
hate, are the first passions a child feeleth: if reason approach, and
they apply themselves unto it; that is virtue.* I have a Dictionary
severally and wholly to myself: I pass the time when it is foul and
incommodious: when it is fair and good I will not pass it: I run it
over again, and take hold of it. *A man should run the bad, and settle
himself in the good.* This vulgar phrase of pass time, and to pass
the time, represents the custom of those wise men, who think to
have no better account of their life, than to pass it over and escape
it: to pass it over and balk it, and so much as in them lieth, to ignore
and avoid it, as a thing of any irksome, tedious, and to be disdained
quality. But I know it to be otherwise; and find it to be both prize-
able and commodious, yea in her last declination; where I hold it.
And Nature hath put the same into our hands, furnished with such
and so favourable circumstances, that if it press and molest us, or if
unprofitably it escape us, we must blame ourselves. *Stulti vita in-
grata est, trepida est, tota in futurum fertur* (SEN. *Epist.* XV.). *A
fool's life is all pleasant, all fearful, all fond of the future.* I therefore prepare and compose myself, to forgo and lose it without
grudging; but a thing that is losable and transitory by its own
condition: not as troublesome and importunate. Nor beseems it a
man to be grieved when he dieth, except they be such as please
themselves to live still. There is a kind of husbandry in knowing
how to enjoy it. I enjoy it double to others. For *the measure in
jovissance dependeth more or less on the application we lend it.*
Especially at this instant, that I perceive mine to be short in time, I
will extend it in weight: I will stay the readiness of her flight, by
325 the promptitude of my hold-fast by it: and by the vigor of custom,

recompense the haste of her fleeting. According as the possession of life is more short, I must endeavour to make it more profound and full. Other men feel the sweetness of a contentment and prosperity. I feel it as well as they; but it is not in passing and gliding; yet should it be studied, tasted and ruminated, thereby to yield it condign thanks, that it pleased to grant the same unto us. They enjoy other pleasures, as that of sleep, without knowing them. To the end that sleep should not dully and unfeelingly escape me, and that I might better taste and be acquainted with it, I have heretofore found it good, to be troubled and interrupted in the same. I have a kind of contentment to consult with myself: which consultation I do not superficially run over, but considerately sound the same, and apply my reason to entertain and receive it, which is now become forward, peevish and distasted. Do I find myself in some quiet mood? is there any sensuality that tickles me? I do not suffer the same to busy itself or dally about senses, but associate my mind unto it: Not to engage or plunge itself therein, but therein to take delight: not to lose, but therein to find itself. And for her part I employ her, to view herself in that prosperous state, to ponder and esteem the good fortune she hath, and to amplify the same. She measureth how much she is beholding unto God, for that she is at rest with her conscience, and free from other intestine passions, and hath in her body her natural disposition: orderly and competently enjoying certain flattering and effeminate functions, with which it pleaseth him of his grace to recompense the griefs, wherewith his justice at his pleasure smiteth us. Oh how availful is it unto her to be so seated, that wherever she casteth her eyes, the heavens are calm round about her; and no desire, no fear or doubt troubleth the air before her: here is no difficulty, either past, or present, or to come, over which her imagination passeth not without offence. This consideration takes a great lustre from the comparison of different conditions. Thus do I in a thousand shapes propose unto myself those to whom either fortune, or their own error doth transport and torment. And these nearer, who so slackly and incuriously receive their good fortune. They are men which indeed pass their time: they overpass the present and that which they possess, thereby to serve their hopes with shadows and vain images, which fancy sets before them,

VIRG. *Æn.* x. 641.

Morte oblita quales fama est volitare figuras
Aut quæ sopitos deludunt somnia sensus.

Such walking shapes we say, when men are dead,
326 Dreams, whereby sleeping senses are misled,

which hasten and prolong their flight, according as they are followed. The fruit and scope of their pursuit, is to pursue: As Alexander said, that *The end of his Travel, was to travel.*

LUCAN. ii. 656.

Nil actum credens cùm quid superesset agendum.

Who thought that nought was done,
When ought remained undone.

As for me then, I love my life and cherish it, such as it hath
pleased God to grant it us. I desire not he should speak of the necessity of eating and drinking. And I would think to offend no less
excusably, in desiring it should have it double. *Sapiens divitiarum
naturalium quæsitor acerrimus* (SEN. *Epist.* cxix.). *A wise man is
a most eager and earnest searcher of those things that are natural.*
Nor that we should sustain ourselves by only putting a little of that
drug into our mouth, wherewith Epimenedes was wont to allay
hunger, and yet maintained himself. Nor that we should insensibly
produce children at our fingers' ends or at our heels, but rather
(speaking with reverence) that we might with pleasure and voluptuousness produce them both at our heels and fingers' ends. Nor that
the body should be void of desire, and without tickling delight. They
are ungrateful and impious complaints. I cheerfully and thankfully,
and with a good heart, accept what nature hath created for me;
and am therewith well pleased, and am proud of it. Great wrong is
offered unto that great and all-puissant Giver, to refuse his gift,
which is so absolutely good, and disanul or disfigure the same, since
he made perfectly good. *Omnia quæ secundum naturam sunt, esti-
matione digna sunt* (CIC. *Fin. Bon.* iii.). *All things that are according to nature, are worthy to be esteemed.* Of Philosophy's opinions,
I more willingly embrace those, which are the most solid, and that
is to say, such as are most human and most ours: My discourses are
suitable to my manners: low and humble. She then brings forth a
child well pleasing me, when she betakes herself to her Quiddities
and Ergoes, to persuade us, that it is a barbarous alliance, to marry
what is divine with that which is terrestrial: wed reasonable with
unreasonable; combine severe with indulgent, and couple honest
with dishonest: that voluptuousness is a brutal quality, unworthy
the taste of a wise man. The only pleasure he draws from the enjoying of a fair young bride, is the delight of his conscience, by performing an action according unto order; As to put on his boots for a
profitable riding. Oh that his followers had no more right, or sinews,
or pith, or juice, at the dismaidening of their wives, than they
327 have in his Lesson. It is not that, which Socrates, both his and our

Master, saith; He valueth rightly as he ought corporal voluptuousness: but he preferreth that of the mind, as having more force, more constancy, facility, variety and dignity. This according to him, goeth nothing alone, he is not so phantastical; but only first. For him, temperance is a moderatrix, and not an adversary of sensualities. *Nature is a gentle guide:* Yet not more gentle, than prudent and just. *Intrandum est in rerum naturam, et penitus quid ea postulet, pervidendum (Ibid. v.). We must enter into the nature of things, and thoroughly see what she inwardly requires.* I quest after her track; we have confounded her with artificial traces. And that Academical and Peripatetical *summum bonum* or sovereign felicity, which is, to live according to her rules: by this reason becometh difficult to be limited, and hard to be expounded. And that of the Stoics, cousin-german to the other, which is, to yield unto nature. Is it not an error, to esteem some actions less worthy, forsomuch as they are necessary? Yet shall they never remove out of my head, that it is not a most convenient marriage, to wed Pleasure unto Necessity. With which (saith an ancient Writer) the Gods do ever complot and consent.

To what end do we by a divorce dismember a frame contexted with so mutual, coherent and brotherly correspondence. Contrariwise, let us repair and renew the same by interchangeable offices: that the spirit may awake and quicken the dull heaviness of the body, and the body stay the lightness of the spirit, and settle and fix the same. *Qui velut summum bonum, laudat animæ naturam, et tanquam malum, naturam carnis accusat, profectò et animam carnaliter appetit, et carnem incarnaliter fugit, quoniam id vanitate sentit humana, non veritate divina* (AUG. *Verb. Apostol.* ser. xiii. c. 6). *He that praiseth the nature of the soul, as his principal good, and accuseth nature of the flesh as evil, assuredly he both carnally affecteth the soul, and carnally escheweth the flesh, since he is of this mind not by divine verity, but human vanity.* There is no part or parcel unworthy of our care in that present, which God hath bestowed upon us. We are accountable even for the least hair of it. And it is no commission for fashion's sake for any man, to direct man according to his condition: it is express, natural and principal: And the Creator hath seriously and severely given the same unto us. Only authority is of force with men of common reach and understanding; and is of more weight in a strange language. But here let us charge again. *Stultitiæ proprium quis non dixerit, ignavè et contumaciter facere quæ facienda sunt: et aliò corpus impellere, aliò animum, distrahique inter diversissimos motus? Who will not call it a property of folly to do slothfully and frowardly what is to be done, and one way to drive the body, and another way the mind, and himself to be distracted into most divers motions?* Which, the better to see, let such a man one day tell you the amusements and imaginations, which he puts into his own head, and for which he diverteth his thoughts from a good repast, and bewaileth the hour, he employeth in feeding himself: you shall find there is nothing so wallowish in all the messes of your table, as is that goodly entertainment of his mind (It were often better for us to be sound asleep, than awake unto that we do) and you shall find, that his discourses and intentions are not worth your meanest dish. Suppose they were the entrancings of Archimedes himself: and what of that? I here touch not, nor do I blend with that rabble or rascality of men, as we are, nor with that vanity of desires and cogitations, which divert us, only those venerable minds, which through a fervency of devotion and earnestness of religion, elevated to a constant and conscientious meditation of heavenly-divine things, and which by the violence of a lively, and virtue of a vehement hope, preoccupating the use of eternal soul-saving nourishment; the final end, only stay and last scope of Christian desires; the only constant delight and incorruptible pleasure; disdain to rely on our necessitous, fleeting and ambiguous commodities: and easily resign the care and use of sensual and temporal feeding unto the body. It is a privileged study. Super-celestial opinions, and under-terrestrial manners, are things, that amongst us, I have ever seen to be of singular accord. Æsope that famous man, saw his Master piss as he was walking: What (said he) must we not etc. when we are running? *Let us husband time as well as we can. Yet shall we employ much of it, both idly and ill.* As if our mind had not other hours enough to do her business, without disassociating herself from the body in that little space which she needeth for her necessity. They will be exempted from them and escape man. It is mere folly, instead of transforming themselves into Angels, they transchange themselves into beasts: in lieu of advancing, they abase themselves. Such transcending humours affright me as much, as steep, high and inaccessible places. And I find nothing so hard to be digested in Socrates' life, as his ecstasies and communication with Dæmones. Nothing so human in Plato, as that which they say, he is called divine. And of our sciences those which are raised and extolled for the highest, seem to me, the most base and terrestrial. I find nothing so humble and mortal in Alexander's life, as his concepts about his immortalization. Philotas by his answer quipped at him very pleasantly and wittily. He had by a letter congratulated with him, and rejoiced that the Oracle of Jupiter Hammon had placed him amongst the Gods; to whom he answered, that in respect and consideration of him, he was very

glad; but yet there was some cause those men should be pitied, that were to live with a man and obey him, who outwent others, and would not be contented with the state and condition of mortal man.

HOR. *Car.* iii. *Od.* vi.

Diis te minorem quod geris, imperas.

Since thou less than the Gods
Bear'st thee, thou rul'st with odds.

The quaint inscription, wherewith the Athenians honored the coming of Pompey into their City, agreeth well, and is conformable to my meaning.

PLUT. *Vit. Pomp.*

*D'autant es tu Dieu, comme
Tu te recognois homme.*

So far a God thou mayest accounted be
As thou a man dost reacknowledge thee.

It is an absolute perfection, and as it were divine for a man to know how to enjoy his being loyally. We seek for other conditions because we understand not the use of ours: and go out of ourselves, forsomuch as we know not what abiding there is. *We may long enough get upon stilts, for be we upon them, yet must we go with our own legs. And sit we upon the highest throne of the World, yet sit we upon our own tail.* The best and most commendable lives, and best pleasing men are (in my conceit) those which with order are fitted, and with *decorum* are ranged to the common mould and human model: but without wonder or extravagance. Now hath old age need to be handled more tenderly. Let us recommend it unto that God, who is the protector of health, and fountain of all wisdom: but blithe and social:

HOR. *Car.* i. *Od.* xxxi. 17.

*Frui paratis et valido mihi
Latoe dones et precor integra
Cum mente, nec turpem senectam,
Degere, nec cythara carentem.*

Apollo grant, enjoy health I may
That I have got, and with sound mind, I pray:
Nor that I may with shame spend my old years,
330 Nor wanting music to delight my ears.

JEAN BODIN

Method for the Easy Comprehension of History
Translated by Beatrice Reynolds

ON THE IDEA OF A GOLDEN AGE

. . . Once there was a golden age, afterwards a silver, then a bronze, and then an iron. At length clay followed. But this opinion must be adjusted, for if anyone examines the meaning of historians, not of poets, certainly he will decide that there is a change in human affairs similar to that in the nature of all things; nor is there anything new under the sun, as that sage master of wisdom says. The age which they call "golden," if it be compared with ours, would seem but iron. Who doubts that the flood came about through divine will on account of the sins of men, which were so many and so great that God himself was grieved that man had been created? Let us then consider the ages which followed the flood and are called "golden," not only by the poets, but also by Cato himself in his book *Of Origins*. He reported that Cameses and Saturn flourished at that time. But no one doubts that Cameses was called the son of Noah by the Hebrews; Saturn, Nimrod by the consent of all; it was his son Jupiter Belus who made an end to the golden age. From this it is plain that the golden age seemed a brief moment if an epoch of six thousand years is taken into account. Cato, following the fables of the poets, limited it to two hundred and fifty years. But how innocent was Cameses, who violated the honor of the best of parents by some new and disgraceful indignity! On this account he earned the curse of his father. It was even so in the case of Nimrod, grandson of Cameses, whom they call the founder of the golden age. What his character was is understood sufficiently from his very name, which in Hebrew means "rebel." He was termed by Moses

331 a "mighty hunter," but he used this word everywhere to indicate

robbers and wicked men, as even Aristotle placed piracy among the kinds of hunting. The next was Jupiter Belus, who with greater audacity, or shall I say impiety, hurled his aged father from power as if from a bridge. I observe there have been other Jupiters (for antiquity worshipped three hundred), but whichever is the one who drove his father from the throne, according to the poets, he is well known not only for parricide but also for all kinds of debauchery and incest with his sister. In that same era someone tried to snatch the tyranny from Jupiter. On this occasion the brothers plotted to rend the skies, and when they had built towers and ramparts, they brought an accursed war against immortal God. They tried to cast him headlong from the sky (and would have succeeded), if they had not been prevented by a thunderbolt or by the confusion of tongues which made it impossible for the rebels to cooperate. On this account the name of Babylon was given to the tower which we call also Babel.

Of course Moses to a certain extent agreed with the poets (who confused the truth of the matter with fables). Yet what significance is there in the statement that the giants bring war against the gods —other than the struggle against nature, as Cicero says?

This, then, is that golden age which produced such monsters for us. I make the same judgment about Hercules who, Manetho reported, was the greatest of the pirates. He allied Theseus and Pirithous with him in criminal association, and when they had carried off Helen and had tried to take the daughter of King Molossus from her father, he threw them into prison. The one was torn by the Cerberean hounds; the other would have been torn in a short time, if he had not been called back from the infernal regions by the prayers of Hercules, or rather if he had not been saved for crueler punishments. Furthermore, who was stronger in all kinds of lust than Hercules, or shall I say more abominable? But lest these things should seem like fables, let us rather agree with Thucydides, the most truthful father of history. He left witness that a little before his time such was the barbarity and ferocity of men in Greece itself that by land and sea piracy was openly practiced. Without any shame travelers usually asked whether those they encountered were robbers or pirates or not. Yet since fortifications did not exist at that time and there were no defenses, justice resided in force, and the old colonists were continually driven from possession by new ones. This custom in Greece little by little became permanent. Moreover, the nations farthest removed from culture lived in this savagery for a long time, as Caesar wrote about the Germans. Piracy committed beyond the frontiers of each state is considered no disgrace among the Germans, and they recommend that this practice be used to train youth and to diminish laziness. From that custom, it happened, I suppose, that robbers, who are commonly called "brigands," take their name from the Brigantini, who hold Lake Podamicus or Brigantinus, as the assassins do from that tribe of Persians which for a long time has labored under the bad reputation of being robbers and murderers. The Spartans, too, thought that there was no crime in the theft of edibles, but only in being caught stealing. Of course both opinions are more criminal than stealing, in so far as it is more wretched and base to permit freely by law anything which is wrong by nature.

These were the golden and the silver ages, in which men were scattered like beasts in the fields and the woods and had as much as they could keep by means of force and crime, until gradually they were reclaimed from that ferocity and barbarity to the refinement of customs and the law-abiding society which we see about us. Thievery, which once incurred only a civil judgment, not only according to the laws of the Hebrews but also to those of the Greeks and the Latins, now everywhere in the world is repaid by capital punishment. On the contrary, if human affairs were becoming worse, long ago we should have reached the extreme limit of vices and improbity, whither indeed I think in times gone by they had arrived.

Since wicked men cannot progress any farther or stand any longer in the same place, it becomes necessary for them to retrace their steps gradually, forced either by shame, which inheres in men naturally, or by necessity, because society can in no way be developed by such crimes, or else they are forced by the goodness of God, which is the truer solution. This, indeed, becomes plain from books of annals and records of our elders, in which so many and such dreadful enormities are reported (and yet not all) that we cannot very easily say which was the worst. The witnesses are Suetonius, Tacitus, Lampridius, and Athenaeus. What more criminal could be conceived than that the most horrible vices should be regarded as virtues? This is to be seen not only in depraved states but also in that republic which flourished under the institutions of Lycurgus and was thought most laudable by the consent of all writers. To omit the abandoned lusts of these people (Oh, that they were buried in eternal oblivion!), what is so impious as that men should be sacrificed most cruelly both at funerals and in religious rites? But this used to be done among almost all peoples. What more cruel than that the most innocent, under pretext of slavery, should be torn to bits in public spectacles, or should wound and kill each other for the delight of the people? Yet nothing was more commonplace among the Romans, who enjoyed the highest reputation for justice.

By some divine retribution, in a spectacle of gladiators at Fidenae fifty thousand persons were overwhelmed in the collapse of one amphitheater. Certainly our men, much more wisely than the Romans (may it be said with due apologies to them), eliminated from the Christian state mortal contests among human beings, as well as the bloodthirsty spectacles of wild beasts, and set up instead a fruitful and useful kind of disputation on all subjects. How much better it is, then, to be formed for the good arts and true ornament than to be trained for the gymnasium? Yet we have not omitted suitable exercises for the body or neglected military training. Our records have also their Catos, Fabricii, Camilli, Alexanders, to say nothing of the others, and Titan did not fashion their hearts of a finer clay than our own.

Was military glory greater in Alexander than in Charlemagne? The former, indeed, was great, but only against the soft Asiatics, as Caesar was wont to say about Pompey after he himself had experienced the strength of our men; the latter, our leader, conquered the most ferocious nations of Europe. Did an equal piety exist in Antoninus and in Louis the Pious? Moreover, what price of all antiquity can be compared to St. Louis the king? Omitting the laws promulgated by him upon which this kingdom rests, certainly no such devotion of any prince toward God, responsibility to his country, love toward his subjects, and justice to all have ever been recorded. Not only the virtues of our men are equal to those of the ancients but also the disciplines. Literature suffers changes of fortune. First the arts arise in some places through the practice and the labor of talented men, then they develop, later they flourish for a while at a fixed level, then languish in their old age, and finally begin to die and are buried in a lasting oblivion by the eternal calamity of wars, or because too great abundance (an evil much to be feared in these times, of course) brings satiety to the frivolous, or because God inflicts just punishments upon those who direct useful knowledge to the ruin of men. Although disciplines had gradually developed among the Greeks, so that they believed these arts had reached their peak, such a change came about afterward that Greece herself, to judge from her present predicament, seems never to have existed.

What of the Latins? Among them talented men were so abundant that almost simultaneously they excelled all peoples in warlike glory and in superiority of culture. Yet by a similar fall they also started to lapse into their early barbarity when the forces of the Scythians, pouring into Italy, burned the well-stocked libraries almost everywhere and all the monuments of antiquity. This horrible deed destroyed all disciplines, so that for about a thousand years they lay prostrate without any prestige and indeed seemed to be dying, until Mansur, prince of Africa and Spain, stirred up the talents of the Arabs with offers of great rewards for the revival of letters. I omit how Egypt, India, and Ethiopia teemed with many philosophers, geometrists, and astrologers; how many well-known mathematicians were in Chaldea before Greece had any literature. I come back to our times in which, after a long eclipse of letters throughout almost the entire world, suddenly such a wealth of knowledge shone forth, such fertility of talents existed, as no age ever excelled.

Not even the Goths themselves have lacked the finest talents in modern times. Olaus Magnus is an evidence of this, as well as Holster and many others, as if nature had decreed that the wounds of knowledge should now be healed by those very people who once inflicted them. Although until recently they retained the custom of their ancestors and the voice of a herald ordered men of letters to depart from the senate (for we have evidence of this in their history), now everywhere they are wont to cultivate letters. This is so definite a change in all respects that no one ought to doubt that the same process occurs in human talent as in the fields, which are wont to repay with greater abundance the privilege of lying fallow. Some one will say, however, that the ancients were inventors of the arts and to them the glory ought to go. They certainly did discover many things—especially the power of the celestial bodies, the calculated courses of many stars—but yet not all—the wonderful trajections of fixed stars and of those called "planets." Then they noted carefully the obscurities of nature and explained many things accurately, and yet they left incomplete many of these things which have been completed and handed down to posterity by men of our time. No one, looking closely into this matter, can doubt that the discoveries of our men ought to be compared with the discoveries of our elders; many ought to be placed first. Although nothing is more remarkable in the whole nature of things than the magnet, yet the ancients were not aware of its use, clearly divine, and whereas they lived entirely within the Mediterranean basin, our men, on the other hand, traverse the whole earth every year in frequent voyages and lead colonies into another world, as I might say, in order to open up the farthest recesses of India. Not only has this discovery developed an abundant and profitable commerce (which formerly was insignificant or not well known) but also all men surprisingly work together in a world state, as if in one and same city-state. Indeed, in geography, one of the most excellent arts, one may understand how much advance has been made from the fact that information about India which used to seem fabulous to many (for Lactantius and Augustine said that men who believed in the antipodes were

335

crazy) have been verified by us, as well as the motion of the fixed stars and the trepidation of the great sphere. Moreover, what is more remarkable than that abstraction and separation of forms from matter (if I may speak thus)? From this the hidden secrets of nature are revealed; hence healthful medicines are daily brought forward. I pass over the method of investigating celestial longitude from equal hours, which could not be calculated by the ancients from the normal to the ecliptic without great error. I will not dwell upon the catapults of our ancestors and the ancient engines of war, which, of course, seem like some boyish toy if compared with our [instruments]. I omit finally countless arts, both handicraft and weaving, with which the life of man has been aided in a remarkable way. Printing alone can easily vie with all the discoveries of all the ancients.

So they who say that all things were understood by the ancients err not less than do those who deny them the early conquest of many arts. Nature has countless treasures of knowledge which cannot be exhausted in any age. Since these things are so and since by some eternal law of nature the path of change seems to go in a circle, so that vices press upon virtues, ignorance upon knowledge, base upon honorable, and darkness upon light, they are mistaken who think that the race of men always deteriorates. When old men err in this respect, it is understandable that this should happen to them—that they sigh for the loss of the flower of youth, which of itself breathes joy and cheerfulness. When they see themselves deprived of every kind of delight and instead of pleasure they feel sharp pains, instead of having unimpaired senses, they suffer weakness in all their members, it happens that they fall to these sad meditations and, deceived by the false picture of things, think that loyalty and friendship of man for man has died. As though returning from a distant journey, they narrate the golden century— the golden age—to the young men. But then their experience is the same as that of men carried out of port into the open sea—they think the houses and the towns are departing from them; thus they think that delight, gentle conduct, and justice have flown to the heavens and deserted the earth.

BONAVENTURE DES PÉRIERS

Cymbalum Mundi,
The Third Dialogue
Anonymous translation

Cupid: Who's that there? Ha! your servant Mercury, is that you?
Pray what news? What good tidings from above in your celestial
court? Is Jupiter still amorous?

Mercury: Amorous! Yes, by the d—l. He does not meddle much
that way at present; but the remembrance of his amours is now
very troublesome and uneasy to him.

Cupid: Why so?

Mercury: Because these rogues of mortals have made a book, which
I unluckily brought him instead of his own, into which he always
look'd, when he was about to order any thing to be done, which
I went to get bound for him; but it was chang'd. I am now going
to have it cry'd by sound of trumpet, that so if any body has it,
he may give it back. He cou'd have eat me for it.

Cupid: I think I heard somebody speak of the most wonderful
book that ever was, which two blades are in possession of, by
which, (as they say) they tell fortunes, and can guess what is to
come, as well as ever Tiresias did, or the Oak of Dodona. Several
astrologers wou'd fain have it, or purchase a copy of it. For they
say, that by the help of it, they cou'd make their ephemerides,
prognostications, and almanacks, a great deal more true and
exact. Moreover, these sparks promise to enrol people in the
Book of Immortality, for a certain sum of money.

Mercury: Indeed? 'sbuddikins, that is the book, or I'm a rogue. I
and afraid of nothing, but that they insert in it usurers, grinders
of the poor, villains, and thieves, and blot out honest people,
because they have not wherewithal to bribe them. Jupiter will
have a fine time on't, by the d—l. And where can I meet with
them?

Cupid: I can't inform you; for I am not curious in such matters. I mind nothing but my little sports and pleasures, and merry diversions, and how to entertain these young damsels. To play at hide and seek in the little apartment of their hearts, which I prick with my light arrows, to flutter in their little brains, tickle their tender fancies, and delicate soft bellies; to shew myself, and take my walks before their wanton eyes; to kiss and suck their vermilion lips, to slide betwixt their little hard bubbies, from whence I steal into the Valley of Pleasure, where is the Fountain of Youth, in which I play, refresh and recreate myself, and make my happy abode.

Mercury: Your mother gave me a memorandum here, to mind you of somewhat. Here you may look into it at your leisure, and perform the contents; for I am in great haste. Adieu.

Cupid: Very well, very well, 'Squire Mercury.

Mercury: 'sbud! you'll pull off my winged shoes: let me go, I intreat you, Cupid; I am not so playsome as you.

Cupid: Tho' I'm young and in life's spring
Think me not unfit for man:
I can better do the thing
Than an older body can.

Mercury: Ha! you have a good time on't, you are not concern'd whether it rains or snows, as our Jupiter is, who has lost his book that should inform him of such things.

Cupid: Tho' it thunder from above,
As Heav'n and Earth wou'd come together,
Still it shall go well with love:
Lovers still shall have good weather.

Mercury: Yes, yes, all goes well with us.

Cupid: Who is that pretty girl, I see below in an orchard all alone? Is not she in love yet? I must look her in the face. No; and yet I know that her admirer dyes for love of her. Ha! you shall be in love, fair lady, without mercy, before I go three paces.

Celia: O ingrate, that I am! What pain is he in at this minute, for love of me? Now I know (but alas! it is too late) that the power of love is wonderfully great, and that none can escape the vengeance of it. Am not I much to blame, thus to despise and deny him who loves me so much, even more than he does himself? Shall I always be as insensible as a statue of marble? Shall I always live thus without society? Alas! 'tis all to be laid at my door; 'tis my fault and foolish fancy alone. Ha! my little birds, how well you sing, and teach me my lesson! How good a mother Nature is, thus to teach me by your little songs, and play, that all creatures must have their mates! I wou'd only make one request to you, and that is, that you importune me no more by your little gibberidge; for I too well understand what you mean; and that you no more shew me the bewitching spectacle of your amorous encounters. That can never comfort me, but rather make me esteem myself the most unhappy creature in the world. Alas! When will my dear come again? I'm afraid, I have been so ill-natur'd and savage to him, that he'll never return any more! He will, if he lov'd me as much, or continues yet to love me as much as I love him at present. I long extremely to see him. If ever he comes again, I'll be more civil to him, and give him a kinder welcome, a more favourable reception, and better treatment than ever I did hitherto.

Cupid: Now the good lady is in a right temper; she has got what she wanted.

Mercury: Is not this a hard case? whether I come to the Earth, or return to Heaven; the world, and the gods always ask me, whether I have heard any news. One wou'd need an ocean, to fish fresh news for them every day. I'll tell you; that the world may forge some, and that I may have some to carry up with me, I am going, this minute, to make that horse there speak to his groom. This will be news, or the Devil's in't. Gargabonado, Phorbantas, Sarmotoragos. O, what have I done? I had almost spoke aloud the words which must be pronounc'd to make beasts speak. I am very foolish, when I think on't. If I had said all, and if any body here had heard me, he might have got that science.

Phlegon: Time was when beasts spoke. But if speech had been preserv'd to us, as well as it was to you, you shou'd not have found us such beasts as you make us.

Statius: What the d—l's to do here? Z—ds, my horse speaks!

Phlegon: Yes, to be sure, I speak: And wherefore not? You men (because speech has been preserv'd to you alone, and we poor beasts have no intelligence among ourselves, because we cannot speak) know well how to usurp authority and command over us, and not only say of us whatever you please, but also get upon our backs, whip us and spur us: We must carry you, we must cloathe you, we must feed you, you sell us, you kill us, you eat us; and whence comes all this? This comes only from our want of speech. But if we could speak, and tell our reason, you are so humane, or at least you ought to be so, that after hearing us speak, you would treat us after another manner, or else I'm mistaken.

Statius: 'sb—d! There never was so strange a thing heard of as this. Good people, come and hear this wonder, I intreat you, or else you won't believe it; Z—ds! my horse speaks!

Ardelio: What's yonder to do? Who do the people run and meet in such crowds? I must go and see what's the matter there.

Statius: Dost not know, Ardelio? 'sbuddikins! my horse speaks!

Ardelio: Say'st thou so? That's wonderful indeed! But what says he?

Statius: I don't know, for I'm so amaz'd to hear words come from such a mouth, that I understand nothing he says.

Ardelio: Have courage, and let us hear him discourse a little. Keep back, gentlemen, if you please, make room; you'll see as well at a distance, as near at hand.

Statius: But now what dost mean, pretty beast, by thy talking?

Phlegon: Good people, since Mercury has been pleas'd to restore my speech, and since you are pleas'd to spare so much time from your affairs, to come and hear the cause of such a poor animal as I am; you must know, that this groom of mine gives me all the hard usage possible, and not only beats me, spurs me, and lets me die of hunger, but——

Statius: I let you die of hunger?

Phlegon: Yes, you let me die of hunger.

Statius: 'sdeath! you lye, and if you maintain this, I'll cut your throat, Egad.

Ardelio: You shall not do it, by the d—l; wou'd you be so bold as to kill a horse that speaks? He is to be made a present of to King Ptolemy; and will be the finest ever was made: And I tell you freely, all the treasure of Crœsus cou'd not purchase him. Therefore, consider well what you do, and touch not a hair of him, if you are wise.

Statius: Why do's he say what's not true then?

Phlegon: Don't you remember, that last time you receiv'd money, to defray the charges of four horses of us, that you made your account thus? *You have abundance of hay and straw, eat heartily of them, you shall have only so much oats, the rest shall be to go and feast with my mistress.*

Statius: Thou hadst better never spoke; never trouble thyself.

Phlegon: I am not concern'd a straw for all this. But when I meet with a mare, in that month when we are in love (which happens only once a year) he will not let me mount her, tho' I let him get upon me so many times a day. You men wou'd have one law for yourselves, and another for your neighbours. You are very well contented to take all your natural pleasures, but you will not let others take them, namely us beasts. How often have I seen thee bring thy doxies into the stable to lie with thee? How often have I been oblig'd to be a witness of thy fine management? I wou'd not desire you to let me bring mares into the stable for myself, as you bring your doxies: But when we go into the fields, you might allow me to give one little stroke at least, in the season. He has rid me these six years, and yet he has not allow'd me to ride so much as once in all that time.

Ardelio: Egad! Thou art in the right, friend; thou art the most gentle horse, and the noblest beast that ever was seen. Hold there. I have a mare at thy service. I will lend her thee with all my heart, because thou art a good fellow, and hast a mind to her. Thou shalt do with her as thou wilt; and for my part, I shou'd be very glad and well pleas'd to have some of thy posterity; if it were but to have it to say; that, *this is of the race of the horse that spoke.*

Statius: 'sbuddikins! I'll take care to prevent that, since you have been so forward in speaking. Come, come along, think of trotting briskly, and don't play the jade, if you are wise, lest I drive you on with this stick.

Ardelio: Adieu, adieu, I see you are heartily vex'd at what the horse told you.

Statius: 'sdeath! I'll fit him soundly for it, when I get him to the stable, let him be as good a speech-maker as he will.

Ardelio: I shou'd never have believ'd a horse cou'd speak, if I had not both heard and seen it. This horse is worth a hundred thousand crowns! He cannot be valu'd too much. I'll go and tell the story to Mr. Cerdonius, who will not forget to put it into his Annals.

Mercury: Here is some news already, or I'm mistaken. I'm glad there was so goodly a company, bless'd be G—, who have both heard and seen the adventure. The noise of it will be thro' the whole town presently. Somebody will put it into writing, and perhaps add something of his own to it, to enrich the story. I'm sure I'll find a copy of it to be sold presently at the Booksellers. In the mean time, till some other news come, I'll go about my commissions, and especially to seek for the city trumpet, to cry if any person has found that devil of a book.

PIERRE CHARRON

A Treatise on Wisdom
Translated by Myrtilla H. N. Daly

INCONSTANCY

Man is, of all creatures, the most difficult to sound and know. He is dual and artificial, and there are in him so many cabinets and dark corners from which he comes forth, sometimes a man, sometimes a satyr; in his actions is a perpetual race of errors; sometimes a god, sometimes a fly; he laughs and weeps for one and the same thing (as the extremity of laughter is mingled with tears); content and discontent; he will and he will not, and in the end knows not what he will; now he is filled with such joy and gladness that he cannot stay within his own skin, and presently he falls out with himself and dares not trust himself.

For the most part men's actions are nothing but impulses, induced by occasions and that have reference to others. Irresolution, inconstancy, and instability are the most common and apparent vices in the nature of man. We follow our inclinations, and as the wind of occasion carries us, not governed by reason.

Constancy, which is a stayed resolution, is always maintained by the wise, in whom the will is governed and subject to the rule of reason, and not by fleeting, inconstant opinions which are commonly false.

MISERY

"Man born of a woman hath but a short time to live, and is full
342 of misery"; sorrow is the only true evil man is wholly born to, and

it is his natural property. The Mexicans thus salute their new-born infants, "Infant, thou art come into the world to suffer. Endure, suffer, and hold thy peace." The empire of sorrow is far greater than that of pleasure. Evil comes of itself without seeking; pleasure must be sought after, and many times we pay more for it than it is worth. Pleasure is not always unalloyed, and there is always something wanting; grief is often entire and absolute, and the greatest pleasures touch us not so nearly as the lightest sorrows. We are not so conscious of our sound health as of the least malady. It is not enough that man is by nature miserable, and that besides substantial evils he forges false ones; but he causes both the true and false to endure longer than necessary by the remembrance of what is past, and in the anticipation of that which is to come. The fearful, and sometimes false apprehension of evils which may come, afflict and darken, as with smoke, all the beauty and serenity of the soul. Let us leave this anticipation of evil, for there is misery in every painful thought, and we have no power over that which is to come, and much less over what is past.

The world has three sorts of people in it who take up much room and carry great sway, both in number and reputation: the superstitious, the formalists, and the pedants, and notwithstanding they differ in opinions they are all of one stamp; they are dangerous people and afflicted with an incurable disease. It is lost labor to try to persuade them to change their minds, for they account themselves the best and wisest in the world. Opinionative obstinacy is there in its proper seat, and for him who is stricken with these evils there is little hope of recovery.

The superstitious are enemies of true religion; they cover themselves with the cloak of piety, zeal, and love toward God, tormenting and punishing themselves more than is needful, thinking thereby to merit much, and that God is not only pleased but indebted to them.

The formalists do nothing against the tenor of the law, and fashion their lives to outward forms, thinking to be free from blame in following their desires, by omitting no outward observance. The rule of duty extends beyond the rule of law. How many good works have been omitted, how many evils committed under the cloak of forms. And therefore it is very truly said that the extremity of the law is the extremity of wrong.

The pedants, with great study and pains filch from other men's writings their learning, and set it out to view with ostentation. Are there any people in the world so foolish in their affairs, more unskilful in everything, and yet so presumptuous and obstinate? They have their memories stuffed with the wisdom of other men, and have

343

none of their own; and it seems their learning serves for no other purpose than to make them arrogant prattlers.

HONESTY

Honesty is the first principle of wisdom. All applaud it whether truthfully or but outwardly, and confess themselves its servants and affectionate followers. It will be difficult to show that true and essential probity we here require. Actions of virtue are many times nothing but masks, they carry the outward countenance but have not the essence. Therefore to know which is the true honesty, we must not look at the outward action, that is but the sign and simplest token, and often a cloak to cover villainy; we must penetrate into the inward part, and know the motive which causes the strings to vibrate, which is the soul and life that gives motion to all.

There are men, honest through accident and occasion, and not in spirit and truth; it is easy to discover them by their want of stability, and by sounding them, for in one and the same action they will give various opinions. This instability proceeds from outward influences which easily move and stir them.

The true honesty which I require in him who will be wise, is free, manly, and generous, uniform and consistent. Every man should be, or should desire to be an honest man, because he is a man; and he who cares not to be such is a monster. It is necessary that honesty should grow in man, by that inward instinct which is God-given, not from any outward cause or inducement.

A man desires to have all his possessions good and sound, his body, judgment, and memory, even his hose and his shoes, and why will he not likewise have his will and conscience good?

What though a man does not receive recompense for his honesty, what can concern him so much as his own character? This is, as it were, not to care how bad the horse is so the saddle is good. If a man is honest for honor or reputation, from fear of the law or punishment, there is an end of his honesty. I would have him good, firm, and honest for the love of himself, because it is absolutely required of him by nature. And the pattern for honesty he will find in this nature itself, which is the universal reason that shines in every one of us. He that works according to it works truly according to God, for it is God, or at least His fundamental law that has brought it into the world. God and nature are in the world as in a state the king,—the author, and founder, and the fundamental law for the preservation and government of the state.

344   Nature is a ray of light from the Divinity, a stream and depend-

ence of the eternal law which is God Himself and His Will. Behold in us, then, an essential, radical, and fundamental honesty, growing in us from its own roots, from the seed of that universal reason which is in the soul, maintaining itself strong and invincible, by which a man works according to God, nature, and the universal order of the world.

"All goodness is natural, vice unnatural."

True honesty is a right and firm disposition of the will to follow the counsels of reason; and as the mariner's needle never rests until it points towards the north, and thus directs aright, so man is never tranquil until he sees this and directs the course of his life, manners, judgment, and will according to the Divine natural law, which is an inward light whereof all others are but beams. To perfect our work we still need the grace of God by which life is given to honesty, goodness, and virtue.

Honesty in the soul is like a good organist, whose touch is true and according to art; the grace and spirit of God is the blast which gives life to the touch, and makes the instrument speak with pleasant melodies.

This last good does not consist in long discourses, precepts, and instructions, neither is it attained by our own act or labor; it is a free gift from above, and so we call it grace. But we must desire it, and ask for it both humbly and ardently. O God, vouchsafe of Thy infinite goodness to look upon me with the eye of Thy clemency, to accept my desire and my work, which Thou hast implanted, to the end that it may return to Thee, and that Thou mayst finish what Thou hast begun, and so be both my Alpha and my Omega. Sprinkle me with Thy grace, keep me and account me Thine.

The true remedy by which we are cleansed and healed of our sin, is a serious and modest confession of our faults; excuse is a remedy invented by the author of evil. There is a proverb which says, "Sin makes itself a garment, but it is without warmth."

Religion consists in the knowledge of God and of ourselves, and the office of religion is to join us to the Author and Giver of all good; and so long as we continue firm in our confidence in God we are preserved, but when He is separated from us we faint and languish. We must be sincere, obedient, and kind, if we would be fit to receive religion, and to believe and live under the law. By reverence and obedience we should subject our judgment, and suffer ourselves to be led by authority, "submitting our understanding to the obedience of faith."

MIDDLE AND
EASTERN EUROPE

JUSTUS LIPSIUS

MARTIN LUTHER

JOHN CALVIN

DESIDERIUS ERASMUS

CORNELIUS AGRIPPA

PARACELSUS

ANDREAS VESALIUS

NIKOLAUS COPERNICUS

JOHANNES KEPLER AND GALILEO GALILEI

JUSTUS
LIPSIUS

Two Books of Constancy
Translated by Sir John Stradling, Modernized

First *That travelling into foreign countries is not available against the*
Book *inward maladies of the mind: That it is a testimony of them, but not*
Chapter *a remedy against them, except only in slight and first motions of the*
Two *affection.* Langius beckoning somewhat with his head: I hear you
(Lipsius) but I had rather you would hearken to the voice of
wisdom and reason. For these mists and clouds that thus compass
you, do proceed from the smoke of OPINIONS. Wherefore, I say with
Diogenes, You have more need of reason, than of a rope. That
bright beam of reason (I mean) which may illuminate the obscurity
of your brain. Behold, you forsake your country: Tell me in good
sooth, in forsaking it, can you forsake yourself also? See that the
contrary fall not out: And that whithersoever you go, you carry not
in your breast the fountain and food of your own grief. As they that
be holden with a fever, do toss and turn themselves unquietly, and
often change their beds through a vain hope of remedy: In like
case are we, who being sick in our minds do without any fruit,
wander from one country to another. This is indeed to bewray our
grief, but not to allay it. To discover this inward flame, but not to
quench it: very fitly said that wise Roman: *It is proper to a sick*
person not to suffer any thing long, but to use mutations instead of
medicines: Hereof proceed wandering peregrinations, and walkings
on sundry shores: And our INCONSTANCY, *always loathing things*
present, one whiles will be upon the sea, and incontinent desires the
land. Therefore you fly from troubles always, but never escape them,
not unlike the Hind that Virgil speaks of,

Whom ranging through the chase, some hunter shooting far by chance
All unaware hath smit, and in her side hath left his lance,
She fast to wilderness and woods doth draw, and there complains,

but all in vain: because as the Poet adds,

—That underneath her ribs the deadly dart remains. So you that are wounded with this dart of affections, do not shake it out, but in travelling carry it with you to another place. He that has broken his thigh or his arm, lists not, I trow, to go on horseback, or into his chariot, but to a Surgeon: And what madness is this in you, to seek remedy of this inward wound by motion, and trudging from place to place?

It is the mind that is wounded, and all this external imbecility, dispair & languishing, springs from this fountain, that the mind is thus prostrated and cast down. The principal and sovereign part has let fall the Scepter, and is become so vile and abject, that it willingly serves his own servants. Tell me, what good can any place or peregrination work in this case? Except happily there be some region in the world which can temper fear, bridle hope, and draw out these evil dregs of vice, which we have sucked from our infancy. But none such is there, no not in the fortunate Islands: Or if there be, show it unto us, and we will all hasten thither in troupes.

But you will say, that the self-mutation and change, has that force in it: And that the daily beholding of strange fashions, men and places does refresh and lighten the mind loaded with oppressions. No (Lipsius) you are deceived. For, to tell you the truth plainly, I do not so much derogate from peregrination and travelling, as though it bare no sway over men and their affections: yes verily, it avails, but yet thus far, to the expelling of some small tediousness and weariness of our minds, not to the curing of maladies rooted so deeply, as that these external medicines cannot pluck them up. Music, wine, and sleep have oftentimes quenched the first enkindled sparks of anger, sorrow, and love: But never weeded out any settled or deep rooted grief. Likewise I say, that travelling might perhaps cure superficial scars, but not substantial sores. For, these first motions having their original from the body, do stick in the body, or at the most do but cleave to the utter velm of the mind (as a man may say). And therefore no marvel is it, though with a sponge they be lightly washed away: Otherwise it is of old festered affections, which hold their seat, yea & scepter in the castle of the mind. When you have gone far, and wandered every sea and shore, you shall neither drown them in the deep sea, nor bury them in the bowels of the earth. They will follow you at an inch: And (as the Poet says) foul care will sit close in the skirts of footman and horseman.

One demanding of Socrates how it came to pass that his travelling did him no good. Because (said he) you forsook not yourself. So say I, that withersoever you flee, you carry with you a corrupt mind, no good companion. And I would to God he were but as your companion, I fear lest he be your captain, in that your affections follow not you, but you them.

Chapter *Examples of necessary alteration, or death in the whole world. That*
Sixteen *heaven and the elements are changed, and shall perish: the like is to be seen in towns, provinces and kingdoms, Finally, that all things here do turn about the wheel: And that nothing is stable or constant.* It is an eternal decree, pronounced of the world from the beginning, and of all things therein, to be born & to die; to begin and end. That supreme Judge of all things, would have nothing firm and stable but himself alone, as says the tragic Poet.

From age and death God only standeth free,
But all things else by time consumed be.

All these things which you behold and admire, either shall perish in their due time, or at least be altered and changed: See you the Sun? He faints. The Moon? She labours and languishes. The Stars? They fail and fall. And howsoever the wit of man cloaks and excuses these matters, yet there have happened and daily do in that celestial body such things as confound both the rules and wits of the Mathematicians. I omit Comets strange in form, situation and motion, which all the universities shall never persuade me to be in the air, or of the air. But behold our Astrologers were sore troubled of late with strange motions, and new stars. This very year there arose a star whose increasing and decreasing was plainly marked, and we saw (a matter hardly to be credited) even in the heaven itself, a thing to have beginning and end again. And Varro (in Augustine) cries out and affirms, that *the Evening star called of Plantus* Vesperûgo, *and of Homer Hesperus, had changed his colour, his bigness, his fashion, & his course.* Next unto the heaven, behold the Air, it is altered daily and passes into winds, clouds, and showers. Go to the waters. Those floods and fountains which we affirm to be perpetual, do sometimes fail altogether, and otherwhiles change their channel and ordinary course. The huge Ocean (a great and secret part of nature) is ever tossed and tumbled with tempests: and if they be wanting, yet has it his flowing and ebbing of waters, & that we may perceive it to be subject to decay, it swells & swages daily in his parts.

Behold also the earth which is taken to be immovable, and to stand steady of her own force: it faints and is stricken with an inward secret blast that makes it to tremble: Some where it is cor-

rupted by the water, other where by fire. For these same things do
strive among themselves: Neither grudge you to see war among
men, there is likewise between the Elements. What great lands
have been wasted, yea wholly swallowed up by sudden deluges, and
violent overflowings of the sea? In old time the sea overwhelmed
wholly a great Island called Atlantis (I think not the story fabulous)
and after that the mighty cities Helice and Bura. But to leave ancient
examples, in our own fathers' age, here in Belgica two Islands with
the towns and men in them. And even now in our time this Lord of
the sea Neptune opens to himself new gaps, and swipes up daily the
weak banks of Frizeland and other countries. Yet does not the earth
sit still like a slothful housewife, but sometimes revenges herself,
and makes new Islands in the mids of the sea, though Neptune
marvel and be moved thereat. And if these great bodies which to
us seem everlasting, be subject to mutability and alteration, why
much more should not towns, common-wealths, and kingdoms;
which must needs be mortal, as they that do compose them? As
each particular man has his youth, his strength, old age, and
death. So fares it with those other bodies. They begin, they increase,
they stand and flourish, and all to this end, that they may decay.
One earthquake under the reign of Tiberius overthrew twelve
famous towns of Asia. And as many in Campania in Constantine's
time. One war of Attila a Scythian prince destroyed above a hundred cities. The ancient Thebes of Egypt is scarce held in remembrance at this day: And a hundred towns of Crete not believed
ever to have been. To come to more certainty, our Elders saw the
ruins of Carthage, Numantia, Corinth, and wondered thereat. And
ourselves have beheld the unworthy relics of Athens, Sparta, and
many renowned cities, yea even that Lady of all things and countries
(falsely termed everlasting) where is she? Overwhelmed, pulled
down, burned over-flowed: She is perished with more than one kind
of destruction, and at this day she is ambitiously sought for, but not
found in her proper soil. See you that noble Byzantium being proud
with the seat of two Empires? Venice lifted up with the stableness of
a thousand years' continuance? Their day shall come at length. And
you also our Antwerp, the beauty of cities, in time shall come to
nothing. For this great Master-builder pulls down, sets up, and
(if I may so lawfully speak) makes a sport of human affairs: And
like an Image-maker, forms and frames to himself sundry sorts of
portraitures in his clay.

I have spoken yet of towns and cities: Countries likewise and
kingdoms run the very same race. Once the East flourished: Assyria, Egypt and Jewry excelled in war and peace. That glory was
transferred into Europe, which now (like a diseased body) seems

unto me to be shaken, and to have a feeling of her great confusion nigh at hand. Yea, and that which is more (and never enough) to be marvelled at, this world having now been inhabited these five thousand and five hundred years, is at length come to his dotage: And that we may now approve again the fables of Anarxarchus in old time hissed at, behold now there arise elsewhere new people, & a new world: O the law of NECESSITY, wonderful, and not to be comprehended: All things run into this fatal whirlpool of ebbing and flowing: And some things in this world are long lasting, but not everlasting.

Lift up your eyes and look about with me (for it grieves me not to stand long upon this point) and behold the alterations of all human affairs: and the swelling and swaging of them as of the sea: Arise: fall: rule: obey: hide your head: lift up yours and let this wheel of changeable things run round, so long as this round world remains. Have you Germans in time past been fierce? Be you now milder than most people of Europe. Have you Britons been uncivil heretofore? Now exceed you the Egyptians and people of Sybaris in delights & riches. Has Greece once flourished? Now let her be afflicted. Has Italy swayed the scepter? Now let her be in subjection. You Goths, you Vandals, you vilest of the Barbarians, peep you out of your lurking holes, and come rule the nations in your turn. Draw near you rude Scythians, and with a mighty hand hold you a while the reins of Asia and Europe: yet you again soon after give place, and yield up the scepter to another nation bordering on the Ocean. Am I deceived? or else do I see the sun of a new Empire arising in the West?

Second Book Chapter Twenty *Now we come to comparison. And first of all the misery of the Low-countries and of this our age, is exaggerated. That opinion is generally confuted. And it is declared how that the natural disposition of men is prone to augment their own griefs.* This earnest & grave communication of Langius was nothing answerable to my hope or expectation: Wherefore interrupting him, whither now? (quoth I.) Was this your promise to me? I expected the sweet wine and honeycombs of histories: But you serve me with such sour sauce, as there is none more sharp among all the store of philosophy. What? Do you think that you have to do with some Thales? No, no: Now you have Lipsius in hand, who as he is a man, and of the Common sort of men: So he desires remedies somewhat more spiced with humanity, than these be. Then said Langius with a mild voice 353 and countenance, I confess indeed I am worthy of blame. For in following the bright beams of reason, I see myself to have strayed out of the high way and declined unwares into the path of wisdom again. But now I will amend the matter, and return to hold on my course in a more familiar known trade-way. Does the sharpness of the wine that I broached, dislike you? I will sweeten it with the honey of examples. Now therefore I come to COMPARISONS, and will prove evidently that there is nothing grievous or great in all these evils which do now about everywhere, if we compare them with those of old time. For in times past the same have been far more heinous and lamentable than now. Hereat I once again more eagerly than before replied: What? Say you so indeed? *And think you to bring me into that belief?* No (Langius) not so long as there is any sense in my head. For what age past, if you examine the matter rightly, has at any time been so miserable as this ours, Or ever shall be? What country, what region has suffered, *So many things grievous to be spoken of and rigorous to be endured,* As we Flemmings do at this day? We are shaken to and from with wars not only foreign, but civil: And not such only, but intestine dissentions even within our own bowels. For there be not only parties among us, but new parties of these same parties. (Alas my dear country what Safety can save you?) Add hereto pestilence, and famine, tributes, rapines, slaughters: Also the uttermost extremity of tyranny; And oppressions not of bodies only, but also of the minds. And what is there in other parts of Europe? war, or fear of war: And if any peace be, it is joined with shameful servitude under petty-lords, and no better at all than any kind of war. Whithersoever we cast our eyes or cogitations, all things hang in suspense and suspicion. And (as it were in an old ruinous house) there be many tokens of falling down. In fine (Langius) like as all rivers run into the Sea: So it seems that all misfortunes are fallen upon this present age. I speak only of those evils which are in action, and now presently tossing us. What need I make mention of such as hang over our heads? To which I may truly apply that saying of Euripides:

I see so great a sea of evils nigh at hand,
So that it seems a matter hard, safely to swim to land.

Langius turning himself towards me angrily, and as it were with intent to rebuke me; What? Do you yet again cast yourself down by these querulous complaints? I thought you had stood fast like a man, and I see you fall: That your wounds had been quite closed up, but I perceive you do open them again. Howbeit you must be endued with contentation of mind, if you will be in perfect health.

354   You say, this age is the unhappiest that ever was. This has been

an old lay long agone used. I know your grandfather said so, and likewise your father. I know also that your children and children's children will sing the same note. It is a thing naturally given unto men to cast their eyes narrowly upon all things that be grievous, but to wink at such as be pleasant. As flies & such like vile creatures do never rest long upon smooth & fine polished places, but do stick fast to rough and filthy corners: So the murmuring mind does lightly pass over the consideration of all good fortune, but never forgets the adverse or evil. It handles and pries into that, yea and oftentimes augments it with a great wit. Like as Lovers do always behold somewhat in their mistress whereby they think her to excel all others: Even so do men that mourn, in their miseries. Yea moreover we imagine things that be false, and bewail not only things present, but also such as be to come. And what gain we by this forereaching wit of ours? Surely nothing else, but that as some espying afar off the dust raised by an army, do thereupon forsake their tents for fear: So the vain shadow of future danger casts us down into the pit of desperation.

MARTIN LUTHER

Concerning Christian Liberty
Translated by R. S. Grignon

Christian faith has appeared to many an easy thing; nay, not a few
even reckon it among the social virtues, as it were; and this they do
because they have not made proof of it experimentally, and have
never tasted of what efficacy it is. For it is not possible for any man
to write well about it, or to understand well what is rightly written,
who has not at some time tasted of its spirit, under the pressure of
tribulation; while he who has tasted of it, even to a very small extent,
can never write, speak, think, or hear about it sufficiently. For it is a
living fountain, springing up unto eternal life, as Christ calls it in
John iv.

Now, though I cannot boast of my abundance, and though I know
how poorly I am furnished, yet I hope that, after having been vexed
by various temptations, I have attained some little drop of faith, and
that I can speak of this matter, if not with more elegance, certainly
with more solidity, than those literal and too subtle disputants who
have hitherto discoursed upon it without understanding their own
words. That I may open then an easier way for the ignorant—for
these alone I am trying to serve—I first lay down these two propositions, concerning spiritual liberty and servitude:—

A Christian man is the most free lord of all, and subject to none;
a Christian man is the most dutiful servant of all, and subject to
every one.

Although these statements appear contradictory, yet, when they
are found to agree together, they will make excellently for my
purpose. They are both the statements of Paul himself, who says,
"Though I be free from all men, yet have I made myself servant unto
all" (1 COR. *ix. 19*), and "Owe no man anything, but to love one
another" (ROM. *xiii. 8*). Now love is by its own nature dutiful and

356

obedient to the beloved object. Thus even Christ, though Lord of all things, was yet made of a woman; made under the law; at once free and a servant; at once in the form of God and in the form of a servant.

Let us examine the subject on a deeper and less simple principle. Man is composed of a twofold nature, a spiritual and a bodily. As regards the spiritual nature, which they name the soul, he is called the spiritual, inward, new man; as regards the bodily nature, which they name the flesh, he is called the fleshly, outward, old man. The Apostle speaks of this: "Though our outward man perish, yet the inward man is renewed day by day" (2 COR. iv. 16). The result of this diversity is that in the Scriptures opposing statements are made concerning the same man, the fact being that in the same man these two men are opposed to one another; the flesh lusting against the spirit, and the spirit against the flesh (GAL. v. 17).

We first approach the subject of the inward man, that we may see by what means a man becomes justified, free, and a true Christian; that is, a spiritual, new, and inward man. It is certain that absolutely none among outward things, under whatever name they may be reckoned, has any influence in producing Christian righteousness or liberty, nor, on the other hand, unrighteousness or slavery. This can be shown by an easy argument.

What can it profit the soul that the body should be in good condition, free, and full of life; that it should eat, drink, and act according to its pleasure; when even the most impious slaves of every kind of vice are prosperous in these matters? Again, what harm can ill-health, bondage, hunger, thirst, or any other outward evil, do to the soul, when even the most pious of men, and the freest in the purity of their conscience, are harassed by these things? Neither of these states of things has to do with the liberty or the slavery of the soul.

And so it will profit nothing that the body should be adorned with sacred vestments, or dwell in holy places, or be occupied in sacred offices, or pray, fast, and abstain from certain meats, or do whatever works can be done through the body and in the body. Something widely different will be necessary for the justification and liberty of the soul, since the things I have spoken of can be done by any impious person, and only hypocrites are produced by devotion to these things. On the other hand, it will not at all injure the soul that the body should be clothed in profane raiment, should dwell in profane places, should eat and drink in the ordinary fashion, should not pray aloud, and should leave undone all the things above mentioned, which may be done by hypocrites.

357   And, to cast everything aside, even speculations, meditations, and

whatever things can be performed by the exertions of the soul itself, are of no profit. One thing, and one alone, is necessary for life, justification, and Christian liberty; and that is the most holy word of God, the Gospel of Christ, as He says, "I am the resurrection and the life; he that believeth in Me shall not die eternally" (JOHN *xi. 25*), and also, "If the Son shall make you free, ye shall be free indeed" (JOHN *viii. 36*), and, "Man shall not live by bread alone, but by every word that proceedeth out of the mouth of God" (MATT. *iv. 4*).

Let us therefore hold it for certain and firmly established that the soul can do without everything except the word of God, without which none at all of its wants are provided for. But, having the word, it is rich and wants for nothing, since that is the word of life, of truth, of light, of peace, of justification, of salvation, of joy, of liberty, of wisdom, of virtue, of grace, of glory, and of every good thing. It is on this account that the prophet in a whole Psalm (PSALM *cxix.*), and in many other places, sighs for and calls upon the word of God with so many groanings and words.

Again, there is no more cruel stroke of the wrath of God than when He sends a famine of hearing His words (AMOS *viii. 11*), just as there is no greater favour from Him than the sending forth of His word, as it is said, "He sent His word and healed them, and delivered them from their destructions" (PSALM *cvii. 20*). Christ was sent for no other office than that of the word; and the order of Apostles, that of bishops, and that of the whole body of the clergy, have been called and instituted for no object but the ministry of the word.

But you will ask, What is this word, and by what means is it to be used, since there are so many words of God? I answer, The Apostle Paul (ROM. *i.*) explains what it is, namely the Gospel of God, concerning His Son, incarnate, suffering, risen, and glorified through the Spirit, the Sanctifier. To preach Christ is to feed the soul, to justify it, to set it free, and to save it, if it believes the preaching. For faith alone, and the efficacious use of the word of God, bring salvation. "If thou shalt confess with thy mouth the Lord Jesus, and shalt believe in thine heart that God hath raised Him from the dead, thou shalt be saved" (ROM. *x. 9*); and again, "Christ is the end of the law for righteousness to every one that believeth" (ROM. *x. 4*), and "The just shall live by faith" (ROM. *i. 17*). For the word of God cannot be received and honoured by any works, but by faith alone. Hence it is clear that as the soul needs the word alone for life and justification, so it is justified by faith alone, and not by any works. For if it could be justified by any other means, it would have no need of the word, nor consequently of faith.

But this faith cannot consist at all with works; that is, if you imagine that you can be justified by those works, whatever they are, along with it. For this would be to halt between two opinions, to worship Baal, and to kiss the hand to him, which is a very great iniquity, as Job says. Therefore, when you begin to believe, you learn at the same time that all that is in you is utterly guilty, sinful, and damnable, according to that saying, "All have sinned, and come short of the glory of God" (ROM. *iii. 23*), and also: "There is none righteous, no, not one; they are all gone out of the way; they are together become unprofitable: there is none that doeth good, no, not one" (ROM. *iii. 10-12*). When you have learnt this, you will know that Christ is necessary for you, since He has suffered and risen again for you, that, believing on Him, you might by this faith become another man, all your sins being remitted, and you being justified by the merits of another, namely of Christ alone.

Since then this faith can reign only in the inward man, as it is said, "With the heart man believeth unto righteousness" (ROM. *x. 10*); and since it alone justifies, it is evident that by no outward work or labour can the inward man be at all justified, made free, and saved; and that no works whatever have any relation to him. And so, on the other hand, it is solely by impiety and incredulity of heart that he becomes guilty and a slave of sin, deserving condemnation, not by any outward sin or work. Therefore the first care of every Christian ought to be to lay aside all reliance on works, and strengthen his faith alone more and more, and by it grow in the knowledge, not of works, but of Christ Jesus, who has suffered and risen again for him, as Peter teaches (1 PETER *v.*) when he makes no other work to be a Christian one. Thus Christ, when the Jews asked Him what they should do that they might work the works of God, rejected the multitude of works, with which He saw that they were puffed up, and commanded them one thing only, saying, "This is the work of God: that ye believe on Him whom He hath sent, for Him hath God the Father sealed" (JOHN *vi. 27, 29*).

Hence a right faith in Christ is an incomparable treasure, carrying with it universal salvation and preserving from all evil, as it is said, "He that believeth and is baptised shall be saved; but he that believeth not shall be damned" (MARK *xvi. 16*). Isaiah, looking to this treasure, predicted, "The consumption decreed shall overflow with righteousness. For the Lord God of hosts shall make a consumption, even determined (*verbum abbreviatum et consummans*), in the midst of the land" (ISA. *x. 22, 23*). As if he said, "Faith, which is the brief and complete fulfilling of the law, will fill those who believe with such righteousness that they will need nothing else for justification." Thus, too, Paul says, "For with the heart man believeth unto righteousness" (ROM. x. 10)

But you ask how it can be the fact that faith alone justifies, and affords without works so great a treasure of good things, when so many works, ceremonies, and laws are prescribed to us in the Scriptures? I answer, Before all things bear in mind what I have said: that faith alone without works justifies, sets free, and saves, as I shall show more clearly below.

Meanwhile it is to be noted that the whole Scripture of God is divided into two parts: precepts and promises. The precepts certainly teach us what is good, but what they teach is not forthwith done. For they show us what we ought to do, but do not give us the power to do it. They were ordained, however, for the purpose of showing man to himself, that through them he may learn his own impotence for good and may despair of his own strength. For this reason they are called the Old Testament, and are so.

For example, "Thou shalt not covet," is a precept by which we are all convicted of sin, since no man can help coveting, whatever efforts to the contrary he may make. In order therefore that he may fulfil the precept, and not covet, he is constrained to despair of himself and to seek elsewhere and through another the help which he cannot find in himself; as it is said, "O Israel, thou hast destroyed thyself; but in Me is thine help" (HOSEA xiii. 9). Now what is done by this one precept is done by all; for all are equally impossible of fulfilment by us.

Now when a man has through the precepts been taught his own impotence, and become anxious by what means he may satisfy the law—for the law must be satisfied, so that no jot or tittle of it may pass away, otherwise he must be hopelessly condemned—then, being truly humbled and brought to nothing in his own eyes, he finds in himself no resource for justification and salvation.

Then comes in that other part of Scripture, the promises of God, which declare the glory of God, and say, "If you wish to fulfil the law, and, as the law requires, not to covet, lo! believe in Christ, in whom are promised to you grace, justification, peace, and liberty." All these things you shall have, if you believe, and shall be without them if you do not believe. For what is impossible for you by all the works of the law, which are many and yet useless, you shall fulfil in an easy and summary way through faith, because God the Father has made everything to depend on faith, so that whosoever has it has all things, and he who has it not has nothing. "For God hath concluded them all in unbelief, that He might have mercy upon all" (ROM. xi. 32). Thus the promises of God give that which the precepts exact, and fulfil what the law commands; so that all is of God alone, both the precepts and their fulfilment. He alone commands; He alone also fulfils. Hence the promises of God belong to the New Testament; nay, are the New Testament.

Now, since these promises of God are words of holiness, truth, righteousness, liberty, and peace, and are full of universal goodness, the soul, which cleaves to them with a firm faith, is so united to them, nay, thoroughly absorbed by them, that it not only partakes in, but is penetrated and saturated by, all their virtues. For if the touch of Christ was healing, how much more does that most tender spiritual touch, nay, absorption of the word, communicate to the soul all that belongs to the word! In this way therefore the soul, through faith alone, without works, is from the word of God justi- fied, sanctified, endued with truth, peace, and liberty, and filled full with every good thing, and is truly made the child of God, as it is said, "To them gave He power to become the sons of God, even to them that believe on His name" (JOHN *i. 12*).

From all this it is easy to understand why faith has such great power, and why no good works, nor even all good works put to- gether, can compare with it, since no work can cleave to the word of God or be in the soul. Faith alone and the word reign in it; and such as is the word, such is the soul made by it, just as iron ex- posed to fire glows like fire, on account of its union with the fire. It is clear then that to a Christian man his faith suffices for every- thing, and that he has no need of works, neither has he need of the law; and if he has no need of the law, he is certainly free from the law, and the saying is true, "The law is not made for a righteous man" (1 TIM. *i. 9*). This is that Christian liberty, our faith, the effect of which is, not that we should be careless or lead a bad life, but that no one should need the law or works for justification and salvation.

Let us consider this as the first virtue of faith; and let us look also to the second. This also is an office of faith: that it honours with the utmost veneration and the highest reputation Him in whom it believes, inasmuch as it holds Him to be truthful and worthy of belief. For there is no honour like that reputation of truth and right- eousness with which we honour Him in whom we believe. What higher credit can we attribute to any one than truth and righteous- ness, and absolute goodness? On the other hand, it is the greatest insult to brand any one with the reputation of falsehood and un- righteousness, or to suspect him of these, as we do when we dis- believe him.

Thus the soul, in firmly believing the promises of God, holds Him to be true and righteous; and it can attribute to God no higher glory than the credit of being so. The highest worship of God is to ascribe to Him truth, righteousness, and whatever qualities we must ascribe to one in whom we believe. In doing this the soul shows itself prepared to do His whole will; in doing this it hallows His name, and gives itself up to be dealt with as it may please God. For it cleaves to His promises, and never doubts that He is true, just, and wise, and will do, dispose, and provide for all things in the best way. Is not such a soul, in this its faith, most obedient to God in all things? What commandment does there remain which has not been amply fulfilled by such an obedience? What fulfilment can be more full than universal obedience? Now this is not accomplished by works, but by faith alone.

On the other hand, what greater rebellion, impiety, or insult to God can there be, than not to believe His promises? What else is this, than either to make God a liar, or to doubt His truth—that is, to attribute truth to ourselves, but to God falsehood and levity? In doing this, is not a man denying God and setting himself up as an idol in his own heart? What then can works, done in such a state of impiety, profit us, were they even angelic or apostolic works? Rightly hath God shut up all, not in wrath nor in lust, but in unbelief, in order that those who pretend that they are fulfilling the law by works of purity and benevolence (which are social and human virtues) may not presume that they will therefore be saved, but being included in the sin of unbelief, may either seek mercy, or be justly condemned.

But when God sees that truth is ascribed to Him, and that in the faith of our hearts He is honoured with all the honour of which He is worthy, then in return He honours us on account of that faith, attributing to us truth and righteousness. For faith does truth and righteousness in rendering to God what is His; and therefore in return God gives glory to our righteousness. It is true and righteous that God is true and righteous; and to confess this and ascribe these attributes to Him, this it is to be true and righteous. Thus He says, "Them that honour Me I will honour, and they that despise Me shall be lightly esteemed" (1 SAM. *ii. 30*). And so Paul says that Abraham's faith was imputed to him for righteousness, because by it he gave glory to God; and that to us also, for the same reason, it shall be imputed for righteousness, if we believe (ROM. *iv.*).

The third incomparable grace of faith is this: that it unites the soul to Christ, as the wife to the husband, by which mystery, as the Apostle teaches, Christ and the soul are made one flesh. Now if they are one flesh, and if a true marriage—nay, by far the most perfect of all marriages—is accomplished between them (for human marriages are but feeble types of this one great marriage), then it

362 follows that all they have becomes theirs in common, as well good

things as evil things; so that whatsoever Christ possesses, that the believing soul may take to itself and boast of as its own, and whatever belongs to the soul, that Christ claims as His.

If we compare these possessions, we shall see how inestimable is the gain. Christ is full of grace, life, and salvation; the soul is full of sin, death, and condemnation. Let faith step in, and then sin, death, and hell will belong to Christ, and grace, life, and salvation to the soul. For, if He is a Husband, He must needs take to Himself that which is His wife's, and, at the same time, impart to His wife that which is His. For, in giving her His own body and Himself, how can He but give her all that is His? And, in taking to Himself the body of His wife, how can He but take to Himself all that is hers?

In this is displayed the delightful sight, not only of communion, but of a prosperous warfare, of victory, salvation, and redemption. For, since Christ is God and man, and is such a Person as neither has sinned, nor dies, nor is condemned, nay, cannot sin, die, or be condemned, and since His righteousness, life, and salvation are invincible, eternal, and almighty—when, I say, such a Person, by the wedding-ring of faith, takes a share in the sins, death, and hell of His wife, nay, makes them His own, and deals with them no otherwise than as if they were His, and as if He Himself had sinned; and when He suffers, dies, and descends to hell, that He may overcome all things, and since sin, death, and hell cannot swallow Him up, they must needs be swallowed up by Him in stupendous conflict. For His righteousness rises above the sins of all men; His life is more powerful than all death; His salvation is more unconquerable than all hell.

Thus the believing soul, by the pledge of its faith in Christ, becomes free from all sin, fearless of death, safe from hell, and endowed with the eternal righteousness, life, and salvation of its Husband Christ. Thus He presents to Himself a glorious bride, without spot or wrinkle, cleansing her with the washing of water by the word; that is, by faith in the word of life, righteousness, and salvation. Thus He betrothes her unto Himself "in faithfulness, in righteousness, and in judgment, and in lovingkindness, and in mercies" (HOSEA ii. 19, 20).

Who then can value highly enough these royal nuptials? Who can comprehend the riches of the glory of this grace? Christ, that rich and pious Husband, takes as a wife a needy and impious harlot, redeeming her from all her evils and supplying her with all His good things. It is impossible now that her sins should destroy her, since they have been laid upon Christ and swallowed up in Him, and since she has in her Husband Christ a righteousness which she may claim as her own, and which she can set up with confidence against all her sins, against death and hell, saying, "If I have sinned, my Christ, in whom I believe, has not sinned; all mine is His, and all His is mine," as it is written, "My beloved is mine, and I am His" (CANT. *ii. 16*). This is what Paul says: "Thanks be to God, which giveth us the victory through our Lord Jesus Christ," victory over sin and death, as he says, "The sting of death is sin, and the strength of sin is the law" (1 COR. *xv. 56, 57*).

From all this you will again understand why so much importance is attributed to faith, so that it alone can fulfil the law and justify without any works. For you see that the First Commandment, which says, "Thou shalt worship one God only," is fulfilled by faith alone. If you were nothing but good works from the soles of your feet to the crown of your head, you would not be worshipping God, nor fulfilling the First Commandment, since it is impossible to worship God without ascribing to Him the glory of truth and of universal goodness, as it ought in truth to be ascribed. Now this is not done by works, but only by faith of heart. It is not by working, but by believing, that we glorify God, and confess Him to be true. On this ground faith alone is the righteousness of a Christian man, and the fulfilling of all the commandments. For to him who fulfils the first the task of fulfilling all the rest is easy.

Works, since they are irrational things, cannot glorify God, although they may be done to the glory of God, if faith be present. But at present we are enquiring, not into the quality of the works done, but into him who does them, who glorifies God, and brings forth good works. This is faith of heart, the head and the substance of all our righteousness. Hence that is a blind and perilous doctrine which teaches that the commandments are fulfilled previous to any good works, and good works follow their fulfilment, as we shall see.

But, that we may have a wider view of that grace which our inner man has in Christ, we must know that in the Old Testament God sanctified to Himself every first-born male. The birthright was of great value, giving a superiority over the rest by the double honor of priesthood and kingship. For the first-born brother was priest and lord of all the rest.

Under this figure was foreshown Christ, the true and only First-born of God the Father and of the Virgin Mary, and a true King and Priest, not in a fleshly and earthly sense. For His kingdom is not of this world; it is in heavenly and spiritual things that He reigns and acts as Priest; and these are righteousness, truth, wisdom, peace, salvation, etc. Not but that all things, even those of earth

364 and hell, are subject to Him—for otherwise how could He defend

and save us from them?—but it is not in these, nor by these, that His kingdom stands.

So, too, His priesthood does not consist in the outward display of vestments and gestures, as did the human priesthood of Aaron and our ecclesiastical priesthood at this day, but in spiritual things, wherein, in His invisible office, He intercedes for us with God in heaven, and there offers Himself, and performs all the duties of a priest, as Paul describes Him to the Hebrews under the figure of Melchizedek. Nor does He only pray and intercede for us; He also teaches us inwardly in the spirit with the living teachings of His Spirit. Now these are the two special offices of a priest, as is figured to us in the case of fleshly priests by visible prayers and sermons.

As Christ by His birthright has obtained these two dignities, so He imparts and communicates them to every believer in Him, under that law of matrimony of which we have spoken above, by which all that is the husband's is also the wife's. Hence all we who believe on Christ are kings and priests in Christ, as it is said, "Ye are a chosen generation, a royal priesthood, a holy nation, a peculiar people, that ye should show forth the praises of Him who hath called you out of darkness into His marvellous light" (1 PETER *ii.* 9).

These two things stand thus. First, as regards kingship, every Christian is by faith so exalted above all things that, in spiritual power, he is completely lord of all things, so that nothing whatever can do him any hurt; yea, all things are subject to him, and are compelled to be subservient to his salvation. Thus Paul says, "All things work together for good to them who are called" (ROM. *viii.* 28), and also "Whether life, or death, or things present, or things to come, all are yours; and ye are Christ's" (1 COR. *iii. 22, 23*).

Not that in the sense of corporeal power any one among Christians has been appointed to possess and rule all things, according to the mad and senseless idea of certain ecclesiastics. That is the office of kings, princes, and men upon earth. Yea, the more of a Christian any man is, to so many the more evils, sufferings, and deaths is he subject, as we see in the first place in Christ the First-born, and in all His holy brethren.

This is a spiritual power which rules in the midst of enemies, and is powerful in the midst of distresses. And this is nothing else than that strength is made perfect in my weakness, and that I can turn all things to the profit of my salvation; so that even the cross and death are compelled to serve me and to work together for my salvation. This is a lofty and eminent dignity, a true and almighty dominion, a spiritual empire, in which there is nothing so good, nothing so bad, as not to work together for my good, if only I believe. And yet there is nothing of which I have need—for faith alone suffices for my salvation—unless that in it faith may exercise the power and empire of its liberty. This is the inestimable power and liberty of Christians.

Nor are we only kings and the freest of all men, but also priests for ever, a dignity far higher than kingship, because by that priesthood we are worthy to appear before God, to pray for others, and to teach one another mutually the things which are of God. For these are the duties of priests, and they cannot possibly be permitted to any unbeliever. Christ has obtained for us this favour, if we believe in Him: that just as we are His brethren and co-heirs and fellow-kings with Him, so we should be also fellow-priests with Him, and venture with confidence, through the spirit of faith, to come into the presence of God, and cry, "Abba, Father!" and to pray for one another, and to do all things which we see done and figured in the visible and corporeal office of priesthood. But to an unbelieving person nothing renders service or works for good. He himself is in servitude to all things, and all things turn out for evil to him, because he uses all things in an impious way for his own advantage, and not for the glory of God. And thus he is not a priest, but a profane person, whose prayers are turned into sin, nor does he ever appear in the presence of God, because God does not hear sinners.

Who then can comprehend the loftiness of that Christian dignity, which, by its royal power, rules over all things, even over death, life, and sin, and, by its priestly glory, is all-powerful with God, since God does what He Himself seeks and wishes, as it is written, "He will fulfil the desire of them that fear Him; He also will hear their cry, and will save them"? (PSALM cxlv. 19) This glory certainly cannot be attained by any works, but by faith only.

From these considerations any one may clearly see how a Christian man is free from all things; so that he needs no works in order to be justified and saved, but receives these gifts in abundance from faith alone. Nay, were he so foolish as to pretend to be justified, set free, saved, and made a Christian, by means of any good work, he would immediately lose faith, with all its benefits. Such folly is prettily represented in the fable where a dog, running along in the water and carrying in his mouth a real piece of meat, is deceived by the reflection of the meat in the water, and, in trying with open mouth to seize it, loses the meat and its image at the same time.

Here you will ask, "If all who are in the Church are priests, by what character are those whom we now call priests to be distinguished from the laity?" I reply, By the use of these words, "priest," "clergy," "spiritual person," "ecclesiastic," an injustice has been

done, since they have been transferred from the remaining body of Christians to those few who are now, by a hurtful custom, called ecclesiastics. For Holy Scripture makes no distinction between them, except that those who are now boastfully called popes, bishops, and lords, it calls ministers, servants, and stewards, who are to serve the rest in the ministry of the word, for teaching the faith of Christ and the liberty of believers. For though it is true that we are all equally priests, yet we cannot, nor if we could, ought we all to, minister and teach publicly. Thus Paul says, "Let a man so account of us as of the ministers of Christ and stewards of the mysteries of God" (1 COR. iv. 1).

This bad system has now issued in such a pompous display of power and such a terrible tyranny that no earthly government can be compared to it, as if the laity were something else than Christians. Through this perversion of things it has happened that the knowledge of Christian grace, of faith, of liberty, and altogether of Christ, has utterly perished, and has been succeeded by an intolerable bondage to human works and laws; and, according to the Lamentations of Jeremiah, we have become the slaves of the vilest men on earth, who abuse our misery to all the disgraceful and ignominious purposes of their own will.

Returning to the subject which we had begun, I think it is made clear by these considerations that it is not sufficient, nor a Christian course, to preach the works, life, and words of Christ in a historic manner, as facts which it suffices to know as an example how to frame our life, as do those who are now held the best preachers, and much less so to keep silence altogether on these things and to teach in their stead the laws of men and the decrees of the Fathers. There are now not a few persons who preach and read about Christ with the object of moving the human affections to sympathise with Christ, to indignation against the Jews, and other childish and womanish absurdities of that kind.

Now preaching ought to have the object of promoting faith in Him, so that He may not only be Christ, but a Christ for you and for me, and that what is said of Him, and what He is called, may work in us. And this faith is produced and is maintained by preaching why Christ came, what He has brought us and given to us, and to what profit and advantage He is to be received. This is done when the Christian liberty which we have from Christ Himself is rightly taught, and we are shown in what manner all we Christians are kings and priests, and how we are lords of all things, and may be confident that whatever we do in the presence of God is pleasing and acceptable to Him.

Whose heart would not rejoice in its inmost core at hearing these
367 things? Whose heart, on receiving so great a consolation, would not

become sweet with the love of Christ, a love to which it can never attain by any laws or works? Who can injure such a heart, or make it afraid? If the consciousness of sin or the horror of death rush in upon it, it is prepared to hope in the Lord, and is fearless of such evils, and undisturbed, until it shall look down upon its enemies. For it believes that the righteousness of Christ is its own, and that its sin is no longer its own, but that of Christ; but, on account of its faith in Christ, all its sin must needs be swallowed up from before the face of the righteousness of Christ, as I have said above. It learns, too, with the Apostle, to scoff at death and sin, and to say, "O death, where is thy sting? O grave, where is thy victory? The sting of death is sin, and the strength of sin is the law. But thanks be to God, which giveth us the victory through our Lord Jesus Christ" (1 COR. xv. 55–57). For death is swallowed up in victory, not only the victory of Christ, but ours also, since by faith it becomes ours, and in it we too conquer.

Let it suffice to say this concerning the inner man and its liberty, and concerning that righteousness of faith which needs neither laws nor good works; nay, they are even hurtful to it, if any one pretends to be justified by them.

JOHN CALVIN

Instruction and Confession of Faith
Which Is Used in the Church of Geneva
Translated by John Charles Nelson

THE DIFFERENCE BETWEEN TRUE AND FALSE RELIGION

Since it is held by common consent that if our life is without religion we live very wretchedly and indeed as though we were in no way better than brute animals, there is no one who wishes to be thought altogether alien to piety and acknowledgment of God. But there is a great deal of difference in the way in which one declares his religion: for the majority of men are not really touched at all by the fear of God. But because, willing or not, they are bound by this thought which constantly comes to their mind, that there is some divinity by whose power they stand or fall, being overawed to think of so great a power, so that they may not provoke it against themselves by too great contempt, they hold it in some kind of veneration. Nevertheless, living in a disorderly fashion and rejecting all honesty they exhibit a great self-confidence in despising the judgment of God. Furthermore because they do not value God by his infinite majesty but by the foolish and heedless vanity of their own mind, they thereby turn themselves away from the true God. Although by great effort they afterward endeavor to serve God, they do not profit one whit since they adore not the eternal God but the dreams and fantasies of their own heart instead of God. Now true piety does not consist in the fear which would gladly indeed flee the judgment of God, but since it cannot do so feels horror of it; but consists rather in a pure and true zeal that loves God altogether like a Father and reveres him exactly as a Lord, embraces his justice, and dreads more to offend him than to die. And all those who have this zeal do not in the least undertake to form such a God as

369

they might wish according to their temerity, but seek the knowledge of the true God from himself and do not conceive him at all otherwise than he manifests and declares himself to them.

MAN

Man was at first made in the image and semblance of God, so that in the adornments by which God had nobly dressed him he would admire his author, and by that recognition properly honor him. But because counting upon the great excellence of his nature, having forgotten whence it derived and subsisted, he tried to raise himself without the Lord, it was necessary for him to be divested of all the gifts of God of which he had become foolishly proud, in order that being denuded and deprived of all glory he might know God, whom man, being enriched by his generosity, had dared to despise. Hence all of us who have our origin from the seed of Adam, this resemblance to God being effaced in us, are born flesh from flesh. For although we are made up of a soul and a body, we nevertheless feel only the flesh: so that to whatever part of man we turn our eyes it is impossible to see anything that is not impure, profane and abominable to God. For man's prudence, blinded and enveloped by infinite errors, is always contrary to the wisdom of God; his malicious will, full of corrupt affections, hates nothing more than divine justice; and man's strength, powerless to do any good work, tends furiously toward iniquity.

FREE WILL

The Scripture often testifies that man is a slave of sin: which signifies that his spirit is so alien to God's justice that he conceives, desires and undertakes nothing that is not base, perverse, wicked and sullied: for the heart, utterly imbued with the poison of sin, can produce nothing but the fruits of sin. Yet one must not for that reason think that man sins as though constrained by violent necessity: because he sins by a very prompt and inclined consent of the will. But because by the corruption of his affection he severely hates all of God's justice and on the other hand is fervent in every kind of evil, he is said not to have free power of choosing good and evil, which is called free will.

SIN AND DEATH

In the Scripture sin means both the perversity of human nature, which is the fountain of all vices, and the vile desires which are born from it and the wicked transgressions which arise from these desires, such as murders, thefts, adulteries, and other sins of this kind. Therefore, sinners from our mothers' wombs, we are all born subject to the wrath and vengeance of God. Having grown up we pile onto ourselves an increasingly heavier judgment of God. Finally through all our life we tend ever nearer to death. For if there is no doubt at all that all wickedness is execrable to the justice of God, what can we expect from the face of God, we wretches who are oppressed by so great a burden of sins and soiled by infinite filth, if not very certain confusion, such as his indignation brings? This thought, although it disheartens man with terror and crushes him with despair, is nevertheless necessary to us in order that divested of our self-righteousness, forsaking confidence in our own virtue, and being barred from any expectation of life, we may learn by the recognition of our poverty, wretchedness and ignominy to prostrate ourselves before the Lord, and by the acknowledgment of our wickedness, impotence and perdition give him all glory of holiness, virtue and salvation.

HOW WE ARE SAVED AND RESTORED TO LIFE

By this knowledge of ourselves, which shows us our nothingness if it enters our hearts in full consciousness, easy access is given to the true knowledge of God. Or rather he himself has opened to us, so to speak, a first door to his kingdom when he had destroyed these two most evil pests, namely the feeling of security from his vengeance and false confidence in ourselves. For then we begin to raise to heaven our eyes which formerly were fixed and arrested on earth, and we who rested in ourselves long for the Lord. And on the other hand this Father of mercy, although our wickedness would deserve something else altogether, nevertheless according to his ineffable kindness he voluntarily shows himself to us who are so afflicted and confused, and by such means which he knows to be expedient for our imbecility, recalls us from error to the straight 371 path, from death to life, from ruin to salvation, from the kingdom of the devil to his kingdom. Since the Lord first established this step for all those whom it pleased him to restore to the heritage of heavenly life—that is, those who being distressed by conscience and weighted by the burden of their sins, are stung and stimulated to fear him—he proposes to us at the beginning his Law which exercises us in this knowledge.

WE APPREHEND CHRIST BY FAITH

As the merciful Father offers us his Son through the word of the Gospel, so do we embrace him by faith and acknowledge him as given to us. It is true that the word of the Gospel calls everyone to participation in Christ, but many, blinded and hardened by unbelief despise such a singular grace. Therefore only the faithful enjoy Christ, who receive him as sent to them, do not reject him after he is given them, and follow him when he calls.

ELECTION AND PREDESTINATION

In such a difference it is necessary to consider the great secret of the counsel of God: for the seed of the word of God takes root and bears fruit only in those whom the Lord by his eternal election has predestined as his children and heirs of the heavenly kingdom. To all others, who by the same counsel of God before the constitution of the world are rejected, the clear and evident preaching of truth can be nothing but the odor of death unto death. Now why does the Lord show his mercy to some and exercise the rigor of his judgment upon the others? We must let the reason be known to him alone, since he has wished it to be hidden from us all, and not without very good reason. For neither could the rudeness of our spirit bear such great clarity, nor our smallness understand such great wisdom. And in fact all those who will try to rise so high and will not repress the temerity of their spirit, will experience the truth of Solomon's saying (PROV. 25) that he who will investigate majesty will be oppressed by glory. Let us only resolve in ourselves that this dispensation of the Lord, although it be hidden from us, is nevertheless holy and just: for if he wished to damn all mankind, he has the right to do it, and in those whom he withdraws from perdition one can contemplate nothing but his sovereign goodness. Let us therefore recognize that the elect are vessels of his mercy (as truly they are), and that the rejected are vessels of his wrath, which yet is only just.

Let us find reason and matter in both cases to exalt his glory. And on the other hand let us not seek (as many are accustomed) to confirm the certitude of our salvation, to penetrate to the interior of heaven, and to investigate what God from his eternity had determined to do with us—a cogitation which can only agitate us with wretched anxiety and perturbation. But let us be content with the testimony by which he has sufficiently and amply confirmed that certitude to us. For as in Christ are elected all those who have been preordained to life before the foundations of the world were constituted, so is he the one by whom the pledge of our election is presented to us if we receive and embrace him through faith. For what do we seek in election but that we may participate in eternal life? And we have that in Christ, who was the life since the beginning and is proposed to us as life to the end that all who believe in him may not perish but enjoy eternal life. If therefore in possessing Christ by faith we likewise possess in him life, we need inquire no further about the eternal counsel of God: for Christ is not only a mirror by which the will of God is represented to us, but a pledge by which it is as sealed and confirmed to us.

WHAT TRUE FAITH IS

It must not be thought that the Christian faith is a bare and mere knowledge of God or understanding of the Scripture, which is revolved in the brain without touching the heart—as is usually the case with opinion about things which are confirmed to us by some probable reason. Rather it is a firm and solid confidence in the heart by which we rest securely in the mercy of God which is promised to us through the Gospel. For thus the definition of faith must be taken from the substance of the promise. Faith rests so much on this foundation that without it faith would immediately fall, or rather vanish. Therefore when the Lord by the promise of the Gospel grants us his mercy, if certainly and without any hesitation we confide in him who made the promise, we are said to apprehend his word by faith. And this definition is in no way different from that of the apostle (HEB. 11) in which he teaches that faith is the substance of things to be hoped for and the demonstration of things not apparent: for he means a certain and sure possession of the things that are promised by God and an evidence of things not apparent—that is to say, of eternal life, hope of which we conceive

373

by our confidence in the divine goodness which is offered us through the Gospel. Now as all the promises of God are confirmed in Christ and so to speak kept and accomplished, it appears without doubt that Christ is the perpetual object of faith, in whom faith contemplates all the riches of divine mercy.

FAITH IS A GIFT OF GOD

If we consider correctly within ourselves how blind our thought is to the heavenly secrets of God and how greatly our heart distrusts everything, we shall not doubt in the least that faith far surpasses all the power of our nature and that it is a singular and precious gift of God. For as St. Paul argues (I COR. 2), if no one but the spirit of man which is in man can testify to the human will, how can man be certain of the divine will? And if God's truth wavers in us even in these things which we see with our eyes, how will it be firm and stable where the Lord promises things which the eye does not see and man's intellect does not at all comprehend?

Hence there is no doubt that faith is a light of the Holy Spirit, by which our intellects are clarified and our hearts confirmed in a certain persuasion—that the truth of God is so certain that it cannot fail to accomplish that which he has promised to do by his holy word. For this reason (II COR. 1 and EPH. 1) the Holy Spirit is called as a guarantee which confirms in our hearts the certainty of divine truth and a seal by which our hearts are sealed in the expectancy of the day of the Lord. For it is the Spirit who testifies to our spirit that God is our Father and that likewise we are his children (ROM. 8).

WE ARE JUSTIFIED IN CHRIST BY FAITH

Since it is manifest that Christ is the perpetual object of faith, we cannot otherwise know what we receive by faith unless we look to him. Now he was indeed given us by the Father so that we might obtain eternal life through him. As he says: (JOHN 17), eternal life is to know one God the Father and Jesus Christ whom he sent. And again (JOHN 11): he who will believe in me shall never die, and if he has died he shall live. Nevertheless, in order that this may be done we who are contaminated by stains of sin must be cleansed 374 in him, for nothing that is soiled will enter the kingdom of God. He therefore makes us participants in himself, so that we who are sinners in ourselves may by his justice be reputed just before the throne of God. And in this manner being divested of our own justice we are dressed with the justice of Christ, and being unjust in our works we are justified by the faith of Christ.

Because we are said to be justified by faith, not that we receive in ourselves any justice, but because the justice of Christ is attributed to us just as if it were ours, our own wickedness not being attributed to us at all. So that in a word one may truly call this justice the remission of sins, as the apostle evidently declares when he often compares justification by works with justification by faith and teaches that the former is destroyed by the latter (ROM. 10, PHIL. 3). . . .

THE LORD'S SUPPER

The promise which is added to the mystery of the supper clearly declares to what end it was instituted and to what it tends. That is, it confirms to us that the body of the Lord has once for all been given for us in such a way that it is now ours and will be so perpetually; and that his blood has once for all been shed for us in such a way that it will always be ours. The signs are the bread and the wine, by which the Lord gives us the true but spiritual communication of his body and his blood. This communication, content with the bond of his spirit, does not require an enclosed presence either of the flesh in the bread or the blood in the wine. For although Christ, elevated into heaven, has left his earthly habitation in which we are still pilgrims, still no distance can dissolve his power of nourishing his own with himself. In the supper he gives us so certain and clear a teaching of this fact that we must be assured beyond any doubt that Christ with all his riches is there present to us no less than if he were placed in the presence of our eyes and were touched by our hands; and that he is even present with such great power and efficacy that he brings there to our spirits not only an assured confidence in eternal life, but also makes us certain of the immortality of our flesh. For our flesh is already vivified by his immortal flesh and communicates in some manner with his immortality.

Hence the body and blood are represented by bread and wine, so that we may learn not only that they are ours, but that they are life and nourishment for us. Thus when we see the bread
375 sanctified as the body of Christ, we must immediately think of this

similitude—that as the bread nourishes, sustains and conserves the life of our body, so is the body of Christ the food and protection of our spiritual life. When the wine is presented to us as a sign of the blood, we must likewise believe that such fruits as he brings to the body we receive spiritually from the blood of Christ.

Now as this mystery is a teaching of such great divine generosity toward us, so likewise should it admonish us not to be ungrateful to such manifest kindness, but rather to exalt it by such praises as are fitting and to celebrate it with acts of thanks. Furthermore, it admonishes us to mutually embrace each other in such unity as binds among themselves and joins together the parts of one same body. For no sharper or more stinging spur could be given to move and excite a mutual charity among us than when Christ, giving himself to us, invites us not only by his example mutually to give and expose ourselves for one another, but by making himself common to all he also makes us all one in himself.

DESIDERIUS ERASMUS

The Praise of Folly.
An Oration, of feigned matter, spoken
by Folly in her own Person.
Translated by John Wilson

And therefore, according to Homer's example, I think it high time to leave the Gods to themselves, and look down a little on the Earth; wherein likewise you'll find nothing frolick or fortunate, that it ows not to me. So provident has that great Parent of Mankind, Nature, been, that there should not be any thing without it's mixture, and as it were seasoning of Folly. For since according to the definition of the Stoicks, Wisdom is nothing else than to be govern'd by reason; and on the contrary Folly, to be giv'n up to the will of our Passions; that the life of man might not be altogether disconsolate and hard to away with, of how much more Passion than Reason has Jupiter compos'd us? putting in, as one would say, 'scarce half an ounce to a pound.' Besides, he has confin'd Reason to a narrow corner of the brain, and left all the rest of the body to our Passions; as also set up, against this one, two as it were, masterless Tyrants—Anger, that possesseth the region of the heart, and consequently the very Fountain of life, the Heart it self; and Lust, that stretcheth its Empire every where. Against which double force how powerful Reason is, let common experience declare, inasmuch as she, which yet is all she can do, may call out to us till she be hoarse again, and tell us the Rules of Honesty and Vertue; while they give up the Reins to their Governour, and make a hideous clamour, till at last being wearied, he suffer himself to be carried whither they please to hurry him.

But forasmuch as such as are born to the business of the world have some little sprinklings of Reason more than the rest, yet that they may the better manage it, even in this as well as in other things, they call me to counsel; and I give 'em such as is worthy of my self, to wit That they take to 'em a wife—a silly thing, God wot, and foolish, yet wanton and pleasant by which means the roughness of the Masculine temper is season'd and sweeten'd by her folly. For in that Plato seems to doubt under which Genus he should put woman, to wit that of rational Creatures or Brutes, he intended no other in it than to shew the apparent folly of the Sexe. For if perhaps any of them goes about to be thought wiser than the rest, what else does she do but play the fool twice, as if a man should 'teach a Cow to dance,' 'a thing quite against the hair.' For as it doubles the crime if any one should put a disguise upon Nature, or endeavour to bring her to that she will in no wise bear, according to that Proverb of the Greeks, 'An Ape is an Ape, though clad in Scarlet'; so a woman is a woman still, that is to say foolish, let her put on what ever Vizard she please.

But, by the way, I hope that Sexe is not so foolish as to take offence at this, that I my self, being a woman, and Folly too, have attributed Folly to them. For if they weigh it right, they needs must acknowledge that they owe it to Folly that they are more fortunate than men. As first their Beauty, which, and that not without cause, they prefer before every thing, since by its means they exercise a Tyranny even upon Tyrants themselves; otherwise, whence proceeds that sowre look, rough skin, bushy beard and such other things as speak plain Old age in a man, but from that Disease of Wisdom? whereas women's Cheeks are ever plump and smooth, their Voice small, their Skin soft, as if they imitated a certain kind of perpetual Youth. Again, what greater thing do they wish in their whole lives, than that they may please the Men? For to what other purpose are all those Dresses, Washes, Baths, Curlings, Slops, Perfumes, and those several little tricks of setting their Faces, painting their Eye-brows, and smoothing their Skins? And now tell me, what higher Letters of Recommendation have they to men than this Folly? For what is it they do not permit 'em to do? and to what other purpose than that of pleasure? wherein yet their folly is not the least thing that pleaseth; which how true it is, I think no one will deny, that does but consider with himself, what foolish Discourse and odd Gambals pass between a man and his woman, as oft as he has a mind to be gamesome? And so I have shown ye whence the first and chiefest delight of man's life springs.

But there are some, you'll say, and those too none of the youngest, that have a greater kindness for the Pot than the Petticoat, and place their chiefest pleasure in good fellowship. If there can be any great entertainment without a woman at it, let others look to 't. This I am sure, there was never any pleasant which Folly gave not the relish to. Insomuch that if they find no occasion of Laughter, they send for 'one that may make it,' or hire some Buffon flatterer, whose ridiculous discourse may put by the Gravity of the company. For to what purpose were it to clogg our Stomacks with Dainties, Junkets and the like Stuff, unless our Eyes and Ears, nay whole Mind, were likewise entertain'd with Jests, Merriments and Laughter? But of these kind of second Courses I am the onely Cook; though yet those ordinary practises of our Feasts, as choosing a King, throwing Dice, drinking Healths, trouling it Round, dancing the Cushion and the like, were not invented by the seven Wise Men but my Self, and that too for the common pleasure of Mankind. The nature of all which things is such, that the more of Folly they have, the more they conduce to Humane Life, which, if it were unpleasant, did not deserve the name of Life; and other than such it could not well be, did not these kind of Diversions wype away tediousnesse, nexte cosyn to the other.

But perhaps there are some that neglect this way of pleasure, and rest satisfi'd in the enjoyment of their Friends, calling friendship the most desirable of all things; more necessary than either air, fire, or water; so delectable, that he that shall take it out of the World had as good put out the Sun; and lastly so commendable, if yet that make any thing to the matter, that neither the Philosophers themselves doubted to reckon it among their chiefest good. But what if I shew you that I am both the beginning and end of this so great good also? Nor shall I go about to prove it by Fallacies, Sorites, Dilemmas, or other the like subtilties of Logicians, but after my blunt way, point out the thing as clearly as 'twere with my finger.

And now tell me, if to wink, slip over, be blind at, or deceiv'd in, the vices of our friends, nay, to admire and esteem them for Virtues, be not at least the next degree to folly? What is it when one kisses his Mistresses freckle Neck, another the Wart on her Nose? When a Father shall swear his squint-ey'd Child is more lovely than Venus? What is this, I say, but meer folly? And so, perhaps you'l cry, it is; and yet 'tis this onely that joyns friends together, and continues them so joyn'd. I speak of ordinary men, of whom none are born without their imperfections, and happy is he that is prest with the least: for among wise Princes there is either no friendship at all, or if there be, 'tis unpleasant and reserv'd, and that too but amongst a very few, 'twere a crime to say none. For that the greatest part of mankind are fools, nay there is not any one that dotes not in many things; and friendship, you know, is seldome made but amongst equalls. And yet if it should so happen that there were a mutual good-will between them, it is in no wise firm nor very long liv'd; that is to say,

379

among such as are morose and more circumspect than needs, as being Eagle-sighted into his friends' faults, but so blear-ey'd to their own that they take not the least notice of the Wallet that hangs behind their own Shoulders. Since then the nature of Man is such that there is scarce any one to be found that is not subject to many errors, add to this the great diversity of minds and studies, so many slips, oversights and chances of humane life, and how is it possible there should be any true friendship between those Argus's, so much as one hour, were it not for that which the Greeks excellently call ευήθειαν? and you may render by Folly or good Nature, chuse you whether, But what? Is not the Author and Parent of all our Love, Cupid, as blind as a beetle? and as with him all colours agree, so from him is it that every one likes his own Sweeter-kin best, though never so ugly, and 'that an old man dotes on his old wife, and a boy on his girle.' These things are not onely done every where but laught at too, yet as ridiculous as they are, they make society pleasant, and, as it were glew it together.

And what has been said of Friendship may more reasonably be presum'd of Matrimony, which in truth is no other than an insepa-rable conjunction of life. Good God! What Divorces, or what not worse than that, would daily happen, were not the converse be-tween a man and his wife supported and cherished by flattery, apishness, gentleness, ignorance, dissembling, certain Retainers of mine also! Whoop holiday! how few marriages should we have, if the Husband should but through-examin how many tricks his pretty little Mop of modesty has plaid before she was marry'd! And how fewer of them would hold together, did not most of the Wife's actions escape the Husband's knowledg through his neglect or sottishness! And for this also ye are beholding to me, by whose means it is that the Husband is pleasant to his Wife, the Wife to her Husband, and the house kept in quiet. A man is laught at, when seeing his Wife weeping he licks up her tears. But how much happier is it to be thus deceiv'd than by being troubled with jeal-ousie, not onely to torment himself, but set all things in a hubbub!

In fine, I am so necessary to the making of all society and manner of life both delightful and lasting, that neither would the people long endure their Governors, nor the Servant his Master, nor the Master his Footman, nor the Scholar his Tutor, nor one friend an-other, nor the Wife her Husband, nor the Userer the Borrower, nor a Souldier his Commander, nor one Companion another, unlesse all of them had their interchangeable failings, one while flattering, other while prudently conniving, and generally sweetning one an-other with some small relish of Folly.

And now you'd think I had said all, but ye shall hear yet greater things. Will he, I pray, love any one that hates himself? Or ever agree with another who is not at peace with himself? Or beget pleasure in another that is troublesome to himself? I think no one will say it that is not more foolish than Folly. And yet, if ye should exclude me, there's no man but would be so far from enduring another that he would stink in his own nostrils, be nauseated with his own actions, and himself become odious to himself; forasmuch as Nature, in too many things rather a Stepdame than a Parent to us, has imprinted that evil in men, especially such as have least judgment, that every one repents him of his own condition and admires that of others. Whence it comes to pass that all her gifts, elegancy and graces corrupt and perish. For what benefit is Beauty, the greatest blessing of Heaven, if it be mixt with affectation? What Youth, if corrupted with the severity of old Age? Lastly, what is that in the whole business of a man's life he can do with any grace to himself or others—for it is not so much a thing of Art, as the very life of every Action, that it be done with a good meen—unlesse this my friend and companion, Self-love, be present with it? Nor does she without cause supply me the place of a Sister, since her whole endeavours are to act my part every where. For what is more foolish than for a man to study nothing else than how to please himself? To make himself the object of his own admiration? And yet, what is there that is either delightful or taking, nay rather what not the contrary, that a man does against the hair? Take away this Salt of life, and the Orator may ev'n sit still with his Action, the Musitian with all his division will be able to please no man, the Player be hist off the Stage, the Poet and all his Muses ridiculous, the Painter with his Art contemptible, and the Physitian with all his Slipslops go a begging. Lastly, thou wilt be taken for an Ugly fellow instead of a Beautiful, for Old and Decrepit instead of Youthful, and a Beast instead of a Wise man, a Child instead of Eloquent, and instead of a well-bred man, a clown. So necessary a thing it is that every one flatter himself, and commend himself to himself before he can be commended by others.

Lastly, since it is the chiefest point of happinesse 'that a man is willing to be what he is,' you havet further abridg'd in this my Self-love, that no man's asham'd of his his own face, no man of his own wit, no man of his own parentage, no man of his own house, no man of his manner of living, nor any man of his own Country; so that a Highlander has no desire to change with an Italian, a Thracian with an Athenian, nor a Scythian for the fortunate Islands. O the singular care of Nature, that in so great a variety of things has made all equal! Where she has been sometime sparing of her gifts she has
381 recompenc'd it with the more of self-Love; though here, I must

confess, I speak foolishly, it being the greatest of all her Gifts: to say nothing that no great action was ever attempted without my Motion, or Art brought to perfection without my help.

And first 'tis agreed of all hands that our passions belong to Folly; inasmuch as we judge a wise Man from a Fool by this, that the one is order'd by them, the other by Reason; and therefore the Stoicks remove from a wise man all disturbances of Mind as so many Diseases. But these Passions do not onely the Office of a Tutor to such as are making towards the Port of Wisdome, but are in every exercise of Vertue as it were Spurs and Incentives, nay and Encouragers to well doing: which though the great Stoick Seneca most strongly denys, and takes from a wise man all affections whatever, yet in doing that he leaves him not so much as a Man, but rather a new kind of God, that was never yet, nor ever like to be. Nay, to speak plainer, he sets up a stony Semblance of a Man, void of all Sense and common feeling of Humanity. And much good to them with this Wise Man of theirs; let them enjoy him to themselves, love him without Competitors, and live with him in Plato's Commonwealth, the Countrey of Ideas, or Tantalus's Orchards. For who would not shun and startle at such a man, as at some unnatural accident or Spirit? A man dead to all sense of Nature and common affections, and no more mov'd with Love or Pity than if he were a Flint or Rock; whose censure nothing escapes; that commits no errors himself, but has a Lynx's eyes upon others; measures every thing by an exact Line, and forgives nothing; pleases himself with himself onely; the onely Rich, the onely Wise, the onely Free Man, and onely King; in brief, the onely man that is every thing, but in his own single judgment onely; that cares not for the Friendship of any man, being himself a friend to no man; makes no doubt to make the Gods stoop to him, and condemns and laughs at the whole Actions of our Life? And yet such a Beast is this their perfect Wise Man. But tell me pray, if the thing were to be carri'd by most voices, what City would chuse him for its Governour, or what Army desire him for their General? What Woman would have such a Husband, what Good-fellow such a Guest, or what Servant would either wish or endure such a Master? Nay, who had not rather have one of the middle sort of Fools, who, being a Fool himself, may the better know how to command or obey Fools; and who though he please his like, 'tis yet the greater number; one that is kind to his Wife, merry among his Friends, a Boon Companion, and easie to be liv'd with; and lastly one that thinks nothing of Humanity should be a stranger to him? But I am weary of this Wise Man, and therefore I'll proceed to some other advantages.

Go to then. Suppose a man in some lofty high Tower, and that he could look round him, as the Poets say Jupiter was now and then wont. To how many misfortunes would he find the life of man subject? How miserable, to say no worse, our Birth, how difficult our Education; to how many wrongs our Childhood expos'd, to what pains our Youth; how unsupportable our Old-age, and grievous our unavoidable Death? as also what Troups of Diseases beset us, how many Casualties hang over our Heads, how many Troubles invade us, and how little there is that is not steept in Gall? to say nothing of those evils one man brings upon another, as Poverty, Imprisonment, Infamy, Dishonesty, Racks, Snares, Treachery, Reproaches, Actions, Deceipts—But I'm got into as endless a work as numbring the Sands—For what offences Mankind have deserv'd these things, or what angry God compell'd 'em to be born into such miseries, is not my present business. Yet he that shall diligently examine it with himself, would he not, think ye, approve the example of the Milesian Virgins, and kill himself? But who are they that for no other reason but that they were weary of life, have hastned their own Fate? were they not the next Neighbours to Wisdom? amongst whom, to say nothing of Diogenes, Xenocrates, Cato, Cassius, Brutus, that Wise Man Chiron, being offer'd Immortality, chose rather to dye than be troubled with the same thing always.

And now I think ye see what would become of the World if all men should be wise; to wit 'twere necessary we got another kind of Clay and some better Potter. But I, partly through ignorance, partly unadvisedness, and sometimes through forgetfulness of evil, do now and then so sprinkle pleasure with the hopes of good, and sweeten men up in their greatest misfortunes, that they are not willing to leave this life, even then when according to the account of the Destinys this life has left them; and by how much the less reason they have to live, by so much the more they desire it; so far are they from being sensible of the least wearisomness of life. Of my gift it is, that ye have so many old Nestors every where, that have scarce left 'em so much as the shape of a Man; Stutterers, Dotards, Toothless, Gray-hair'd, Bald; or rather, to use the words of Aristophanes, 'Nasty, Crumpt, Miserable, Shrivel'd, Bald, Toothless, and wanting their Baubles': yet so delighted with life and to be thought young, that one dies his gray hairs; another covers his baldness with a Periwigg; another gets a set of new Teeth; another falls desperately in love with a young Wench, and keeps more flickering about her than a young man would have been asham'd of. For to see such an old crooked piece, with one foot in the grave, to marrie a plump young Wench, and that too with a portion, is so common that men almost expect to be commended for 't. But the best sport of all is to see our

383

old Women, even dead with age, and such skeletons one would think they had stoln out of their graves, and ever mumbling in their mouths, 'Life is sweet'; and as old as they are, still catterwawling, daily plaistering their face, scarce ever from the glasse, gossipping, dancing, and writing Love-letters. These things are laught at as foolish, as indeed they are; yet they please themselves, live merrily, swimme in pleasure, and in a word are happy, by my courtesie. But I would have them to whom these things seem ridiculous, to consider with themselves whether it be not better to live so pleasant a life, in such kind of follies, than, as the Proverb goes, 'To take a Halter and hang themselves.' Besides though these things may be subject to censure, it concerns not my fools in the least, in as much as they take no notice of it, or if they do, they easily neglect it. If a stone fall upon a man's head, that's evil indeed; but dishonesty, infamy, villany, ill reports, carrie no more hurt in them than a man is sensible of; and if a man have no sense of them, they are no longer evils. What art thou the worse if the people hisse at thee, so thou applaud thy self? And that a man be able to do so, he must ow it only to Folly.

But methinks I hear the Philosophers opposing it, and saying 'tis a miserable thing for a man to be foolish, to erre, mistake, and know nothing truly. Nay rather, this is to be a man. And why they should call it miserable, I see no reason; forasmuch as we are so born, so bred, so instructed, nay, such is the common condition of us all. And nothing can be call'd miserable that suits with its kind, unless perhaps you'l think a man such because he can neither flie with Birds, nor walk on all four with Beasts, and is not arm'd with Horns as a Bull. For by the same reason he would call the Warlike Horse unfortunate, because he understood not Grammar, nor eat Chees-cakes; and the Bull miserable, because he'd make so ill a Wrestler. And therefore, as a Horse that has no skill in Grammar is not miserable, no more is man in this respect, for that they agree with his Nature. But again, the Virtuosi may say that there was particularly added to Man the knowledge of Sciences, by whose help he might recompence himself in Understanding for what Nature cut him short in other things. As if this had the least face of truth, that Nature, that was so sollicitously watchful in the pro-duction of Gnats, Herbs and Flowers, should have so slept when she made Man, that he should have need to be helpt by Sciences, which that old Devil Theuth, the evil Genius of mankind, first invented for his Destruction, and are so little conducing to happiness that they rather obstruct it; to which purpose they are properly said to be first found out, as that wise King in Plato argues touching the invention of Letters.

Sciences therefore crept into the world with the other pests of mankind, from the same head from whence all other mischiefs spring; wee'l suppose it Devils, for so the name imports when you call them Dæmons, that is to say, Knowing. For that simple people of the golden Age, being wholly ignorant of every thing call'd Learning, liv'd only by the guidance and dictates of Nature; for what use of Grammar, where every man spoke the same Language and had no further design than to understand one another? What use of Logick, where there was no bickering about the double-meaning of words? What need of Rhetorick, where there were no Law-suits? Or to what purpose Laws, where there were no ill manners? from which without doubt good Laws first came. Besides, they were more religious than with an impious curiosity to dive into the secrets of Nature, the dimension of Starrs, the motions, effects, and hidden causes of things; as believing it a crime for any man to attempt to be wise beyond his condition. And as to the Inquiry of what was beyond Heaven, that madness never came into their heads. But the purity of the golden age declining by degrees, first, as I said before, Arts were invented by the evil Genii; and yet but few, and those too receiv'd by fewer. After that the Chaldean Superstition and Greek newfangledness, that had little to do, added I know not how many more; meer torments of Wit, and that so great that even Grammar alone is work enough for any man for his whole life.

Though yet amongst these Sciences those only are in esteem that come nearest to common sense, that is to say, Folly. Divines are half starv'd, Naturalists out of heart, Astrologers laught at, and Logicians slighted; onely the Physician is worth all the rest. And amongst them too, the more unlearned, impudent, or unadvised he is, the more he is esteem'd, even among Princes. For Physick, especially as it is now profest by most men, is nothing but a branch of Flattery, no less than Rhetorick. Next them, the second place is given to our Law-drivers, if not the first; whose Profession, though I say it my self, most men laugh at as the Ass of Philosophy; yet there's scarce any business, either so great or small, but is manag'd by these Asses. These purchase their great Lordships, while in the mean time the Divine, having run through the whole Body of Divinity, sits gnawing a Raddish, and is in continual Warfare with Lice and Fleas. As therefore those Arts are best that have the nearest Affinity with Folly, so are they most happy of all others that have least commerce with Sciences, and follow the guidance of Nature, who is in no wise imperfect, unless perhaps we endeavor to leap over those bounds she has appointed to us. Nature hates all false-colouring, and 385 is ever best where she is least adulterated with Art.

Go to then, don't ye find among the several kinds of living Creatures, that they thrive best that understand no more than what Nature taught them? What is more prosperous or wonderful than the Bee? And though they have not the same judgement of sense as other Bodies have, yet wherein hath Architecture gone beyond their building of Houses? What Philosopher ever founded the like Republique? Whereas the Horse, that comes so near man in understanding and is therefore so familiar with him, is also partaker of his misery. For while he thinks it a shame to lose the Race, it often happens that he cracks his wind; and in the Battel, while he contends for Victory, he's cut down himself, and, together with his Rider, 'lies biting the earth': not to mention those strong Bits, sharp Spurrs, close Stables, Arms, Blows, Rider, and briefly, all that slavery he willingly submits to, while, imitating those men of Valour, he so eagerly strives to be reveng'd of the Enemy. Than which how much more were the life of flies or birds to be wish'd for, who living by the instinct of Nature look no further than the present, if yet man would but let 'em alone in 't. And if at any time they chance to be taken, and being shut up in Cages endeavour to imitate our speaking, 'tis strange how they degenerate from their native gaiety. So much better in every respect are the works of Nature than the adulteries of Art.

In like manner I can never sufficiently praise that Pythagoras in a Dung-hill Cock, who being but one had been yet every thing; a Philosopher, a Man, a Woman, a King, a private man, a Fish, a Horse, a Frog, and I believe too, a Sponge; and at last concluded that no Creature was more miserable than man, for that all other Creatures are content with those bounds that Nature set them, onely Man endeavours to exceed them. And again, among men he gives the precedency not to the learned or the great, but the Fool. Nor had that Gryllus less wit than Ulysses with his many counsels, who chose rather to lie grunting in a Hog-sty than be expos'd with t' other to so many hazzards. Nor does Homer, that Father of trifles, dissent from me; who not only call'd all men 'wretched and full of calamity', but often his great pattern of Wisedom, Ulysses, 'Miserable'; Paris, Ajax, and Achilles no where. And why, I pray? but that, like a cunning fellow and one that was his craft's-master, he did nothing without the advice of Pallas. In a word he was too wise, and by that means ran wide of Nature. As therefore amongst men they are least happy that study Wisedom, as being in this twice-Fools, that when they are born men they should yet so far forget their condition as to affect the life of Gods; and after the Example of the Gyants, with their Philosophical gimcracks make a War upon
386 Nature: so they on the other side seem as little miserable as is

possible, who come nearest to Beasts and never attempt any thing beyond Man. Go to then, let's try how demonstrable this is; not by Enthymems or the imperfect Syllogisms of the Stoicks, but by plain, downright and ordinary Examples.

And now, by the immortal Gods! I think nothing more happy than that generation of men we commonly call fools, ideots, lack-wits and dolts; splendid Titles too, as I conceive 'em. I'le tell ye a thing, which at first perhaps may seem foolish and absurd, yet nothing more true. And first they are not afraid of death; no small evil, by Jupiter? They are not tormented with the conscience of evil acts; not terrify'd with the fables of Ghosts, nor frighted with Spirits and Goblins. They are not distracted with the fear of evils to come, nor the hopes of future good. In short they are not disturb'd with those thousand of cares to which this life is subject. They are neither modest, nor fearful, nor ambitious, nor envious, nor love they any man. And lastly if they should come nearer even to the very ignorance of Brutes, they could not sin, for so hold the Divines. And now tell me, thou wise fool, with how many troublesome cares thy mind is continually perplext; heap together all the discommodities of thy life, and then thou'lt be sensible from how many evils I have delivered my Fools. Add to this that they are not onely merry, play, sing, and laugh themselves, but make mirth where ever they come, a special priviledge it seems the Gods have given 'em to refresh the pensiveness of life. Whence it is, that whereas the world is so differently affected one towards another,—that all men indifferently admit them as their companions, desire, feed, cherish, embrace them, take their parts upon all occasions, and permit 'em without offence to do or say what they list. And so little doth every thing desire to hurt them, that even the very Beasts, by a kind of natural instinct of their innocence no doubt, pass by their injuries. For of them it may be truly said that they are consecrate to the Gods, and therefore and not without cause do men have 'em in such esteem. Whence is it else that they are in so great request with Princes, that they can neither eat nor drink, go any whither, or be an hour without them? Nay, and in some degree they prefer these Fools before their crabbish Wise-men, whom yet they keep about them for State-sake. Nor do I conceive the reason so difficult, or that it should seem strange why they are prefer'd before t' others, for that these wise men speak to Princes about nothing but grave, serious matters, and trusting to their own parts and learning do not fear sometimes 'to grate their tender ears with smart truths'; but fools fit 'em with that they most delight in, as jeasts, laughter, abuses of other men, wanton pastimes, and the like.

387   Again, take notice of this no contemptible blessing which Nature

hath giv'n fools, that they are the only plain, honest men and such as speak truth. And what is more commendable than truth? for though that Proverb of Alcibiades in Plato attributes Truth to Drunkards and Children, yet the praise of it is particularly mine, even from the testimony of Euripides; amongst whose other things there is extant that his honourable saying concerning us, 'A fool speaks foolish things.' For whatever a fool has in his heart, he both shews it in his looks and expresses it in his discourse; while the wise men's are those two Tongues which the same Euripides mentions, whereof the one speaks truth, the other what they judge most seasonable for the occasion. These are they 'that turn black into white,' blow hot and cold with the same breath, and carry a far different meaning in their Breast from what they feign with their Tongue. Yet in the midst of all their prosperity, Princes in this respect seem to me most unfortunate, because, having no one to tell them truth, they are forc't to receive flatterers for friends.

But, some one may say, the ears of Princes are strangers to truth, and for this reason they avoid those Wise men, because they fear lest some one more frank than the rest should dare to speak to them things rather true than pleasant; for so the matter is, that they don't much care for truth. And yet this is found by experience among my Fools, that not onely Truths but even open reproaches are heard with pleasure; so that the same thing which, if it came from a wise man's mouth might prove a Capital Crime, spoken by a Fool is receiv'd with delight. For Truth carries with it a certain peculiar Power of pleasing, if no Accident fall in to give occasion of offence; which faculty the Gods have given onely to Fools. And for the same reasons is it that Women are so earnestly delighted with this kind of Men, as being more propense by Nature to Pleasure and Toyes. And whatsoever they may happen to do with them, although sometimes it be of the seriousest, yet they turn it to Jest and Laughter; as that Sexe was ever quick-witted, especially to colour their own faults.

But to return to the happiness of Fools, who when they have past over this life with a great deal of Pleasantness, and without so much as the least fear or sense of Death, they go straight forth into the Elysian Field, to recreate their Pious and Careless Souls with such Sports as they us'd here.

CORNELIUS AGRIPPA

Selected Letters and Other Writings
Translated by Henry Morley

One *Letter to a new magistrate, citing the case of a woman whose mother had been burnt as a witch, and who was herself accused of the same offense, seized, beaten, imprisoned, tortured. He pleads for the dismissal of Nicolas Savin, the Inquisitor, 1519:* You have seen lately, most honorable man, from the acts themselves, those impious articles of a most iniquitous information by virtue of which brother Nicolas Savin, of the Dominican convent, Inquisitor of heretics, has fraudulently dragged into his slaughter-house this innocent woman, in spite of God and justice, in spite of law and equity, contrary to Christian conscience, brotherly kindness, contrary to sacerdotal custom, the profession of his rule, the form of laws and canons: and has also, as a wicked man, wickedly and wrongfully exposed her to atrocious and enormous torments; whereby he has earned for himself a name of cruelty that will not die, as the lord official John Leonard, your predecessor now departed, himself testified upon his death-bed: and the lords of the chapter themselves know it with abhorrence. Among those articles of accusation one and the first is, that the mother of the said woman was burnt for witchcraft. I have excepted against this man as impertinent, intrusive, and incompetent to exercise in this case the judicial function; but lest you be led astray by false prophets who claim to be Christ, and are Antichrist, I pray your reverence to bear with a word of help, and only pay attention to a conversation lately held with me upon the position of this article, by the before-named bloodthirsty brother. For he asserted superciliously that the fact was in the highest degree decisive, and enough to warrant torture; and not unreasonably he asserted it according to the

knowledge of his sect, which he produced presently out of the depths of the *Malleus Maleficarum* and the principles of peripatetic Theology, saying: "It must be so, because it is the custom with witches, from the very first, to sacrifice their infants to the demons, and besides that" (he said), "commonly, or often, their infants are the result of intercourse with incubi. Thus it happens that in their offspring, as with an hereditary taint, the evil sticks." O egregious sophism! Is it thus that in these days we theologize? Do figments like these move us to the torturing of harmless women? Is there no grace in baptism, no efficacy in the priests bidding: "Depart, unclean spirit, and give place to the Holy Ghost," if, because an impious parent has been sacrificed, the offspring must be given to the devil? Let any one who will, believe in this opinion, that incubi can produce offspring in the flesh. What is the fruit of this impossible position, if it be admitted, unless, according to the heresy of the Faustinians and Donatists, we get a greater evil as result? But to speak as one of the faithful, what matters it if one is the child of an incubus, what hurt is it to have been devoted as an infant to the devil? Are we not all from the nature of our humanity born one mass of sin, malediction, and eternal perdition, children of the devil, children of the Divine wrath, and heirs of damnation, until by the grace of baptism Satan is cast out, and we are made new creatures in Jesus Christ, from whom none can be separated, except by his own offence. You see now the worth of this position as a plea for judgment, at enmity with law, perilous to receive, scandalous to propound. Farewell, and either avoid or banish this blaspheming brotherkin. Written this morning in the city of Metz.

Two *Selection from* ON MARRIAGE: They sin heavily, whether they be parents, relations, tutors, guardians, who (not looking to the lifelong good-will, or to the prospect of children, or to the maintenance of chastity, but through avarice and ambition, for the dignity of lands, the power of nobility, wealth, or the like) urge beyond their duty the divine rule of obedience to parents (by a sort of tyranny), and fettering the free will of their sons or daughters, force them into unwelcome nuptials; prompted by no reason of age, kindness, condition, manners, love, or any divine precept. Out of such marriages are bred adultery, dissension, scorn, continual anger, perpetual scoldings, discords, hatreds, repudiation, and other unending ills. Sometimes there follow even poisonings, slaughterings, or sudden deaths, so that not God, but Satan, appears to have joined those pairs together. Add to this that in many places some princes and

lords of this world, under the name of Christians—foes to God, blasphemers of the Lord, overturners of the Church, defilers of things sacred, arrogating to themselves divinity—by their arbitration, sometimes even by their command as tyrants, compel the marriages of subjects, taking, moreover, tithes of the dowries, not without most wicked sacrilege, for their private treasuries: thus, leaving adultery untaxed, they punish marriage. There is, moreover, yet another custom to condemn, which has grown up in many nations—that second marriages are pursued everywhere with I know not what contempt. Moreover, they levy a fine of a certain sum on those who marry twice, and give the money to be devoured by a certain fraternity of theirs, making Joseph, the husband of the blessed Virgin Mary, patron of this scorn of a divine mystery. Of this fraternity the devil was the founder, and the wrath of God delivers it to its own reprobate sense, which, applauding fornication, decries second nuptials; as if, destitute of divine grace, mocking the sacrament, to which is due all honor, reverence, and freedom. . . .

You, therefore, who wish to take a wife, let love be your inducement, not opinion: choose a wife, not a dress; marry a wife, not a dowry. In this temper having prayed to the omnipotent God, who alone gives a true wife to man, having sought also the consent of her parents, and shown to them a due obedience, putting away all avarice, ambition, envy, and fear: with mature self-communing, with free consent, with fervent but yet chaste and reasonable love, accept the wife given to you for a perpetual companion, not for a slave, by the hand of God: let your wisdom guide her with all gentleness and reverence. Do not submit her, but admit her to your counsels; let her be in your house the mistress, in your family the mother.

Three *Letters after being dismissed as physician to the Queen-mother of France, 1526:* Hear what rules I have prescribed for myself, if ever I am tempted to return to the court service: to make myself a proper courtier, I will flatter egregiously, be sparing of faith, profuse of speech, ambiguous in counsel, like the oracles of old; but I will pursue gain, and prefer my own advantage above all things: I will cultivate no friendship save for money's sake; I will be wise to myself, praise no man except through cunning, decry any man you please. I will thrust forth whom I can, that I may take what he is forced to leave, will place myself on half a dozen seats, and despise every one who offers me his hospitality but not his money, as a barren tree. I will have faith in no man's word, in no man's friend-

391

ship; I will take all things ill and brood on vengeance; the Prince only I will watch and worship, but him I will flatter, I will agree with, I will infest, only through fear or greed of my own gain. You may admire me for that I have become so good a courtier only now, when I am liberated from the court. . . . The astrological judgments, as I before told you, I have not finished, and will not finish, until the Queen has replied to my letter, and herself required them of me. . . . But I should like you to tell me who my evil genius is by whom the Queen's mind is possessed, to the obliteration of her good will, so recently expressed towards me: because I ought to cast him out by some religious exorcism, or appease him by some magical sacrifice, or fortify myself against him with barbarous names of the gods and cabalistic pentacles. . . .

All hail! my dearest Chapelain. Blessed be the Lord, I am a rich man, if there be truth in fable. A man of consideration, long my friend, has brought me seeds of gold, and planted them over my furnace, within long-necked flasks, putting underneath a little fire, as of the sun's heat; and as hens brood over eggs, we keep the warmth up night and day, expecting forthwith to produce enormous golden chicks. If all be hatched we shall exceed Midas in wealth, or at least in length of ears, and I shall say a long farewell to those great Ninuses and Semiramises. A rich and prosperous farewell to you!—From Lyons, from your soon to be long-pursued or long-eared Agrippa. . . .

I know that Bourdon was an enemy, but I did not think he was so pestilent that one might even be poisoned by uttering his name. I remember now how a good mathematician and astrologer, Orontius of Paris, was vexed with a long imprisonment for prophesying what was true. Certainly, if I had sent the rest of my prognostication I should have passed through the smoke into the fire. Because, like Balaam, I could not curse Bourbon, I am guilty already, marked as Bourbon's friend and the court's enemy. How far I am so, many of that duke's noble followers can testify, who, when I was leaving Friburg, tried to divert me, both by prayers and large promises, into his service. How I answered them and what I did, there are some captains to testify, cousins of mine, named von Eylens, who would have favored Bourbon had I not caused them to come hither with the four thousand foot-soldiers under their command. I induced them to serve the King of France, and trusted my whole fortunes on the faith which has been kept neither with them nor me. Our men have been carried to slaughter: one of my relatives is lost, another seriously wounded, but neither pledges, promises, nor the usual public military contract, have secured for us what is our due. Had we served Bourbon we should have grown rich upon your spoil, and I, a soldier and a knight, should never have been basely used as the physician to your Queen. Your King in absence has forgotten and neglected me; your Queen, for candid speech, impatient of the truth, immoderate in vengeance, has spurned, repulsed, expelled me. . . .

Hitherto I have fought in the ranks, now I will fight alone; armed cap-à-pie, you shall see me act more boldly, hear me speak more boldly. But you must forgive my wrath, for there is no animal created so infirm as never to break out into anger. I know your honesty, or I would not have written words like these. Be of good courage, and say no more to the Queen in my behalf, make no further attempt to appease her; our Seneschal may try this if he pleases, since he gave occasion to her fury, through, in truth, by no fault of his own. Take care never to address to me again as Counsellor, or Queen's Physician. I detest this title. I condemn all hope it ever raised in me. I renounce all fealty that I ever swore to her. She never more shall be mistress of mine (for already she has ceased to be so), but I have resolved to think of her as some atrocious and perfidious Jezebel, if she thus heeds rather dishonest words than honest deeds. Salute for me Jacques Lefevre (Faber), Cop, and Bode, patriarchs of literature and virtue, and all others who love you and me. I wish them all peace and good fortune: the rest of the courtiers, may the gods confound! I now hate princes and courts equally. Again farewell. Remembrance to you from my dearest wife, the most faithful companion of my fortune. . . .

Four *On hearing that the French court was bringing from Germany at considerable cost a magician said to have power over demons, 1527:* You see where they put their faith who seek to subject the elements, nature, Providence, God, to the command of one magician, saying as Saul, when the Lord answered him not, said to the witch, I pray thee divine unto me by the familiar spirit. This is done by the most Christian king and by his mother; bishops and cardinals connive and suffer the counsels of the Father of Lies to be rewarded from the sacred treasures of the Church. What profit had the mighty ones of eld from the diviners who deluded them with promises of happy fortune? Did they not all come to the dust, and perish miserably in their sins? Those impious follies lead to ruin, and make none more miserable than the men who trust them most. I do not deny that there are arts, wise thoughts, by which, without offence to God, injury to faith or religion, kingdoms may be defended, counsel tested, wealth increased, enemies overcome, the good-will of mankind conciliated, sicknesses be combated, health preserved, life prolonged, the vigor of youth restored: there are also holy intercessions, public supplications, private prayers of good men, by which not only the Divine wrath may be averted, but the Divine blessing obtained. But if there is beyond this any art of prescience, or of working miracles, certainly to these triflers and slaves to the demons it remains unknown. By the grave counsels of wise men, who have sought to be filled with the spirit of God, states may be served, not by the follies which produced the ruin of the greatest empire in the world. . . . In vain the watchman wakes, except the Lord be keeper of the city. There is only one way of averting evil, by the change of perfidy and malice into repentance and charity, then it may be to any man against whom judgment has been decreed, as it was with Ahab, when the Word of the Lord came, saying, Seest thou how Ahab humbleth himself before me? Because he humbleth himself before me, I will not bring the evil in his days.

Five *Letters from Erasmus to Agrippa, 1531, 1533:* Greeting to you, illustrious man, your name here is in everybody's mouth, especially on account of the book you have issued on the Vanity of Studies, concerning which many of the learned have written to me—I myself not yet having seen it—that it contains, in all conscience, liberty enough, though as to other things opinions differ. I will take care to get it as soon as I can, and devour the whole. This Andrew, a priest, in my opinion modest and pious, has come hither to see Erasmus; but having hoped for a treasure, has found coals. Now he is hastening to you, expecting to draw from your breast a greater flow of wisdom. He seems to have a special love for your talent, and carries your book on Occult Philosophy as his constant companion on the way. I do not commend him to you, but ask rather to be commended to you through him. When I shall have read your book, I will write to you more fully. In the mean time, I pray for your prosperity. From Friburg in Brisgan. Sept. 17, 1531. . . .

I wrote to you at first in few words, to the effect that the doctrine of your book on the Vanity of Sciences had pleased some of the most learned in these parts. I had not then read the book, but soon afterwards, having obtained it, I bade a famulus read it aloud at supper, for I had no other vacant time, and am myself compelled to abstain after supper from all study. I liked the courage and the eloquence, nor do I see why the monks should have been so angry. As you attack the bad, you praise the good, but they like altogether to be praised. What I advised you before, I would advise you now, that if you conveniently can, you extricate yourself from this contention. Take Louis Barguin for a warning, whom nothing ruined but his simple freedom towards monks and theologians, he being a man otherwise of unstained character. I often advised him dexterously to disentangle himself from that business, but the hope of victory misled him. But if you cannot fly, and must hazard the fortune of war, see that you fight from a tower, and do not trust yourself into their hands. Of this, before everything, take heed that you do not mix me up with the matter: I am burdened with more than enough ill will, and this would trouble me, while doing you more harm than good. I asked the same of Barguin, and he promised, but deceived me, trusting more to his own courage than to my advice. You see the end. There would not have been the smallest danger had he yielded to my counsel. Many a time I harped to him that monks and theologians are not to be overcome, even if one had a better cause than St. Paul had. Now, therefore, if I have any influence with you, again and again I would warn you that the task you have undertaken leads to perilous encounters, and may cost you the power of advancing in your studies. At present I have not leisure to say more, for I am writing to several friends. Farewell. Friburg, April 21, 1533.

Six Apology *for his* Vanity of Arts and Sciences *in answer to forty-three articles of accusation preferred against his book by the theologians of Louvain, 1532:* I have been commended by the learned for the Declamation now attacked, and from them never heard that it was heretical, though they have indeed objected against it a too fearless use of liberty of speech. If that be a vice in me, it is mine in company with many great and holy men, and I would not have fallen into it but for the example they had set. I am not afraid to confess that it is an inbred vice which makes me unable to flatter, and apt now and then to speak more freely than is thought expedient for tender ears. I own that I have offended many by true speech. . . . I know, too, that I am a man liable to err, but always of a sincere mind, and I profess myself to be a Catholic, nor do I think that I have pushed so far the licence of my Declamation as to have separated myself from the orthodox faith, or that I need fear to receive the admonition and correction of superiors, who will themselves remember that they are men capable of erring in their judgment. . . .

395

[He had called Luther "the unconquered heretic."]

I know not whether by chance there may not be some superstitious theologians who would grudge Luther the name of heretic,
as one shared by him with the Apostle Paul, who, before Felix,
professed that he served God after the sect which the Jews called
heresy; but I make no doubt that our masters of Louvain approve of
me for having called Luther a heretic, only it offends them much
that I have called him unconquered whom they and their associates
at Cologne were the first men dogmatically to condemn. But I am
not ignorant that Luther has been condemned for heresy, only I do
not see that he is vanquished, when to this day he gains ground in
his battle, and reigns in the mind of the people which is won to
him in spite of authority by the dishonesty, ignorance, malice, and
falsehood of many of our priests, and monks, and masters. I speak
of the event, not of the doctrine, against which, though it has been
opposed in the best manner of the schools, judged with all strict-
ness and subjected to the most august condemnation, all efforts end
unprosperously. . . .

First, there descended into this arena Hochstraten and Eckius, so
fighting as to earn nothing but ridicule. Then succeeded monks,
vociferating among the common people rude abuse of Luther; what
did they thereby but scatter among the multitude those questions
which before were discussed in Latin by the learned, and confined
within the limits of the schools. So they impelled Luther to write
in the vernacular, and heresy was then sown broadcast. The schools
of Louvain, Cologne and Paris afterwards came out with their bare
articles and dogmatical censures, which, while they spread abroad
the smoke and fire of books committed to be burnt—as if fire could
put out fire—made Luther's works more to be sought after, more
sold. At length there appeared the terrific bull of Leo, which is so
much scorned by the Lutherans that they have not hesitated openly
to jest at it, with contemptuous scholiae and glosses. An Imperial
decree was added, with no better success. The slaughter-houses
were next opened: what else resulted but the cutting off heads from
a hydra? Is this the conquest of Luther? I speak of the event, not
of the doctrine, and I wish that Christ were not preached as
religiously by some of these heretics as by our teachers. Was Arius
conquered when his sect occupied more churches than the orthodox?
Is Mahomet conquered when there are more men of his creed
than Christians? Again, I say, I speak of the event, not of the
doctrine. How have I sinned, then, if I have called Luther an unconquered heretic? Would that I lied, and that Luther had been
conquered as happily as he has been boldly provoked to war. I wish
he were not unconquered heretic, and even, also, conquerer of

heretics, to the great shame of our teachers. For who conquered the Anabaptists? Who has withstood the Sacramentarians? Was it not Luther alone? Show me one writing out of your academies by which you have moved them so much as a finger's breadth. Of what use are you in the Church, if it be enough to say: We condemn, because so has the Church decided? (And to decrees of the Church our teachers fly whenever they are hardly pressed, and there abide, unable to produce the Scripture that defends them.) Certainly, rustics who have not learnt the alphabet, and idiots, can profess as much. If that sufficed for the reconquest of heretics, oh, now would I welcome Martin Luther, who, while our masters slept and snored, alone watched for the Church, and alone freed it from the strong and violent heresies of Anabaptists and Sacramentarians, who were getting possession of almost all Germany. But I seem here to approve of Luther, and herein I do, indeed, approve of him. But be not enraged; I approve of him as of the serpent in theriaca, which though in itself deadly, is in this form poisonous to poison. . . .

Seven *Complaint Against the Calumnies of Theologians and Monks, 1532:* I think, therefore, that in these days, my Eustochius, there is no bliss greater than ignorance, nothing safer than to teach men nothing, when almost nothing can be written at which there shall not be some to take offence; but they who teach and know nothing, or nothing but the meanest and the basest things, are far removed from this fear, from these dangers, for of little things large ruin is impossible; and he who grovels cannot tumble far; but he who seeks to climb the heights, seems to be seeking his misfortune. As pleasant— and with more safety, as pleasant—is the marsh to the frogs, the mire to the hogs, the gloom to the bats, as to the doves the housetop, or the clear sun to the eagle. Therefore Pythagoras in Lucian, having wandered through all shapes in his own round of metamorphoses, confesses that he enjoyed life far more when he was a frog than when he was a king and a philosopher. Which persuasion seems to me so suited to the present time, that to know nothing and teach nothing, and to differ, as one might say, in nothing from a beast, is now the happiest and safest course; at the same time it is that which makes a man the most acceptable to those courtiers and satraps, who commonly bestow their favors upon creatures having most resemblance to themselves.

397

PARACELSUS

The Sixth Defence,
To Excuse His Strange Manner and Wrathful Ways (from Seven
Defensiones, the Reply to Certain Calumniations of His Enemies)
Translated by C. Lilian Temkin

Not enough to attack me in various articles, but I am said to be a strange fellow with an uncivil answer, I do not wash up to the satisfaction of everyone, I do not answer everyone's contention in humility. This they consider and deem a great vice in me. I myself, however, deem it a great virtue and would not that it were otherwise than it is. I like my ways well enough. In order, however, that I may justify myself as to how my strange manner is to be understood, pay heed: I am by nature not subtly spun, neither is it usual in my country to attain anything by spinning silk. Neither are we raised on figs, nor on meat, nor on wheaten bread, but on cheese, milk and oatcakes. This cannot make subtle fellows; besides what one received in youth sticks to one all one's days. The same is almost coarse to the subtle, the cat-clean, the superfine. For those who are brought up in soft raiment and in the women's apartments, and we who grow up among fir-cones do not understand one another well. Therefore must the coarse be judged coarse, though the same think himself utterly subtle and charming. Thus it is with me too: what I think is silk, the others call ticking and coarse cloth.

But pay heed further how I justify myself in this accusation that I give a rough answer. The other physicians know little of the arts; they resort to friendly, pleasing, charming words; they advise people with breeding and fine words; they set forth all things at length, delightfully, with distinct differentiations, and say: Come again soon, my dear sir; my dear wife, go and accompany the gentleman, etc. I say thus: What wilt thou? I have no time now; it is not so urgent. Now I have upset the applecart! They have made such fools of the patients that they are completely of the belief that a friendly, affectionate manner, ceremony, ingratiating ways, much ado, constitute art and medicine. They call him 'young sir' who only comes from the shopkeeper's; they call another 'Sir, wise Sir' who is a cobbler and a dullard, where I say 'Thou'; but with this I throw away my resources. My intention is to gain nothing with my tongue, but only with works. As they, however, are not of this opinion, they can well say in their way that I am a strange, queer-headed fellow, that I give little good advice. I do not believe in feeding myself on friendly caresses, wherefore I cannot use what befits me not, nor what I have not learned. For it is not necessary to use such flattery and to deal tenderly with every boor who is not fit to be carried in a dung-barrow. Medicine should be such, that the physician may answer according to his flesh and blood, his country's customs and his own nature: rough, rude, stern, gentle, mild, virtuous, friendly, delightful—according to how he is by nature and by acquired habit. But let this not be his art, but only the briefest answer. And on with the works! That's the way to oil the wheels!

Thus I consider in this respect I am sufficiently defended. Still, it happens that I have other strange ways, for instance towards the sick, if they do not follow my prearranged injunctions. Anyone can judge that such strange ways are not unjustified, in order that medicine may be found true, the patient become well, and I may still remain without blame. A turtle-dove would grow angry with such lousy muddle-heads.

There is a further complaint against me, with regard in part to the servants who have left me, in part also to my Pupils, that none of them could stay with me because of my strange ways. Now note my answer: the hangman has taken from me into his favour one and twenty servants, and removed them from this world, God help them all. How can a man stay with me, when the hangman will not leave him with me? And what has my strange way done to them? If they had fled the hangman's way, that would have been true art. And there are yet some who have thus kept with me and have also fled the hangman; and in rejecting me, they have excused themselves, for I was strange, no one could cope with me. But how should I not be strange, when a servant is no servant, but a master? He looks for his advantage, ruins me with it, brings shame upon me, and rejoices in it. Thus they lie about me to the patient, they receive them behind my back, without my knowledge and consent, make a contract with them for half the money, say they know my art, have copied it from me. After such disloyalty they cannot and would not be with me, nor the patients either. Afterwards, when I hear of it, the knavery is a bargain. Let anyone judge how honest the bargain is! *Doctores,* barbers, bath-keepers, pupils, servants and lads too, have done it to me. Should this make a lamb of me? A wolf should result in the end! Moreover, I must go afoot while they ride. For this comforts me always, that I linger and remain when they run away and their falsity is understood. Not less do the *Doctores* complain about me and not without justification. For telling the truth hurts the one whose cunning is revealed. How many, however, are there who for this speak good of me?—they too are *Doctores.* Thus are the apothecaries, too, inimical to me; they say I am strange, eccentric, etc., no one can do right in my opinion. Yet to me, every-one can do right who acts righteously. But as for giving *Quid pro Quo, Merdum pro Musco*—it suits me not to acknowledge the *Quid pro Quo* book of the travelling scholars, to accept it nor yet to allow its use. Besides, of what they give me themselves, not a third is good, sometimes indeed none is good. And the same is sometimes not what they say it is. Should I subject my patient to the *Quid pro Quo,* even if it is no good? Thus should I come to shame, my patients to disaster, perhaps even to their death. When I proclaim this in my native way, which I consider and deem very friendly, the idlers call it an angry, strange manner. Other *Doctores* do not thus, I alone do so. And furthermore, I write short prescriptions, not forty to sixty ingredients, I prescribe little and seldom, I do not empty their boxes for them, I do not bring much money into their kitchens. Yet this is the business for which they calumniate me. Now judge for yourselves, to whom do I owe most? Or to whom have I pledged myself as *Doctor?* To help the apothecary empty the bags in his kitchen, or the patient from the kitchen to his benefit? Now behold, dear sirs, how strange I am and in what a plight is my head! If I should defend my angry manner to the end, they would blush with shame and be frowned upon. For to tell of those who thus accuse me and criticise me because they think thus to belittle me, will bring too much of their knavery to light for them, and will greatly damage them with all pious judges and interrogators. If I were now to attack some barbers and bathkeepers a little and make public what they have against me, why they call me eccentric and a strange man, I rather think there would be few of them and they would fare very much as some others have fared whom I have mentioned. Wherefore, understand me in this sixth defence, that you who hear such things may please to measure them with true judgment and true balance; and remember that not everything comes of a pure heart, but from filth with which their mouths run over, to glorify themselves and to belittle me.

On the Miners' Sickness
and Other Miners' Diseases, First book, First Tractate
Translated by George Rosen

The In order that you may understand the cause of asthma as quickly
Third as possible, know then that the heaven is the element fire and that
Chapter its elemental movement produces the chaos which shall be discussed
here. And in the same manner as water is brought to boil by fire,
the chaos is that which is boiled by the element of heaven. And just
as the meat in water gives up its strength to the water, so the stars
are like the meat and give their strength to the afore-mentioned
chaos. And just as the soup from the meat is food for man, so the
chaos, of which we are speaking here, is also food for man. Just as
the food is digested in the stomach and has its special gullet, thus
the chaos is digested in the lung and it also has its own gullet. Just
as the things, that are placed in water, have their properties and
make people sick or healthy according to them, so do the stars, that
are placed in the chaos also produce a soup that is healthy or un-
healthy. For this is the soup in which the plague is prepared, that
enters through the lung tube and which proceeding further according to its anatomy, flies like a bird to its nest. If God had not
determined at the beginning, that some should be protected and
leave children behind whose seed should remain, who would have
remained blessed then? Know then also concerning the lung-sick-
ness that it comes through the power of the stars, in that their peculiar characters are boiled out, settling on the lungs in three
different ways: in a mercurial manner like a sublimated smoke that
coagulates, like a salt spirit which passes from resolution to coagu-
lation, and thirdly, like a sulphur which is precipitated on the walls
by roasting. In the same manner as you see a clean barrel, that is
filled with clear wine in the fall and the wine has no palpable and
congealed components. But at the end of the year, when the wine is
poured out again, these three kinds of mercury, sulphur and salt are
found to have settled on this barrel; this is the winestone (tartarus).
Thus in the same manner, just as there is something in the wine
which was not seen in it, there is also a body (corpus) in the chaos,
which attaches itself to the lungs, as to its barrel, and which then
hardens there like a mucus in its viscosity, after which the coagula-
401 tion starts, which is the matter of the lung sickness.

I do not want to describe the species of the lung sickness, but what
has been reported here is an instruction, so that you will understand concerning the heaven and the chaos and that they are also
in the earth. That is to say that those who are instructed in the
philosophy of the earth will also explain the lung sickness, since in
its origin and rise the miners' sickness shares the species and the rise
of the lung sickness, which is why the one explains the other and
allows it to be understood. Anyone who has been instructed concerning the terrestrial diseases, also knows those in the firmament.
One who writes correctly concerning the diseases of the firmament
will also hit upon the diseases of the earth correctly. One who does
not strike the earth will also shoot astray in the heavens. The physician should be so grounded in the light of nature, that he not only
knows seven stars, but all the stars that the firmament contains. He
doesn't stop with this knowledge, since he also knows the earth if
he knows this, and therefore also the other two elements in their
astronomy and philosophy. Therefore know further, just as the
chaos is born, so is the earth a heaven of this generation, and the
minerals that lie in the earth are the firmament of this heaven. Fire
arises out of this element of the earth and makes a chaos in the
earth of the same kind as the chaos between heaven and earth. And
this same chaos becomes a soup of its minerals in the same manner
as the external chaos is a soup of the stars. Now such people as seek
and make their dwellings in the earth must carry on and nourish
their lungs with the chaos that is there. And that which has been
cooked in the chaos is the mineral impression, is the tartarus of
the lung, which I call the miners' sickness here. And therefore the
mode of origin (modus generandi) is the same process in both
diseases, which ends according to the three kinds of mercury,
sulphur and salt, the type depending on the definite property contained in this flesh. It is well to consider this point, that this chaos
acts in two kinds of bodies; since you know that the Earth's own
inhabitants were made for her, just as we were made from Adam
to live in the air between heaven and earth, just as you also know
similar things about the nymphs. The chaos of the earth has been
given to the inhabitants of the earth as air, the chaos of the water
as air to the nymphs, they live therefore from this air. The one body
is that of the inhabitants of the earth; for this I recommend the
Archidoxa and the books Paramiris. But it should be understood,
the other body is that of people who become inhabitants in the
mines, and they are not people of the earth. From which it follows

that the human chaos must be carried with them into the mines, since their lungs are maintained by their chaos, that is by the human chaos. But there it comes to a mixture of the earthly and the firmamental, and the two kinds become as one there, just as in a marriage; now the individual is suited for this constellation of the earth, from which constellation the miners' sickness takes its origin.

The Diseases That Deprive Man of His Reason
Translated by Gregory Zilboorg

Chapter Three **On the Origin of Truly Insane People** In previous chapters I have spoken of the deprivation of reason, but it is not the case that patients remain without reason until they die. They suffer from attacks time and again, so that they lose their reason and then regain it, as we have indicated. Now we shall speak of those who are permanently insane and of insane body, rather than of those subject to recurring attacks. The period is irregular, once long, then short, in correspondence with the stars; it does not always occur, behave, and stay in the same way, but is irregular in accordance with the course of the stars.

There are four kinds of insane people: *Lunatici, Insani, Vesani* and *Melancholici. Lunatici* are those who get the disease from the moon and react according to it. *Insani* are those who have been suffering from it since birth and have brought it from the womb as a family heritage. *Vesani* are those who have been poisoned and contaminated by food and drink, from which they lose reason and sense. *Melancholici* are those who by their nature lose their reason and turn insane. We must, however, note that apart from these four kinds there is another kind: these are the *Obsessi* who are obsessed by the devil; the various ways in which this happens are treated by us in *De Spiritibus*. But here we deal with those who are insane by nature, and sufferers of these four kinds cannot become obsessed by the devil and his company, as many people say; for the devil and his crew do not enter an insane body which is not being ruled by the entire reason according to its quality. Therefore, the devil does not enter those four kinds of insane people for, due to causes that will be explained later, they have no power of reason. While they are out of their senses they are possessed by, but safe against, the devils and *Vatis,* as we have said. The reason for this will be given in the proposed chapter *De Spiritibus et Vatis.*

403

Although there are four kinds of insanity, each with a separate origin and derivation, they all end in depriving man of his reason, not in the same way, as we announce in the first four chapters, but without any other disease, so that there is no pain, as in epilepsy, in *mania,* in *chorea lasciva,* in *suffocationis intellectus;* but these people always live in madness and, in the cases in which it is apparent that there is going to be another sick day, increasing insanity. When reason announces such sick days, death is not far, because the origin of the disease is so evident that it hurts the *spiritus vitae* and poisons it, and death results.

Now we shall take up the lunatics and the reason for their disease, so that the discussion of them in the second chapter on *Methods of Cure* will be understandable. The stars have the power to hurt and weaken our body and to influence health and illness. They do not fall into us materially or substantially, but influence reason invisibly and insensibly, like a magnet attracting iron, or a scarab dust, or asphalt fibers and wood. Such power of attraction is possessed by the moon, which tears reason out of man's head by depriving him of humors and cerebral virtues. The moon does not enter us and work in us, as has been affirmed, for no star has the power to possess us, as many state falsely; but we must believe that it takes reason from us as the stars do by virtue of their power of attraction. Just so the sun takes the humidity out of the earth, not by entering the earth and driving out the water as if it had been poured into fire, but by attracting it. Not only the moon acts thus; many planets deprive the organs of the whole body of their humors, as we discuss not here but in *De Astris et Superioribus.* Thus many people are deprived of their senses only by the moon's attraction which takes out the cerebral humor so that the whole head rages without reason. Those lunatics are ruled by the moon. The power of attraction is at its height during the full moon, and therefore it attracts most strongly and the lunatics suffer most then. It is somewhat the same with the new moon, because the newly conceived moon has new virtues which cause greater or lesser insanity; it is not that the moon because of its weakness weakens the limbs, as if all our power lay in the moon, as we shall point out in *De Firmamento.* But owing to the unusual nature of the moon there are various degrees of attraction. It so happens that the humor is drawn out of the brain when the moon is smallest. The explanation is that the new moon does not draw out the same humor as the old one: the new moon draws out the body's humor less than the old moon, which is rough and hard and therefore draws out the rough and hard humor. Just so, a young fire which has no great burning capac-

404 ity does not drive out oils and hard substance, while a great fire

takes out hard *and* soft. When the sun rises it takes away only the moisture which is not heavy but light, while at noon the heavy waters are taken. The removing of moisture is more noxious to the earth and its strength than the removal of the rough, great humidity, due to reasons given by us in *On Dew*. The sun at noon absorbs dew and fine particles, rough particles, and vapors. But this is not the case with the moon; it is not in its nature and quality. When it first comes out it takes the fine humor from the brain so that the full moon is compelled to take the rough, for nothing fine is left; under the waning moon the humor grows like dew at night, and when the moon is on the increase it is driven out again. Many people are more insane and frantic during the waning moon than during the waxing moon, because the full moon has already taken the humor from them and they suffer more acutely the more the moon wanes. Just so the splitting of the earth from lack of humor cannot take place in the forenoon but only in the afternoon after the sun at noon has taken away the humidity. It may happen with man that his insanity shows only at the end of the moon's period. There are various reasons why the powers of nature struggle increasingly until they can do no more. While the moon exerts its attraction, as long as there is humor in the head it will draw it out. This is the main reason for its drawing out and attracting most at the end of its period, and this explains why the end is most troublesome for those who begin the sick days of their nature during the moon.

In the same way we can explain those people who have received insanity from the mother's womb as a heritage, such as a family which is insane or a child who has been born insane: the seed and its function may be defective, or it may be inherited from the part of father or mother. The first reason is that the sperm in itself and in the operation may be lacking in the power of matter which makes and builds the brain. If the matter of a limb dissolves, its proper shape and nature dissolve too, as we have said in *De Generatione Hominis* in Volume One of our *Philosophy*. If there is such a deficiency in the sperm, reason is not complete since matter is not complete; therefore, there cannot be completeness of reason in the child. There is another cause for insanity in people, which is produced during the development; if, at its height, the power of attraction of the moon interferes with the generation and conception of the child, the moon can take away reason, so that complete sanity can never be restored. Such deprivation does not happen every day, although the moon rises every day, because the matter and the moon must be in accord with each other, and not every cerebral humor can be attracted by the moon, only the one

405

adjusted to it, as we have stated in *De Generatione Humana.* If it does happen, the deprivation of the senses takes place too. The moon can take away man's reason at birth; when, however, this is hereditary, the circumstance is such that if there is insanity in the brain, the child's mother also has some deficiency in her brain, for the brain of the parents is continued in the brain of the son, as we have said in *De Generatione Hominis,* because the nature and qualities of the one originate in those of the other. This does not always happen, because the sperma become mixed, and either the man or the woman may or may not be insane, and the child may follow the insanity or take after the one who has the greater influence. It may even happen that if both are insane they still would give birth to a healthy child. This is due to the power of nature, which drives out the impediments and adversities.

Now we must also speak about *Vesani* who become insane from eating and drinking. It often happens that food offered by whores causes deprivation of the senses, and this in many ways. Such insanity may lead to love, so that the *Vesani* put all their being into the whores; some are bent on war only, and therefore they have to do with war only, and there is no sanity; some climb and run; some act in various ways which we do not wish to enumerate and shall not describe, but which should be remembered. Let us not be amazed that it should be possible for food to cause this, for it is possible; and much less should we be astonished at the effects they produce. And why? Because food and drink have affected them greatly. Now we shall describe the fourfold insanity that comes from food and drink; we shall have more to say about it in the chapter *On Treatment.*

First of all, there are those that have so eaten and drunk that they have to and are compelled to love a woman. We shall leave out a few points here. If a person offers something to eat to another, whether man or woman, unbreakable, eternal love is the result; for this reason some servants give food to their masters so as to flatter them and to make love spring up in them, with the result that servants are above the masters, as we shall mention in *De Republica.* Further, unreasonable animals, dogs and others, can be brought to such love for those who offer it to them. It is natural that women should give such things to men, so that the latter should think only of making love to them; and they have no reason, and their melancholy is directed toward those women who have offered it. We shall leave it at that, because of other proposed topics.

The others who are bent only on war have been given some food intended to make them insane, and if they are choleric by nature they think only of war; their insane behavior has been given them

406

through the food. We must also speak about the melancholic and phlegmatic ones, who exhibit their nature and constitution in like behavior.

The third, who jump up and run around all the time, have received their insanity from eating the kind of thing that gives them an urge to mount and climb; this comes from the nature of this food and not from that of man. If it were up to us to write about it we would reveal everything here, but some things must remain unmentioned as there exists a great body of philosophy and contemplation on the nature of this insanity, and that must suffice.

The same is true of the fourth kind, which we shall not describe at all; it may deprive man of his reason in the way described above. Some incantations are able to do the same; we shall not describe that here but put it under *De Influentiis*. After the first accounts in this chapter we shall speak about melancholy persons, of whom there are four kinds. If such complexions deprive man of his reason, it is due to their driving the *spiritus vitae* up toward the brain so that there is too much of it there. We shall not speak of this here but leave it to those who write on philosophy.

A Book on Nymphs,
Sylphs, Pygmies, and Salamanders, and on the Other Spirits
Translated by Henry E. Sigerist

Tractatus Four As we came to the end of the treatise, we had sufficiently discussed the necessities of these beings, and how they come to man. You must now, furthermore, know about their disappearance from man, and about their doings with us, with many such tales and stories that have happened with them, in many queer ways. And first about those who married men and bore them children, as was said before. When they have been provoked in any way by their husbands while they are on water, they simply drop into the water, and nobody can find them any more. To the husband it is as if she were drowned, for he will never see her again. And yet, although she dropped into the water, he may not consider her dead. She is alive and he may not take another wife. If he did, he would have to pay with his life and could never return to the world, for the marriage is not dissolved but is still valid. It is the same as in the case of a wife who has run away. She is not divorced from her husband, nor he from

407

her. It still is a valid marriage that has not been dissolved and that nobody can ever dissolve, as long as there is life. When she has dropped into the water and has abandoned husband and children, her marriage is still valid, and she will present herself on the Day of Judgment on account of her union and pledge. The soul, namely, is not taken away nor separated from her. She must follow the soul and hold to her pledge to the end. Although she remains a water woman and nymph, she must behave as the soul requires and the pledge she has given, except that she is separated from her husband, and that there is no return, unless he takes another wife. Then she returns and brings him death, as has happened many times.

It also happens that sirens are born. They are water women too, but live more on the water than in it. They are not split like fish, but are more like a virgin, yet their form is not quite that of a woman. They bear no children but are monsters, just as a strange human being can be born from two normal parents. I would like to put it thus: the water people reproduce themselves like humans, but when it happens that they produce a monster, these monsters are sirens that swim on the water, for they repudiate them and do not keep them. This is why they occur in many forms and figures, as it happens and is the case with all monsters. Thus we marvel not only at the water people but also at the sirens, who have many strange features and are very different from people. Some can sing, some can whistle with reeds, some can do this and that. Monks are also born from nymphs, that is, a monster which is shaped just like a monk. This you must know, namely, that such growths that are comparable to men and are found in some places, come from men, that is, they come from water people, earth manikins and similar beings. In order to understand the matter correctly, remember that God effects strange things in his creations. It is the same as with a comet. Born from other stars, the comet is nothing but a super-growth, that is, a growth that has not a natural course, as a star should have, but has been directed by God on purpose into another course. This is why the comet has great significance. And so have the sea wonders and similar things which thus come from water people. They too are such regular comets that God presents to man on purpose, not without meaning and significance. There is no need to write about it here, but this you must know, that great things come from such people, who should be great mirrors held before man's eyes. But love has cooled down in many, and thus they pay no attention to the signs, intent only on usury, self-interest, gambling, drinking, matters that are interpreted by these beings, as if they were saying: look at the monsters, thus you shall be after death; let yourself be warned, beware—but nothing is done about it.

To continue the discussion of these beings, know that such people also convene and assemble in one place, where they may live together and seek intercourse with man, for they love him. The reason is that flesh and blood hold to flesh and blood. There are more women than men in such groups, few men, many women; hence they are after men whenever they have a chance. From such people a group originated that is called the Venusberg. It consists of nothing else but a kind of nymphs, thrown together in a cave and hole of their world, yet not in their own chaos, in man's chaos, but in their regionibus. Know about them that they reach a very old age, but you cannot notice it, because their appearance remains the same from beginning to end, and they die unchanged. Venus was a nymph and undine who excelled others and reigned for a long time, but she died and the succeeding Venus was not as endowed as she had been. She died in the course of time and her kingdom vanished. There are many tales about her. Some people believe that she will live until the Day of Judgment, meaning: she and her seed, not she alone. And on the Day of Judgment, all these beings will appear before God, will dissolve and come to an end. It is also said that those who come to them do not die either. But this is not true, for all beings end in death and nothing remains, neither they nor other people, nothing is without an end. It is on account of the seed that all kinds survive to the Day of Judgment. There is a story about a different beginning. It tells of a queen who resided there and sank into the earth. It was a water woman who resided there. She went into the mountain, under the pond that was above her, in her region. There she took her abode, and for making love, she built a gallery, for her to get to the lads and they to her. Such strange things happened there that nobody was able to report about these beings, what they were or where they were from, until it came to an end. It is quite possible that this could happen again should another nymph come, equal to her. How often does it not happen that a man is amazingly superior to others, and then for many years there is nobody equal to him. Thus a special portent occurred about the nymphs, was called the Venusberg, after the idol of unchastity. Many such strange stories have happened on earth, but they have been greatly despised. Yet, it should not be, because no such thing occurs without great attention being paid to it. Hence, they should not be despised. There is no need of writing about it here.

There is also a true story of the nymph in Staufenberg who sat on the road in all her beauty and served the lord she had chosen. It is quite correct that to the theologians such a being is a devilish ghost, but certainly not to the true theologians. What greater admonition is there in the Scriptures than to despise nothing, to ponder everything in mature understanding and judgment, to explore all things and dismiss nothing without previous exploration. It becomes easily apparent that they have little understanding of these beings. Making it short, they call them devils, although they know little enough about the devil himself. This you must know, that God lets such miracles happen not to have us all marry nymphs and live with them, but once in a while, in order to demonstrate the strange doings of divine creatures and that we may see the work of his labor. If it were the devil's work it should be despised, but it is not, for this he is not able to do; God alone is. Our nymph was a water woman. She promised herself to von Staufenberg and stayed also with him, until he married another wife, and took her for a devil. Taking her for a devil and considering her such, he married another woman and thus broke his promise to her. Therefore, at the wedding, she gave him the sign, through the ceiling, during the banquet, and three days later, he was dead. It requires great experience to judge in such matters, for the breaking of a pledge never remains without sanction, whatever it may be, to uphold honor and honesty and to prevent other evil and vice. If she had been a ghost, from where would she have taken blood and flesh? If she had been a devil, where would she have hidden the devil's marks which always go with it? If it had been a spirit, why should it have needed such a being? She was a woman and a nympha, as we have described them, a woman in honor, not in dishonor, and this is why she wanted duty and loyalty to be kept. Since they were not kept, she herself, from divine destiny, punished the adulterer (for no judge would have passed a sentence at her request, since she was not from Adam). Thus God granted her the punishment that is appropriate for adultery, and permitted her to be her own judge, since the world repudiated her as a spirit or devil. Many more such things have happened that are despised by men, badly so and it is a sign of great stupidity.

We must pay equally great attention to Melusine, for she was not what the theologians considered her, but a nympha. It is true, however, that she was possessed by the evil spirit, of which she would have freed herself. if she had stayed with her husband to the end. For such is the devil that he transforms these beings into different shapes, as he also does with the witches, transforming them into cats and werewolves, dogs, etc. This happened to her also, for she never was free of witchcraft but had a part in it. A superstitious belief resulted, that on Saturdays she had to be a serpent. This was her pledge to the devil for his helping her in getting a man. Otherwise, she was a nympha, with flesh and blood, fertile and well built to have children. She came from the nymphs to the humans on earth and lived there. But then, as *superstitio* seduces and vexes all beings, she went away from her people in her superstitious belief, to the places where the seduced people come who are bewitched in *superstitionibus* and spell-bound. Mind you, she remained the same serpent to the end of her life, and God knows how long it lasted. Thus these beings are warnings to us, to make us understand what we are on earth, and in what strange ways the devil deals with us and is after us in every corner. Nothing is hidden to him, neither in the depth of the sea nor in the center of the earth, where he whiles. But wherever we are, there is also God who redeems those who are his, in all places. It is stupid, however, to consider such women ghosts and devils on the basis of such happenings and because they are not from Adam. It is holding God's works in low esteem to assume that they are rejected because they have *superstitiones*. Yet there are more *superstitiones* in the Roman Church than in all these women and witches. And so it may be a warning that if *superstitio* turns a man into a serpent, it also turns him into a devil. That is, if it happens to nymphs, it also happens to you in the Roman Church. That is, you too will be transformed into such serpents, you who now are pretty and handsome, adorned with large diadems and jewels. In the end you will be a serpent and dragon, like Melusine and others of her kind.

Therefore, consider such things carefully, and be not blind with seeing eyes and dumb with good tongues, particularly since you will not let yourselves be called dumb and blind.

ANDREAS VESALIUS

The Epitome of Andreas Vesalius
The Epitome of His Books on the Fabric of the Human Body by
Andreas Vesalius of Brussels
Translated by L. R. Lind

To the Most Serene Prince Philip, Son and Heir of the Divine Emperor Charles the Fifth, Mightiest and Most Invincible Andreas Vesalius Sends Greetings: Within the slender compass of these pages, greatest prince Philip, adorned with the splendor of your immortal name and under its good auspices, there is set forth unto the common use of learning the description of the human body, which I have so divided in the manner of an enumeration, and singly related, that the principal branch of natural philosophy, treating the finished product of a creation most perfected and nigh the most worthy of all, may in the manner of an image be set before the eyes of those studious of the works of Nature. This has been done with as much conciseness as possible, and with less labor it describes those matters which I have embraced more amply in my seven books upon the subject. To those books this Epitome is, as it were, a footpath, or as it will also be rightly considered, an appendix, gathering into summary form the chapters which are set forth with detail in those books; it lays out everything in such a fashion I may prophesy that you, with the amazing liberality of culture in which you eagerly welcome whatsoever slightest offering of the writer's craft, will not utterly cast it from your sight. Moreover, as you are now entering upon a period in your life distinguished by such various virtues, you are held fast by a wondrous and most generous love of all art and learning. And when your spacious spirit shall one day rule the whole world, you may perhaps at times consider it pleasant to be acquainted with my work and to
412 regard it as a situation wretched and unworthy of the greatest

Emperors, Kings, and Consuls, that in the pursuit of studies so
varied, the harmony of the human body which we shall publish
to the world should lie constantly concealed; that man be completely unknown to himself; and that the structure of instruments
so divinely created by the Great Artificer of all things should remain
unexamined: since it is by the function of these instruments that
those things we look upon as most, and almost solely, important are
brought to pass.

Truly, although for this reason my undertaking will perhaps be
not wholly displeasing to your admirable judgment, if I should
nevertheless refuse to give forth this companion to physicians because, while I strive to be useful to them yet at the same time I
am anxious to snatch opportunity from the hands of certain rascally
printers who may later seize in possession upon the labors of another to reduce them ineptly into small space and publish them
under their own names (creatures born for the destruction of letters!), I might in either case prove a grievous hindrance. For no one
is ignorant how much is lost in all sciences by the use of compendiums. Though indeed they seem to provide a certain way and
systematic approach to the perfect and complete knowledge of
things and seem to contain in short and in sum that which is set
down elsewhere with more space and prolixity and are for this
reason considered in the light of an index or the very abode of
memory, in which matters written down at length are fitly reduced
to their proper place, nevertheless, compendiums do signal injury
and wreak a great havoc upon literature; for, given to the use of
compendiums alone, we read scarcely anything else through to the
end these days. This is true even for those who have delivered
themselves completely to learning, to this degree aspiring only to the
shadow and superstructure of science, digging little or not at all
beneath the surface.

However, although this evil wanders widely amid almost all
studies, it is a charge to be laid most gravely at the door of the mob
of physicians that they perform their duty so carelessly in distin-
guishing the parts of the human body that not even enumeration
is made use of in learning them. For when, beyond the function
and use of each part, its location, form, size, color, the nature of its
substance, and the principle of its connection with the other parts,
and many things of this sort in the medical examination of the parts
may never be sufficiently perceived, how many can be found who
know even the number of the bones, cartilages, ligaments, muscles,
and veins, arteries, and nerves running in a numerous succession
throughout the entire body and of the viscera which are found in
413 the cavities of the body? I pass over in silence those pestilent doctors

who encompass the destruction of the common life of mankind, who never even stood by at a dissection: whereas in the knowledge of the body no one could produce anything of value who did not perform dissections with his own hands as the kings of Egypt were wont to do and in like manner busied himself frequently and sedulously with dissections and with simple medicines. Whence also those most prudent members of the household of Asclepius will never be sufficiently praised, who, as children in the home learn reading and writing, so they exercised the dissection of cadavers and, learned in this wise, under the happy auspices of the Muses, they bent to their studies. Furthermore, whatever our sloth in the thorough mastery of Anatomy as the basis and foundation of the medical art, I have assumed that no demonstration is required of how necessary the knowledge of human parts is for us who have enlisted under the banner of medicine, since the conscience of each and all will bear full testimony to the fact that in the cure of illness the knowledge of those parts lays rightful claim to first, second, and third place; and this knowledge is to be sought primarily from the affected portion, without, of course, neglecting the due application of subsidiary remedies. Indeed, those who are now dedicated to the ancient study of medicine, almost restored to its pristine splendor in many schools, are beginning to learn to their satisfaction how little and how feebly men have labored in the field of Anatomy to this day from the times of Galen, who, although easily chief of the masters, nevertheless did not dissect the human body; and the fact is now evident that he described (not to say imposed upon us) the fabric of the ape's body, although the latter differs from the former in many respects.

But as to my own audacity, by virtue of which this slight offering, unworthy of your majesty and uniquely commended by such a patronage, hazards the dubious fortune of critical judgment, I shall defend myself with no excuse except that this is the grain and salt whereby I am permitted to obtain favorable omens for my systematic studies; and meanwhile I should wish this book to be an indication of my complete obedience and sense of duty toward my country's ruler until such time as it shall be possible to offer incense also.

At Padua, on the Ides of August, in the Year of the Virgin Birth, MDXLII.

Chapter Concerning the Organs Which Minister to Nutrition by Food and
Three Drink Since man has been unable to form the substance of an immortal being by means of the genital semen and the menstrual blood
(the origins of our generation and of those parts of which we are
composed), the great Creator of things has carefully devised that
man should live as long as possible and that his species, never
failing, should continue to exist forever. In order that man might
attain to the stature for which he was intended and that those elements upon which his innate heat is continually fed might be restored as quickly as possible, he possesses organs which serve to
nourish him in many ways.

The food is broken up by the teeth in order that the task may later
be completed more easily. Food, as well as drink, passes from the
mouth to the stomach as into a storehouse along a path called the
esophagus or gullet. This is extended by two special tunics appropriately formed to descend from the fauces behind the rough artery
and then along the vertebrae of the thorax through the transverse
septum to the upper, or left-hand, orifice of the stomach.

The stomach lies between the liver and the spleen under the
septum. It is particularly roomy and rather long transversely, larger
on the left-hand region of the body than on the right; it is equipped
with two tunics suitable for distending and contracting and enclosed by a third covering derived from the peritoneum. The
stomach is intertwined with many veins, arteries, and nerves. It
concocts what is sent down to it from the mouth and changes this
by an innate force into a thick milky juice. This passes through the
lower orifice of the stomach from the higher region of its right side
and is sent into the intestines.

The intestines are rounded, extending from stomach to anus in a
continuous course made tortuous by innumerable coils and turns;
like the stomach, they are fashioned from two tunics. To these is
added from the peritoneum a third tunic adapted for relaxing and
contracting no less than the first two tunics proper to the intestines
but not everywhere equally extensive. The origin of the intestines
proceeds from the stomach; along the posterior side of the stomach,
reflected toward the back, lies the organ we call the duodenum.
Following this is the part of the intestines known as the jejunum and
that which is called the ileum or volvulus. The coils of the latter fill
the ilia and the region lying under, and contiguous on all sides to,
the umbilicus; it is of almost constant diameter. The narrowness of
415 this organ provides the reason for designating as small intestines

the parts just mentioned. The part of the intestines in which the terminus of the ileum lies is broad and very thick: in its entire course it constitutes the colon. Joined to it is a small appendage, narrow and curled like an earthworm; this has one orifice and is therefore called blind by the masters of dissection. The thick part of the intestines itself ascends from the region of the right kidney to the concavity of the liver. Thence it proceeds along the base of the stomach to the region of the spleen, then turns downward along the region of the left kidney, and bends back to the left region of the pubis in a sort of coil. This last passes above the beginning of the os sacrum straight down to the anus, thereby obtaining the name of the straight and principal intestine.

Thus, whatever has been prepared in the stomach is sent down through these intestines to be forced through their various coils. Veins in innumerable series pass from the concavity of the liver, together with the arteries drawn off from the great artery, between the two membranes which fasten the intestines to the back. These veins are quite thick and dense, abounding in much fat and glands; they are called the mesentery and extend to the intestines. The veins suck out from the intestines (especially the small ones) whatever is suitable for the making of the blood, together with the aqueous and thin refuse of the stomach's concoction, and carry it to the workshop of the liver, where the blood is made. But that refuse which is thicker and less adaptable to suction is gradually collected in the thick intestine; it is kept there only until, it becoming troublesome to man, the muscle surrounding the rectum in circular fashion relaxes, and the refuse is borne forth at once and completely at the will of man.

The liver is not divided into fibers or lobes; it occupies a position higher than that of the organs ministering to it and for the most part lies in intimate relation to the stomach; the liver is placed close beneath the transverse septum and fills the right, rather more than the left, region of the body. It is gibbous above and hollow below, conforming exactly to the shape of the parts lying near it. It is formed by the intertwining of many veins and is surrounded by the substance proper to the liver, similar to recently coagulated blood. It is clothed with a thin membrane proceeding from the ligaments with which it is secured to the peritoneum. It admits two small nerves and one artery. It is the tinder of the natural or nutritive faculty, or, as Plato said, of the part of the soul which desires the pleasures of love, food, and drink.

NIKOLAUS COPERNICUS

The Commentariolus
Translated by Edward Rosen

Our ancestors assumed, I observe, a large number of celestial spheres for this reason especially, to explain the apparent motion of the planets by the principle of regularity. For they thought it altogether absurd that a heavenly body, which is a perfect sphere, should not always move uniformly. They saw that by connecting and combining regular motions in various ways they could make any body appear to move to any position.

Callippus and Eudoxus, who endeavored to solve the problem by the use of concentric spheres, were unable to account for all the planetary movements; they had to explain not merely the apparent revolutions of the planets but also the fact that these bodies appear to us sometimes to mount higher in the heavens, sometimes to descend; and this fact is incompatible with the principle of concentricity. Therefore it seemed better to employ eccentrics and epicycles, a system which most scholars finally accepted.

Yet the planetary theories of Ptolemy and most other astronomers, although consistent with the numerical data, seemed likewise to present no small difficulty. For these theories were not adequate unless certain equants were also conceived; it then appeared that a planet moved with uniform velocity neither on its deferent nor about the center of its epicycle. Hence a system of this sort seemed neither sufficiently absolute nor sufficiently pleasing to the mind.

Having become aware of these defects, I often considered whether there could perhaps be found a more reasonable arrangement of circles, from which every apparent inequality would be derived and in which everything would move uniformly about its proper center, as the rule of absolute motion requires. After I had addressed myself to this very difficult and almost insoluble problem, the suggestion at length came to me how it could be solved with fewer and much simpler constructions than were formerly used, if some assumptions (which are called axioms) were granted me. They follow in this order.

ASSUMPTIONS

1. There is no one center of all the celestial circles or spheres.
2. The center of the earth is not the center of the universe, but only of gravity and of the lunar sphere.
3. All the spheres revolve about the sun as their mid-point, and therefore the sun is the center of the universe.
4. The ratio of the earth's distance from the sun to the height of the firmament is so much smaller than the ratio of the earth's radius to its distance from the sun that the distance from the earth to the sun is imperceptible in comparison with the height of the firmament.
5. Whatever motion appears in the firmament arises not from any motion of the firmament, but from the earth's motion. The earth together with its circumjacent elements performs a complete rotation on its fixed poles in a daily motion, while the firmament and highest heaven abide unchanged.
6. What appear to us as motions of the sun arise not from its motion but from the motion of the earth and our sphere, with which we revolve about the sun like any other planet. The earth has, then, more than one motion.
7. The apparent retrograde and direct motion of the planets arises not from their motion but from the earth's. The motion of the earth alone, therefore, suffices to explain so many apparent inequalities in the heavens.

Having set forth these assumptions, I shall endeavor briefly to show how uniformity of the motions can be saved in a systematic way. However, I have thought it well, for the sake of brevity to omit from this sketch mathematical demonstrations, reserving these for my larger work. But in the explanation of the circles I shall set down here the lengths of the radii, and from these the reader who is not unacquainted with mathematics will readily perceive how closely this arrangement of circles agrees with the numerical data and observations.

Accordingly, let no one suppose that I have gratuitously asserted, with the Pythagoreans, the motion of the earth; strong proof will be found in my exposition of the circles. For the principal arguments by which the natural philosophers attempt to establish the immobility of the earth rest for the most part on the appearances;

it is particularly such arguments that collapse here, since I treat the earth's immobility as due to an appearance.

The Narratio Prima of Rheticus
The Arrangement of the Universe

Aristotle says: "That which causes derivative truths to be true is most true." Accordingly, my teacher decided that he must assume such hypotheses as would contain causes capable of confirming the truth of the observations of previous centuries, and such as would themselves cause, we may hope, all future astronomical predictions of the phenomena to be found true.

First, surmounting no mean difficulties, he established by hypothesis that the sphere of the stars, which we commonly call the eighth sphere, was created by God to be the region which would enclose within its confines the entire realm of nature, and hence that it was created fixed and immovable as the place of the universe. Now motion is perceived only by comparison with something fixed; thus sailors on the sea, to whom

land is no longer
Visible, only the sky on all sides and on all sides the water

are not aware of any motion of their ship when the sea is undisturbed by winds, even though they are borne along at such high speed that they pass over several long miles in an hour. Hence this sphere was studded by God for our sake with a large number of twinkling stars, in order that by comparison with them, surely fixed in place, we might observe the positions and motions of the other enclosed spheres and planets.

Then, in harmony with these arrangements, God stationed in the center of the stage His governor of nature, king of the entire universe, conspicuous by its divine splendor, the sun

To whose rhythm the gods move, and the world
Receives its laws and keeps the pacts ordained.

The other spheres are arranged in the following manner. The first place below the firmament or sphere of the stars falls to the sphere of Saturn, which encloses the spheres of first Jupiter, then Mars; the spheres of first Mercury, then Venus surround the sun; and the centers of the spheres of the five planets are located in the

419

neighborhood of the sun. Between the concave surface of Mars' sphere and the convex of Venus', where there is ample space, the globe of the earth together with its adjacent elements, surrounded by the moon's sphere, revolves in a great circle which encloses within itself, in addition to the sun, the spheres of Mercury and Venus, so that the earth moves among the planets as one of them.

As I carefully consider this arrangement of the entire universe according to the opinion of my teacher, I realize that Pliny set down an excellent and accurate statement when he wrote: "To inquire what is beyond the universe or heaven, by which all things are over-arched, is no concern of man, nor can the human mind form any conjecture concerning this question." And he continues: "The universe is sacred, without bounds, all in all; indeed, it is the totality, finite yet similar to the infinite, etc." For if we follow my teacher, there will be nothing beyond the concave surface of the starry sphere for us to investigate, except insofar as Holy Writ has vouchsafed us knowledge, in which case again the road will be closed to placing anything beyond this concave surface. We will therefore gratefully admire and regard as sacrosanct all the rest of nature, enclosed by God within the starry heaven. In many ways and with innumerable instruments and gifts He has endowed us, and enabled us to study and know nature; we will advance to the point to which He desired us to advance, and we will not attempt to transgress the limits imposed by Him.

That the universe is boundless up to its concave surface, and truly similar to the infinite is known, moreover, from the fact that we see all the heavenly bodies twinkle, with the exception of the planets including Saturn, which, being the nearest of them to the firmament, revolves on the greatest circle. But this conclusion follows far more clearly by deduction from the hypotheses of my teacher. For the great circle which carries the earth has a perceptible ratio to the spheres of the five planets, and hence every inequality in the appearances of these planets is demonstrably derived from their relations to the sun. Every horizon on the earth, being a great circle of the universe, divides the sphere of the stars into equal parts. Equal periods in the revolutions of the spheres are shown to be measured by the fixed stars. Consequently it is quite clear that the sphere of the stars is, to the highest degree, similar to the infinite, since by comparison with it the great circle vanishes, and all the phenomena are observed exactly as if the earth were at rest in the center of the universe.

Moreover, the remarkable symmetry and interconnection of the motions and spheres, as maintained by the assumption of the foregoing hypotheses, are not unworthy of God's workmanship and not

420

unsuited to these divine bodies. These relations, I should say, can be conceived by the mind (on account of its affinity with the heavens) more quickly than they can be explained by any human utterance, just as in demonstrations they are usually impressed upon our minds, not so much by words as by the perfect and absolute ideas, if I may use the term, of these most delightful objects. Nevertheless it is possible, in a general survey of the hypotheses, to see how the inexpressible harmony and agreement of all things manifest themselves.

For in the common hypotheses there appeared no end to the invention of spheres; moreover, spheres of an immensity that could be grasped by neither sense nor reason were revolved with extremely slow and extremely rapid motions. Some writers stated that the daily motion of all the lower spheres is caused by the highest movable sphere; but when a great storm of controversy raged over this question, they could not explain why a higher sphere should have power over a lower. Others, like Eudoxus and those who followed him, assigned to each planet a special sphere, the motion of which caused the planet to revolve about the earth once in a natural day. Moreover, ye immortal gods, what dispute, what strife there has been until now over the position of the spheres of Venus and Mercury, and their relation to the sun. But the case is still before the judge. Is there anyone who does not see that it is very difficult and even impossible ever to settle this question while the common hypotheses are accepted? For what would prevent anyone from locating even Saturn below the sun, provided that at the same time he preserved the mutual proportions of the spheres and epicycle, since in these same hypotheses there has not yet been established the common measure of the spheres of the planets, whereby each sphere may be geometrically confined to its place? I refrain from mentioning here the vast commotion which those who defame this most beautiful and most delightful part of philosophy have stirred up on account of the great size of the epicycle of Venus, and on account of the unequal motion, on the assumption of equants, of the celestial spheres about their own centers.

However, in the hypotheses of my teacher, which accept, as has been explained, the starry sphere as boundary, the sphere of each planet advances uniformly with the motion assigned to it by nature and completes its period without being forced into any inequality by the power of a higher sphere. In addition, the larger spheres revolve more slowly, and, as is proper, those that are nearer to the sun, which may be said to be the source of motion and light, revolve more swiftly. Hence Saturn, moving freely in the ecliptic, revolves in thirty years, Jupiter in twelve, and Mars in two. The center of the earth measures the length of the year by the fixed stars. Venus passes through the zodiac in nine months, and Mercury, revolving about the sun on the smallest sphere, traverses the universe in eighty days. Thus there are only six moving spheres which revolve about the sun, the center of the universe. Their common measure is the great circle which carries the earth, just as the radius of the spherical earth is the common measure of the circles of the moon, the distance of the sun from the moon, etc.

Who could have chosen a more suitable and more appropriate number than six? By what number could anyone more easily have persuaded mankind that the whole universe was divided into spheres by God the Author and Creator of the world? For the number six is honored beyond all others in the sacred prophecies of God and by the Pythagoreans and the other philosophers. What is more agreeable to God's handiwork than that this first and most perfect work should be summed up in this first and most perfect number? Moreover, the celestial harmony is achieved by the six aforementioned movable spheres. For they are all so arranged that no immense interval is left between one and another; and each, geometrically defined, so maintains its position that if you should try to move any one at all from its place, you would thereby disrupt the entire system.

JOHANNES KEPLER AND GALILEO GALILEI

Letters Between Galileo and Kepler

GALILEO TO KEPLER

Padua, August 4th, 1597   Your book, highly learned gentleman, which you sent me through Paulus Amberger, reached me not days ago but only a few hours ago, and as this Paulus just informed me of his return to Germany, I should think myself indeed ungrateful if I should not express to you my thanks by this letter. I thank you especially for having deemed me worthy of such a proof of your friendship. . . . So far I have read only the introduction, but have learned from it in some measure your intentions and congratulate myself on the good fortune of having found such a man as a companion in the exploration of truth. For it is deplorable that there are so few who seek the truth and do not pursue a wrong method of philosophizing. But this is not the place to mourn about the misery of our century but to rejoice with you about such beautiful ideas proving the truth. So I add only this promise that I will read your book in peace, for I am certain that I will find the most beautiful things in it. . . . I would certainly dare to approach the public with my ways of thinking if there were more people of your mind. As this is not the case, I shall refrain from doing so. The lack of time and the ardent wish to read your book make it necessary to close, assuring you of my sympathy. I shall always be at your service. Farewell, and do not neglect to give me further good news of yourself.

> Yours in sincere friendship,
> Galilaeus Galilaeus
> Mathematician at the Academy of Padua

Graz, October 13th, 1597   I received your letter of August 4th on September 1st. It was a double pleasure to me. First, because I became friends with you, the Italian, and second because of the agreement in which we find ourselves concerning Copernican cosmography. As you invite me kindly at the end of your letter to enter into correspondence with you, and I myself feel greatly tempted to do so, I will not let pass the occasion of sending you a letter with the present young nobleman. For I am sure, if your time has allowed it, you have meanwhile obtained a closer knowledge of my book. And so a great desire has taken hold of me, to learn your judgment. For this is my way, to urge all those to whom I have written to express their candid opinion. Believe me, the sharpest criticism of one single understanding man means much more to me than the thoughtless applause of the great masses.

I would, however, have wished that you who have such a keen insight [into everything] would choose another way [to reach your practical aims]. By the strength of your personal example you advise us, in a cleverly veiled manner, to go out of the way of general ignorance and warn us against exposing ourselves to the furious attacks of the scholarly crowd. (In this you are following the lead of Plato and Pythagoras, our true masters.) But after the beginning of a tremendous enterprise has been made in our time, and furthered by so many learned mathematicians, and after the statement that the earth moves can no longer be regarded as something new, would it not be better to pull the rolling wagon to its destination with united effort. . . . For it is not only you Italians who do not believe that they move unless they feel it, but we in Germany, too, in no way make ourselves popular with this idea. Yet there are ways in which we protect ourselves against these difficulties. . . . Be of good cheer, Galileo, and appear in public. If I am not mistaken there are only a few among the distinguished mathematicians of Europe who would dissociate themselves from us. So great is the power of truth. If Italy seems less suitable for your publication and if you have to expect difficulties there, perhaps Germany will offer us more freedom. But enough of this. Please let me know, at least privately if you do not want to do so publicly, what you have discovered in favor of Copernicus.

Now I want to ask you for an observation; as I possess no instruments I must turn to other people. Do you possess a quadrant which shows minutes and quarterminutes? If so, then, please, observe at about the time of the 19th of December the smallest and the largest altitude of the middle star of the tail in the great dipper. Likewise observe about December 26th both heights of the polar star. Also observe the first star about the 19th of March 1598 in its height at midnight, the second about September 28th, also around midnight. If, as I wish, there could be shown a difference between the two observations of one or another minute or even 10' to 15', this would be proof of something of great importance for all astronomy. If there is no difference shown, however, we shall earn all the same together the fame of having become aware of an important problem hitherto not noticed by anybody. [Fixed-star parallax]. . . . Farewell and answer me with a very long letter.

KEPLER TO GALILEO

Prague, August 9, 1610   I have received your observations on the Medicean stars from the Ambassador of his Highness the Grand Duke of Tuscany. You have aroused in me a passionate desire to see your instruments, so that I at last, like you, might enjoy the great performance in the sky. Of the oculars which we have here the best has a tenfold enlargement, the others hardly a threefold; the only one which I have gives a twentyfold enlargement, but the light is very weak. The reason for this is not unknown to me and I see how the intensity could be improved, but one hesitates to spend the money.

. . . In my opinion, no one is entitled to charge a person with having taken over another's ideas unless he is able to recognize and . . . understand the new, rare, and beautifully original ideas which the other has pronounced. To me it is an insult . . . if someone wants to praise me because of my reputation in order to slander others. Nothing annoys me more than the praise of such a man; what an outcast of a human being! He fantastically ascribes to me doubts about the value of your discoveries, because I allow everyone his own opinion. What lack of judgment! The considerations of others need not necessarily be in accord with my own. Regarding something as true, I am, nevertheless, able to tolerate others who are not of the same opinion.

. . . O, you wise Pythagoras, who believed that the majesty of philosophy is present in nothing but silence! But now the die is cast. You, my Galileo, have opened the holy of the holiest of the skies. What else can you do but despise the noise which has been created. . . . The crowd takes vengeance on itself by remaining in eternal ignorance in consequence of its contempt for philosophy. . . .

GALILEO TO KEPLER

Padua, August 19, 1610 . . . What is to be done now? Shall we follow Democritus or Heraclitus? We will laugh at the extraordinary stupidity of the crowd, my Kepler. What do you say to the main philosophers of our school, who, with the stubbornness of vipers, never wanted to see the planets, the moon or the telescope although I offered them a thousand times to show them the planets and the moon. Really, as some have shut their ears, these have shut their eyes towards the light of truth. This is an awful thing, but it does not astonish me. This sort of person thinks that philosophy is a book like the Aeneid or Odyssey and that one has not to search for truth in the world of nature, but in the comparisons of texts (to use their own words).

Why have I no time to laugh a little longer with you! How you would burst out laughing, my dear Kepler, if you would hear what the greatest philosopher of the "Gymnasium" told the Grand Duke about me when, with logical reasons as if they were magic formulas, he wanted to tear the planets from the heavens and dispute them away till nothing was left of them! But night begins, I cannot continue to chat with you. Farewell, highly learned gentleman, and continue to show your good will toward me.

Memorandum to Foreign Bookdealers, especially in Italy

JOHANNES KEPLER

Linz, Spring 1619 I have written this work as a German, after the German fashion and with German frankness. The greater the freedom of thought the more will faith be awakened in the sincerity of those who are devoted to scientific research. I am a Christian, a son of the Church, and accept the doctrine of Catholicism not only with my heart but also with my head as far as I have been able to grasp it up to my present age; I give proof of this in more than one passage of my book. What else is written in my book does not bring you any danger and can stand the censorship in your country. 426 . . . Only one difficulty arises in the teaching of the movement of the earth around the sun, because of the rough procedure of some few who have lectured about it at the wrong place and not in an adequate manner; this has led to the interdiction of the reading of Copernicus, until the book might be corrected even though it has been entirely free for almost eighty years (since the dedication of the work to Pope Paul III). . . . Though being by this time a rather old pupil of Copernicus—I have been his follower now for twenty-six years—I have only quite recently heard this about the interdiction of the Copernican doctrine. But there are men in high positions of the State and the Church who encourage the astronomers by saying the censorship did not take place and that the freedom to discuss problems of nature and to elucidate the works of God would not be squelched even by censorship. Though the die be cast already or danger lie ahead, I must openly confess a guilt. Having hesitated far too long with the publication of my works, I let it happen that the new philosophy remained undefended. . . . For indeed, if I am entitled to have any opinion at all, even the most learned among the Italians and philosophers and the most ardent amongst the theologians will have to say after having read this work on harmonies: the sublimity and fineness in the harmonious order of the divine work is so great, that Copernicus could not possibly have been understood sufficiently before the publication of this work. Therefore philosophy requires and Copernicus asks for the favor of being entirely replaced in his right . . . without hurting the honor of the judges; he . . . asks them to open a new proceeding and to examine newly available evidence which has not been understood up to the present day through carelessness of his advocates.

  You bookdealers, it is true, will act according to law and order, if, considering the given judgment, you will not openly offer copies of my book for sale. But you must realize that you have to serve philosophy and the good writers, so to speak, as "notaries," who must provide the judges with the written defense. Therefore, please, sell the book only to the highest clergy, the most important philosophers, the experienced mathematicians and the profoundest metaphysicians, to whom I, personally, as the advocate of Copernicus have no other approach. These may decide whether it is only the fabrications of an eccentric imagination which are at issue or whether it is something which can be verified by evident facts as the result of the investigation of nature. These men may decide whether one should make these immeasurable beauties of the divine works known to the common people or rather diminish their glory and suppress them by censures. And as the theologians have requested

427 the improvement of Copernicus' teaching from the scholars, they

themselves may judge whether . . . the harmonious construction of the heavenly movements, as it is interpreted in my present book, can exist at all if one sets aside the movement of the earth and accepts that of the sun. The theologians may decide which of the two hypotheses confronted in the title page of Book V—that of Copernicus or that of Brahe—should henceforth be regarded as valid (the old Ptolemaic is surely wrong). Whatever the decision may be after all the reasons are objectively examined, the mathematicians belonging to the Catholic Church will doubtless acknowledge it [the Copernican hypothesis] as legitimate and unassailable.